THE 100 BEST ART TOWNS IN AMERICA

A Guide to Galleries, Museums, Festivals, Lodging, and Dining

Fourth Edition

John Villani

The Countryman Press
Woodstock, Vermont

Library of Congress Cataloging-in-Publication Data
Villani, John.
The 100 best art towns in America : a guide to galleries, museums, festivals, lodging,
and dining / John Villani.—4th ed.
p. cm.
Includes index.

1. Art patronage—United States. 2. Artist colonies—United States. 3. Cities and
towns—Ratings—United States. 4. United States—Description and travel. I. Title: One
hundred best art towns in America. II. Villani, John. 100 best small art towns in
America. III. Title.

NX503.V55 2005
700' .973—dc22

2004061796

ISBN-13 978-0-88150-641-9
ISBN-10 0-88150-641-9

Book design and map by Hespenheide Design
Cover painting © Gregory Effinger

Published by The Countryman Press, P.O. Box 748, Woodstock, Vermont, 05091

Distributed by W.W. Norton & Company, Inc., 500 Fifth Avenue, New York,
NY 10110

Printed in the United States of America

10 9 8 7 6 5 4 3

For Denise Kusel, a great teacher.
Special thanks to Fran Elliot, a great motivator.

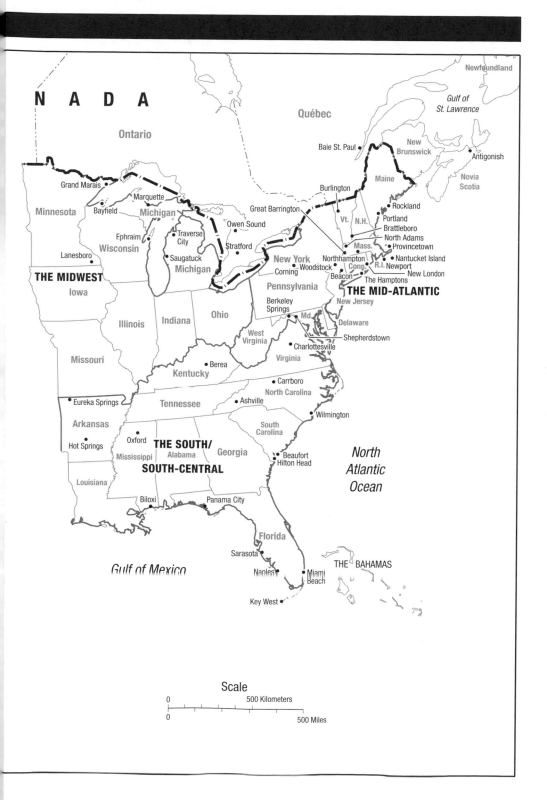

Contents

The Southeast/South-Central Region 81

The Midwest 165

The Rocky Mountains/Southwest 205

Introduction

In the early 1990s, before the first edition of this book was published, I changed the way I traveled. Instead of planning vacations around elaborate dinners at highly regarded restaurants, I started spending more time in art museums. Visits to clothing shops and antiques stores that I once couldn't pass up were replaced by afternoons of wandering in and out of art galleries. I started planning my vacations around outdoor art festivals, street fairs, and poetry slams. Practically overnight I'd become a cultural tourist. About that same time, I also began noticing that most magazine and newspaper travel articles that focused on journeys to communities such as Bisbee, Arizona, and Newport, Rhode Island, failed to acknowledge the important contributions being made by local arts sectors to those places' economies and quality of life. So I decided to write a book addressing this shortcoming.

If you're the kind of traveler who builds your perceptions of a place through visits to art museums, art galleries, theatre performances, music festivals, and art fairs, this book is meant for you. It's an honest recognition of the new priorities many of us place on enjoying life's experiences through an arts and culture perspective. It's also an acknowledgment of an arts explosion taking place in small and mid-sized communities from coast to coast.

That this book is now in its fourth edition is largely the result of a broadly based diversification and democratization of the national arts conscience. In recent years a rapid expansion in all sectors of the arts has resulted in a proliferation of art galleries, theatre companies, and music festivals in places where they had either been nearly invisible or been completely off the radar screen. In many instances, these communities have blossomed into Art Towns, places that have expanded their tourism sectors or even revitalized their downtown neighborhoods through arts-related development. As these Art Towns flourished, newly arrived artists, as well as individuals with rich experiences in the arts, have burst onto local art scenes with creative energy, big dreams, and the kind of fresh thinking that maintains creative momentum.

The Ten Best Large and Small Art Towns

Top 10 Art Towns with a population above 30,000 and less than 100,000:

1. Santa Fe, New Mexico
2. Loveland, Colorado
3. Sarasota, Florida
4. Hot Springs, Arkansas
5. Asheville, North Carolina
6. Boulder, Colorado
7. Portland, Maine
8. Lawrence, Kansas
9. Bellingham, Washington
10. Chico, California

Top 10 Art Towns with a population below 30,000:

1. Naples, Florida
2. Ashland, Oregon
3. Provincetown, Massachusetts
4. Taos, New Mexico
5. Northampton, Massachusetts
6. Aspen, Colorado
7. Eureka, California
8. Marfa, Texas
9. Salt Spring Island, British Columbia
10. Brattleboro, Vermont

We're living in an era when there are few, if any, limits placed on the artistic expressions found in North America's Art Towns. For travelers, this explains why installations of conceptual art are now found in places like Rockland, Maine, and why challenging works of modern stagecraft are regularly presented in Ashland, Oregon. An astonishing diversity of cultural amenities now exists in places where the pickings had been slim in years past. From Shakespeare under the stars in Boulder, Colorado, to gallery walks in New London, Connecticut, and street-busker festivals in Nelson, British Columbia, there's now a wealth of exciting, well-staged art events from which to choose when planning a getaway. Those who build their travel itineraries with a yen toward enjoying an arts festival, a chamber music concert, or a stroll through intriguing neighborhoods filled with art galleries and coffee bars that serve as alternative venues exhibiting locally created works of art are now faced with a broad array of inspirations to hit the highway in search of art adventures. Many of the artists, theatre directors, arts administrators, and art gallery owners interviewed in this book are individuals with track records of success in the ultracompetitive setting of metropolitan-area arts scenes. But they've made conscious decisions based on personal, professional, familial, and economic criteria to get off the urban racetrack and restart their lives in communities where they can afford a home, get to know their neighbors, and create their art in a setting with fewer pressures and distractions. While the motivations for making these lifestyle changes vary, what's universal is the impact these individuals have had on the small and midsized Art Towns where they've settled. This book recognizes 100 places in the United States and Canada where an influx of creative field professionals has dovetailed with the development of local art talents as well as new sources of financial support from the public and private sectors, resulting in the evolution of creative communities. This book was also written to serve as a guide for those who are considering major lifestyle changes in the form of moving to a small town where there's support of the arts. Densely populated cities and their suburbs are filled with jewelers working in basement studios, musicians juggling two jobs and a family, writers whose laptops occupy valuable space on kitchen tables, and painters working in the corners of two-car garages. Many of these individuals dream about relocating to a community where they can afford a home and build the studio of their dreams. While real-estate values in some Art Towns have rocketed skyward, this book also includes dozens of communities that offer their residents the opportunity to live in a place where artists can qualify for a mortgage without sentencing themselves to a future of tortillas and beans. All an artist needs is the courage to live her or his dreams, a one-way rental of a moving truck, and the willingness to become part of a supportive, talented community of artists.

The experience of writing four editions of this book has meant that I've spent many nights on the road traveling to meet the artists and creative field professionals whose lives are invested in these communities. It also means that I've benefited from feedback proffered by numerous individuals tipping me off to places that fit into the concept of an Art Town. In this edition, Forks, Washington, Chico, California, Owen Sound, Ontario, Antigonish, Nova Scotia, and Traverse City, Michigan, are prime examples of the results of this process. That's also why each edition of this book has been different from its previous versions. Constantly changing communities and rapidly evolving art scenes have spread the Art Town phenomenon from coast to coast, and it seems as if I'm continually being told about places that are attracting substantial numbers of artists. I've set the parameter of what qualifies as an Art Town to a population limit of 100,000, which is the reason places such as Miami Beach, Florida, and Galveston, Texas, are now profiled in these pages. Population figures are based on 2000 U.S. Census results as reported by Rand McNally, adjusted for growth. If you have a tip for upcoming editions of this book regarding a community that's becoming an Art Town, visit the www.arttowns.com Web site and tell me about it. This is also the place to contact me for scheduling conference and lecture appearances as well as book signings. In previous editions this book's title was *The 100 Best Small Art Towns in America*. And while the current edition's title has been changed to acknowledge its inclusion of mid-sized communities, it still strives to include as many small towns as possible. Art Towns whose populations are measured in the hundreds or thousands remain prominent in this fourth edition, which is good news for artists in places like Tubac, Arizona, North Adams, Massachusetts, Ephraim, Wisconsin, and Friday Harbor, Washington. Some communities profiled in this book have been included in its previous editions. Conversely, a number of Art Towns profiled in earlier editions have not been included in this current edition. Those communities repeating from previous editions typically have taken major steps forward in the development of their art scenes, such as the opening of new art centers and museums in places like Charlottesville, Virginia, Lawrence, Kansas, Santa Fe, New Mexico, and Northampton, Massachusetts.

Earlier editions of this book had ranked the profiled communities from 1 to 100 as a way of distinguishing the truly outstanding Art

Towns from the ones that were in the more formative stages of development. This proved to be an arbitrary process when trying to decide why one town should be ranked 64th while another should be 39th. In the interest of injecting more objectivity into the rating system, I'm using two rating categories: One category ranks the Top 10 Art Towns with populations of less than 30,000; the other category rates the Top 10 Art Towns with populations falling between 30,000 and 100,000. (This way, everyone else gets to tout his or her town as "Number 11 in the nation!")

In communities such as Aspen, Colorado, Provincetown, Massachusetts, Santa Fe, New Mexico, and Key West, Florida, their high costs of living places them out of reach for some artists (and in Aspen's case that includes most rock stars). But each community also has an arts scene that stands out for its quality and depth. Conversely, many Top 10 Art Towns offer costs of living that are much more within the reach of artists surviving on income from the sales of their work, which is why places like Chico, California, Brattleboro, Vermont, Bellingham, Washington, and Northampton, Massachusetts, continue to attract relocating artists and are deserving of Top 10 Art Town recognition. Cribbing a nifty trick from the Catholic school nuns and priests who wired my brain for thinking creatively, I also rate all 20 of the Top 10 Art Towns on a flexible curve. For some towns, their sheer numbers of galleries and art festivals make them obvious choices, while for others affordability and location in areas of astounding natural beauty have helped vault them to the Top 10. Each Art Town was considered on its individual merits, which is why a place like Loveland, Colorado, which supports a sculpture industry on a grand scale, is in the Top 10 with Chico, California, which is a highly livable college town and an affordable refuge for increasing numbers of artists priced out of the Bay Area's warehouse studios and ethnic neighborhoods.

My Top 10–ratings criteria included, but were not limited to, the number of art galleries; affordability; natural beauty; local support for the arts; availability of suitable studio and rehearsal space; frequency and impact of art festivals; cohesiveness of the local arts community; diversity of creative statements being made by local visual and performing artists; and infrastructure in the form of theatres, art schools, art museums, and alternative exhibition and performance venues. Each town's creative vibe was also taken into consideration, that undercurrent experienced as a sixth sense when our normal perceptions fall short. In culinary terms this is known as *umami*, a Japanese word used to describe hard-to-pin-down flavors. Umami can best be described as the feeling I got when I first visited Santa Fe, New Mexico, in early 1989. Walking around the town's snow-covered plaza on a late-January day, I was struck by the feeling that I had been there before, even though it was my initial contact with the City Different (Santa Fe's all-too-apropos nickname). I felt like I had returned home to a place where everything felt just right. Fortunately, I still connect with that feeling whenever I'm in an Art Town whose wealth of artistic creativity and environmental beauty leaves me breathless.

I sincerely hope that this book guides its readers to exciting and intriguing communities across North America, allowing them to appreciate the contributions being made by artists in 100 places that have become Art Towns.

John Villani,
Santa Fe, New Mexico, August 2004
www.arttowns.com

New England

New London, Connecticut

Best known as the home of the U.S. Coast Guard Academy and a nearby navy submarine base, New London is a surprisingly well-preserved waterfront community whose downtown wraps along the Thames River and whose Ocean Beach Park borders the Long Island Sound. Located about an hour's drive southwest of Providence, Rhode Island, New London's the jumping off point for a ferry system operating between here and Long Island, Block Island, and Fishers Island. Connecticut College, home to both the Cummings Art Center and the OnStage Performing Arts series is here, and just across the Thames, the University of Connecticut (UConn) at Avery Point operates the Avery Point Playhouse and the Alexey von Schlippe Gallery, home to year-round exhibitions and an independent film series. Connecticut artists have long been attracted to this quiet and affordable stretch of coastline, starting with Florence Griswold and the Lyme Art Colony in the early 20th century, a movement that attracted the likes of Childe Hassam and dozens more. Today, the nearby community of Old Lyme, just a half-hour drive along the shoreline west of New London, is home to the Lyme Academy College of Fine Arts, a half-dozen art galleries specializing in early American painting, the Florence Griswold Museum, one of the nation's foremost institutions dedicated to American Impressionism, and the Lyme Art Association, which has operated and exhibited in the same structure since 1921.

To New London's east is historic Mystic Seaport, once home to a fleet of whaling vessels, now a tourism and education center whose spectacular harbor is filled with beautifully restored sailing ships and whose dockside lanes have been turned into an agglomeration of T-shirt shops, ye olde trinket shoppes, and overpriced pubs, with nary a sailor in sight. On the other hand, among Mystic's redeeming qualities are Hollywood-famous Mystic Pizza, the visual arts gallery and studio complex operated by the 90-year-old Mystic Art Association, and a half-dozen or so galleries selling exquisite examples of maritime art.

Arts Scene

Downtown New London is home to several art galleries and alternative venues such as coffee bars and restaurants exhibiting locally made art. The community's gallery scene survives because of low overheads, a steady trickle of tourist interest, and an increasing number of savvy collectors who make their way here from New York and Boston in search of reasonably priced, well-executed art. The Lyman Allyn Art Museum of Connecticut College on Williams Street is the community's most prominent visual arts venue, staging exhibitions that pay homage to the region's seafaring past while accommodating the progressive forces of change that have impacted the contemporary art world. The museum adjoins a children's art park and a sculpture garden. The Garde Arts Center, a complex of restored commercial buildings as well as a 1,458-seat, restored theatre built in 1926, is home to a year-round series of performing-arts events including the October to May concert series of the 75-member Eastern Connecticut Symphony Orchestra. The Hygenic Artist Cooperative & Galleries, a historic Bank Street structure and an adjacent sculpture garden/amphitheatre, is an 1844 commercial building that's been renovated into a working studio and live/work complex for local artists. Home to monthly exhibitions as well as being the driving force behind the annual Hygenic Art Show, this cooperative gallery's reopening in 2000 following several years of renovations provided a huge boost to the regional art scene's viability and visibility.

The marquee attraction of the region's performing-arts scene is the Eugene O'Neill Theater Center in the adjacent town of Waterford. This revered American playwright, whose childhood home is in downtown New London, was the inspiration for the center's six ongoing educational programs covering everything from drama criticism to playwriting and puppetry. Since the early 1960s more than 700 plays and musicals have been developed and/or premiered here, including dozens that went on to Broadway success. Soaking in the O'Neill's summer plays and its many readings is one of the must-do highlights of the annual arts season. From June to August, prominent classical music organizations from the Northeast perform under the seaside concert tent of Summer Music at Harkness State Park. Across the mouth of the Thames River, during that same stretch of summer, Shakespeare by the Sea stages its annual production of a Bard classic in the Avery Point Playhouse on the UConn campus. Secret Theatre uses the Playhouse and various local venues for its year-round presentations of innovative, new theatrical works, while the Flock Theatre uses several venues for its performances, ranging from puppetry at local schools to summer Shakespeare on the Connecticut College campus.

Essentials

Visual Arts Venues
Hygenic Artist Cooperative & Galleries (79–83 Bank Street; 860/443-8001; www.hygenic.org) Downtown live/work space and studio complex.

Lyman Allyn Art Museum (625 Williams Street; 860/443-2545; www.lymanallyn.org) Exhibits historic and regional work, as well as national contemporary art.

Florence Griswold Museum (96 Lyme Street, Old Lyme; 860/434-5542; www.flogris.org) One of the nation's best collections of American Impressionism.

Performing Arts & Events

Eugene O'Neill Theater Center (305 Great Neck Road, Waterford; 860/443-5378; www.oneilltheatercenter.org) Readings, full-scale productions, and theatre education.

Art Talk

Christopher Steiner, interim director of the Lyman Allyn Art Museum. I've been here since 1997, starting as an art instructor at Connecticut College. At the museum we're on our way to becoming an independent institution and more of a regionally influential institution. We're redefining our curatorial direction, which in the past has embraced a bit of everything, with an emphasis on American art and the art of this region. My feeling is that the museum needs to expand beyond that to contextualize our American collection in a broader view. We're now looking at American artists who worked overseas, and we're planning an African art exhibition and more ethnic shows. New London has a youthful and energetic arts scene, and we want to bring some of that energy and vision into our exhibitions programs.

Art Talk

James Stidfole, wood turner and founder of the Hygenic Artist Cooperative & Galleries.
New London's filled with young artists, and each month, it seems, new plans are announced to turn some down-town building into lofts or studios. Our artist population has quadrupled, with lots of them moving in from New York City and Boston, as well as other parts of Connecticut. The newer galleries have a contemporary art emphasis. We don't have all the buyers we need yet, but the big city art dealers make a point of coming here for the shows, which are interesting, exciting, and giving us all a sense that something great is just starting to happen here. The whole town is affordable right now, and while we've had our ups and downs there's a damn good chance that one day New London will become the next Providence.

Annual Hygenic Art Show
(79–83 Bank Street; 860/443-8001; www.hygenic.org) January arts event plus the Annual Night Kitchen fiesta of late-nite food, music, and art shows.

Fourth Friday (see New London Chamber of Commerce below) Monthly coordinated openings.

Wine & Dine

Zavala (2 State Street; 860/437-1891; www.zavalarestaurant.com) Best mole Oaxaqueño north of Las Cruces.

Village Beanery (27 Coogan Boulevard, Mystic; 860/536-1175) Coffee and desserts by the harbor.

Bank Street Lobster House (194 Bank Street; 860/447-9398) Get a harborside table, order a two-pounder, and don't pass on dessert.

Accommodations

Queen Anne Inn (265 Williams Street; 860/447-2600; www.queen-anne.com) Historic, downtown, and with views.

Lighthouse Inn & Resort (6 Guthrie Place; 860/443-8411; www.lighthouse inn-ct.com) Historic estate overlooking the Long Island Sound.

Red Roof Inn (707 Coleman Street; 860/444-0001; www.redroof.com) Affordable, with a pool.

Information

New London Chamber of Commerce: 105 Huntington Street; 860/464-7373; www.chamberect.com

Population: 25,700

Portland, Maine

from its vantage point on a peninsula jutting into Casco Bay, Maine's largest community is a relative metropolis in a state filled with small towns. Located on the New England coast just a two-hour drive northeast of Boston, Portland has developed a strong local arts scene that's filled with a diverse range of activities taking place in sophisticated facilities catering to the visual and performing arts. For blockbuster shows and full-throttle opera, Boston's amenities are close enough to be just a day trip away, so the challenge for Portland's arts organizations is to develop and present at a quality level that keeps local arts and entertainment dollars from being spent elsewhere.

One of the most appealing aspects of Portland's quality of life is the community's emphasis on historic preservation. The city's Old Port neighborhood is a warren of cobblestone streets, waterfront walkways, and brick structures whose architectural roots are firmly planted in the vibrant expressions of the Victorian era. There are monuments to the past at practically every intersection, from banks and libraries erected in the late 1800s to pylons and plaques commemorating the tradition of military service that's deeply ingrained into Maine's heritage.

Downtown Portland is a place that's come to grips with its destiny and has decided to restore, renovate, and rebuild not only its historic infrastructure but to add into its mix the elements that were missing from its original composition. A thriving art school has flourished in the midst of what once was a dreary corner of downtown,

7

infusing the city's streets with a year-round flow of creative types whose spiked hair and wild styles of dress present an interesting contrast with the more sedate, L.L. Bean and Sebago flourishes favored by lifelong Mainers. During the summer months ferries depart from Portland's waterfront on a sometimes harrowing, open ocean journey to Nova Scotia. Mainers shrug off the rough seas as a minor inconvenience, adroitly sidestepping the steady flow of seasick tourists making a beeline for the ferry rest rooms. Portland's coastal location tends to moderate the impact of Maine's winters, though less than an hour's drive northwest, in the White Mountains foothills, are several of New England's most challenging ski areas. Come summer's glory, Maine takes on four months of warm-weather personality, and the social action shifts southward to places such as Old Orchard Beach and Rye Beach in neighboring New Hampshire.

Arts Scene

Nearly two dozen commercial art galleries and an equal number of alternative venues in the form of coffee bars and restaurants are the prime contact points for locally and regionally created visual art. There's a healthy art market during the summer months when out-of-state tourists are clogging Portland's streets and sidewalks, but the trick to staying alive as a local artist is to make sure your work is also represented in the summer-season galleries farther up the coast in places such as Deer Isle, as well as in the busy winter galleries close to major Vermont and New Hampshire ski resorts. Old Port harbors the majority of Portland's downtown art venues, making its First Friday gallery walks an easy way to catch up on the comings and goings of the local arts scene.

The Maine College of Art (MCA), a nationally respected training ground for students aspiring toward careers as painters, video artists, ceramists, and other art disciplines, occupies the shell of what once had been downtown's largest department store before mall mania wormed its way into the local suburbs. The institution's students provide a breath of edgy air for the area's street life and make it possible for a range of new coffee bars and cafés to stay in business. Regular exhibitions in the MCA galleries are showcases for the often remarkably strong work created by its art students and have become a must-see stop on First Fridays. The best time of the year to experience downtown's revived arts spirit is during June's Old Port Festival, an event whose preparations keep the community on edge for the better part of May. Part freak show, part art festival, and part fashion parade, the Old Port Festival is above all a legitimate excuse for half the town to get sloshed and enjoy the arrival of summer.

The jewel in Portland's visual arts tiara is the Portland Museum of Art, an architectural masterpiece designed by I. M. Pei that anchors Congress Square, the site of a summer-long series of free concerts and special events such as the One World Portland multicultural celebration, and the dances hosted by the Maineiac Swing Dance Society. The art museum has developed a strong reputation for its year-round exhibitions of regional, national, and international artists and has also originated a number of touring exhibitions featuring the work of Maine artists. It has an extensive collection strong on works by the likes of Andrew Wyeth, John Singer Sargent, Winslow Homer, and Marsden Hartley, exhibiting these masterpieces in regular exhibitions, as well as offering shows by other key figures in American art history. Opened in its new building in 1983, Portland Museum of Art was one of the nation's first "new generation" art museums (San Francisco, Cincinnati, St. Louis, and Denver are among those cities that have followed suit) whose nontraditional architecture allowed curators to redefine the art-viewing experience. It has been nothing less than a resounding success, in part because of its constant flow of great exhibitions but also as the result of its year-round programs of art education workshops, artist and curator lectures, summer art camps for kids, and concerts during its popular Jazz Breakfasts program on Sunday mornings during the year's colder months.

Portland's performing-arts scene is in large part centered around events at the Merrill Auditorium, an elegant, restored, 1912 concert hall that's also home to the world-famous Kotzschmar Memorial Organ. The Merrill's 1,900 seats are often sold out for performances of companies such as the Portland Symphony Orchestra, which uses this venue for its very popular Tuesday and Sunday concert programs as well as its America's Pops Series. The Merrill's Great Performances Series brings touring national and international theatre, music, and dance companies into Portland, and the venue is also used as a perfect downtown environment for presenting top folk, world, and new music acts. When it's not touring the state, delivering Verdi to the plaid-shirted masses, Portland Opera Repertory uses the Merrill for its full-scale productions. Portland Chamber Music Festival's summer concerts take place at Ludcke Auditorium, while Shoestring Theatre uses a variety of venues, including the St. Lawrence Arts Center, for its imaginative puppetry shows. Portland Stage Company presents

Art Talk

Jessica Tomlinson, director of public relations for the Maine College of Art.

Portland's a very accessible yet urban place where you can get a sense of something important happening in the arts. People here tend to be interested in dialogue, in conversing about the shows and talking about the impact they're having on the larger community. There are a variety of venues showing local art, and artists here have proved to be very resourceful in developing alternative outlets for showing their work. Affordability of housing and studio space is an issue for many artists and for graduates of MCA who want to stay in Portland but have a hard time making ends meet. Things change constantly here, and that's great.

year-round performances of Broadway dramas, musicals and comedies, while the Portland Players Community Theatre uses its own playhouse on Cottage Road for its season of comedies and musicals.

Essentials

Visual Arts Venues

Portland Museum of Art (7 Congress Square; 207/775-6148; www.portland museum.org) Year-round regional, national, and international shows.

Maine College of Art (97 Spring Street; 207/775-3052; www.meca.edu) Contemporary art exhibitions and multidisciplinary programs.

St. Lawrence Arts Center (76 Congress Street; 207/775-5568; www.stlawrencearts.edu) Historic church renovated as an exhibition and performance space.

Performing Arts & Events

Old Port Festival (see Portland Convention & Visitors Bureau below) June downtown arts celebration.

Portland Symphony Orchestra (477 Congress Street; 207/773-6128; www.portlandsymphony.com) Presents its season at Merrill Auditorium.

The Portland Players (420 Cottage Road; 207/799-7337; www.portland players.org) Community theatre presenting comedies and musicals.

Wine & Dine

Benkay (2 India Street; 207/773-5555) Sushi with a fresh, Maine twist.

Flatbread Company (72 Commercial Street; 207/772-8777) Wood-fired pizzas.

Portland Coffee Roasting Co. (111 Commercial Street; 207/772-9044) Favorite downtown buzz shop.

Accommodations

Inn at St. John (939 Congress Street; 207/773-6481; www.innatstjohn.com) Downtown B&B close to major arts amenities.

Doubletree Hotel (1230 Congress Street; 207/774-5611; www.doubletree hotels.com) Large, downtown hotel with a pool.

Holiday Inn by the Bay (88 Spring Street; 207/775-2311; www.innbythe bay.com) Affordable and in a great location.

Information

Portland Convention & Visitors Bureau: 245 Commercial Street; 207/772-5800; www.visitportland.com

Population: 67,000

Art Talk

Susan Danly, curator of contemporary art, graphics, and photography for the Portland Museum of Art.
We work fairly closely with the local arts community, and in our last biennial exhibition we had 830 regional artists apply. I'm constantly doing studio visits and making inroads into the statewide arts community. Portland has an active gallery scene and some older commercial buildings that have been converted into artists' studios. The influence of the studio scene and the impact of MCA are starting to show results, and what's being generated by local artists is quite interesting and innovative. You also see lots of interesting art on the walls of coffee bars and restaurants, places where there's also local musicians performing. There's both a youthful art scene in Portland and an established one, but there's enough venue diversity so all the community's artists can find places to show their work.

Rockland, Maine

waterfront community on the west shores of Penobscot Bay, Rockland is a historic town whose seafaring roots are still evident in its year-round fishing fleet and its stature as the homeport of a regional ferry system. Located less than two hour's drive northeast of Portland, Rockland is famous for its legendary beautiful summers, a four month window of shoulder-to-shoulder tourist activity that clogs local roadways, backs up service at restaurants, and gets well under the skin of all year-round residents by the time Labor Day rolls around. Late summer starts the headlong evacuation of rented homes and cottages, returning Rockland to its normal, somnambulant condition. While summers are lived at local beaches and in backyard gardens, the early-arriving Maine winter lays down thick carpets of snow, thereby shifting the region's outdoor recreation focus to Camden Snow Bowl, a ski area just a short drive north of town.

The entire Penobscot Bay area is loaded with artists, galleries, and community theatres. Thirty miles north of here is the Art Town of Belfast, home to galleries as well as the highly regarded Maskers Theatre drama troupe. Between Belfast and Rockland are the charming towns of Camden and Rockport, each of which is home to a dozen or so art galleries as well as theatre and music organizations, and in Camden's case, the Maine Center for Contemporary Art. Artists from across the globe have been coming here since the early part of the twentieth century, buying homes on the islands and mainland and using these as their summer studios. The foremost of these artists are the members of the distinguished Wyeth family, whose long-standing Rockland roots are celebrated at the Wyeth Center, part of the Farnsworth Art Museum and located in a converted United Methodist Church and in the Study Center building. Ruidoso, New Mexico, another of the nation's best Art Towns, is home to a branch of this enormously talented family.

Arts Scene

In this spectacular region, where Belfast has its waterfront Maskers Theatre, Camden has its lovely Opera House and contemporary art museum, and Rockport has its cluster of galleries and fine restaurants, what makes Rockland stand out from the rest are the Wyeth Center, the Farnsworth Art Museum, and the arts-focused Lincoln Street Center, an in-progress renovation of the old Rockland High School into a broadly scoped, year-round community arts center.

The Center for Maine Contemporary Art keeps its focus on the statewide pulse of Maine's contemporary arts community, delivering year-round, rotating exhibitions in its galleries as well as artist lectures and community forums on contemporary art issues. Rockport College, an internationally respected training ground for photographers, filmmakers, and video artists, is located on the same campus used during the summer months by Maine Photographic Workshops, an organization that for more than three decades has attracted top fine art photographers, photojournalists, and documentary photographers to Rockland for summer workshops. Through its Wyeth Center, the Farnsworth Art Museum offers exhibitions of work by N.C. Wyeth, Andrew Wyeth, James Wyeth, and other members of the Wyeth family. The center also draws scholars who are interested in the museum's extensive archives of Wyeth heirlooms and research materials. The Farnsworth has an outstanding collection of works by many of the key figures in American art history, including those of sculptor Louise Nevelson, who made Rockland her childhood home. The museum balances shows of historic art and contemporary works in its year-round exhibitions schedule and presents lectures as well as art workshops and music performances for the Rockland community.

Bay Chamber Concerts, which uses the 400-seat Rockport Opera House and the restored, 500-seat Camden Opera House for its year-round programs of chamber music, international performing-arts companies, and jazz concerts, is the region's premier performing-arts and

Art Talk

Christopher Crosman, executive director of The Farnsworth Art Museum & Wyeth Center.

We're one of two independent art museums in the state, and our focus heavily emphasizes Maine's role in the development of America's art history. This gives us an interesting focus in our exhibitions programs, and as a small art museum we can use this focus to direct shows by living artists who are doing work with a Maine connection. Clearly, we have a lot of summer visitors, so we mount those shows with a very high visibility quotient in mind, and during the off-season we can do a lot more with emerging artists. The local arts climate is very encouraging. We've had our exhibitions reviewed in the *New York Times*, and even though we're located in rural Maine there's a feeling that we're connected to the mainstream of art practices.

music presenter. Maine Grand Opera, which stages its performances during the winter arts season, also uses the Camden Opera House, as does Camden Civic Theatre, the community's year-round stage company.

Essentials

Visual Arts Venues

The Farnsworth Art Museum & Wyeth Center (356 Main Street; 207/596-6457; www.farnsworth museum.org) Traditional and contemporary works by Maine and national artists and masterworks by the Wyeth family.

Center for Maine Contemporary Art (162 Russell Avenue, Rockport; 207/236-2875; www.artsmaine.org) Year-round exhibitions and lectures.

Rockport College (2 Central Street, Rockport; 207/236-8581; www.rockport college.edu) Home of the Maine Photographic Workshops.

Performing Arts & Events

Bay Chamber Concerts (10 Summer Street, Rockport; 207/236-2823; www.baychamberconcerts.org) Year-round music, dance, and workshop presenter.

Country Roads Artists & Artisans Tour (Camden-Rockport-Lincolnville Chamber of Commerce; 207/236-4404; www.camdenme.org) September studio tour with more than two dozen, self-guided sites.

Annual Fall Festival of Arts & Crafts (Camden-Rockport-Lincolnville Chamber of Commerce; 207/236-4404; www.camdenme.org) Staged in early October on the Camden waterfront.

Wine & Dine

Café Miranda (15 Oak Street; 207/594-2034; www.cafe-miranda.com) Great wood-fired pizza with an Armenian twist.

Primo Restaurant (2 S. Main Street; 207/596-0770; www.primorestaurant.com) Innovative takes on local ingredients by an acclaimed chef.

Harbor View Restaurant (Public Landing, Thomaston; 207/354-8173; www.harborviewrestaurant.com) Great spot for king-sized lobsters.

Accommodations

Captain Lindsey House (5 Lindsey Street; 207/596-7950; www.lindsey house.com) Downtown B&B with Maine charm.

Camden Harbour Inn (83 Bayview Street, Camden; 207/236-4200; www.camdenharbourinn.com) Within an easy walk to the Camden Opera House.

Towne Motel (68 Elm Street, Camden; 207/236-3377) Affordable and conveniently located.

Information

Rockland-Thomaston Chamber of Commerce: P.O. Box 508, 207/596-0376; www.therealmaine.com

Population: 7,650

Art Talk

Oliver Wilder, president and C.E.O. of the Center for Maine Contemporary Art.

We try to be the leading resource on contemporary art in Maine, with our strength being artists who have pushed their vision forward, whether they're established, emerging, deceased, or mid-career. Because we're so in touch with the pulse of artists who are on the rise, many other art institutions look to us for direction. The area where we're located is a great example of how the pursuit of creative endeavors can drive an economy forward. A number of contemporary artists have moved here in order to be close to our programs, and we're now at the point where one of our future interests is in spreading our exhibitions and programs out across the state.

Great Barrington, Massachusetts

The home of civil rights pioneer W.E.B. du Bois, this one-time manufacturing community in southwest Massachusetts is less than a three-hour drive from Boston in a corner of the Berkshire Mountains that's home to ski areas, rivers, nature preserves, and small colleges. The Appalachian Trail skirts Great Barrington's eastern flank, while to its north is the historic community of Stockbridge, home to the Norman Rockwell Museum and a number of fine restaurants. Great Barrington has grown slowly and smartly through the past two decades, and its low-key Berkshires chic has meant that this is still an affordable, accessible place to live. Artists have long appreciated the community's cheap studio quarters, and in recent years a sizeable studio glass community has moved into the region. Great Barrington is a perfect place for artists who like to slave away the mornings in their studios, then toss their skis into the back of their trucks and head up to the slopes for a half-day of letting the steam out of their psyches.

Downtown Great Barrington is a compact, vibrant place whose 1920's architectural heritage was largely spared from the urban renewal movements of the past few decades. It's a district filled with record shops, pubs, hardware stores, coffee bars, hair salons, cafés, and art galleries, reflecting an authenticity that many other American towns would like to recapture. Railroad Street and Main Street are favorite spots for the community's galleries, but there are also many working studios located on the upper levels of downtown's commercial buildings. There's a sense of cohesiveness in the local arts community, which tends to be appreciative of newcomers who want to build strong ties to the local artsinfrastructure.

Arts Scene

A number of art galleries and studios compensate for the lack of a community visual arts center in Great Barrington. The Guthrie Center, named after the family of musicians that includes Arlo and Woody Guthrie, is an Interfaith center in nearby Van Deusenville that attempts to fill some of this gap through its Troubadour Concert Series and an arts education program for kids. South of Great Barrington, the Sheffield Art League stages its member and invitational shows in the Dewey Memorial Hall and Bushnell-Sage Library. Chesterwood Estate, the Stockbridge home of Daniel Chester French, best known for his sculpture of Abraham Lincoln at the Lincoln Memorial, organizes a summer and autumn juried invitational exhibition of contemporary sculpture on its manicured grounds.

Nearby Stockbridge is home to one of America's art treasures, the Norman Rockwell Museum. This hilltop facility is home to a year-round series of rotating exhibitions of Rockwell's art, as well as exhibitions surveying his decades of *Saturday Evening Post* magazine covers, along with guest artist shows, artist lectures, and occasional music performances filling out its offerings. IS 183, a community arts center in Stockbridge, uses its IS 183 Gallery for regional and national visual arts exhibitions and also offers year-round artworkshops, artist lectures, and performances. In Housatanic, about 10 miles northwest of Great Barrington, the Monument Mills textile-manufacturing complex has attracted a thriving community of artists and several art galleries. Dozens of artists have moved into the area, renovating cottages once lived in by Eastern European industrial workers. A half-dozen galleries have taken root here, including Great Barrington Pottery, which has built its Chasbitsu Tea House for daily tea ceremonies. The two biggest visual arts events on Great Barrington's annual calendar, both of which take place in July, are the Berkshires Summer Arts Festival at Butternut Ski Resort and the Berkshire Woodworkers Guild Annual Furniture Show in the Berkshire Botanical Garden.

The Mahiwe Performing Arts Center on Railroad Street hosts the Great Barrington performances of the Berkshire Opera Company as well as Club Helsinki's series of concerts by leading folk and

Art Talk

Robin Schmitt, owner of Tokonoma Gallery.

Things go up and down in Housatonic, where there are several galleries in these old textile mill buildings and an association of local artists with about 30 members. We all work together, organizing the art walks, planning other events, and building our sense of community. There's an oversupply of artist live/work spaces and an available arts infrastructure that can be somewhat expensive, depending on the individual landlord. The artists moving here are a variety of New York City and Boston types, and our buyers tend to mostly come from the New York area. Our art walks happen several times a year and get a good turnout, but the sales are usually disappointing.

independent label musicians. Music & More, a series of summer and autumn classical music concerts, takes place at the Meeting House in New Marlborough just outside of Great Barrington, while Aston Magna's summer chamber music concerts are performed at St. James Church, the same venue used by the Berkshire Bach Society for its winter concerts. Close Encounters with Music, whose season is also staged in Scottsdale, Arizona, is another presenter using St. James Church for classical music performances. Barrington Stage Company presents its season of Broadway and off-Broadway comedies, dramas, and musicals at the Consolati Performing Arts Center in Sheffield. The Berkshire Theatre Festival, one of the nation's premier summer theatre festivals, uses the Stockbridge Casino for its Main Stage season of new American works and its Unicorn Theatre for a series of smaller scale and experimental plays.

Essentials

Visual Arts Venues

The Norman Rockwell Museum (Rte. 183, Stockbridge; 413/298-4100; www.nrm.org) Dedicated to the work of an American master.

Tokonoma Gallery (402 Park Street, Housatonic; 413/274-1166) One of the region's best spots for fine crafts by Berkshires artists.

Iris Gallery (47 Railroad Street; 413/644-0045;www.irisgallery.net) Fine art photography.

Performing Arts & Events

The Berkshires Summer Art Festival (see the Southern Berkshire Chamber of Commerce below) July outdoor art show with more than 200 artists.

Aston Magna Festival
(323 Main Street; 413/528-3595;
www.astonmagna.org) Summer series
of early music.

Berkshire Theatre Festival (P.O. Box
797, Stockbridge; 413/298-5536;
www.berkshiretheatre.org) Outstanding
summer season of new, innovative
works.

Wine & Dine

Jack's Grill (1063 Main Street;
Housatonic; 413/274-1000; www.jacks
grill.com) Great food and local art.

Castle Street Café (10 Castle Street;
413/528-5244) Jazz on weekends and a
great wine list.

Limey's (650 N. Main Street, Sheffield;
413/229-9000) Fish & chips and a
draft, mate.

Accommodations

Holiday Inn Express
(415 Stockbridge Road; 413/528-1810;
www.hiexpress.com) Affordable, with
room for families.

The Red Lion Inn (30 Main Street, Stockbridge; 413/298-5545;
www.redlioninn.com) Historic quarters in the middle of
Stockbridge.

Berkshire 1802 House (48 S. Main Street, Sheffield; 413/229-2612;
www.berkshire1802.com) Comfortable, historic B&B.

Information

Southern Berkshire Chamber of Commerce: 362 Main Street;
413/528-1510; www.southernberkshires.com

Population: 2,500

Art Talk

Ronnie Boriskin, director of
the Aston Magna Festival.
We're the only organization doing a
summer festival of chamber music on
early instruments, and while we add a
lot to the cultural diversity of the
Berkshires, we're one of those hidden
treasures that's not as well known as
we could be. We're in our 32nd season,
and we're the result of a partnership
between a musician and an arts patron
who wanted to stage a concert series
on a local estate called Aston Magna.
Now we're performing in town at the
St. James Church and present small and
large programs each summer. Local
businesses give us plenty of support, as
we've carved out this niche for ourselves and attract larger and larger audiences each year. In the coming years
we will take on more touring responsibilities and do more recordings.

Nantucket, Massachusetts

So compact it's easily navigable by bicycle, Nantucket island lies 30 miles off the New England coast and is reached year-round by a ferry system. Nantucket's long attracted individuals seeking a quieter, calmer way of life, and for much of the year the island is peaceful and slow. But during the summer months things take a turn toward the manic when the entire 14.5-mile length of Nantucket is invaded by weekending urbanites from New York, Boston, and beyond. For four months they throw money around like grog-sodden sailors, compelling the island's permanent residents to lock their doors while praying for Labor Day weekend's arrival and the exodus of summer residents. Like many other places with seasonal popularity, Nantucket has become a pricey version of paradise. Artists who bought homes here in the 1980s have prospered from rising real-estate values, and they watched some fellow artists practically run off the island by soaring prices.

More than 80 miles of beaches wrap around Nantucket's boomerang-shaped configuration. The south shore beaches lure surfers, while the north shore beaches are ideal for families. Nantucket harbor, once home to one of the world's largest fleets of whaling vessels, is a historic and beautiful spot where the ferry dock is practically in the middle of town. Cobblestone streets, historic residences from the mid-1800s, and quaint shops are among the commercial center's most charming features. Nearly 40 percent of the island is protected conservation land, and islanders are justifiably proud of their wild moors, sandy beaches, and marshy wetlands. Those actually walking through these areas, however, need to be on the lookout for disease-laden deer ticks.

Arts Scene

In many ways, the arts scene on Nantucket is similar to that in the island Art Town of Friday Harbor, Washington. Both places seem to have just enough of a visual arts presence and performing-arts energy to keep their permanent populations happy, yet they also have the talent reserves to get cranked up to full-throttle summer volume when the need arises. More than a dozen art galleries are sprinkled around downtown Nantucket, exhibiting everything from seascapes to sculptor David Hostetler's hand-carved female forms, as well as the international roster of artists featured at the Art Cabinet gallery space on Union Street. Several of the galleries, including the contemporary art space of Sailor's Valentine, are clustered around the spectacularly beautiful South Wharf, while others, including the top-notch visual arts venue operated by the Artists' Association of Nantucket (AAN), are sited along the business district's commercial streets.

As one of the island's most prominent visual arts venues, the association pursues a vigorous, year-round program of rotating art exhibitions by local, regional, and national artists. It offers lectures by artists and art-world luminaries, exhibits its permanent collection of more than 600 works of art by Nantucket artists in venues such as bank lobbies and the Nantucket Atheneum's first-floor gallery, conducts year-round educational programs for adults and kids in its workshop on Gardner Perry Lane, and even screens art flicks in its AAN Gallery. The island's other leading nonprofit venue for visual arts is the Silo Art Gallery on the campus of the Nantucket Island School of Art & Design, a year-round arts education center offering a range of adult and student workshops in its SeaView Farm Art Center, as well as presenting a highly regarded series of Silo Gallery exhibitions featuring local, regional, and national artists.

The Nantucket Atheneum, a historic structure built in the mid-1800s, uses its Great Hall for a series of poetry readings and lectures by authors, historians, and university professors. During the summer months there's a children's storytelling series in its Weezie Library. In June the Nantucket Film Festival screens 30 independent films at three venues while the Nantucket Arts Council stages a free summer

Art Talk

Doerte Neudert, owner of Art Cabinet of Nantucket.

In the 10 years I've been here I've developed a great group of collectors, many of whom have permanent homes on the island. Contemporary art is gaining more local prominence, and the artists who create that type of work feel very comfortable here. There's this incredibly busy three-month period where we all work very hard to create and sell art, but most artists still need to have winter jobs to make a living here. Younger artists are still coming to Nantucket, getting temporary jobs to get time to work in their studios and experiment with developing their styles and expressions. I prefer keeping my gallery a small space where people can focus on the art, and younger collectors seem to appreciate this kind of approach.

concert series at the Coffin School. The Nantucket Musical Arts Society uses First Congregational Church on Centre Street for its Tuesday-evening summer concert series, while the Nantucket Community Music Center uses its Centre Street location for year-round music education and performances. The two major theatre companies on the island are the Actors Theatre of Nantucket and the Theatre Workshop of Nantucket. The workshop, a year-round community theatre, uses Bennett Hall for its performances of classic and off-Broadway material, while Actors Theatre uses both the upstairs and downstairs of the Historic Methodist Church for its wide-ranging season of comedies, music, readings, short plays, and cabaret nights.

Essentials

Visual Arts Venues

Artists' Association of Nantucket (19 Washington Street; 508/228-0294; www.nantucketarts.org) Year-round education and exhibition programs.

Nantucket Island School of Design & the Arts (23 Wauwinet Road; 508/228-9248; www.nisda.org) Home of the Silo Art Gallery, numerous workshops, and residency programs.

Art Cabinet of Nantucket (2 Union Street; 508/325-7202; www.artcabinet.com) Local, regional, and international contemporary artists.

Performing Arts & Events

Annual Wet Paint Art Auction (Artists' Association of Nantucket; 19 Washington Street; 508/228-0294; www.nantucketarts.org) October event featuring local artists painting the island landscape and auctioning their art that same day.

Nantucket Arts Council Concert Series

(see Nantucket Island Chamber of Commerce below) Free summer concerts at the Coffin School.

Actors Theatre of Nantucket

(12 Alexandria Drive; 508/325-4549; www.nantuckettheatre.com) June to September season of theatre, music, and children's presentations.

Wine & Dine

Nantucket Lobster Trap (23

Washington Street; 508/228-4200; www.nantucketlobstertrap.com) Get a steamed lobster and a bottle of sauvignon blanc.

The Rose & Crown (23 South Water

Street; 508/228-2595; www.theroseand crown.com) Great burgers, cold brew, and the Red Sox on the tube.

Fog Island Café (7 South Water Street;

508/228-1818; www.fogisland.com) Try the Fog-Style Chicken Hash.

Accommodations

Brant Point Inn (6 North Beach Street; 508/228-5442; www.brantpointinn.com) Luxurious B&B within walking distance to the ferry dock.

Roberts House Inn (11 India Street; 508/228-0600; www.robertshouseinn.com) Four historic buildings just off Main Street.

The Wauwinet (Wauwinet Road; 508/228-0145; www.wauwinet.com) Nine miles from town, with waterfront views.

Information

Nantucket Island Chamber of Commerce: 48 Main Street; 508/228-1700; www.nantucketchamber.org.

Population: 3,830

Art Talk

Robert Foster, gallery director for the Artists' Association of Nantucket. We have started an art-reference library that's a nonlending resource intended to expand upon what's available at the Atheneum, which also is one of the main locations for rotating exhibitions of work from our permanent collection. We've tripled our office and workshop spaces, which has allowed us to expand our programs for the island's year-round community of artists. The art market here is very strong, especially in the summertime. We're seeing lots of off-island art dealers trying to establish a retail presence here. Contemporary art has really increased in its presence on the island, and many of our newer members work in contemporary styles.

North Adams, Massachusetts

This small town in northwest Massachusetts is a former manufacturing hub whose brick factory buildings once produced shoes, horse-drawn wagons, textiles, and even electronics. By the late 1980s these industries had run their course, leaving North Adams with an intact infrastructure that the director of the nearby Williams College Museum of Art identified as ideal for large-scale installations of contemporary art. In 1999, after an investment of more than $30 million, buildings with more than 100,000 square feet of visual arts exhibition space covering 19 galleries as well as a 200-seat outdoor cinema, two performance courtyards, a theatre seating up to 850, and two restaurants, opened as MASS MoCA, the Massachusetts Museum of Contemporary Art. Dedicated to exhibiting national and international contemporary art on its 13-acre facility, MASS MoCA is now one of the region's foremost cultural institutions with a contemporary art focus, and its presence has had a dramatic impact on the local and regional economy, attracting more than 100,000 annual visitors.

The landscape surrounding North Adams is pure New England. The college town of Williamstown (home to the Williams College Museum of Art) is a short drive west, while Mt. Greylock to the south, the state's highest peak (3,487 feet), is a popular hiking destination. There are rivers, forests, and state parks around every corner, and just to the north, across the Vermont state line, is Bennington County and its collection of five historic covered bridges. The North Adams of today is a place that's undergone a cultural, social, and economic transformation that mirrors the changes under way in the Art Town of Beacon, New York. Art collectors from across the globe find their way here for MASS MoCA's year-round exhibitions, performances, and public programs, and their spending has led to a substantial local development of restaurants and lodging facilities. Dozens of artists have relocated their full-time residences to North Adams since MASS MoCA's opening, wanting to be close to MASS MoCA's arts programs, with many finding jobs that allow them to also pursue their fine arts careers. . Boston, which is a three-hour drive east, has roped North Adams into its arts orbit, making this Art Town a favored destination for Beantown's cultural tourists.

Arts Scene

Art Talk

Katherine Myers, marketing and public relations director for MASS MoCA.

Since we opened there have been lots of changes in North Adams. You can find cappuccino and wrapped sandwiches, for instance, and downtown's storefronts are 70-percent occupied instead of being 70-percent vacant. We've become a hip, happening place to live, with rising property values and gentrified homes and new businesses. There are lots of studio spaces being developed out of old warehouses, and we've now got lots of venues interested in exhibiting the work of local and national artists. Our exhibitions are centered around broad themes and trends, and if a local artist's work fits into that theme, we'll exhibit their work.

From exhibits of hand-painted movie posters from Ghana to performances by members of the Bang on a Can festival to screenings of *Rebel Without a Cause* to swing dance parties to installations by the likes of Robert Wilson and Joseph Beuys in the separate buildings that house MASS MoCA's 19 galleries, there's no end to the top-rate cultural programming taking place year-round and across all forms of creative media at MASS MoCA. This is one of those rare, small-town places (the Chinati Foundation in the art town of Marfa, Texas, is another) that's plugged into the very essence of the international contemporary art matrix, and artists living in this part of the state don't feel a pressing need to travel far in their quests to stay abreast of the latest developments in the art world.

Even though MASS MoCA's programs and exhibitions are comprehensive, the local arts scene continues outside the doors of the museum. A prime example of this is the Contemporary Artists Center, a working studio and gallery complex in another of North Adams's industrial buildings. Home to a year-round program of exhibitions and artist lectures, the center is located in a 130,000-square-foot brick structure and is also included in the monthly First Friday ArtWalk through downtown North Adams's art businesses.

Nearby Williamstown is home to the Clark Art Institute, an art-education and exhibition center whose focus is historic European and American art, with a special emphasis on Impressionist works. The Williams College Museum of Art emphasizes modern and contemporary works in its exhibitions programs and has developed a strong national reputation for organizing touring exhibitions by many of the nation's top established and emerging artists. The museum also exhibits historic works from its permanent collection and hosts faculty and student exhibitions.

The Williamstown Theatre Festival, a summer event (June–August) emphasizing new American works and stagecraft classics, presents its plays in the 520-seat Adams Memorial Theatre and the 99-seat Nikos Stage. From September to April, the Williams College Center for Theatre & Dance uses both a 200-seat black box and a 550-seat Main Stage for its theatrical presentations. The college also offers more than 100 classical music concerts and recitals annually through its music department. The Williamstown Jazz Festival in late April heralds in the full-bore of New England's spring, while the Williamstown Film Festival screens its features and documentaries in late October and early November.

Essentials

Visual Arts Venues

MASS MoCA (1040 MASS MoCA Way; 413/662-2111; www.mass moca.org) Year-round contemporary art, film, performance, and lectures.

Contemporary Artists Center
(189 Beaver Street; 413/663-9555; www.thecac.org) Working studios, galleries, and performances.

Williams College Museum of Art
(15 Lawrence Hall Drive; 413/597-2429; www.williams.edu) Contemporary art and historical works.

Performing Arts & Events

Williamstown Theatre Festival
(P.O. Box 517; 413/597-3400;
www.wtfestival.org) Summer festival
of new and classic stage works.

Williamstown Jazz Festival
(Williamstown Chamber of Commerce;
800/214-3799; www.williamstown
jazz.com) World-class musicians at the
height of spring.

Williamstown Film Festival (P.O. Box
81; 413/458-9700; www.williamstown
filmfest.com) Fall festival of new,
documentary work.

Wine & Dine

Dora's Café (34 Holden Street;
413/664-9449) Mediterranean classics.

eleven (1040 MASS MoCA Way; 413/662-
2111; www.massmoca.org) Contemporary cuisine on MASS MoCA's campus.

Spice Root (23 Spring Street; 413/458-
5200) Modern Indian cuisine.

Art Talk

Karyn Behnke, director of the
Contemporary Artists Center.
This is a community that continues to
change. There's a great deal of interest
in renovating more buildings and in
expanding the arts community. Many
artists come here just for the summer
months, and a few come back during
the year to work on special projects.
MASS MoCA put the idea into artists'
minds that you could come here, live
in a small community, yet somehow
stay connected to the creative ideas of
international-style work. We dedicate
half of our space to artists creating
work, with exhibition and residential
areas at below-market rates. The cost
of living here is so low that many
artists can actually make a profit by
subletting their city places and moving
here to create art.

Accommodations

Porches Inn (231 River Street; 413/664-0400; www.porches.com)
Converted row houses with a pool.

Holiday Inn Berkshires (40 Main Street; 413/663-6500; www.holiday
innberkshires.com) Room for families and RVs.

Jae's Inn (1111 South State Street; 413/664-0100; www.jaesinn.com)
Affordable rooms, with tennis court and a pool.

Information

Berkshire Chamber of Commerce: 57 Main Street,
413/663-3735; www.berkshirechamber.com
Population: 14,700

Northampton, Massachusetts

framed by the Connecticut River to its east and the Berkshire Mountains to its west, this one-time manufacturing town in rural Massachusetts is ringed by five colleges, each infusing the local culture with a constantly shifting sense of the cutting edge in art, lifestyles, fashion, and music. Settled in the mid-1600s, Northampton retains much of the architectural legacy of its prosperous past. Grand residences built in the 19th century line the tree-shaded streets of its neighborhoods, and its downtown Main Street is filled with multi-story buildings that once housed watchmakers, accountants, and medical offices. Today, Main Street has a vital and beautiful Art Town commercial core and ranks with the likes of Massachusetts Street in Lawrence, Kansas, as a prime example of what small towns dream of when they envision reenergizing their downtowns. Art galleries, ethnic restaurants, nightclubs, independently owned clothing stores, and locally owned booksellers occupy Main Street's prime retail spaces, while the upper levels of these same buildings have been renovated into apartments for the community's college students and young professionals.

Living here means being just two hours away from ball games at Boston's Fenway Park and four hours from the gleaming art museums of New York City. Northampton has turned out to be one of the cultural nerve centers of New England, and artists who years ago fled rising real-estate prices in the distant urban areas have staked a claim to this community's much more affordable and safer quality of life. The local school system is one of the best in the state, a direct result of the numbers of education graduates who complete their studies locally and elect to stay in Northampton to pursue their careers. The community offers an intriguing combination of city conveniences wrapped around the benefits of small-town living. There are great pizzerias as well as several live-music venues bringing national and international music acts into town. There are also two dairies in the area, which is why the town offers its residents some of the best ice-cream shops and restaurant cheese selections in New England. For artists, Northampton offers a supportive arts community and a well-developed arts infrastructure, with studio spaces priced within reach. The town's proximity to major art markets in Vermont, New York City, and Boston makes Northampton an ideally affordable setting in which to base a regional arts career.

The Connecticut River is home to a state park and the well-used Norwottuck Rail Trail Line, a former railroad right of way that's been converted into a paved pathway whose level, winding route crosses rivers and roadways and is a favorite recreation destination for bicyclists, roller bladders, and winter's cross-country skiers. The Connecticut River and Deerfield River are used by kayakers, sailors, tubers, and fishermen, and the Connecticut is also home to the 60-passenger *Quinneticut,* a tourist boat that takes families on summer river cruises. Northampton is also home to Look Park, a tree-shaded refuge whose lawns are the town's favorite places for Frisbee games, picnics, and music performances in the Pines Theatre.

Arts Scene

Communities across the Pioneer Valley region are filled with a sense of excitement about arts and culture. A small town like Easthampton, just a short drive from Northampton, is justifiably proud of the diverse, year-round programming offered through its Pioneer Arts Center, while Charlemont, a community about a 30-minute drive north of here, is home to the highly acclaimed Mohawk Trail Concerts of chamber music in a historic, converted church. Two of the nation's top performing-arts festivals, the Boston Symphony Orchestra's summer residency at Tanglewood and the Jacob's Pillow Dance Festival, are staged about an hour's drive west of Northampton. Four of the five colleges surrounding Northampton offer both theatre and visual arts

programs, and many of their faculty members are intimately connected to the regional arts scene. Right in the middle of Northampton
is Smith College, whose Smith College Museum of Art has received a
$35 million makeover, turning this facility into an ideal environment
for exhibitions of traditional works from its extensive permanent collection as well as traveling national and international contemporary
art shows. With its year-round series of art lectures, exhibitions, and
films, the museum understandably serves as Northampton's contemporary arts focal point.

The Mount Holyoke College Art Museum, one of the nation's oldest teaching museums, is located a short drive away in South Hadley.
It also offers an inspired, year-round slate of contemporary and traditional art exhibitions. The exhibitions programming at the Mead Art
Museum on the Amherst College campus, 15 miles northeast of
Northampton, is decidedly contemporary in its focus, attracting exhibitions from regional, national, and international art institutions. Also
in Amherst is the University of Massachusetts (UMass), whose Fine
Arts Center is home to the University Gallery, a regional venue for traveling national and international exhibitions, as well as the Hampden
Gallery, a small space specializing in local and regional contemporary
art. The nearby community of Williamsburg is home to Snow Farm,
a year-round institute for fine crafts, sculpture, painting, studio glass,
and woodworking.

There are more than a dozen visual arts venues in downtown
Northampton, including the Northampton Center for the Arts, which
is also home to dance classes, film screenings, poetry readings, concerts, and art workshops. The most prominent commercial venue, R.
Michelson Galleries, is located in the soaring spaces of what once was
a bank building. Two of Northampton's movie theatres, the Academy
of Music and Pleasant Street Theatre, specialize in independent and
foreign films and are used as screening venues for the Northampton
Independent Film Festival. Iron Horse Music Hall is the region's top
venue for touring ethnic, folk, and independent record label acts,
while the Pearl Street Nightclub presents bands on the leading edge
of new rock and alternative music. The Calvin Theatre, Northampton's
premier concert venue, hosts major touring music and comedy acts.
The Northampton Community Music Center is home to an extensive,
year-round, children's music education program. Transperformance,
the Northampton Arts Council's annual music bash in August at the
Pines Theater in Look Park, puts a closing note on the community's
summer arts season, while its Four Sundays in February event presents

dance, theatre, film, and music performances in several downtown venues.

Smith College, Amherst College, and Mount Holyoke College each present a season of stage works in their own theatre department playhouses. The UMass Center Series presents an October to April season of top international dance companies, touring symphony orchestras, and theatre companies. New Century Theatre, Northampton's resident professional stage company, presents contemporary plays and Broadway classics. The Massachusetts International Festival of the Arts, which is staged in both Northampton and Holyoke, takes place from late September through October and features a stellar group of experimental and established international performing artists in theatre, dance, film, and music. Commonwealth Opera uses various Northampton venues, including the Pines Theatre and St. John's Episcopal Church, for its November to June series of performances. Musicordia, a summer residency program on the Mount Holyoke College campus, presents a series of July and August concerts and recitals in Chapin Auditorium.

Art Talk

Rich Michelson, owner of R. Michelson Galleries.

The nature of our art scene is changing as the older generation of master artists has stepped aside to make way for the art leaders of tomorrow. There are still lots of creative professionals of all types moving into this area, and the regional museum infrastructure continues to be expanded and renovated, which has allowed for a substantial enhancement of the types of exhibitions being brought into this area. The community's nationally recognized for the number of children's books illustrators who have settled here. Many of the artists coming into Northampton have spent a number of years living in and dealing with the environments of big cities and trade that setting for a town that's supportive, friendly, and close to the Northeast's major cities.

Essentials

Visual Arts Venues

Smith College Museum of Art (Elm Street; 413/585-2760; www.smith.edu) A $35-million makeover has made this on-campus facility one of the nation's premier university art museums.

Northampton Center for the Arts (17 New South Street; 413/584-7327; www.nohoarts.org) Visual art exhibitions, performances, and film.

Art Talk

Linda Muehlig, curator of painting and sculpture for the Smith College Museum of Art.

We're now in a renovated facility with a new, third-floor exhibition space and much more room to fulfill the college's teaching mission. Physically, the renovated museum looks nothing like our former building, and we're now much more opened up in architectural terms to the community. The expanded structure allows us to mount exhibitions that are much more in-depth and also enhances our options for collaborating with the community on town-wide programs. We encourage local artists to come in and take advantage of this museum, to give lectures and participate in our programs. Our collections are growing, and we're moving away from being an institution focused on Western art traditions.

R. Michelson Galleries (132 Main Street; 413/586-3964) Located in a former bank building, this gallery exhibits regional, national, and international contemporary art.

Performing Arts & Events

Massachusetts International Festival of the Arts (274 Main Street; 413/584-4425; www.mifafestival.org) Five weeks of international dance, theatre, and music.

Transperformance (Northampton Arts Council; 240 Main Street; 413/587-1269; www.northamptonartscouncil.org) Summer music and arts festival.

Paradise City Arts Festivals (30 Industrial Drive East; 413/587-0772; www.paradise-city.com) October and May outdoor art shows drawing top national talents.

Wine & Dine

Mulino's Trattoria (41 Strong Ave.; 413/586-8900; www.mulinos.com) Affordable, authentic, casual Italian dining.

Bart's Homemade (235 Main Street; 413/584-0049; www.bartshome made.com) Local, fresh, and delicious ice cream.

Smokin' Lil's (82 Cottage Street, Easthampton; 413/527-5566; www.amysplace.biz) Can't miss with the gumbo of the day.

Accommodations

Allen House Victorian Inn (599 Main Street, Amherst; 413/253-5000; www.allenhouse.com) Within walking distance of Emily Dickinson's house.

The Hotel Northampton (36 King Street; 413/584-3100; www.hotelnorthampton.com) Historic, grand hotel in downtown.

Clarion Hotel (One Atwood Drive; 413/586-1211; www.hampshire hospitality.com) Large, modern, with room for families and a pool.

Information

Greater Northampton Chamber of Commerce: 99 Pleasant Street; 413/584-1900; www.northamptonuncommon.com.

Population: 29,100

Provincetown, Massachusetts

Tucked away at the far end of Cape Cod, a sandy spit of land curling eastward into the Atlantic Ocean from New England's mainland, the Art Town of Provincetown has attracted artists, writers, playwrights, and other creative types for more than a century. Henry Thoreau wandered out this way in the mid-1800s, and Eugene O'Neill not only wrote his first play while holed up in a summer cottage here, but his first produced play was presented by the Provincetown Players in 1916. The community's stature as a visual artists' colony began in 1899 with the arrival of Charles Hawthorne, whose presence attracted the likes of Emily Dickinson and Karl Knaths to a row of Pearl Street studios that are now the Fine Arts Work Center. Those same studios have served as working environments for many of the top names in modern art history, including luminaries such as Helen Frankenthaler, Adolph Gottlieb, Marsden Hartley, and Hans Hofmann. Robert Motherwell was one of the founders of the center, which also serves American writers and displays local art in its Stanley Kunitz Common Room.

Once home to a population of Portuguese fishermen and Yankee traders (June's Portuguese Festival & Blessing of the Fleet is almost as big an event on Provincetown's calendar as is August's Carnival Week of gay and lesbian madness), Provincetown gained art world historical acclaim for its exploration of the white line block print process as developed by the Provincetown Printers. The technique caught on like wildfire and is showcased today in the printmaking studios of several local art businesses.

Much of the land surrounding Provincetown and heading down the Cape past Eastham, about a half-hour's drive south, is protected from development by the Cape Cod National Seashore, whose northernmost tip curls around Provincetown's harbor and includes the granite tower of Pilgrim Monument & Provincetown Museum. The museum also serves as one of the community's many visual arts exhibition venues, explaining through some of its exhibition programs the impact the likes of O'Neill and Hofmann had on the region's arts development. The Pilgrim forefathers of Provincetown would have deeply frowned upon the current laissez-faire attitude that's contributed to Provincetown's standing as one of the nation's premier gay and lesbian residential and resort communities. On the other hand, just how much fun were those Pilgrim nightclubs, anyway? They couldn't have held a candle to the drag shows at Esther's or the x-rated comedians who circuit through the Alibi and the cabaret shows at the Paramount. Those frowning Englishmen never would have fit in with today's micro-dressed, bicycle-pedaling, whale-watching Provincetown tourists.

Arts Scene

From one end of Cape Cod to the other, there are so many art galleries crowded onto this narrow strip of sea grass and sand that if they all were to disappear one mysterious night the entire Cape would be in danger of blowing away in the next big storm. There are more than 200 art galleries calling the Cape their home, and no fewer than 60 of them are scattered across Provincetown's enjoyably walkable streets. Just down the road a few miles in Wellfleet there's another dozen or so galleries, while also nearby is the Truro Center for the Arts at Castle Hill, a facility concentrating on arts education and workshops but also offering a visual art exhibition series, artist lectures, art films, and music performances on a year-round basis. The Fine Arts Work Center on Pearl Street is in many ways emblematic of the continuing legacy of creative integrity that's provided a century's worth of inspiration for the Provincetown arts scene. Its reputation among artists and writers is one of the best anywhere, and its capacity to attract writers and artists for its year-round readings, lectures, and workshops has elevated the center to the forefront of the nation's creative edge.

The town's premier visual arts venue is the Provincetown Art Association and Museum, whose quarters on Commercial Street are being expanded into the sort of full-scale, museum-quality exhibition, storage, and education facility the community has so long deserved. Established in 1914, the museum's galleries have a strong focus on the work of historic and contemporary Cape Cod and New England artists, exhibiting paintings and sculpture through both one-artist and themed shows. Home to a schedule of year-round classes in various visual arts disciplines, the museum also organizes events such as the annual Secret Garden Tour in July, the Blue Door Concert Series of chamber music from June through September, and the Dick Miller and Friends jazz nights.

One of the more recent entrants on the local arts scene is the Schoolhouse Center for Art & Design on Commercial Street in the East End gallery district. Home to the Silas-Kenyon Gallery, which is used year-round for contemporary art from local and regional artists, and the Driskel Gallery, which emphasizes historic photography, the center also is home to Manso Hall, a performance space used for theatre, dance, and music. The region's largest exhibition space, the Cape Museum of Fine Arts, is located in the town of Dennis, itself home to a cluster of art galleries, about an hour's drive south of Provincetown. Two of the annual highlights of the Provincetown arts calendar are the Spring Arts Showcase Weekend in early May and the Fall Arts Festival, which spreads across four weekends in September and October. Both events are organized by the Fine Arts Work Center, with the spring weekend featuring an outdoor art fair in Bas Relief Park as well as numerous exhibition openings at various galleries, artist lectures at several venues, and concerts at local restaurants. The Fall Arts Festival is a much larger production that embraces all of the spring event's functions and adds in studio tours, an art auction at the museum, a playwright's festival at the Schoolhouse Center, and concerts at the Universalist Unitarian Meeting House on Commercial Street, which is also home to the Sundays at 5 concert series of classical music performances.

The Provincetown International Film Festival of more than 50 screenings takes place in June, while the Provincetown Fringe Festival of new theatrical works is staged from late June through July at the Provincetown Inn. In nearby North Truro, the Payomet Performing Arts Center is home to a year-round slate of music, dance, and theatre productions for adults and kids. Things really get up to full speed during the summer performing-arts season when the venue is home to a jammed schedule of Shakespeare, off-Broadway, and children's programs. The Provincetown Theatre on Bradford Street is home to the two most prominent performing-arts organizations in the nation, Provincetown Theatre Company and Provincetown Repertory Theatre Company. The repertory company is a summer professional theatre organization whose material tends to be drawn from new American drama and whose season runs from June through September. The theatre company is a year-round community theatre group whose new and classic material is oriented toward both adult and youth audiences and is widely recognized. Fall Playwright's Festival is one of the highlights of the Fall Arts Festival.

Essentials

Visual Arts Venues

Fine Arts Work Center (24 Pearl Street; 508/487-9960; www.fawc.org) Year-round literary and visual arts programs.

Provincetown Art Association and Museum (460 Commercial Street; 508/487-1750; www.paam.org) Expanding into a new, multidimensional facility.

The Schoolhouse Center for Art & Design (494 Commercial Street; 508/487-4800; www.schoolhousecenter.com) Includes a historic photography gallery.

Performing Arts & Events

Spring Arts Weekend & Fall Arts Festival (Fine Arts Work Center; 24 Pearl Street; 508/487-9960; www.fawc.org) Signaling the beginning and conclusion of Provincetown's busy summer arts season.

Art Talk

Larry Collins, director of the Front Gallery of the Schoolhouse Center for Art & Design.

We're set up to exhibit photography in the Front Gallery and contemporary art in the Back Gallery, with our photography emphasis on vintage work. Photographers have been working in this area since the 1950s, but Provincetown is mainly a place interested in paintings. We also show things that are not normally part of what's exhibited here, like science photography and anonymous studio work, as well as the blue-chip stuff. The community attracts big-time art dealers from New York City and Boston who are sophisticated buyers and a large part of our collector base. Our presence in town has done a lot to establish Provincetown as the kind of place where serious photography professionals want to show their work.

Art Talk

Thom Egan, executive director of the Provincetown Theatre Foundation.

The history of Provincetown as a theatre community dates back to 1915 and Eugene O'Neill. As a foundation we're now building a performance space for two theatre companies, the Provincetown Rep, which is our equity company, and the Provincetown Theatre Company, which is our long-standing community theatre organization. To have community and equity theatre companies exist in the same building is practically unheard of, but both organizations are committed to using this facility equally. The building will also be rented, from time to time, to outside promoters, which will help keep the place affordable for the theatre companies. Serious theatre tends to be staged during the shoulder seasons, as is the case with our Playwrights Festival, while in summer we do the popular, more broadly appealing shows.

Provincetown Repertory Theatre Company & Provincetown Theatre Company (238 Bradford Street; 508/487-7487; www.provincetown theatre.org) Summer drama, musicals and comedies, plus year-round classics.

Sundays at 5 (see Provincetown Chamber of Commerce below) Summer classical music series.

Wine & Dine

The Lobster Pot (321 Commercial Street; 508/487-0842; www.ptown lobsterpot.com) A not-to-be-missed, P-Town tradition.

Ciro & Sal's (4 Kiley Court; 508/487-6444; www.cirosandsals.com) Best Italian food in town, try the vitello picatto.

Esther's (186 Commercial Street; 508/487-7555; www.estherlives.com) Downstairs piano bar, patio dining.

Accommodations

The Red Inn (15 Commercial Street; 508/487-7334; www.theredinn.com) Historic inn close to the galleries.

The Brass Key Guesthouse (67 Bradford Street; 508/487-9005; www.brasskey.com) Quiet, upscale inn with a pool.

Bill White's Motel (29 Bradford Street Extension; 508/487-1042; www.billwhitesmotel.com) An authentic slice of the old Cape Cod.

Information

Provincetown Chamber of Commerce: 307 Commercial Street; 508/487-3424; www.ptownchamber.com

Population: 3,600

Newport, Rhode Island

This maritime community, less than a two-hour drive south of Boston, is home to a treasure trove of historic mansions as well as one of the nation's most active sailing centers, a navy base, and a jam-packed summer tourist season. Newport's filled with art festivals as well as gala events catering to the substantial numbers of New England socialites who spend their days riding polo ponies and dreaming of another Newport-based America's Cup winner.

Founded in 1639, Newport retains much of the architectural flavor of its historic past. Seafood and shipping formed the town's economic base up to the late 1800s, when the Astors, Vanderbilts, and other super-rich industrialist families decided that Bellevue Avenue and Ocean Drive would be the perfect places to build America's first neighborhood of palatial mansions. Soon, grand European-style estates became all the rage among The 400, as the Gilded Age's wealthy were known. About this same time, Newport developed a large community of professionals who the wealthy patronized for assistance with matters of style and substance. Today, many of the so-called summer cottages built by The 400 are open to the public. Some would say it's only fitting that the ghosts of Caroline Astor and Cornelius Vanderbilt are doomed to an eternity of watching families traipse through their sitting rooms.

Arts Scene

Newport's arts scene is as varied as the summer Evening Picnics concert series on the grounds of the Newport Art Museum. The concert series takes place in venues such as the 1864 Griswold House, the Kahn Building, and the 1919 Cushing Gallery, with local artists showcased at the DeBlois Gallery, an artist-run cooperative on Bellevue Avenue. The Art Museum serves as the core force behind Newport's creative community, using its Artists' Open Space for year-round shows by local and regional artists, and its Wright and Ilgenfritz galleries for changing exhibitions of traveling national and international art, as well as the museum's permanent collection. There are year-round art classes in the Kahn Building, a popular Winter Lectures series, and gala events such as the Artists' Ball in April and Wet Paint in August. There are about a dozen commercial art galleries in Newport, and an important nonprofit visual arts group is Island Arts. Operating from an upstairs facility on Pelham Street, Island Arts focuses on local and regional contemporary work and also organizes a kids' summer art camp. Project One, another local nonprofit, produces public art events such as the September and October show called "Wind, Sea & Sky," a performance and sculpture event on First Beach. The state's premier outdoors arts and crafts show, the Newport Arts Festival, is staged in September at Fort Adams State Park.

On its performing-arts side, Newport offers everything from summer Shakespeare in Queen Anne Square to the huge crowds at three summer music festivals dedicated to classical, jazz, and folk music. The Newport Jazz Festival and the Newport Folk Festival take place on consecutive August weekends in Fort Adams State Park. Each festival showcases top-name acts and draws huge crowds. The Newport Music Festival, staged across two weeks in July, uses a variety of local venues for its slate of more than 60 classical music concerts and recitals, including several staged in historic mansions. The Swanhurst Chorus and the Newport Baroque Orchestra both present their concerts mainly during the winter months and will likely use the Newport Performing Arts Center when it's completed in 2007. Beechwood Theatre Company performs period pieces about Newport's past at the Beechwood Mansion, while Island Moving Company, a resident troupe of dancers, is affiliated with the Newport Academy of Ballet. The Firehouse Theatre stages its year-round slate of off-Broadway works in its own facility on Equality Park Place.

Essentials

Visual Arts Venues

Newport Art Museum (76 Bellevue Avenue; 401/848-8200; www.newport artmuseum.com) Local, national, and international exhibitions of traditional and contemporary artwork.

Deblois Gallery (138 Bellevue Avenue; 401/847-9977; www.debloisgallery.com) Local and regional contemporary art.

Island Arts (3 Pelham Street; 401/848-2775) Contemporary art space with a community focus.

Performing Arts & Events

Newport Folk Festival (see Newport Visitors Center below) August weekend of top-name acts.

Newport Arts Festival (see Newport Visitors Center below) September shows of fine arts and crafts in Fort Adams State Park.

The Newport Music Festival (850 Aquidneck Avenue; 401/849-0700; www.newportmusic.com) More than 60 classical music concerts in July.

Wine & Dine

The Market-Newport Gourmet (43 Memorial Boulevard; 401/848-2600; www.newportgourmet.com) Great salads and sandwiches, including a true mussel salad.

Twenty-Two Bowen's
(Bowen's Wharf; 401/841-8884; www.22bowens.com) Great wine bar and restaurant.

Art Talk

Valorie Sheehan, sculptor.
The Deblois Gallery is the only non-profit cooperative in town, and our mission is to promote the work of emerging and member artists. We have 14 member artists and 4 associate members. Most of our exhibitions focus on artists from the southern New England area. We do one open show each year that includes artists from around the community. Newport is a double-edged sword of a place. It's beautiful and inspirational for the dozens of traditional-style artists who live here and paint the landscape. But it's also a very expensive place and a tough place for contemporary artists to find buyers for their work. The availability of low-cost studio space is such an issue here that many artists are thinking of moving away.

Art Talk

Nancy Grinnell, curator of the Newport Art Museum.

On a historic level, we have a large, permanent collection of art by painters and sculptors from Newport's past. On the contemporary level, we do a lot with artists associated with RISD Rhode Island School of Design. We try to partner with all of the state's art institutions, and we do a lot of collaborative work throughout the region with non-profits, commercial galleries, and educational institutions. There's a group of avant-garde artists living in Newport and we work with them on events such as Project One, a month-long installation of art on the beach. Those artists also exhibit in the annual "Visions" show in a church, our annual juried show, and the exhibitions in our non-juried Artists Open Space gallery.

Sardella's Italian Restaurant (30 Memorial Boulevard, West Newport; 401/849-6312; www.sardellas.com) Typically great, Rhode Island take on Italian food. Get the calamari.

Accommodations

The Hotel Viking (One Bellevue Avenue; 401/847-3300; www.hotel viking.com) Old-fashioned-style in the historic Hill district.

Sea Whale Motel (150 Aquidneck Avenue; 401/846-7071; www.sea whale.com) Affordable, with ocean views.

Aunt Polly's B&B (349 Valley Road; 401/847-2160; www.pollysbnb.com) A mile from the tourist hubbub, comfortable and peaceful.

Information

Newport Visitors Center: 23 America's Cup Avenue; 401/845-9123; www.gonewport.com

Population: 26,900

Brattleboro, Vermont

Vermont's southeast corner is framed by the Connecticut River on its eastern boundary and the majestic Green Mountains to its west. Brattleboro, a former industrial community located close to the river amid a confluence of valleys, has made a name for itself as one of New England's most arts-supportive communities. It has successfully used the presence of artists, galleries, and art organizations as a key leveraging point in a broad-scale effort to revitalize its downtown business district. In the past decade, empty storefronts have been returned to life as bakeries, coffee bars, cafés, and fine crafts shops selling the work of hundreds of talented artists living in Brattleboro as well as in neighboring communities such as Putney, Marlboro, and Guilford. Brattleboro grew like topsy in its early years, benefiting from a manufacturing economy that cranked out organs, sewing machines, wood products, and textiles. The arrival of the Vermont Valley Railroad brought trainloads of dyspeptic tourists who flocked here for baths in mineral spring waters, and while those same waters are today used by local residents for canoe excursions and tubing trips down the West River and Whetstone Brook, the railroad's historic presence has been memorialized by the conversion of Union Station into the Brattleboro Museum & Art Center.

Artists have found southeast Vermont to be an ideal place to base themselves and build their studios while remaining close to the Northeast's major urban centers as well as the lucrative marketing opportunities in Vermont and New Hampshire galleries catering to the region's year-round flow of tourists. It seems that every possible means of exploiting urban dwellers' passions for rural experiences has been folded into the region's tourism initiatives, and from spring's sugaring season to autumn's foliage spectaculars, Windham County roads are clogged with out-of-state vehicles filled with weekending city folks. Winters are loaded with tribes of snowboarders headed toward the slopes at Mts. Snow and Stratton. For artists living in the region, the name of the game is to have some sort of a local gallery presence but to also focus one's efforts on developing market outlets elsewhere.

Arts Scene

Brattleboro has not only been exceedingly wise in its strategy to use the presence of street-level galleries, upper-story artist studios, and a broad array of arts events in implementing its downtown revitalization strategy, it's also hooked a dramatic expansion of its downtown's vitality into the redevelopment of a triplex cinema and hotel into a state-of-the-art performing and visual arts center. The Latchis Hotel project is part of a multimillion dollar effort to turn the hotel into the sort of performing-arts venue that the region's many theatre and music organizations have longed for. The Latchis Performing Arts Center is expected to serve as an anchor for even further development of the downtown arts and cultural scene. At present, the Hooker-Dunham Theater and Gallery on Main Street are Brattleboro's most popular performing-arts venues. Managed by Wild Root Arts, the theatre is used for screenings of films as well as occasional presentations of concerts by touring national acts. Community music and theatre organizations such as the Apron Theatre Company, which stages its plays and readings on a year-round basis, use the Hooker-Dunham, as do performing-arts presenters such as Acting on Impulse and Folk Poetry. The building's art gallery is a nonjuried art space that's open to the community at large for rotating exhibitions of work ranging from photography to painting, sculpture, and fine crafts.

The town's visual arts jewel is the Brattleboro Museum & Art Center, housed in a beautifully restored railroad depot whose grounds include the Green River Watershed Garden. The center presents eight exhibitions annually, featuring local, regional, and national artists. Year-round art workshops for adults and kids are held at the center, as are monthly artist lectures. The popular Twilight Wandering series of rural hikes during the year's warmer months are another of the center's programs, as is the WindowWorks visual art exhibition program, which installs art in downtown Brattleboro business locales. One of the most successful of all the Art Town art walks is Brattleboro's Gallery Walk, a First Friday event that organizes exhibitions of primarily local and regional work in more than two dozen downtown venues that include cafés, coffee bars, and retail shops. Though much of the local arts community seems to prefer exhibiting in these alternative venues, several commercial art galleries have managed to find a stable niche in the local economy, including the Vermont Center for Photography, a facility offering year-round workshops, lectures, and exhibitions. Marlboro College, located just a short drive west of town, is home to the Drury Gallery, which presents regional and national visual art exhibitions during the academic year.

The star of Brattleboro's performing-arts scene is its classical music side, which is anchored by the Marlboro Music School and Festival, a program offering advanced music studies to an international roster of emerging music talent. The festival uses Persons Auditorium on Marlboro College's hilltop campus for its classes as well as for more than a dozen concerts. During the summer months there's a varied slate of music offered on weekend nights as part of Stratton Mountain's Village Concerts series. The New England Bach Festival uses All Souls Church, Persons Auditorium, and Centre Congregational Church for its series of October concerts and recitals. The festival is a program of the Brattleboro Music Center, which also presents a winter Chamber Music Series as well as September to May concerts in various southern Vermont communities through the Windham Orchestra. During the summer months the Yellow Barn Music School and Festival in nearby Putney emphasizes chamber music during its three-month season of classes and nearly 30 concerts. Whittemore Theatre on the Marlboro College campus is home to the college's winter performing-artists series, while the Vermont Jazz Center uses a restored facility on Cotton Mill Hill for its Wednesday-evening jazz jams and year-round music classes.

New England Youth Theatre presents its programs in a downtown, converted retail storefront, while the Vermont Renaissance Festival stages its historic pageantry during June and July in nearby Vernon. Sandglass Theatre, which hosts an annual festival of puppet theatre in September, presents its year-round slate of puppet-theatre productions in a 60-seat Putney venue. The Vermont Theatre Company, which presents an annual Shakespeare in the Park production in Living Memorial Park, is a community theatre company that presents

Art Talk

Linda Rubinstein, acting director of the Brattleboro Museum & Art Center.

Brattleboro's a real community that's friendly and beautiful, with six nearby villages. There's even an international presence here, with a very well-traveled arts community that's brought a strong sense of creative possibilities to this area. Our monthly gallery walk has become enormously popular and has turned into the town's favorite excuse to party. We stay very realistic in terms of deciding the things we can and cannot do within our budgetary limitations. Accessibility to our programs by the community's children is a top priority, as is attracting more visitors into town. The arts are seen as one of the main vehicles through which Brattleboro can build a prosperous future.

its season of contemporary and classic works in venues that include Brattleboro High's auditorium and the Hooker-Dunham Theater.

Essentials

Visual Arts Venues

Brattleboro Museum & Art Center (10 Vernon Street; 802/257-0124; www.brattleboromuseum.org) Art center in an historic train depot.

Hooker-Dunham Theater & Gallery (139 Main Street; 802/254-9276) Nonjuried, public space.

Vermont Center for Photography (49 Flat Street; 802/251-6051; www.vcphoto.org) Exhibiting top regional photographers.

Performing Arts & Events

The Vermont Arts & Fine Crafts Festival (P.O. Box 597, Stratton Mountain; 802/362-0110; www.vtarts festival.com) Ten-day, late-summer, outdoor art show with more than 300 artists at Stratton Mountain.

Yellow Barn Music School & Festival (63 Main Street, Putney; 802/387-6637; www.yellowbarn.org) Six summer weeks of chamber music workshops and concerts.

Vermont Theatre Company (P.O. Box 11; 802/258-1344; www.vermonttheatrecompany.com) Year-round performances.

Wine & Dine

Mocha Joe's Café (82 Main Street; 802/257-7794; www.mochajoes.com) Great buzz shop and arts venue.

Amy's Bakery Arts Café (113 Main Street; 802/251-1071) European hearth breads and local art.

Chelsea Royal Diner (487 Western Avenue; 802/254-8399; www.chelsea royaldiner.com) Authentic diner, with a daily Blue Plate Special.

Accommodations

The Putney Inn (57 Putney Landing Road; Putney; 802/387-5517; www.putneyinn.com) Historic B&B with a great restaurant.

Colonial Motel & Spa (889 Putney Road; 802/257-7733; www.colonial motelspa.com) Traditional comfort and relaxation.

EconoLodge (515 Canal Street; 802/254-2360; www.econolodge.com) Affordable, with a pool and RV parking.

Information

Brattleboro Area Chamber of Commerce: 180 Main Street, 802/254-4565, www.brattleborochamber.org

Population: 12,400

Art Talk

Christine Triebert, board president of the Vermont Center for Photography.

We were founded in 1998 by a photographer who had rented out the old cooperative market space, and we've now grown to become a self-sustaining membership organization that appeals to photographers across New England. We still organize photography workshops, do portfolio critiques, and put on some amazing exhibitions of work by photographers with national reputations. There are a number of local artists who are doing quite well in their careers, but for most of us the challenge is to be exhibited in other regions. Brattleboro is full of venues that welcome the work of younger artists, and lots of local people turn out to see these shows.

Burlington, Vermont

As the largest city in a state filled with small towns, Burlington has developed its own, self-contained arts scene. Located on the east shores of Lake Champlain, about a two-hour drive south of Montréal, Burlington is loaded with architectural legacies of its historic past yet has successfully defined itself as a can-do type of community that's fully embraced modern technology. In many ways, Burlington serves as a miniature model of Seattle, a politically and socially progressive waterfront community with a large cadre of college students, regional power brokers, and independent, creative thinkers. The University of Vermont's (UVM) campus takes up a chunk of Burlington's residential landscape, as does the St. Michael's College campus in nearby Winooski. To the east, the tallest peaks of the Green Mountains are home to several top-notch ski resorts less than an hour's drive from downtown's Church Street Marketplace, a pedestrian-oriented cluster of art-exhibiting cafés, nightclubs, used-record shops, bookstores, and art galleries. Ferries cross Lake Champlain year-round, carrying summer's tourists to Port Kent, New York, and winter's skiers toward the powder slopes at Lake Placid.

As a community with two universities, Burlington is home to a vibrant music scene that supports several live-music venues booking national talents on a year-round basis. During the summer months the Battery Park Free Concert Series on the lakeshore features both national and regional acts, and historic landmarks such as Shelburne Farms, a 1,400-acre facility that's part art center, part dairy farm, and part venue for everything from chamber music performances to the annual Flynn Performing Arts Center's Fine Wine and Food Festival, lure locals from tending their backyard vegetable gardens. In recent years the industrial warehouses and strip malls of South Burlington have turned out to be ideal terrain for the region's blossoming contemporary arts scene, a development in large part fueled by the talented art grads who finish their studies each spring at UVM and elect to stay on in Burlington's arts supportive, affordable, and friendly climate. The annual South End Art Hop, a September event featuring art in dozens of indoor and outdoor venues, is the best time to get a handle on the local, contemporary arts scene.

Arts Scene

Burlington's visual art's venues include a larger than average number of alternative spaces in the form of restaurants, cafés, and even the lobby of the Flynn Performing Arts Center. Arts Alive, which maintains a public gallery space in Union Station, coordinates a great deal of this activity as well as an annual downtown arts festival in June. Monthly First Friday Art Walks coordinate openings at more than a dozen of these downtown spaces, including the Firehouse Center for the Visual Arts, an exhibiting and educational facility whose year-round contemporary shows, lectures, art workshops, children's summer art camp, and performances provide the focal point for Burlington's arts scene. The center also coordinates the community's public art program as well as the summer concerts series in Battery Park. While year-round exhibitions also take place at the Shelburne Farms historic landmark, located just a short drive south of downtown, the jewel of Burlington's visual arts scene is the Fleming Museum on the UVM campus. Founded in 1931, the museum has evolved into a highly regarded exhibiting and collecting entity whose year-round exhibitions accommodate talents from the local and regional arts community as well as touring national and international shows. It participates in the First Friday Art Walk and offers a range of year-round programs including lectures, film screenings, and children's art classes.

The Flynn Performing Arts Center, a fully restored art deco masterpiece, was once exclusively the home of the Lyric Theatre Company, which still uses the Flynn for its two annual music theatre productions. In the early 1980s the facility was turned into a performing-arts center whose Main Stage and FlynnSpace black box are used

Art Talk

Caroline Whiddon, executive director of the Vermont Youth Orchestra Association.

Adults in Burlington are excited about the opportunity to involve the community's young people in music, which is why we've had little difficulty putting together a three-year, $2-million capital campaign to fund our new concert hall, which also includes classroom and administrative space as well as a rehearsal hall. The level of interest and respect for what music means at all stages of a person's life is at a very high level in Vermont, and kids get started in music at an early age. While we're successful in reaching our yearly fundraising goals, it will be interesting to see how things pan out with school-based music education funding in the coming legislative session.

year-round by many regional performing-arts organizations, including the Vermont Symphony Orchestra and UVM for its Lane Series of national and international performing-arts groups. The Flynn itself presents more than 60 annual performances on its stages, including a Student Matinee Series, concerts, and touring Broadway theatre. The Vermont Youth Orchestra, which once used the Flynn for its four annual concerts, has renovated a former gymnasium on the St. Michaels College campus into the Elley-Long Music Center, which is now its home base as well as the preferred venue for the Vermont Mozart Festival's winter series of concerts (the youth festival summers at Shelburne Farms).

UVM Theatre uses the Royall Tyler Stage on campus for its season of six plays during the academic year, while Theatre on a Shoestring stages its two annual productions in the FlynnSpace. Vermont Stage Company, the region's most prominent theatre group, presents its September to May season of five contemporary plays and local works at FlynnSpace. In June the Discover Jazz Festival takes downtown Burlington's indoor and outdoor performance venues by storm with its week of shows by top-name national acts, while the Vermont International Film Festival in October is staged across several days in several downtown venues.

Essentials

Visual Arts Venues

The Firehouse Center for the Arts (149 Church Street; 802/865-7156; www.burlingtoncityarts.com) Year-round exhibitions and art programs.

Fleming Museum (University of Vermont campus; 802/656-0750; www.flemingmuseum.org) Contemporary and traditional exhibitions by local, regional, and national artists.

Vermont State Craft Center (85 Church Street; 802/863-6458; www.froghollow.org) One of the Northeast's top fine crafts galleries, representing more than 250 artisans.

Performing Arts & Events

South End Art Hop (180 Flynn Street; 802/859-9222; www.seaba.com) Annual weekend of open studios and exhibitions.

Arts Alive Festival of Fine Arts (1 Main Street; 802/864-1557) June weekend of outdoor art exhibitions and indoor shows at several venues.

Flynn Performing Arts Center (153 Main Street; 802/652-4500; www.flynncenter.org) Art deco classic with two performance stages.

Art Talk

Stephen Doll, co-owner of the Doll-Anstadt Gallery.

I've been in the contemporary art market for six years, and in some ways having a gallery like this in Burlington has been difficult, but in other ways it hasn't. We've filled a niche here and have tapped in to a great audience for contemporary art by being one of the few places willing to exhibit this kind of work. But what's not here is that critical mass of buyers you need as a gallery in order to economically justify what you're doing. Lots of folks enjoy what we're doing, and finding artists who create good, strong work has never been a problem. Eighty percent of the gallery's artists are from the Burlington area.

Wine & Dine

New England Culinary Institute (250 Main Street, Montpelier; 802/223-6324; www.neculinary.com) Gourmet dining in a culinary arts center.

Ali Baba's Kabob Shop (163 Main Street; 802/862-5752) Great Middle Eastern food.

Uncommon Grounds (42 Church Street; 802/865-6227) Buzz shop with local art shows.

Accommodations

Willard Street Inn (349 S. Willard Street; 802/651-8710; www.willardstreetinn.com) Historic B&B in a great location.

Liberty Inn (462 Shelburne Road; 802/862-5754) Affordable, with a pool.

Anchorage Inn (108 Dorset Street; 802/863-7000; www.vtanchorageinn.com) Affordable, with a pool and room for families.

Information

Lake Champlain Regional Chamber of Commerce: 60 Main Street, 802/863-3489; www.vermont.org

Population: 39,500

The Mid-Atlantic

Beacon, New York

Until May 2003, there wasn't enough arts action taking place in Beacon, a one-time manufacturing town in New York's Hudson River Valley about 90 miles north of New York City, to have made a strong enough case for this community's inclusion as one of the 100 Best Art Towns. Certainly, organizations such as the Howland Cultural Center and the Tallix foundry had long provided arts programming and arts-related employment in Beacon, but there wasn't a sufficient concentration of arts-related amenities that normally round out a community's arts scene.

All that changed when the Dia Art Foundation, the nation's most forward-looking contemporary arts institution, opened the doors of what not very long ago had been a 300,000-square-foot building used to print cookie packages and boxes. The 1929 steel, concrete, and glass structure, which has more than 34,000 square feet of skylights, has been extensively renovated into Dia:Beacon, a 240,000-square-foot complex of galleries (the rest is used for administration and storage) that's home to a permanent collection and changing exhibitions of the very best international contemporary art. With the opening of Dia: Beacon, this quiet community has vaulted into the ranks of the world's must-see art sites, and the Dia Art Foundation, which among its many efforts supports the Chinati Foundation in the Art Town of Marfa, Texas, the Lightning Fields in Quemado, New Mexico, and the Roden Crater Project near the Art Town of Flagstaff, Arizona, has brought into existence yet another sterling example of how arts can transform a community and a region.

The Beacon of today has been flipped around into a community that's finely attuned to the flow of the international contemporary art world. Most of downtown's retail locations have been either spiffed up or reopened as businesses whose fates are at least in some way tied to the contemporary art lovers who trek up the Hudson River Valley for Dia: Beacon events and exhibitions. Some of these newcomer businesses and newly arrived resident artists are drawn from the ranks of New York City dwellers who were searching about for the right set of creative circumstances that would allow them to once and for all put the city's stresses and expenses behind them. A surprising number have also been drawn here from across the globe as well as from the Hudson Valley region, and it has been their efforts that have combined with the energy of the refugee urbanites to forge a new Beacon culture that's set this community's arts scene on a path toward a promising future.

Arts Scene

Dia:Beacon has provided a home for works of art by Andy Warhol, Agnes Martin, James Turrell, Bruce Nauman, Donald Judd, Dan Flavin, and many other stars of the world's contemporary arts scene. Dia has also brought a top-notch bookstore to Beacon as well as initiated an artist lecture series, must-do opening receptions, and a model Arts in Education program for Beacon's schools at the elementary and high school levels. Immediately preceding the opening of Dia:Beacon, the community experienced a startling influx of arts-related investment in the form of everything from sleek coffee bars to nearly a dozen sophisticated galleries to the arrival of another well-funded contemporary art venture, the Beacon Project Space. One of the most visible efforts initiated by this venture is its redevelopment of the former Beacon High School into a creative community center, called Bulldog Studios, modeled along lines similar to those found at the Emerson Cultural Center in the Art Town of Bozeman, Montana. By mid-2005 it will be a place as attractive to artists needing affordable studio space as it will be to architects and designers seeking a supportive, creative environment in which they can pursue their projects. Beacon Project Space also has launched a contemporary art exhibition series in its Main Street gallery location, as well as a Talking Beacon lecture series and a Beacon Performing Arts series presenting music, dance, and theatre programs at various Beacon venues. All of these efforts focus on bringing top international and national talents to Beacon.

The breakneck pace of contemporary art development has had a decided impact on the Howland Cultural Center. The center, founded in 1872 as Beacon's library, is home to the Howland Chamber Music Circle's Sunday concert series, the Coffeehouse Series of jazz, blues, and world music on first Saturdays from September through June, a Concert Performances series by members of Local 238–291 of the American Federation of Musicians, a monthly visual arts exhibitions series focusing on Hudson Valley artists, and year-round art classes for kids.

The 90-acre Beacon campus of the University Settlement uses its 150-seat theatre as a venue for the May to September concerts and performances of US Arts, a recently established summer festival series that brings dance companies and other performing artists to Beacon. The community of Garrison, a short drive south of Beacon, is home to the Hudson Valley Shakespeare Festival and the Garrison Art Center. Storm King Art Center, just across the Hudson River from Beacon, is home to one of the world's premier collections of monumental scale, American and European modern sculpture from the 1960s to the present.

Artist 1

Florence Northcutt, board president of the Howland Cultural Center.

It's been amazing to have the Dia Foundation here. The quality of what they're doing and the impact they're having on this community is unbelievable. Main Street has been renovated, restored, and saved through an influx of galleries, restaurants, and new shops, and our architectural legacy has been retained. Dia has, from the get-go, worked to be a good neighbor to all of Beacon. Their old Nabisco building had been a problem for years, but now it's the jewel of the community. Dia's done wonderful work in our school system, and their impact has led to the town having its first-ever gallery association. The Howland now has more visitors than ever before, and art collectors are walking our downtown's streets seven days a week.

Essentials

Visual Arts Venues

Dia:Beacon (3 Beekman Street; 845/440-0100; www.diabeacon.org) Top-notch contemporary art, public programs, and a great bookstore.

Beacon Project Space (211 Fishkill Avenue; 845/831-1277; www.beaconprojectspace.org) Contemporary art exhibitions, performances, and an artists' studio project.

Artist 2

Stephen Evans, assistant director of Dia:Beacon.
We've approached our presence here from a perspective that has us working with local schools and teachers to get their students into our facility and use Dia:Beacon as an educational tool. Our education program is innovative and works to make this building an integral part of the entire community. We've also worked to be part of the local arts community. We're a member of the area cultural association, which includes galleries, shops and restaurants, and has led to the establishing of a dialogue among the town's cultural institutions. Our long-term interests involve the redevelopment of Beacon's waterfront and working to promote an arts-based economy that will serve the needs of the entire community.

Howland Cultural Center (477 Main Street; 845/831-4988; www.howland culturalcenter.org) Focused on music, poetry readings, and regional art exhibitions.

Performing Arts & Events

Second Saturday Beacon (see Dutchess County Tourism below) More than two dozen venues coordinating monthly openings.

Garrison Art Center Fine Arts & Crafts Fair (23 Garrison's Landing, Garrison; 845/424-3960; www.garrisonart center.org) August outdoor art show with more than 100 artists.

Coffeehouse Series (Howland Cultural Center; 477 Main Street; 845/831-4988; www.howlandculturalcenter.org) Jazz, blues, and chamber music on first Saturdays from September through June.

Wine & Dine

Chthonic Clash (418 Main Street; 845/831-0359; www.chthonicclash.com) Fresh-roasted java and rotating exhibitions in the Two Sevens Gallery.

The Piggy Bank (448 Main Street; 845/838-0028; www.piggybankrestaurant.com) Memphis-style barbecue, plus Smokin' Fridays blues nights, and racks of ribs.

Brother's Trattoria (465 Main Street; 845/838-3300) Home-style foods; famous for the lasagna.

Accommodations

Hudson House Inn (2 Main Street, Cold Spring Harbor; 845/265-9355; www.hudsonhouseinn.com) Comfortable, historic inn close to the Hudson River.

Marriott Courtyard (17 Westage Drive, Fishkill; 845/897-2400; www.marriott.com) Affordable, with room for RVs and a pool.

Pig Hill Inn (73 Main Street, Cold Spring Harbor; 845/265-9247; www.pighillinn.com) Victorian inn with great views.

Information

Dutchess County Tourism: 845/463-4000; www.dutchesstourism.com

Population: 13,800

Corning, New York

for many of the 100 Best Art Towns, the concept of a corporate head-quarters translates into the two-story home of a locally owned real-estate business, or perhaps a white-water river-rafting company that's grown into a manufacturer of outdoors recreation clothing. But in the upstate New York Art Town of Corning, located along the Chemung River about a two-hour drive south of Rochester, things are different. Two of the nation's largest corporations, Corning, Inc. and Dresser Rand, are located here and employ substantial numbers of tech-nicians, scientists, sales pros, and even artists. Their presence has imbued the Corning region with a sense of stability and purpose. Corning, one of the world's leading developers of advanced glass tech-nologies and building systems, attracted many of the world's top glass artists into town through its many decades of growth. Some came here to develop projects such as fiber optics, while others came to work in the fine art operations of Steuben Glass, a studio-glass design and fab-rication company whose creations are sold to collectors worldwide.

Long before artists in the Pacific Northwest started training under Dale Chihuly in Stanwood, Washington, the Corning region was known for its concentration of glass artists. Though most of them were employed by a corporation, there nonetheless was—and continues to be—a great deal of local expertise and interest in all facets of the art glass field. So it's little wonder that this community is now home to the Corning Museum of Glass, the nation's premier fine arts institu-tion with an emphasis on glass fine art. What is starting to take root here is a significant community of glass artists working from their own hot shops, as is the case in fine art glass hotbeds such as Penland, North Carolina, and Whidbey Island, Washington. Several Corning area artists work in this medium, and their ranks are growing.

For local residents one of the joys of living here is visiting the five-block stretch of Historic Market Street, the heart of Corning's gallery and restaurant district. Rebuilt after a devastating 1972 flood, this street captures the charm and laid-back friendliness that so many communities are seeking to incubate in their own downtowns. From the Thursday-morning Farmers' Market held in Riverfront Centennial Park to the free Corning Summer Song community concert series staged in Centerway Square, the essence of Corning's quality of life is expressed along Historic Market Street.

Arts Scene

The Corning Museum of Glass is a collecting, exhibiting, and educational institution whose year-round programs expose the region's residents to the finest examples of contemporary and historic glass art and glass objects through a balanced exhibitions program. Hot-glass studios allow visiting and resident artists to demonstrate the glass art process, while year-round classes teach adults and kids the finer points of glassblowing, lamp work, and other glass art techniques. The nation's largest collection of fine art glass is housed here, and the museum's galleries exhibit both historic and contemporary work.

Another treasure in this upstate New York Art Town is the Rockwell Museum of Western Art, an institution in downtown Corning whose exhibitions range from traditional handcrafts of the Plains Indians to cowboy art by Sedona's (Arizona) large group of Western realist painters, to contemporary works by Santa Fe's (New Mexico) celebrated community of Native American artists. The museum, which is home to an annual celebration called West Fest, offers diverse programs such as art workshops, a Dia de Los Muertos fiesta, summer music on its terrace, artist lectures, and Native American cultural programs for families.

While both the Rockwell Museum and the Corning Museum of Glass mount exhibitions of contemporary art, the Arnot Art Museum in nearby Elmira is the closest place to find a year-round series of contemporary art shows featuring major national and international artists. The 171 Cedar Arts Center is Corning's multidimensional, community arts center, and its Houghton Gallery exhibitions in Drake House are well tuned to the needs of the region's contemporary arts community.

Artist 1

Cindy Weakland, director of public programs for the Rockwell Museum of Western Art.
We completed a major renovation three years ago for our Western art collection. It allowed us to develop better concepts about the American West of today and the Native American of today. Our programs now discuss traditions of cultures from other parts of the world, which has broadened the museum's scope. So far, that expanded type of programming has been well received by the community and has put us on the path to exceeding our expectations of what we can accomplish. Our Native American programs have been taken into regional schools in partnership with art teachers' lessons and programs exploring indigenous cultures.

The center also offers an extensive, year-round program of adult and kids' art classes, with an emphasis on ceramics, photography, textiles, painting, and jewelry. Its Studio Theatre is used for performing-arts programs that include an eight-month Jazz Series, ethnic dance performances, classical music recitals, and children's theatre. The West End Gallery in downtown Corning uses its two floors of exhibition space for works by the region's top artists in a variety of media.

The Corning Civic Music Association uses the Corning Museum of Glass auditorium for its September through May slate of touring national and international jazz, classical, and world music professionals, while the Orchestra of the Finger Lakes uses the same venue for its Corning concerts, as well as the Clemens Center in Elmira for many of its performances.

Essentials

Visual Arts Venues

171 Cedar Arts Center (171 Cedar Street; 607/936-4647; www.171cedar arts.com) Exhibitions, performances, art classes, and lectures.

Rockwell Museum of Western Art (111 Cedar Street; 607/937-5386; www.rockwellmuseum.org) Great collection of Native American artifacts and Western realism.

Corning Museum of Glass (One Museum Way; 800/732-6845; www.cmog.org) Year-round exhibitions and performances.

Performing Arts & Events

ARTSfest (171 Cedar Arts Center; 607/936-4647; www.171cedar arts.com) July weekend outdoor show along Market Street.

Crystal City Jazz Festival (see Corning Area Chamber of Commerce below) September weekend event in outdoor and indoor venues along Market Street.

Corning Summer Song (see Corning Area Chamber of Commerce below) Summer Thursday-night concerts in Centerway Square.

Wine & Dine

Soul Full Cup Coffeehouse (81 W. Market Street; 607/936-9030; www.soul fullcup.com) Great coffee plus live music.

London Underground (69 E. Market Street; 607/962-2345) Popular downtown spot for lunch and dinner, with local wines.

Cap'n Morgan Sports & Seafood (36 Bridge Street; 607/962-1616; www.capn morgan.com) Crabcakes, live music, and cold brews.

Accommodations

Rosewood Inn (134 E. First Street; 607/962-3253; www.rosewoodinn.com) Victorian style, in a great location.

Comfort Inn (66 West Pulteney Street; 607/962-1515; www.choice hotels.com) Affordable, with a swimming pool.

Lando's Hotel and Lounge (41 Bridge Street; 607/936-3612) Affordable, comfortable, and close to everything.

Information

Corning Area Chamber of Commerce: 1 West Market Street; 607/936-4686; www.corningny.com

Population: 13,000

Artist 2

Jan Newcomb, executive director of the 171 Cedar Arts Center. We're still dealing with the impacts of a fluctuating technology-based economy, but in 2001 we completed a renovation and expansion of our facility, so we now have two gorgeous buildings for exhibitions and performances. We bring in students from across Steuben County for art classes and programs. The visual arts community in this region is thriving, with artists moving in from across the Northeast because we have affordable housing and a state of the art arts infrastructure. Plus, you can have a rural studio quite easily, if working in solitude and quiet is what best suits your creative process.

The Hamptons, New York

Strung along the east end of Long Island's South Shore, the communities of Southampton, East Hampton, Bridgehampton, and Westhampton are the key towns that make up what is commonly known as "the Hamptons." Several other places, such as Sag Harbor, Amagansett, Montauk, and Quogue, are also considered to be part of this recreation and arts haven. Settled in the 1640s, the region is home to numerous architectural remnants of its past, from the homes of Revolutionary War heroes to a Southampton art community founded in the late 1800s by painter William Merritt Chase. In the 1950s many of the world's premier abstract expressionist painters found their way to the Hamptons, escaping their stifling, humid, cold-water flats in Manhattan's East Village. Among these artists were Jackson Pollock and his wife, Lee Krasner, who parlayed a cash advance from international art dealer Peggy Guggenheim into a summer rental on several acres near East Hampton. Today, that same complex of buildings has been turned into the Pollock-Krasner House & Study Center, a facility that's home to a summer Round Table Lectures series focused on the continuing legacy of Pollock, Krasner, and American Abstract Expressionism.

With its miles of unspoiled Atlantic Ocean beaches, dozens of harbors, coves, bays, and rolling landscape of seagrass-covered dunes, it's not surprising that urban New Yorkers have adopted the Hamptons as their favorite summer destination. In much the same way that Seaside, Florida, serves as a place where wealthy southerners can park their Hummers, so do the Hamptons lure the city's wealthy to build sprawling homes and throw black-tie gala fundraisers for favored charities. Summers here are impossibly crowded, but they're also a nonstop carnival of sun, fun, and dancing. Things return to a more normal pace the rest of the year, and winters are absolutely quiet.

Arts Scene

The Dia Arts Foundation has a presence here in its Dan Flavin Art Institute in a converted Bridgehampton firehouse. A permanent installation of nine Flavin works occupies the building's upstairs level, while its ground floor is home to changing exhibitions. While there are several commercial art galleries scattered throughout Southampton, Westhampton, Bridgehampton, Sag Harbor, and Amagansett, the most concentrated cluster of galleries is in East Hampton, which is also home to Guild Hall, a year-round arts center whose galleries exhibit work by historical and contemporary artists associated with the region, and whose John Drew Theater serves as a venue for music, theatre, dance, and poetry by regional and national artists. Throughout the year, Guild Hall offers art workshops featuring leading members of the Hamptons arts community. Amagansett is home to Artists' Woods, a 16-acre site that's the site of a summer artists' workshop series as well as a slate of outdoor and gallery exhibitions. The Art Barge, another Amagansett venue, operates as the Victor D'Amico Institute of Art, (also known as the Art Barge), a summer art program with weekend and weeklong workshops.

The Parrish Art Museum in Southampton is the region's premier visual arts facility. Its year-round exhibitions have a national and international focus, paying homage to both the Northeast's fine art traditions and to the changing landscape of the contemporary art world. The museum's collection includes many paintings by William Merritt Chase as well as the Chase Archives. A Monday Night Movies series of screenings of new cinema works is one of the many summer programs offered at the Parrish, as is an arts lecture series, curator talks, and art workshops for adults.

The Westhampton Beach Performing Arts Center is the region's most prominent, year-round venue for theatre, music, dance, and independent film. During July and August the Hamptons Shakespeare Festival stages its productions in Montauk's Roosevelt Park and holds a kids art camp in Southampton's Agawam Park, which is the same venue used for the Southampton Cultural Center's July and August Concerts in the Park. The center is the home of the Southampton

Art Talk

Helen Harrison, director of the Pollock-Krasner House & Studio Center. We're a historical home and studio facility that maintains a scholarly research center and also presents exhibitions and lectures. It's an important legacy to maintain in the context of the history of the Hamptons as an arts colony. There's not really a sense of Pollock's legacy in this community, but there is an awareness that the Abstract Expressionists had a significant local impact. We attract a lot of visitors from around the world, especially people interested in Pollock and Krasner who may be doing research or have pursued their styles in their own artwork. About once a year we even get a Pollock look-alike wandering around the grounds.

Artists Association, which organizes several member exhibitions yearly, as well as the annual Memorial Day and Labor Day arts festivals in Agawam Park. Bay Street Theatre in Sag Harbor presents its March through December series of comedies, cabarets, musicals, and dramas in a 300-seat facility on the town's Long Wharf.

Essentials

Visual Arts Venues

The Parrish Art Museum (25 Job's Lane, Southampton; 631/283-2118; www.thehamptons.com) Outstanding collection of early–20th-century American paintings.

Guild Hall (158 Main Street; East Hampton; 631/324-0806; www.guild hall.org) Shows of regional art and year-round programs.

Pollock-Krasner House & Study Center (830 Fireplace Road., East Hampton; 631/324-4929) Tours of Pollock's and Krasner's studios.

Performing Arts & Events

Bay Street Theatre (P.O. Box 810, Sag Harbor; 631/725-0818; www.baystreet.org) Favorite spot for adult and kids' theatre.

Hamptons Shakespeare Festival (P.O. Box 63, Amagansett; 631/267-0105) The Bard, outdoors, in the summer.

Concerts in the Park (Southampton Cultural Center, 2 Pond Lane; 631/287-4377) July and August offer free family music series in Agawam Park.

Wine & Dine

The Stephen Talkhouse (161 Main Street, Amagansett; 631/267-3117; www.stephentalkhouse.com) Top national music acts.

Chinda's Thai House (3284 Noyac Road, Sag Harbor; 631/725-1374) Best Thai on the East End.

Fellingham's (17 Cameron Street, Southampton; 631/283-9674) Sports bar and burgers.

Accommodations

The J. Harper Poor Cottage (181 Main Street, East Hampton; 631/324-4081; www.jharperpoor.com) B&B in the middle of town.

The Dutch Motel & Cottages (488 Montauk Highway, East Hampton; 631/324-4550; www.thedutch motel.com) Comfortable and quiet.

The Ocean Dunes (379 Bluff Road, Amagansett; 631/267-8121; www.oceandunes.net) Affordable and on the beach.

Information

Hamptons Visitors Council: 76 Main Street, Southampton; 631/283-0402; www.hamptonstravelguide.com

Population: 9,800

Art Talk

Alicia Longwell, curator of the Parrish Art Museum.

Local artists are part of our core audience. They're knowledgeable, sophisticated, and well-traveled individuals whose interests extend into folk art, contemporary art, fine crafts, film, and literature. Our mission is to bring art and people together and local artists are an important part of it. It's challenging to program a small art museum in the shadow of New York City, so we operate on a very creative scale with an emphasis on artists who have some sort of connection to this area. We've announced plans to build a new museum on the grounds of Southampton College. We envision a 70,000-square-foot facility that will give us a theatre and a performing-arts hall for a fuller range of programs.

Woodstock, New York

A turn-of-the-20th-century utopian dream brought the first wave of Woodstock artists to this bucolic corner of New York's Catskills Mountains in 1903. Since then, the community's constant inflow and export of talent in all forms of creative media has allowed Woodstock to retain its status as America's Colony of the Arts. What connects the Woodstock of today to the ideals of its beginning as an outpost of the nation's Arts and Crafts Movement are the continuing efforts of its artists to develop a sense of community woven around the concept that creative pursuits unite friends and neighbors. Unlike many small towns where artists tend to keep to themselves, somewhat the prisoners of their studios, the arts community in Woodstock is exemplified by its sense of cohesiveness, which lends the daily pace of life a neighborhood feeling that's no doubt the result of the town's large numbers of New York City transplants. Woodstock's enduring appeal to artists from across the globe has resulted in the community's developing into an artist's version of the United Nations, a place where meetings at the Woodstock Artists Association are filled with nearly as many French, Brazilian, and Australian accents as there are speakers of Brooklynese.

Though life for much of the year tends to be lived at a laid-back, snail's pace, the development in recent years of Woodstock as a Shangri-La for urbanites' weekend homes has meant that summer weekends and holiday periods tend to be acted out in the breakneck manner dictated by the weekend crowd. Restaurants tuned to city standards (on both price and quality levels) seem to fare quite well in the Woodstock economy, while the gallery scene has experienced a higher degree of turnover than one would expect for an Art Town so close to a major population center. For those who have logged their stays here in terms of years rather than seasons, there's an audible sigh of relief each September when the fast pace of summer gives way to a languorous, brilliantly colored autumn, followed by a snowy winter that keeps the weekend crowd at bay and allows the spirit of Ralph Radcliffe Whitehead, founder of the Byrdcliffe Art Colony in 1903, to wander the streets freely without fear of being run over by socialites driving Range Rovers.

Arts Scene

The Woodstock Guild, which oversees the Byrdcliffe Arts Colony's property in a joint effort with Cornell University, operates the Kleinert/James Art Center, the Fleur de Lis Gallery, the Byrdcliffe Barn, and the Byrdcliffe Theatre. The art center is used for major exhibitions of traveling and historic local art, while the gallery's focus includes the work of nearly 100 local artists, with a strong emphasis on fine crafts. The barn is used for art instruction as well as exhibitions, while the theatre is a venue for music, lectures, drama, and dance. Byrdcliffe Theatre is also used by many local organizations, including the Woodstock Poetry Festival in August and the Woodstock Fringe Festival, which from late July through August stages a half-dozen new works of American theatre as well as a series of readings of plays in progress.

Woodstock's long-standing visual arts center, the Woodstock Artists Association, was founded in 1920 and continues in its mission as the community's primary visual arts exhibition venue, as well as serving as a place for artist lectures, community meetings, and art workshops. Its facility on Tinker Street houses three visual arts galleries that are used for juried and nonjuried group and individual exhibitions featuring local and regional artists. A more casual environment for art exhibitions is offered at practically all of Woodstock's restaurants and coffee bars, especially the Colony Café, a venue on Rock City Road that mounts visual arts shows, offers live-music events, and also stages outdoor sculpture exhibitions. The Center for Photography at Woodstock, one of the nation's premier organizations in the fine art photography field, offers year-round workshops and residency programs, using its two gallery spaces for exhibitions by local, national, and international talents.

Yet another art retreat, the Maverick Colony, established by Hervey White as a spin-off of Byrdcliffe, has existed since 1916 and offers a

Art Talk

Linda Freaney, director of the permanent collection of the Woodstock Artists Association.

We have a great permanent collection that covers artists from the turn of the century to the present, from traditional styles to very modern work. We serve as a museum for artists of this area as well as a gallery venue for changing exhibitions of work by local, regional and national artists. Many of our local artists also have representation in New York City galleries because Woodstock is one of the more popular places for gallery owners to take weekend trips. The Woodstock Festival gave people a certain idea about what Woodstock was about, but we've embraced artists and creativity since the turn of the 20th century.

summer chamber music series that runs from June into September and includes a children's concert series. The concerts take place in the 1916 Maverick Concert Hall. The Woodstock Chamber Orchestra performs regionally throughout the year. The community is also home to the contemporary dance troupe of Linda Diamond and Company, which stages a series of summer performances and oversees a dance academy.

The Woodstock Playhouse is home to the Bird-on-a-Cliff Theatre Company, which presents a season of comedies and dramas as well as a highly popular slate of children's theatre productions and an annual Shakespearean play in Comeau Park. Woodstock Playhouse is also used by independent promoters as a venue for folk, jazz, and world music concerts.

Essentials

Visual Arts Venues

Woodstock Artists Association
(28 Tinker Street; 845/679-2940; www.woodstockart.org) Favorite venue for local and regional art.

The Center for Creative Photography at Woodstock
(59 Tinker Street; 845/679-9957; www.cpw.org) Workshops, residency programs, and exhibitions.

Byrdcliffe Arts Colony (Kleinert/James Art Center; 34 Tinker Street; 845/679-2079; www.woodstockguild.org) Artist residencies, workshops, and exhibitions.

Performing Arts & Events

Woodstock Playhouse (103 Mill Hill Road; 845/679-2764; www.woodstockplayhouse.org) Home of the Bird-on-a-Cliff Theatre Company.

Maverick Concerts (P.O. Box 9; 845/679-8217; www.maverick concerts.org) Summer chamber music series in a historic barn.

Woodstock Fringe Festival (P.O. Box 157, Lake Hill; 845/679-0167; www.woodstockfringe.org) New plays and readings during July and August.

Wine & Dine

New World Home Cooking (1411 Route 212; 845/246-0900; www.new worldhomecooking.com) Innovative, ethnic foods plus live music on weekends. Try the ropa vieja (Cuban shredded beef).

Bread Alone Bakery (22 Mill Hill Road; 845/679-2108; www.bread alone.com) Artisanal loaves and great coffee.

Taco Juan's (18 Tinker Street; 845/679-9673) Healthy burritos.

Art Talk

Ariel Shanberg, executive director of the Center for Creative Photography at Woodstock.

We're truly a center in terms of the photographic world, bringing international voices to Woodstock and helping regional photographers reach out to the world. Our workshop programs attract students from across the world, and we have a very active, year-round exhibition program as well as a monthly, area photographers' salon. We do about 25 workshops a year, including contemporary photography and new fields such as film and Web-based work. Artists in Woodstock have a desire to live in an interesting but rural place where you can get a decent cappuccino.

Accommodations

Woodstock Country Inn (Cooper Lake Road; 845/679-9380) Just a short drive from town, with great views.

Wild Rose Inn (66 Rock City Road; 845/679-8783) Victorian elegance in the heart of town.

The Woodstock Inn by the Millstream (48 Tannery Brook Road; 845/679-8211; www.woodstock-inn-ny.com) Quiet rooms by a swimming hole and close to town.

Information

Woodstock Chamber of Commerce & Arts: P.O. Box 36; 845/679-6234; www.woodstockchamber.com

Population: 2,200

Berkeley Springs, West Virginia

P art new age paradise, part weekend retreat for frazzled urbanites, and part ongoing experiment to see exactly how far one community's group of artists and arts promoters can drive a town's economic destiny, historic Berkeley Springs in West Virginia's eastern panhandle has successfully walked a delicate tightrope since artists started pouring into town in the early 1980s. What they discovered was a place that had given up the ghost, so to speak, when its once-prosperous fruit, mining, and forestry industries pulled up stakes and headed elsewhere. Just a two-hour drive outside the sprawl of the Washington, D.C. area, Berkeley Springs also came up on artists' radar screens because the real estate was affordable and its proximity to several other population centers made it an ideal place for independently minded artists to set up their studios and raise their families. Today, the few blocks of Berkeley Springs's downtown are home to several artists' studios and galleries.

What also made a difference in the fate of this Art Town was the powerful lure of the essential element of water. Since 1776 (the year George Washington and his business pals established farms in this scenic community) water, fresh and crystal clear, has drawn people here. It flows year-round at 74.3 degrees F into a collection of pools and bathhouses clustered around Berkeley Springs State Park, a beautifully manicured, tree-shaded refuge situated just across Fairfax

Street from the town's art galleries and cafés. These mineral springs draw a large and ever-expanding group of spiritual healers, masseuses, acupuncturists, physical therapists, crystal healers, and skin-care specialists to this healing Mecca, which is why Fairfax Street is now home to one of the East Coast's largest concentrations of alternative-medicine practitioners.

Arts Scene

Berkeley Springs has an ace up its sleeve with its Ice House Arts Center, a former fruit-storage facility that not long ago was the town's biggest eyesore. In the mid-1990s the building was sold to the Morgan Arts Council for a buck; this started a renovation project that's still taking place and which has so far resulted in the community's benefiting from the Ice House in many far-reaching ways. The Ice House Artists' Co-op Gallery represents the work of nearly three dozen local and regional artists and has become an important stop on the evening ArtWalk events that are held nearly every month in downtown Berkeley Springs. The facility is also home to a Youth Theatre Project and Summer Theatre Workshop, as well as an Adult Theatre Project that produces four plays annually in the Ice House Theatre. There are several art galleries scattered around Berkeley Springs's historic downtown, including one called Wild Women Fine Art that operates from the backroom of Tari's Café, one of the town's most popular watering holes.

During the summer months there's a weekend farmers' market on Fairfax Street, and the arts council presents a weekly series of free concerts in Berkeley Springs State Park. There's also live music at the Troubadour Lounge, a local institution whose Friday Steak Night parties are not-to-be-missed events, as is its annual Bluegrass Festival held on an August weekend. The vintage Star Theatre movie house, with its legendarily good popcorn and a slate of mainly independent films, is another of the community's only-in-Berkeley Springs kind of places. The year's biggest arts events are the outdoor arts show that takes place during October's Apple Butter Festival and the annual Ice House Art Auction, an important fundraising affair held in late August. The Coolfont Resort, a 1,300-acre retreat in the mountains outside of town, is home to a year-round music series hosted by the Coolfont Foundation. The concerts, which range from classical music to jazz and world music, are held in the Manor House, a 1912 home on the resort's grounds. On Saturday evenings the resort's Fireside Lounge features live jazz music.

Art Talk

J. W. Rone, director of the Ice House Arts Center.

We've been working through a period when even though funds got tight, our programming expanded, especially for our cooperative gallery, which is set up as a separate organization operating inside the Ice House. Our immediate goal is to renovate our second-floor space and create several classrooms. On our programming end, we've got a part-time person coordinating our visual arts shows, which has allowed a number of artists living in Morgan County to get their careers started. The town is loaded with artistic talent, and there are no empty storefronts in the community. Just about everything has been renovated and is occupied.

Essentials

Visual Arts Venues

Ice House Arts Center (Independence & Mercer Streets; 304/258-2300; www.icehouseartistsco-op.com) Featuring nearly three dozen regional talents in various media at the Artists' Co-op Gallery.

Wild Women Fine Art (123 N. Washington Street; 304/258-1196; www.tariscafe.com) Local art in a popular hangout.

Mountain Laurel (101 N. Washington Street; 304/258-1919) Local arts and fine crafts.

Performing Arts & Events

Ice House Theatre Project (Independence & Mercer Streets; 304/258-2300; www.macicehouse.org) Year-round plays plus a summer theatre camp for children.

Apple Butter Festival (see Travel Berkeley Springs below) October event with an outdoor arts fair.

Coolfont Foundation Music Series (3621 Cold Run Valley Road; 304/258-4500; www.coolfont.com) Year-round concerts by a range of musicians.

Wine & Dine

Troubadour Lounge (25 Troubadour Lane; 304/258-9381; www.troubadourlounge.com) Friday Steak Night and NASCAR Sundays.

Tari's Café (123 N. Washington Street; 304/258-1196; www.taris cafe.com) Local ingredients a specialty; try the Filet Merlot.

Panorama Steakhouse (Route 9 West; 304/258-9370; www.panorama wv.com) Three miles west of town on a ridgetop overlooking the Potomac River.

Accommodations

Inspirations B&B (174 N. Washington Street; 304/258-2292) Cozy inn and bakery right in town.

Coolfont Resort (3621 Cold Run Valley Road; 304/258-4500; www.coolfont.com) Quiet, remote, beautiful location, with a spa and private cabins.

Berkeley Springs Motel (268 Wilkes Street; 304/258-1776) Affordable, with room for RVs.

Information

Travel Berkeley Springs: 127 Fairfax Street; 304/258-9147; www.berkeley springs.com

Population: 600

Art Talk

Tari Hampe-Deneen, owner of Tari's Café.

I represent about 90 artists in my gallery, most of them from Berkeley Springs. I see a lot of strong talent moving into this area, and the galleries are expanding to meet the needs of the tourists coming here looking for art. I've sold art out of my café since 1989 and have always thought it was important to promote local talent. First it was part of an effort to brighten up the café's atmosphere, but now the art sales are more than supporting themselves. We also sponsor a local music program, with Thursdays being jam night with lots of blues, country, and West Virginia traditional music. I've got a six-month waiting list for artists wanting to show their work here. The whole community just always has been very supportive of the arts.

Shepherdstown, West Virginia

A quiet, historic, college town just 90 miles west of Washington, D.C., this Potomac River community is a popular destination for day-tripping city dwellers whose year-round spending makes it possible for Shepherdstown's business district to support a half-dozen art galleries and a similar number of art-exhibiting restaurants and cafés. Settled in the early 1700s, the community is coming to grips with the redevelopment of its historic riverfront, home to a 1788 tobacco warehouse as well as a stretch of the Chesapeake & Ohio Canal National Historic Park. The community's Norfolk & Western Railway depot, built in 1908, has been turned into a community center, and the Entler Hotel, parts of which were built in 1786, has been turned into the Historic Shepherdstown Museum. The Shepherdstown Opera House, built in 1909, now serves as a venue for independent and foreign-film screenings. Post–Civil War acrimony led to Shepherdstown turning its Courthouse into a place of higher learning, which is how Shepherd University, a state-supported, four-year institution in the middle of town, was founded. Home to the Robert Byrd Science & Technology Center, the college is also the site of the Guy & Alice Frank Center for the Performing & Visual Arts, a 450-seat venue used year-round for theatre, music, and art exhibitions.

For artists, Shepherdstown represents an ideal, small-town environment where homes are affordable and where community life has a long-standing tradition of support for the arts. The town's proximity to Washington, D.C.'s galleries as well as the art fairs in the D.C./Baltimore and Pittsburgh metro areas makes Shepherdstown a perfect home base for artists who make their living selling at art festivals. They enjoy long bicycle rides along the C & O Canal's 184 miles of trails, or slip a canoe into the Potomac's waters for a twilight paddle. And if they happen to be in town on a Thursday night they are always welcome to drop by O'Hurley's General Store for the free, weekly bluegrass concert.

Arts Scene

There are a half-dozen art galleries and fine crafts galleries in town, as well as rotating art exhibitions of student, faculty, and regional art in the visual art gallery at the Frank Center, and exhibitions of local artists' work at the War Memorial Building. The premier events on Shepherdstown's visual arts front take place during autumn when the Over the Mountain Studio Tour winds up for its November weekend of home-based shows by more than a dozen local artists, and during the Mountain Heritage Arts & Crafts Festival, a three-day weekend affair in late September featuring more than a hundred artists as well as performances by the top names in the region's music scene.

The heart and soul of Shepherdstown's cultural scene is connected to the music and theatre programs offered at Shepherd University. During the academic year the drama department uses the Studio Theatre at Cree Hall for its presentations of Broadway and off-Broadway material, while the college's Performing Arts Series uses the Frank Center Theatre for its active slate of national and international dancers, musicians, and stage companies. The annual highlight of Shepherdstown's performing-arts calendar is the Contemporary American Theatre Festival, a July and August event that draws large crowds from across the region that share an interest in the cutting-edge of American stagecraft. Using both the Studio Theatre and Frank Theatre for its performances, the festival produces main stage plays as well as a Staged Reading Series, a lecture series, and a Contemporary Music Series. More mainstream theatrical fare is presented year-round in nearby Charles Town by the Old Opera House Theatre Company, which also presents its New Voices Play Festival during a July weekend.

While Shepherd College's Millbrook Orchestra uses the Frank Center for its season of six concerts during the academic year, the homegrown aspect of Shepherdstown's music scene is expressed in

Art Talk

James Cooper, gallery director for the J. Cooper Gallery.

John Landis, my partner, is from this area. A few years ago we noticed that Shepherdstown was turning into a destination for D.C. and Baltimore tourists. Since we arrived here there's been more local development, the result of people coming into town to enjoy the quaint, independently owned shops. Now there are a number of people living here who commute into D.C. for work, and that's changing things. Shepherdstown has a sense of itself as a town filled with creative individuals. It's friendly and very welcoming and gets very busy from September to January. There is a lack of appreciation on local government's part for how much of a contribution the arts community makes to Shepherdstown's attractiveness for visitors, and we need to fix those damn sidewalks.

events such as the Upper Potomac Dulcimer Festival in September and the Shenandoah Coffeehouse Series of concerts held monthly from October to April on third Saturdays at the War Memorial Building.

Essentials

Visual Arts Venues

War Memorial Building (Shepherdstown Visitors Center; 102 German Street; 304/876-2786; www.shepherdstown.org) Monthly exhibitions of local and regional artists.

Frank Center for the Performing & Visual Arts (Shepherd University; 304/876-5000; www.shepherd.edu) Student and faculty shows, as well as exhibitions by local and regional artists.

J. Cooper Gallery (140 E. German Street; 304/876-3589) Fine furnishings crafted locally.

Performing Arts & Events

Contemporary American Theatre Festival (Shepherd University; 304/876-5000; www.catf.org) Summer festival of plays, readings, and music.

Over the Mountain Studio Tour (Arts & Humanities Alliance of Jefferson County; P.O. Box 2051; 304/267-5468; www.ahajc.org) November weekend event with more than a dozen studio stops.

Mountain Heritage Arts & Crafts Festival (see Shepherdstown Visitors Center below) September event with artists' booths and local music.

Wine & Dine

The Blue Moon Café (200 E. High Street; 304/876-1920) Favorite artists' spot with local shows.

Yellow Brick Bank (3 E. German Street; 304/876-2208) Shepherdstown's finest dining spot.

Three Onions (117 E. German Street; 304/876-3462; www.threeonions .com) Great wine list, local ingredients, and wood-fired pizzas.

Accommodations

Bavarian Inn & Lodge (164 Shepherdgrade Road; 304/876-2551; www.bavarianinnwv.com) Full-service hotel and the Rathskeller Pub.

Clarion Hotel (233 Lowe Drive; 304/876-7000; www.clarion shepherdstown.com) Affordable, with a pool.

Thomas Shepherd Inn (300 W. German Street; 304/876-3715; www.thomasshepherdinn.com) Comfy B&B close to all the arts action.

Information

Shepherdstown Visitors Center: 102 German Street; 304/876-2786; www.shepherdstown.org

Population: 825

Art Talk

Cheryl Mansley-Ford, photographer and coordinator of the Mountain Stage New Songs Festival.

The festival's in its second year and takes place in Charles Town, but it originated in Charleston as a radio show quite a while ago. We now do it as a live stage event on a three-day weekend in September with all kinds of Appalachian, bluegrass, folk, and country music. I've lived here 18 years and enjoy being in a place that's overflowing with talent. We have performances in town like the Thursday-night bluegrass jam session and places like the Mecklenburg Inn and the Three Onions that have live music on weekends. The theatre festival's three-week run is the best time of the year to be in Shepherdstown.

The Southeast/ South-Central Region

Eureka Springs, Arkansas

This well-preserved resort town in northwest Arkansas has much in common with resort communities located near large lakes and natural springs. And while there are few individuals who can be heard shouting "Eureka!" as they bathe in the healing waters of Basin Spring, several of the town's historic spa hotels are still standing, which drew many thousands here in the late 19th century. These establishments are among the primary reasons why Eureka Springs has been made a Distinctive Destination by the National Trust for Historic Preservation.

Artists started trickling into Eureka Springs in the early-1970s, which is about the same time the downtown started becoming more oriented to the needs of tourists than of locals. The ready availability of studio space in the upper levels of downtown's commercial buildings is still one of the community's big lures for artists, as is the large inventory of Victorian residences built in the early 1900s for the town's spa-owning oligarchy. Northwest Arkansas is a spectacular place whose countryside is filled with lakes, streams, and mountains. Beaver Lake, just to the west of Eureka Springs, is the town's summer recreation hub, while during the winter months it's home to a colony of bald eagles. Many a local artist has marked the end of a long, productive day in the studio by cracking open a cold beer while tossing a fishing line into Beaver Lake during a summer sunset.

Arkansas's artists live in a place where the traditions of rural tourism are still strong. Where, after all, would Eureka Springs be if it weren't for the T-shirt shops and fudge stores that have always done great business? This is, after all, a town that not only supports a Sacred Arts Center with its 70-foot-tall Christ in the Ozarks statue, but which has also learned how to economically develop part of its tourism base by promoting the annual Great Passion Play, a melodrama about Jesus Christ and his followers. Typically, the lead role goes to a fellow with Nordic features, stretching the concept of who was typically found in Israel two thousand years ago.

Arts Scene

The visual arts are thriving in Eureka Springs because a new generation of galleries has blossomed throughout its winding, steep-sided downtown. While Eureka Springs lacks a visual arts center, there are more than a dozen commercial galleries as well as several restaurants and coffee bars exhibiting local art. Much of what's shown here are fine crafts produced by the legions of furniture makers, metalsmiths, wood turners, and jewelers who have arrived in Eureka Springs over the past 30 years. One of the more interesting aspects of the local arts scene is its steady influx of new talent, a dynamic fueled in part by graduates of the fine art programs at the University of Arkansas, which is just down the road in Fayetteville.

The art deco Historic City Auditorium serves as home to the Eureka Theatre Company and the year-round pop, rock, folk, jazz, and world music concert programming presented by the Center for the Performing Arts. Eureka Theatre Company, which presents adult and children's material during its year-round season, balances its season's offerings with time-proven classics and newer, edgier material. The Original Ozark Folk Festival in October attracts national musicians to its presentations in Basin Spring Park, which is also the site of a free, Saturday concert series. Summers get off to a roaring start over Memorial Day weekend when the Eureka Springs Blues Festival fills downtown's bars, coffee bars, and the City Auditorium with national acts from far and wide, while Jazz Eureka in mid-September does the same for its roster of national artists.

While the annual Eureka Springs UFO Conference turns the town on its pointed ears in April, and May is celebrated as the Festival of the Arts, one of the true standouts in the local arts scene is the summer season of productions staged by Opera in the Ozarks, which for more than 50 years has delivered arias and tenors to thousands of residents of northwest Arkansas. The opera's brief but action-packed season runs from mid-June through July at the Inspiration Point Fine Arts

Colony on the outskirts of Eureka Springs and presents three crowd-pleasing productions.

Essentials

Visual Arts Venues

W. Fox Gallery (7 Center Street; 479/363-9029; www.wfox.biz) Fine crafts gallery representing top regional artists.

Satori Arts (81 Spring Street; 479/253-9820) One of the region's most established galleries.

Zarks Gallery (67 Spring Street; 479/253-2626) Broad selection of paintings, sculpture, and ceramics.

Performing Arts & Events

Festival of the Arts (see Greater Eureka Springs Chamber of Commerce below) Coordinated gallery exhibitions and special events for visual artists every May.

Opera in the Ozarks (16311 Highway 62 West; 479/253-8595) Three-production season staged in June and July.

Eureka Theatre Company (P.O. Box 2134; 479/363-0363; www.eurekatheatrecompany.com) Year-round season of adult and children's theatre.

Wine & Dine

Mud Street Café (22 South Main Street; 479/253-6732; www.mudstreetcafe.com) Popular buzz shop with rotating exhibits of local art.

DeVito's of Eureka Springs (5 Center Street; 479/253-6807) Best meatballs west of Philadelphia.

Smokehouse Café (580 W. Van Buren; 479/253-9842) Country ham is its world-renowned specialty.

Art Talk

Steve Shell, president of Eureka Theatre Company.

We've been performing in a 975-seat auditorium that was built 75 years ago and is just now undergoing major renovations that will give us improved lighting, sound, and seating. We use the auditorium for three or four plays a year and share the facility with other arts groups. Our Eureka Creatives program is a banding together of parties from various arts disciplines in an effort to coordinate the arts advocacy agenda for northwest Arkansas and prevent grant-application overlap. We're in a sense transitioning from the older model of community theatre into an approach that accommodates fresher, newer ideas from lesser known and local playwrights.

Art Talk

L. J. Smole, owner of the W. Fox Gallery.

I had the White Fox workshop for 20 years and have just finished my first year in this gallery, which is all about the work of artists from Arkansas and Mississippi, especially members of the different crafts guilds in the Ozarks. We're an area of considerable talent, and there's a fledgling arts school that's now looking to purchase its own building. Eureka Springs is very peaceful, not noisy, and it's the kind of place you can socialize with other artists while nurturing your creative and spiritual sides. Tourism here is very strong and, so far, I'm far exceeding the goals of my business plan.

Accommodations

Flatiron Flats (25 Spring Street; 479/253-9434) Historic, former commercial building in the middle of downtown, with affordable rooms.

The Ridgeway House (28 Ridgeway; 479/253-6618; www.ridgeway house.com) Victorian-era B&B in a quiet neighborhood.

Palace Hotel and Bath House (135 Spring Street; 479/253-7474; www.palacehotelbathhouse.com) One of the first luxury spas in Eureka Springs.

Information

Greater Eureka Springs Chamber of Commerce: 137 W. Van Buren; 479/253-8737; www.eurekasprings chamber.com

Population: 2,000

Hot Springs, Arkansas

entral Avenue, a winding route that's the main thoroughfare of this historic town, is the dividing line between Hot Springs National Park on one side of the road, and a National Historic Landmark District across the street. On its National Park side, Central Avenue reflects the Park Service's ongoing interest in preserving the Victorian majesty of eight, turn-of-the-19th-century bathhouses that were erected during an era when Hot Springs and the mineral waters that flow from its rocky, wooded ground were considered to be America's answer to the miracle healing waters of Lourdes. Across from the bathhouses, Central Avenue and its Landmark District are elegantly preserved treasures of ornate commercial structures erected during the heyday of Bathhouse Row, a period of time that saw Hot Springs evolve from a healing center where trainloads of the elderly and the ill would journey to in hopes of curing their assorted ailments, to a wide-open speakeasy town in which gambling, prostitution, and opium use were pursued with abandon and sanctioned by a wink, nod, and cash payment to local authorities. In its prime, Hot Springs was America's early– 20th-century answer to Las Vegas, a place where fast bucks flowed like the healing waters spurting out of its substrata.

Today's Hot Springs is a place whose architectural legacy beautifully reflects the Victorian aesthetics and dreams of its founders, but whose sidewalks and loft apartments have been cleansed of unsavory characters. It's a place where public fountains along Central Avenue gurgle with the spring-fed waters that flow underneath the community, and where it's not uncommon to see families filling dozens of plastic jugs with genuine Hot Springs water before loading them into their trucks and heading home to Ozark Mountain towns. While the bathhouses inside the National Park's boundaries are carefully preserved, they're no longer places filled with true believers. To find those places you need to enter one of the several, privately owned bathhouses still doing business along Central Avenue's tributaries. There, sitting inside huge bathtubs filled with hot mineral waters, and laying on massage tables while their aching muscles are tended to by massage masters, is where Hot Springs's community of artists comes to recharge its body, mind, and spirit.

Until the early 1990s, when artists first began finding their ways here from various points across the globe, Hot Springs was struggling to make a few bucks from tourists attracted for boat rides, soaks in hot tubs, horse racing, and visits to the National Park. But artists understood that the affordably priced real estate along Central Avenue was ideally suited for studios and galleries and quickly snapped up buildings and went to work restoring them. Soon, newspapers in Memphis, Dallas, and St. Louis caught a whiff of what was shaping up as a civic revitalization driven by artists, and after a few articles were published, Hot Springs's reputation as an Art Town was sealed. Today the rising fortunes of Hot Springs have turned around a decades-long slide in real-estate values, and the town is loaded with great restaurants, art galleries, interior furnishings shops, and coffee bars. To be sure, not all of Hot Springs looks as gussied up as does Central Avenue. There are some marginal neighborhoods filled with junked cars and boarded up buildings. But there is widespread hope for the community's future, and that feeling of hope can largely be traced to the existence of Hot Springs's community of artists.

Arts Scene

One of the high-profile expansions of the local arts scene is an ongoing effort to convert the old Hot Springs High School into the Clinton Cultural Campus, an acknowledgment that Hot Springs was the boyhood home of President Bill Clinton. Half of the project, the rehabilitation of what had been an annex into 38 units of middle-market housing, has been completed. The renovation of the remainder of the structure into a complex of galleries, studios, performance spaces, and workshops remains in its fundraising phase, though the project's local organizers hope to soon move the project's second phase toward completion.

Hot Springs is one of those Art Towns where the initiative to drive forward the local arts scene and expand its impact through key alliances with local businesses, tourism-development officials, politicians, and the regional public has largely come through the efforts of artists and gallery owners. It's not as if the local arts community wouldn't appreciate having a dynamic, multidisciplinary arts center serving all the arts, it's just that the two-word phrase "art center" seems to get loaded down with political and emotional baggage. Regardless, the entrepreneurial spirit of local gallery owners has performed an end run around the naysayers and provided the energy to get things done. A dozen art galleries representing local, national, and international artists are surviving the fluctuations of the regional economy, and they've built tremendous awareness of their existence through year-round, monthly Gallery Walks on First Fridays. Today, collectors pour into Hot Springs from not only Little Rock and Memphis but also Dallas, Houston, St. Louis, and New Orleans, seeking a bit of heat relief to accompany the monthly fulfillment of their art-buying needs. And some of the best exhibitions in Hot Springs are those mounted in the lobby of the town's new convention center.

The Hot Springs Music Festival, which takes place across the first half of June in various downtown venues, has given the town an outstanding reputation in classical music circles for its educational and performance programs featuring student and professional musicians. There's a weekend jazz festival in September, weekly blues nights at a downtown café, a summer outdoor concert series at Timberwood Amphitheater in Magic Springs, and free summer concerts by the Hot Springs Community Band in Whittington Park. Songwriters, poets, and playwrights have an open venue for readings of their new work at the Poet's Loft, a former USO club above a downtown gallery. The Pocket Theatre, founded in the early 1990s, is Hot Springs's community theatre group, performing in its own playhouse on Higdon Ferry Road and staging its productions year-round. The material favors comedies and musicals, and there's a kids' summer theatre camp as well as an annual Christmas show.

The most successful arts event on the community's annual calendar is the Hot Springs Documentary Film Festival, a two-week affair staged in late October and early November. The festival, which attracts international filmmakers and audiences of more than 30,000 movie lovers, has purchased its own theatre in downtown and has developed a reputation as one of the major stops for any documentary filmmaker

Art Talk

Laura Rosenberg, cofounder of the Hot Springs Music Festival.
Our audiences have been up every year during the festival's 10-year existence. It's a fantastic trend, and it has allowed us to offer things like opera. We've air-conditioned our fieldhouse concert space, because the new convention center's acoustics aren't suitable to the needs of an orchestra, so now we've got an acoustically excellent performance facility with a whisper-quiet climate-control system. We've recorded four CDs on Naxos and are working on our fifth. We've started our Symphony Sam program in the public schools and on public television. Our festival has exerted a significant impact on Hot Springs by allowing people to get over their reluctance and lack of familiarity with classical music.

wanting national exposure for his or her projects. The festival has established a year-round series of local programs as well as an extensive educational outreach effort and has grown in the past decade from a weekend screening of 10 films to its current form as a two-week festival screening more than 100 films.

Essentials

Visual Arts Venues

Hot Springs Convention Center (see Hot Springs Convention & Visitors Bureau below) Organizes major shows in its soaring, light-filled lobby.

Artists Workshop Gallery (810 Central Avenue; 501/623-6401; www.artistsworkshopgallery.com) Features work from more than three dozen of the region's top fine crafts and contemporary artists.

Taylor's Contemporanea Fine Arts (516 Central Avenue; 501/624-0516; www.taylorsarts.com) Regional and national artists and fine crafts.

Performing Arts & Events

Hot Springs Documentary Film Festival (819 Central Avenue; 501/321-4747; www.docufilminst.org) Two-week screening of more than 100 films along with filmmaker workshops, lectures, and other events.

Hot Springs Music Festival (634 Prospect Avenue; 501/623-4763; www.hotmusic.org) Annual June series of performances and workshops for classical musicians.

The Pocket Theatre (2138 Higdon Ferry Road; 501/525-7529; www.pockettheatre.com) Year-round musicals and comedies as well as a summer kids' presentation.

Wine & Dine

Maxine's Puzzle Bar (700 Central Avenue; 501/623-0653) Downtown buzz shop and an artists' favorite hangout.

The Pancake Shop (216 Central Avenue; 877/426-4887; www.pancake shop.com) Best hotcakes and country ham in the state.

McClard's Bar-B-Q (505 Albert Pike; 501/623-9665; www.mcclards.com) Fabulous pork ribs and world-famous sauce.

Accommodations

Spring Street Inn (522 Spring Street; 501/624-1901; www.springstreet inn.net) Comfortable B&B in a quiet corner of downtown.

Arlington Resort Hotel (239 Central Avenue; 501/623-7771; www.arling-tonhotel.com) Grand hotel, with an underground bathhouse.

Travelodge (1204 Central Avenue; 501/ 321-1332; www.travelodge.com) Affordable rooms, with a swimming pool.

Information

Hot Springs Convention & Visitors Bureau: 134 Convention Boulevard; 501/321-2835; www.hotsprings.org

Population: 36,000

Art Talk

Melanie Masino, executive director of the Hot Springs Documentary Film Festival.

I moved here from Atlanta in the 1990s and started as a volunteer. In impact, in scope, and in every way this festival continues to grow, if not explode, on the national and international levels. We've been selected to nominate documentaries for the Academy Awards, and now there are documentary filmmakers and producers actually moving to Hot Springs from other parts of the country. Through some grants we've been able to offer a year-round documentary-film workshop program. I like to think we've contributed to the community's quality of life by screening films from across the globe and by educating local schoolkids as to the possibilities that lay in front of them.

Key West, Florida

T his wacky and wonderful Art Town at the southernmost tip of the United States is so close to Havana that Fidel Castro can practically stand on his Havana balcony and wave to the hundreds of jugglers, mimes, sunburned tourists, and Deadheads who gather nightly at Mallory Square to watch Key West's legendary sunsets across the Gulf of Mexico. Key West is America's playtime paradise. To be sure, places like Sun Valley, Idaho, Provincetown, Massachusetts, La Jolla, California, and Galveston, Texas, catch the same spirit from time to time, but here in the Conch Republic (motto: We Seceded Where Others Failed) the culture of wild abandon is so deeply embedded into the local mindset that for 365 days a year there's little attention paid to the concept of throttling back on the pursuit of pleasure. Needless to say, there's a price to pay, and for many former Conchs the condition known as "island burnout" is the gateway to twelve-stepping one's way back home.

Antonio de Herrera was the first European to set foot on the Florida Keys. Its early industries were seafood, smuggling, and salvage, and things stayed bleak until the Florida Overseas Highway linking Key West and the other Florida Keys to the mainland opened in 1938. Papa Hemingway, who arrived here in 1929, convinced other writers and artists to join up with the Key West Conchs, and soon Duval Street was being visited by the likes of Tennessee Williams and Lou Gehrig. The Key West of old is almost gone, though parts of it are preserved in places like Bahama Village and the Key West Bight, the community's restored seaport. What's taken its place is a town that's profuse in its turquoise-and-pink celebration of all things gay, yet it's also a community where being different is not an issue; it's just a fashion statement, or a design scheme for one's home, or in choosing the people one socializes with.

Despite its Duval Street concentration of t-shirt shops and bars, there's still a great deal of charm in Key West, though like some of the most popular small Art Towns, authenticity has become quite pricey. One can pretty much dodge the community's crazed and overpriced facade by sticking to its side streets, though that would eliminate those chance encounters that make life here so much fun. In dealing with Key West it's best to just slap a smile onto your face and wade into the middle of the day's action.

Arts Scene

There's an incredible vibrancy to Key West's arts scene, and alongside this energy there's a wealth of talent that drives things forward. In a place where thousands of tourists search for cheeseburgers and paradise, it's no wonder that big-time art festivals and cultural festivals are exploding throughout the year. There's the Cuban Festival in November, the gay and lesbian Fantasy Fest in October, the Hemingway Days Festival in July, the African-American Festival in June, Art in the Park at Fort Zachary Taylor in January, and Old Island Days in February. On any given year, anywhere from 60 to 80 art galleries are slugging it out in Key West's competitive arts scene. Figuring out the right balance of serious art and fast-selling kitsch is the key to any gallery's staying solvent, though many fold before ever finding their footing. The Key West Art Center, an artist-run cooperative, is located on a prime corner of Front Street in the heart of the tourist district. The Key West Museum of Art & History is located in the 1891 Custom House and features several gallery spaces used for rotating exhibitions of local and regional art. The East Martelo Museum and Gallery, located in a dingy fort modeled after an Italian military facility, houses a permanent collection of works by historical figures in the island's past and also uses a rotating gallery for locally themed exhibitions.

Three main venues serve the island's performing-arts community. The most prominent of these is the Tennessee Williams Theatre, a professionally equipped facility seating 480 and serving as home to the Key West Symphony Orchestra's December to April season, the Key West Pops, Keys Chorale, Island Opera Theatre, and the Founders

Art Talk

Florence Recher, treasurer of the Key West Art Center.

Our building was a grocery store and was condemned in 1960, so the town just allowed some artists to move in and renovate it. We've got 900 square feet of gallery space downstairs and 500 square feet upstairs, with shows through the year that usually last about two weeks each. All of the work we show is on consignment, and to exhibit here you've got to not only live in Monroe County but be willing to put time in at the gallery. Our commissions are a fraction of what's charged in the commercial galleries. Certain members teach art classes to the public, but we also bring in out-of-area artists to teach some of our classes. We feel we give our member artists an opportunity to get their careers rolling and to establish their sales histories.

Society, a presenting organization that brings national and international performing-arts talent to Key West from November to April. Waterfront Playhouse, located in the tourist center of Mallory Square, presents its December to June season of comedies, dramas, and musicals in the same facility used for its Second Stage series of newer works as well as for its Children's Theatre Workshops. The Red Barn Theatre presents a December to June season of comedies, dramas, and new plays.

Essentials

Visual Arts Venues

The Key West Museum of Art and History (281 Front Street; 305/295-6616; www.kwahs.com) First-rate exhibition venue for local, regional, and national art.

Key West Art Center (301 Front Street; 305/294-1241) Ideally located gallery representing island talents.

Gallery on Greene (606 Greene Street; 305/294-1669) Large art space representing contemporary and traditional artists.

Performing Arts & Events

Tennessee Williams Theatre (5901 West College Road; 305/296-1520; www.tennesseewilliamstheatre.com) State-of-the-art venue serving several performing-arts organizations.

Art in the Park (see Key West Chamber of Commerce below) Large, outdoor sculpture and art exhibition in February on the grounds of Fort Zachary Taylor.

The Red Barn Theatre (319 Duval Street; 305/293-3035; www.red barntheatre.com) Presents a seven-month season of drama, comedies, and new works.

Wine & Dine

Half Shell Raw Bar (231 Margaret Street; 305/294-7496; www.halfshell rawbar.com) One of the top places in South Florida for crustaceans.

Sloppy Joe's (201 Duval Street; 305/294-5717; www.sloppyjoes.com) Since 1933, the most famous place in the Keys to wet your whistle.

Virgilio's La Trattoria (Applerouth Lane; 305/296-8118; www.latrattoria keywest.com) Best spot in the Keys for veal cutlets and sambucca cocktails.

Accommodations

Artist House Key West (534 Eaton Street; 305/296-3977; www.artist housekeywest.com) Classy B&B in the heart of town.

The Colony (714 Olivia Street; 305/294-6691; www.thecolony keywest.com) Nine cottages set among tropical gardens.

El Patio Motel (800 Washington Street; 305/296-6531; www.elpatiomotel.com) Affordable rooms with a nice touch of Key West style.

Information

Key West Chamber of Commerce: 402 Wall Street; 305/294-2587; www.keywestchamber.org.

Population: 25,400

Art Talk

Claudia Pennington, executive director of the Key West Museum of Art and History.

We put $9 million into restoring this building and opened it in late 1999. We think of Key West as being a special place with a deep cultural history and an important art history, dating dack at least to the depression era when the WPA sent artists and writers here for their projects, with many of them staying on as permanent residents. Contemporary art is a large part of our exhibitions program, with 13 shows a year in a mix of painting, sculpture, and photography. A lot of those artists have South Florida connections, but we will do shows by national artists occasionally, especially shows that deal with our culture and history.

Miami Beach, Florida

from the Roaring Twenties through the Wheezing Eighties, the buzz about Miami Beach was that it housed thousands of geezers who spent their days gazing across the community's white sand beaches before flooding into local restaurants for their 4 PM, $2.49 senior citizen, early-bird specials. Since then, things have definitely been turned upside down for this fun-crazed, fashion paradise just a short drive across the MacArthur Causeway from downtown Miami. The Miami Beach of today has become the promised land for a never-ending stream of Venezuelan models, Italian restaurateurs, Long Island divorcees, British bookies, and Cuban financiers all wanting to get in on the action in this round-the-clock carnival of hopes and dreams. The community is home to the Miami Beach Architectural District, known to most as the Art Deco District, a historic treasure of America's highest concentration of 1920s and 30s resort architecture. Across Miami Beach's residential and commercial districts are stunning examples of art deco's streamlined motifs, alongside of which are Mediterranean mansions, postwar moderne apartments, and the occasional Arts & Crafts bungalow. Rising real-estate values have resulted in an overseas investment inflow, which is the reason most of the community's historic infrastructure has been restored to its original glory, and why even the new Miami Beach construction conforms to art deco–influenced design guidelines.

The Miami Beach revival wasn't closely associated with an expansion of the community's arts presence until recent years, when local government made a strong effort to embellish the community's lifestyle by developing an arts infrastructure. Though other areas of metropolitan Miami have more to offer artists in the way of cheap studio space and access to other artists, what Miami Beach offers is audience and location. The community's reputation as a world-class nightclub district plus its large inventory of stylish people, hotels, and restaurants makes Miami Beach a perfect place for performances, art fairs, and the international art community's favorite activity of constantly checking each other out.

Arts Scene

Two art museums, a diverse and vibrant community arts center, and two international art fairs headline Miami Beach's visual arts scene. The biggest impact on the community's evolution as an Art Town has been the recent arrival of Art Basel Miami Beach, a North American art fair organized by Swiss-based Art Basel, the world's most respected annual art show. Starting in 2002, Art Basel swept into Miami Beach for an early December week loaded with explosive economic impact, filling its hotels and sophisticated restaurants with art dealers and collectors from across the globe, and stuffing its Convention Center with hundreds of booths displaying the creations of the world's top contemporary artists. The community's other annual art fair, Art Miami, is a smaller, January show whose focus is on contemporary Latin American and South American art.

The Bass Museum of Art, located in the wooded haven of Collins Park just a stone's toss from the beach, is a recently expanded, world class contemporary and traditional art museum with an international focus and extensive community outreach programs. The Bass also is a collecting institution with extensive holdings from the Renaissance and Baroque eras of European art history. The Wolfsonian, whose focus is on modern art and design, is located on Washington Avenue in the middle of the Architectural District's restored masterworks. The museum is home to one of the world's premier collections of Modern Era artifacts, a period covering from 1885 to 1945, and its exhibitions showcase not just objects from the permanent collection but also touring shows. ArtCenter/South Florida, located in three buildings along the Lincoln Road Mall, is an exemplary community arts center whose 60,000 square feet are used for 45 artist studios, several art galleries, a storefront exhibition program, and year-round arts-education programs. Widely acknowledged as the focal point of the Miami Beach visual arts community, the ArtCenter/South Florida's low studio rents

Art Talk

Isabel Block, director of exhibitions at ArtCenter/South Florida.

Our purpose is to help artists develop their careers and their creative potential in a noncommercial atmosphere and to offer educational programs in various arts disciplines. In order for an artist to get a studio here they've got to go through a four-times-a-year jurying process in front of a panel of artists and arts educators. Our artists are from all over the world, and they're required to be in their studios at least 40 hours a week, which allows the public to come in and see what they're doing. Artists who are part of ArtCenter/South Florida are aware of the challenges of this environment and enjoy the results it gets them in their own careers.

and innovative, year-round programs are the key reasons why more of Miami Beach's artists haven't relocated to the Miami Design District's cheaper warehouse studio spaces.

New World Symphony, an international caliber music organization under the direction of Michael Tilson Thomas, operates its Orchestral Academy from the Lincoln Theatre on the Lincoln Road Mall. Its performances, which embrace the classics as well as new works, are presented from September through May. Miami Beach's major performing-arts venue, the Jackie Gleason Theatre, is presently used by the Miami City Ballet, Miami Symphony, and the Concert Association of South Florida for their seasons of international orchestras, dance companies, and chamber music concerts.

Essentials

Visual Arts Venues

Bass Museum of Art (2121 Park Avenue; 305/673-7530; www.bass museum.org) Nationally known for its contemporary arts exhibitions and permanent collection.

Wolfsonian (1001 Washington Avenue; 305/531-1001; www.wolf sonian.fiu.edu) Focused on modern-era arts and objects.

ArtCenter/South Florida (800, 810 & 924 Lincoln Road; 305/674-8278; www.artcentersf.org) Artist studios, classrooms, and several galleries.

Performing Arts & Events

Art Basel Miami Beach (Miami Beach Convention Center; 305/674-1292; www.artbasel.com) December contemporary arts fair with international artists, art dealers, and galleries.

Art Miami (see Miami Beach Chamber of Commerce below) January arts fair with a contemporary South American and Latin American focus.

ArtsBeach 2nd Thursdays (see Miami Beach Chamber of Commerce below) Monthly, mini-festival of visual arts, performing arts, and music.

Wine & Dine

Joe's Stone Crab (11 Washington Avenue; 800/780-2722; www.joes stonecrab.com) A Miami Beach institution serving famous crab claws and much more.

Wish (801 Collins Avenue; 305/674-9474; www.wishrestaurant.com) Contemporary French and Brazilian fusion cuisine.

Van Dyke Café (846 Lincoln Road; 305/534-3600; www.thevandyke.com) Great place for scoping out the beautiful people.

Art Talk

Diane Camber, executive director of the Bass Museum of Art.

I was brought on here in 1980, at a point when one of the museum's biggest challenges was dealing with the decay of its urban neighborhood. We worked closely with the preservation movement and now feel we're the vanguard of what's taking place in Miami Beach. We're expanding our facility and building our collections, and I'm convinced that finding the money to achieve our goals is achievable. The Art Basel show's arrival in Miami Beach only enhances the museum's ability to fulfill its mission, so we've worked closely with the show's organizers to help them publicize the great things happening in the Miami area to a new generation of art supporters.

Accommodations

Aqua Hotel (1530 Collins Avenue; 305/538-4361; www.aqua miami.com) Modern, sophisticated, affordable, and on the beach.

Fairfield Inn (4101 Collins Avenue; 305/673-3337; www.marriott.com) Oceanfront hotel on the broadwalk.

Days Inn North Beach (7450 Ocean Terrace; 305/866-1631; www.daysinn.com) Affordable, with amenities for families.

Information

Miami Beach Chamber of Commerce: 1920 Meridian Avenue; 305/674-1300; www.miamibeachchamber.com

Population: 89,000

Naples, Florida

This fast-growing community on the southwest Florida coast is an arts powerhouse overdue for national attention. Naples, along with neighboring Marco Island, is surrounded by an amazing range of natural splendor. To the west lies the Gulf of Mexico and its reliable supply of year-round, technicolor sunsets. To the east are Big Cypress National Preserve and the Everglades National Park. To the north and south are state parks and wildlife preserves such as Ten Thousand Islands, Rookery Bay National Estuarine Research Reserve, and Picayune Strand State Forest, home to the endangered Florida panther as well as alligators, egrets, and tropical butterflies. First settled by Calusa Indians, modern Naples began rapidly growing in the 1920s with the arrival of train service and the building of the Tamiami Trail East, which connected Naples to Miami. Soon, the Orange Blossom Express was unloading its steady stream of sun-starved northerners, many of whom stayed on to help build what today has become a community whose steep growth curve has spawned a lucrative real-estate and tourism economy. Evidently, things are working out to Naples's advantage. There are still plenty of quiet, unassuming neighborhoods in both Naples and Marco, but their fringes are leapfrogging at an astounding rate as an unrelenting wave of retirees and relocating professionals continue to pursue the Holy Grail of Gulf Coast living.

Naples is an Art Town whose older commercial districts have a dressed-up feeling reflecting both a tropical aesthetic and the upscale nature of places such as Carmel, California, and Vail, Colorado. Naples also has a thriving nightlife, a scene fueled by the surprising numbers of younger professionals who have relocated to this moderately laid-back paradise. Along with its active nightlife Naples offers a sophisticated restaurant scene, made possible by the talents of top-trained chefs attracted here initially by the area's many resort hotels, but who later branched out to open their own cafés, bistros, and boulangeries. When they're not chasing Naples's ever-expanding range of business opportunities, local residents can usually be found on the dozens of championship-caliber golf courses that line this part of Florida's coast, or flopped down on a stretch of the pristine, world class, beaches gleaming along miles of the region's coastline. Needless to say, the Naples area is also a paradise for a sailor, yachtsman, or fisherman. Weekending in the whirlwind of Miami Beach is a simple matter involving a two-hour drive across Alligator Alley, an expressway bisecting the Everglades and connecting Florida's coasts.

Arts Scene

Naples is loaded with sophisticated and serious art galleries representing the full spectrum of contemporary and traditional visual art genres. Nearly three dozen commercial art galleries, plus at least as many more artists' studios with more irregular hours, are scattered across the community's walkable downtown streets, with the main concentrations being along 5th Avenue South and Broad Avenue South. The area is so arts-friendly that it supports two highly regarded community art centers, one in downtown Naples and the other on Marco Island, serving as exemplary models of the multipurpose art centers whose programs, exhibitions, and events are indispensable markers of a region's high quality of life. Downtown's nationally renowned von Liebig Art Center, located in a lovely park setting just a stone's toss from the busy gallery and restaurant cluster of 5th Avenue South, is a gleaming, 16,000-square-foot facility whose four art galleries and six well-equipped teaching studios are busy year-round. Though the structure was opened in 1998, its facilities are so much in demand that an expansion campaign is underway to provide even more education and exhibition space for Naples's artists and arts-savvy residents.

The von Liebig and its surrounding Cambier Park are home to one of the nation's premier outdoor art fairs, the Naples National Art Festival. This February show, which attracts artists from all corners of the continent, is filled with serious art buyers and marks one of the high points of Naples's exciting winter arts scene. During the rest of the year, a number of Art in the Park exhibitions serve as an important sales venue for regional artists. The von Liebig's galleries are dedicated to exhibiting primarily local and regional work, with a special emphasis on contemporary Florida artists and members of the Naples Art Association. During much of the year a monthly lecture series known as ARTalks brings leading figures in the art world to Naples for speaking engagements. The Beth Rhodes Center is the Marco Island Art League's newly expanded community art center. Its two visual arts galleries and several workshop/studios are in constant, year-round use by the fast-growing community's adult and youth artists. Three winter art fairs take place on the art center's grounds. Two juried exhibitions, the Marco Island Art Show in early February and the Craft Fair in mid-March, have established themselves as being among the region's best sales venues for visual and fine crafts artists.

The jewel in Naples's arts crown, and what sets this community's arts scene above and beyond that of most other Art Towns, is the Philharmonic Center Cultural Complex. This sparkling, $21-million facility opened in two phases, with the first being the Philharmonic Center for the Arts in 1989. Its main concert hall is a 1,221-seat acoustic and aesthetic masterpiece, while its companion stage is a state-of-the-art, 200-seat black box theatre. In late 2000 the complex opened its second phase, the Naples Museum of Art, as a 30,000-square-foot exhibition venue with 15 separate galleries and a glassed-in lobby dominated by a spectacular Dale Chihuly Venetian chandelier. With the opening of the art museum the entire region gained access to a sophisticated facility whose directors and community members are determined to chart a course guiding the institution into the upper tier of American art museums. Many of the exhibitions brought to the Naples Museum of Art are the same that tour to major art museums across the continent, shows originated by top institutions and international curatorial services, showcasing important works of art to this community's enthusiastic, year-round audiences.

The Philharmonic Center for the Arts is home to the Naples Philharmonic Orchestra, an 85-piece symphony orchestra. The organization also sponsors the Philharmonic Youth Orchestra as well as the 110-voice Philharmonic Center Chorale. Now in its 20th year, the orchestra and its affiliate companies perform more than 120 concerts annually in programs ranging from pops to chamber music, with four programs incorporating the Naples Ballet Company into its performances. Naples is also home to Classic Chamber Concerts, the presenter of a concert chamber music series performed at Edison Community College and Sugden Community Theatre.

Naples also has a lively and broadly supported theatre scene anchored by three stage companies. The Naples Players use Sugden Community Theatre for an eight-month mainstage season of dramas, musicals, and comedies, as well as the Tobye Theatre for its presentations of newer, experimental works. The Pelican Players, which uses Norris Community Center as its home, presents a season of mainstage classics. Naples Dinner Theatre produces a year-round season of Broadway musicals in its own playhouse, and also stages an innovative, kids-oriented season of plays called the Ice Cream Theatre. Instead of typical dinner theater fare of prime rib and chicken soup, the kiddies are served burgers, pizza, and hot fudge sundaes, along with their educational doses of Chekhov. The annual kickoff to the region's winter art season is the Marco Island Film Festival, a weeklong event staged in November at various regional venues.

Art Talk

Jim Daichendt, director of education for the von Liebig Art Center.

The von Liebig is in a town that has a plethora of art galleries and art museums. It's a community with enough interest in the arts and enough wealth to support a strong visual and performing-arts scene. Much of that support comes from our part-time residents who want to have access to an arts infrastructure when they're spending time here, and from gallery owners who take a great deal of interest in representing work made by local artists. We use 42 instructors in our visual arts programs, and most are local residents who have thriving studio careers. There's more support from local collectors for art that's representational than there is for contemporary work, but that's changing as more and more individuals with contemporary art collections are putting down roots here.

Essentials

Visual Arts Venues

Naples Museum of Art (5833 Pelican Bay Boulevard; 239/597-1900; www.thephil.org) State-of-the-art, multifaceted art museum with regional, national, and international exhibitions.

The von Liebig Art Center (585 Park Street; 239/262-6517; www.naplesartcenter.org) Year-round exhibitions, workshops, and art activities.

Art Talk

Myra Daniels, CEO and chairman of the Naples Museum of Art and the Naples Philharmonic Orchestra.

We're doing exciting things here, like our opening a Dale Chihuly show that drew 100,000 visitors, and our continuing series of important, national exhibitions since then. We were built with the concept that the visual and performing arts can be presented in a single, umbrella facility that shares administrative resources but allows for individual attention to the specific needs of the visual and performing arts. We're also a collecting institution with a focus on Mexican modernism and American modernism. Having a facility like this has given us unexpected access to an incredible amount of private art collections. We're the center for the arts in southwest Florida, and we've had great success in getting the public to come through our doors.

Beth Rhodes Center (1010 Winterberry Drive, Marco Island; 239/394-4221; www.marcoisland art.com) Exhibitions and workshops in an expanded, new facility.

Performing Arts & Events

The Naples Players (701 5th Avenue South; 239/263-7990; www.naples players.org) Energetic slate of dramas, musicals, and comedies.

Naples Philharmonic Orchestra (5833 Pelican Bay Boulevard; 239/597-1111; www.thephil.org) More than 120 concerts for adults and children in a state-of-the-art facility.

Naples National Art Festival (P.O. Box 839; 239/513-2492; www. naplesartcenter.org) Hundreds of top regional and national artists participate in this February event in Cambier Park.

Wine & Dine

The English Pub (2408 Linwood Avenue; 239/774-2408) Bangers and mash for the homesick, Guinness for everyone else.

P.F. Chang's China Bistro (10840 U.S. 41 N.; 239/596-2174) Asian fusion, a thriving bar scene, and Paul Fleming's famous lettuce wraps.

Campiello (1177 Third Street S.; 239/435-1166) A great wine list and Northern Italian cuisine.

Accommodations

Lakeside Inn (155 First Avenue, Marco Island; 800/729-0216; www.marcoislandlakeside.com) Charming rooms by the waterfront.

The Lemon Tree Inn (250 9th Street S.; 239/262-1414; www.lemontreeinn.com) Affordable, comfortable, and close to the galleries.

Comfort Inn on the Bay (1221 5th Avenue S.; 239/649-5800; www.choicehotels.com) Beachfront access right in the middle of town.

Information

Greater Naples Chamber of Commerce: 3620 Tamiami Trail North; 239/262-6376; www.napleschamber.org

Population: 25,000

Panama City, Florida

his diverse Art Town on Florida's panhandle is closer to New
Orleans than it is to Orlando, bringing its cultural spirit more in
line with the tenor of the Deep South's funkiness than South
Florida's multinationalism. Founded as a fishing community in the late
1800s, Panama City has evolved into an ethnically diverse place in
which its affordable and human-scaled downtown is one of the few
remaining places that locals say reminds them of "the old Florida."
There's a military base in town, as well as a constant inflow of retirees,
but it's been the more recent arrival of relocating entrepreneurs as well
as the influx of Asians and Latin Americans who have infused Panama
City with a new sense of vitality.

For most residents, life here revolves around the region's many
miles of unspoiled, white sand beaches. From the Apalachicola Bay's
oyster beds on its eastern flank, to the sand dunes sheltering the new
urbanist community of Seaside to the west, this region is home to more
than 100 miles of coastline, sheltered coves, and amazingly beautiful
places to watch the sunset over the Gulf of Mexico's shimmering
waters. Because it's relatively isolated (Tallahassee is 100 miles east)
Panama City has been compelled to develop its own fine arts infrastructure, which is why this community now has a wealth of venues
for music, theatre, and the visual arts. It's also why Panama City and
neighboring places such as Seaside and Grayton Beach have been able
to successfully sustain a range of arts festivals and events. There's every
incentive for locals to stay close to home base and make the best of

what's on their doorstep when the alternative involves long drives over the panhandle's hot, humid, and much less interesting interior. All an arts organization has to do to raise the likelihood of an event's being a success is to make sure it takes place within a short walk of the Gulf's waters.

Arts Scene

The region's premier arts venue is the Visual Arts Center of Northwest Florida, a multidisciplinary organization located in a 1925 structure originally built as Panama City's government center. Despite its aesthetically conflicted exteriors, the structure still functions as an important exhibition facility and arts-education center whose year-round schedule of shows is supplemented by an energetic calendar of adult and kids' art workshops and classes.

While there are a few art galleries as well as some alternative exhibition venues in downtown Panama City, the most prominent cluster of commercial galleries is located in the sublimely engaging community of Seaside, a 35-mile drive west of Panama City's marina and fishing piers. Founded in the mid-1980s, Panama City is a place whose high architectural standards and traditional street layouts recall a town that looks old, functions new, and serves its residents by kindling a tightly woven sense of neighborhood relationships. Early on, some of Seaside was bought up by real-estate investors whose motives for buying into the developer's high ideals had other goals in mind besides becoming a good, or even a somewhat compatible, neighbor. Nonetheless, Seaside continues to be a place where at least some interesting and artistic individuals are working hard at trying to fit themselves into a new type of life, though the values of its plethora of urbanite weekenders is at odds with those whose standards are fixed on the higher planes of developing new approaches to community.

Panama City is home to the Junior Museum, dedicated to children's programs, as well as two major venues for the performing arts, the Martin Theatre and the Marina Civic Center. The Bay Arts Alliance, which manages the civic center, presents a season of touring, mainstream musicals as well as summer series of free concerts in McKenzie Park. The Panama City Music Association is the community's main presenter of national and international orchestral and classical music talent, using the civic center for its December to April concert season. The Orchestra of St. Andrew Bay stages its October to May concert series at

Art Talk

Tina Dreyer, executive director of the Visual Arts Center of Northwest Florida. I've lived here 18 years, and in the past 10 of those there's been a major boom in this community's arts. It's a decision people have made in the way they run their lives, and we see that in our expanded educational programs, which are attracting more and more adults. We're part of Panama City's downtown resurgence and participate in all the major events happening here. Our shows change out every six weeks, and there are lots of annual events like our photography showcase in November and our annual big exhibition in September. Our other shows tend to pair art by a locally relevant artist with bold works by regional or national artists in our upper gallery.

the Tapper Center on the Gulf Coast Community College campus. Kaleidoscope Theatre uses its own playhouse for a season of six musicals and comedies. Downtown's art deco masterpiece, the 1936 Martin Theatre, is a 460-seat venue used for a year-round series of mainstream theatre presentations as well as the occasional pop orchestra and jazz band. Seaside Repertory Theatre stages its May to August season in both indoor and outdoor venues, presenting an interesting mix of newer and classic material, as well as improv shows by the Seaside Professional Fools.

Essentials

Visual Arts Venues

The Visual Arts Center of Northwest Florida (19 East 4th Street; 850/769-4451; www.visual artscenter.org) Several galleries and education facilities in a renovated, downtown courthouse.

Fusion Art Glass (63 Central Square, Seaside; 850/231-5405; www.fusionartglass.com) National and regional glass artists.

J. Proctor Gallery (123 Quincy Circle; 850/231-1091; www.jproctorgallery.com) Represents a national group of painters and sculptors.

Performing Arts & Events

Martin Theatre (409 Harrison Avenue; 850/763-8080; www.martin theatre.com) Downtown art deco theatre with a resident group of actors.

Fall Arts & Crafts Festival (see Panama City Chamber of Commerce below) Mid-October, outdoor arts fair on the waterfront.

ArtsQuest (Sandestin Baytowne Wharf, Sandestin; 850/231-0885; www.culturalartsassociation.org) May outdoor show with a national group of artists.

Wine & Dine

HammerHead's (137 Fisherman's Cove, Sandestin; 850/351-1997) Chargrilled lobster, seafood gumbo, cold beer.

Big Kahuna Surf Bar (14896 Front Beach Road; 850/233-5706) Great daiquiris and the fastest bartenders on the beach.

Saltwater Grill (11040 Middle Beach Road; 850/230-2739) Best piano bar in town.

Accommodations

Sugar Sands (20723 Front Beach Road; 850/234-8802; www.sugar sands.com) Reasonably priced rooms on the beach.

Quality Inn Gulf Front (15285 Front Beach Road; 800/874-7101; www.frontbeachresort.com) Spacious, luxury rooms on the beach.

The Shores (22500 Front Beach Road; 850/234-6591; www.shorespcbeach.com) Townhouses on the beach.

Information

Panama City Chamber of Commerce: 235 West 5th Street; 850/785-5206; www.panamacity.org

Population: 36,750

Art Talk

Barbara McMinis, executive director of the Martin Theatre.

We have a resident company that offers an educationally based program for both the community and educators, exposing them to live theatre and getting them comfortable with the idea of being here. Because of our educationally based programs, we've been able to increase the numbers of young people coming to our performances by 50 percent, which shows me they feel at home in the theatre. We're also a presenting organization with a January to March series that brings in national musicians and road shows that appeal to the snowbirds, and we target more contemporary shows through the year for our local audience.

Sarasota, Florida

estled along a beautiful stretch of Florida's Gulf Coast, this dynamic and diverse community sits on the east shore of Sarasota Bay, a pristine environment whose west shores are formed by a series of barrier islands known as Longboat Key, Lido Key, and Siesta Key. While much of the region's vaunted quality of life revolves around Sarasota's doorstep access to the Gulf of Mexico's turquoise waters, miles of beaches, and year-round harvests of seafood, this Art Town also revels in its rich cultural scene. Founded in the late 1800s, by the time the Roaring Twenties hit, Sarasota had already carved out a reputation for itself as a winter playground for wealthy northern industrialists. People still come here for golf and the Gulf, building even more mansions in sprawling suburbs as well as the tree-lined residential areas of this well-preserved community.

Perhaps the most influential person in Sarasota's early history was John Ringling, the impresario whose Ringling Brothers and Barnum & Bailey Circus was the continent's premier entertainment organization during the 20th century. In 1927 Ringling made Sarasota the permanent winter home for his hundreds of clowns, elephants, sword swallowers, and bearded ladies, forever stamping this community as the nation's premier circus town. While it's still the organization's winter home, Sarasota is more than a place where the traveling circus pitches its rehearsal tents. Much of Sarasota's arts infrastructure was developed either by the Ringling family or through their generous underwriting of efforts in which the family played a quiet yet crucial role. It was through this decades-long (and continuing) spirit of noblesse oblige that Sarasota built its regional reputation as a place where the arts were given the venues and support they need in order to flourish. And while today's audiences for performances of *La Traviata* by the Sarasota Opera still include a few of the sword swallowers and clowns who Ringling lured here (as well as their descendants), what drives the ongoing development of Sarasota's arts scene are the many thousands of arts supporters who were attracted here by the fine arts legacy the Ringling family's wealth established and nurtured.

Arts Scene

One of the nation's most successful Art Town gallery districts is Towles Court, a 30-gallery cluster of art spaces that range from sculpture and ceramics studios to fine crafts galleries, interior design shops, visual arts galleries, and jewelers' garrets. Originally developed as a residential subdivision in the late 1920s, a significant part of Towles Court's appeal as a gallery district is its architectural diversity. The neighborhood's galleries and studios are, for the most part, located in a series of beautifully preserved homes representing a timeline of Florida's tastes in residential architecture, from Arts & Crafts masterpieces to Modernesque 1950s ramblers. Tossed in among these gems are newer structures whose architectural references meld with, rather than assault, the neighborhood's visual harmony. As is the case with older neighborhoods in general, Towles Court is an eminently walkable place whose sidewalks and lawns are shaded by towering trees and the occasional palm. The district's wildly popular series of Third Friday Gallery Walks is the best place to catch a sense of Sarasota's creative energies. Galleries and studios coordinate their opening receptions, drawing hundreds of art lovers who socialize, buy art, network, and enjoy their community's sense of creative pride. Downtown Sarasota has a smattering of galleries and coffee bars exhibiting local art, including the Mira Mar Gallery, a nationally known venue representing top artists from the region as well as places such as Santa Fe and New York City.

The top venue in Sarasota's arts scene is the John and Mable Ringling Museum of Art, a spectacular facility located on a 66-acre estate, programming exhibitions throughout the year in its 21 art gallery spaces. The museum, whose educational outreach programs lend the entire region a sense of artistic integrity through their multidimensional depth, exhibits works from its permanent collection as well as traveling national and international exhibitions surveying the broad scope of ancient and contemporary art history but with a decided emphasis on historical works from Europe. The Italianate museum building is located on an estate that also includes the Museum of the Circus, the Ringling family's Ca d'Zan mansion, and the Asolo Theatre, an Italian Baroque–era theatre that the Ringling family purchased, shipped, and rebuilt on the estate's grounds. Now administered by Florida State University, the Ringling estate adjoins the New College campus of the University of South Florida, an institution whose own facilities include the Caples Fine Arts Complex, as well as the Sainer Pavilion Theatre and Isermann Gallery. The gallery exhibits mainly student and faculty work, while the theatre's 257-seat venue is the home of the Banyan Theatre Company, whose year-round season balances traditional dramas and new works.

Sarasota's neighboring community of Longboat Key is home to the Longboat Key Center for the Arts, a facility whose classrooms and three galleries are used for year-round workshops as well as rotating exhibitions of works by local and regional artists. The center also coordinates a jazz concert series as well as the free Sunday in the Park concerts in Durante Community Park. Art Center Sarasota, a downtown facility in the process of acquiring its own building, exhibits rotating shows of contemporary work by its members as well as themed shows of work by regional talents. Another nonprofit exhibition facility is the Center for Arts and Humanities, which mainly features local work. Sarasota's also home to the Museum of Asian Art, a facility whose exhibitions feature traveling shows from Japan, China, Thailand, Nepal, and elsewhere, as well as pieces from its own permanent collection. Through the winter months the museum's lecture series brings national experts to Sarasota for public presentations.

The Asolo Theatre Festival is home to two companies, a resident group of Equity actors and a group of students from Florida State University. Performing in a reconstructed, 500-seat Italian opera house on the grounds of the Ringling Museum of Art, as well as in a smaller, modern black box, Asolo's season of mainstage and black box works covers classic American productions as well as newer pieces from the cutting-edge of international theatre. Florida Studio Theatre, which presents its plays year-round, focuses on Broadway and off-Broadway plays, as well as a Festival of New Plays and an annual Playwrights Festival. The Players Theatre focuses its year-round presentations on musical theatre and a performing-arts academy.

Sarasota's also home to the Florida West Coast Symphony, the Sarasota Ballet and Sarasota Opera. The Symphony uses Holley Hall and the Sarasota Opera House for its September to May season, as well as the much larger, 1,700-seat Van Wezel Performing Arts Hall for its

Masterworks concert series. Sarasota Opera's downtown venue, once a Vaudeville theatre, is a beautifully restored, 1,033-seat performance space that's home to the opera's eight-month season of operas and recitals. Sarasota Ballet uses the Van Wezel and FSU's Performing Arts Center for its seven-month season, while La Musica presents its season of chamber music concerts and recitals in the downtown Opera House.

Essentials

Visual Arts Venues

Ringling Museum of Art
(5401 Bay Shore Road; 941/351-1660; www.ringling.org) Located on a sprawling estate, this museum has earned its national reputation as the East Coast peer of Los Angeles's J. Paul Getty Museum.

Art Talk

Katharine Butler, president of the Towles Court Artists Association.

Every year, the quality of the artists in our group improves, the size and range of our events improves, and the number of people attracted to our openings increases. We have about 45 artists in our group, and they're a varied lot, from artists who create work for tourists to high-end craftsmen and artists with outstanding reputations. We're set up as a live/work zone, and our buildings are privately owned. It's a nice, campuslike atmosphere with a mix of residential and commercial activity. Affordability is becoming an issue around here, and it's preventing some of the art school's gradutes from staying in Sarasota to start their careers.

Longboat Key Center for the Arts
(6860 Longboat Drive South, Longboay Key; 941/383-2345; www.longboatkeyartscenter.org) Year-round exhibitions and educational programs.

Museum of Asian Art (640 S. Washington Boulevard; 941/954-7117; www.museumasianart.org) One of the nation's top museums specializing in the arts of Asian cultures.

Performing Arts & Events

Asolo Theatre Festival (5555 N. Tamiami Trail; 941/351-9010; www.asolo.org) Sarasota's premier theatre company, performing in a rebuilt opera house imported from Scotland.

Arts Day (The Sarasota County Arts Council; 941/365-5118; www.sarasota-arts.org) January, community-wide event featuring performing artists, musicians, and visual artists along downtown's streets.

Art Talk

Howard Millman, producing artistic director of Asolo Theatre Festival. We have four Equity theatre companies, an opera company with its own opera house, a symphony orchestra, and a ballet company. This community, for the past 40 years, has been the Florence of Florida. In this state you can find great beaches everywhere, but it's an intense cultural scene that's hard to find. We're a wealthy place, with a lot of deep-pocketed individuals who support the arts. Our county's tourism tax is 25-percent dedicated to the arts, and that helps all of us a great deal, which is why most organizations own their own buildings. We have an acting conservatory here with a group of resident actors who perform in a rotating repertory that runs for eight months.

Florida West Coast Symphony (709 N. Tamiami Trail; 941/953-4252; www.fwcs.org) Presents a very active season of concerts and recitals from October through May.

Wine & Dine

Javier's Peruvian Cuisine (6621 Midnight Pass Road; 941/349-1792; www.javiersrestaurant.com) A touch of Japan, a hint of Mexico, a whisper of Portugal altogether make Sarasota's take on Peruvian food irresistible.

Sarasota News & Books (1341 Main Street; 941/365-6332; www.sarasota newsandbooks.com) European-style café in one of the South's best literary havens.

The Columbia Restaurant (411 St. Armands Circle; 941/388-3987; www.columbiarestaurant.com) Spanish/Cuban fusion with an emphasis on seafoods.

Accommodations

The Calais (1735 Stickney Point Road; 941/921-5797; www.thecalais.com) Affordable rooms on the beach.

American Inn Hotel & Suites (5931 Fruitville Road; 941/342-8778) Great for families with room for RVs.

Comfort Inn (5778 Clark Road; 941/921-7750; www.choice hotels.com) Affordable and convenient to downtown.

Information

Greater Sarasota Chamber of Commerce: 1945 Fruitville Road; 941/955-8187; www.sarasotachamber.org

Population: 55,000

Berea, Kentucky

This talent-laden college town 35 miles south of Lexington, Kentucky, has earned its reputation as the "Folk Arts and Crafts Capitol of Kentucky." While much of the credit for establishing Berea's national stature as a community that takes fine crafts seriously is the result of Berea College's guiding hand in developing an internationally known fine crafts education program, in more recent years this unassuming place has also been the beneficiary of a new wave of resident artists and entrepreneurs attracted here by the community's growing impact as a must-see destination for cultural tourists.

Surrounded by rolling hills, lakes, and rivers, Berea is the kind of town that's taken hold of its destiny by realizing that when you're already a magnet for a creative community that's steadily increasing its local economic and political impact, it's best to jump on board the wagon and fully develop the potential right at your doorstep. While there's a steady flow of commuters who live in Berea and commute to corporate jobs in Lexington, the real strength of this town lies in its strong sense of entrepreneurial independence.

Established in 1855, the fledgling town was the home of Berea College by 1869. In the 1890s the college's president started selling textiles created by the school's students and faculty to shops in Louisville, Lexington, and Cincinnati, which ultimately led to the establishment of the Berea College Fireside Industries. The college, which still provides a full-ride scholarship to each of its students and requires all of them to work at least 10 hours weekly in on-campus jobs, is now home to Berea College Crafts, a business that markets a wide range of fine crafts products produced by the college's students and faculty to a growing group of worldwide art collectors and galleries. Nearly 250 students and two dozen faculty members work for the Student Crafts Program, which collaborates with the Southern Highland Craft Guild and the Kentucky Guild of Artists and Craftsmen in marketing Berea College's creations.

Arts Scene

Downtown Berea is home to two art galleries selling the creations of Berea College crafts: the Boone Tavern Gift Shop and the Log House Crafts Gallery, the latter a historic, free-standing structure whose expansive interior spaces are ideally suited to displaying the sophisticated, elegantly crafted home furnishings turned out by the college's workshops. The gift shop, much smaller in size, is nonetheless a great place to find the amazing array of Broomcrafts whisks, fantail, and hearthsweep brooms created by students.

Downtown Berea is a charming and walkable place whose Southern Colonial–style architecture is home to several commercial art galleries as well as the coffee bars, pubs, and burger joints that are vital to the lifeblood of any college town. The Upstairs Gallery is an especially great place to find visual arts by regional talents. A short walk from the polished charm of downtown Berea leads to the more gritty version of Southern style, the commercial mishmash architecture of Old Town, a cluster of galleries built in the part of town that's home to the Louisville and Nashville railroad depot. Needless to say, this is also the part of town where another group of artists has decided to set up their own versions of a gallery and studio district, and from one end of the neighborhood to the other, Old Town is filled with artist-run businesses, fine crafts shops, and the occasional antiques store.

The biggest news on Berea's arts scene has been the opening of the $6-million Kentucky Artisan Center, a 26,000-square-foot exhibition and education facility built alongside an interstate highway at one of the main entrances into Berea. The venue gives Berea's arts community, as well as artists from across Kentucky, an incredibly powerful marketing tool for their creations.

While the Berea Arts Council organizes events such as the Sunday Series of artist performances at ArtSpace, one of the town's main arts events is the mid-October Fall Guild Fair, which attracts more than 120 artists to Berea's Indian Fort Theater for its weekend run. There's also the Spring Showcase, an April open studios tour weekend, the Spring

Fair organized by the Kentucky Guild of Artists and Craftsmen in May, and the Berea Crafts Festival in June.

Essentials

Visual Arts Venues

Berea College Crafts Log House Gallery (Dixie Court; 859/985-3220; www.bereacollegecrafts.com) Home furnishings and accessories created by Berea College students and faculty.

Kentucky Artisan Center (575 Walnut Meadow Road; 859/985-5448; www.kentuckyartisancenter.org) Large, multipurpose facility representing fine crafts artisans from across the Bluegrass State.

Upstairs Gallery (114 Main Street; 859/986-4434) Represents top regional painters and sculptors.

Art Talk

Debby Giannini, assistant director of the Kentucky Artisan Center.
We opened in July 2003 and have received lots of favorable response to our presence, which is right on I-75. We have helped people understand that there's lots of great art being created all across the state. Our mission is to get people to understand the bigger picture of what's happening in Kentucky arts, then direct them into Berea to see the local arts community. We exhibit mostly furniture and crafts in our front gallery, and we have weekend musician performances and weaving demonstrations. We try to get work by Berea artists into our exhibitions, and we have a rural partners program that develops marketing opportunities for artists elsewhere in the state.

Performing Arts & Events

Berea Crafts Festival and Arte Vida (see Berea Tourism Center below) Outdoor summer arts fair in Indian Fort Theater with music performances on the James Hall lawn.

Fall Guild Fair (Kentucky Guild of Artists & Craftsmen; 859/986-3192; www.kyguild.org) October outdoor arts show featuring more than 120 national artists and craftspeople.

Pioneer Playhouse (840 Stanford Road, Danville; 859/236-2747; www.pioneerplayhouse.com) Summer outdoor theatre with camping facilities.

Wine & Dine

Boone Tavern (100 Main Street; 800/366-9358; www.boonetavern hotel.com) Dining room and hotel operated by Berea College students.

Art Talk

Peggy Burgio, marketing manager of Berea College Crafts.

Our primary function is to promote college crafts and regional crafts, and over 50 percent of what we sell is made in our student crafts program. In terms of quality and sophistication the work created by our students holds up to the best of what you'll find at galleries across the country. We also have works from a number of local and regional crafts artists mixed into the range of what we sell. We try to present Berea College Crafts in a home-like setting, and that seems to work well with developing word-of-mouth advertising among the collectors who seek us out. Our emphasis is on keeping traditional pieces of craft art up to modern standards, and we're not being dictated to by trends in the national crafts markets.

Population: 9,900

Berea Coffee & Tea Co. (124 Main Street; 859/986-7656; www.berea coffee.com) Favorite local buzz shop.

Papaleno's Italian Restaurant (106 Center Street; 859/986-4497) Pastas, lasagne, and canolli for those on a student budget.

Accommodations

Boone Tavern Hotel (100 Main Street; 800/366-9358; www.boone tavernhotel.com) Historic luxury in the heart of Berea.

The Doctor's Inn (617 Chestnut Street; 859/986-3042) Historic, Greek revival mansion, with gourmet breakfasts.

Comfort Inn & Suites (1003 Paint Lick Road; 859/985-5500; www.choicehotels.com) Affordable rooms plus pool.

Information

Berea Tourism Center: 201 N. Broadway; 800/598-5263; www.berea.com

Biloxi, Mississippi

Once a sleepy community best known for its military base and the fleet of shrimp boats moored in its harbor, the Biloxi of today has revived itself into a confident, prosperous and spiffed up jewel of the Gulf Coast. The short and long of how it happened traces back to 1992 when gaming became a legal business and millions of Las Vegas dollars started pouring into Biloxi construction projects. Today, eight major casino resorts have shouldered their way onto stretches of Biloxi's white sand beaches, and their thousands of hotel rooms attract not only vacationing gamblers from across the middle part of the nation but also the top name talent one normally associates with Las Vegas. Want to catch Jay Leno's stand-up show and follow it with dinner at a French restaurant and a midnight jazz show in a sprawling nightclub? You can now do that in Biloxi, and not just once in a blue moon. High-end restaurants and top-name entertainers have become part of the fabric of everyday life in this beach town, and with these changes Biloxi and its neighboring community of Ocean Springs have developed the ability to financially sustain two art museums and a range of arts groups.

Founded as a French trading post, Biloxi honors its past with an annual Mardi Gras whose madness and mayhem is second only to that of New Orleans, which is just a 90-mile drive west. The maritime and fishing industries are still important enough in Biloxi's economy to where they share a museum, and two of the biggest events on the annual social calendar are the Christmas-season boat parade and mid-September's Biloxi Seafood Festival, home of the world championship of gumbo cooking. Life here is intimately wrapped around Biloxi's Gulf Coast locale, and family outings at one of the many state parks and public beaches lining the shore are a local tradition. For those with a taste for outdoors adventure there are the wild environs of the Gulf Coast National Seashore, a collection of barrier islands connected to the mainland by a ferry ride, and many a local Biloxian prefers just pointing their own powerboat or sailboat in that same direction on weekends.

Arts Scene

The Mississippi Gulf Coast's highest concentration of art galleries is in the Depot District of Bay St. Louis, a small town about an hour's drive west of Biloxi, making it a perfect day trip for heat-stroked urbanites from New Orleans. Biloxi's visual arts action mainly takes place at the area's two art museums, the Ohr-O'Keefe Museum and the Walter Anderson Museum of Art, as well as in the galleries of the Biloxi Maritime and Seafood Industry Museum.

Named after ceramist George Ohr and members of the Biloxi O'Keefe family who underwrote the venture, the Ohr-O'Keefe Museum showcases its collection of pottery and other ceramics made by a man known as the "Father of Modern American Pottery." The museum's exhibition and education programs have a determinedly contemporary and national vision, embracing visiting artist residencies by many of the nation's top ceramics talents, as well as traveling regional and national exhibits in its Frank Gehry–designed main facility. The exhibited work ranges from paintings and sculpture to photography by local, regional, and national artists. Each October, the George E. Ohr Fall Festival of the Arts on Biloxi's town green is one of the highlights of the community's annual arts calendar. The Biloxi Maritime and Seafood Industry Museum has an energetic range of exhibitions and programs that include year-round educational workshops for kids, exhibitions of regional and national artwork (not limited to sketches of shrimp boats and sand dunes), and programs using the two reproduction Biloxi Schooner craft moored at its dock.

Just across Biloxi Bay, Ocean Springs has since the early 1990s built its arts scene around the Walter Anderson Museum of Art, a facility dedicated to the legacy of one of America's leading 20th-century artists. As was the case with William Faulkner in Oxford, so was Walter Anderson inspired by the day-to-day life stories he saw unfolding around him in Ocean Springs, and his ornate images of plants, animals, and people reflect this amazing vision. The museum's exhibition programs tend to focus on the work of Walter Anderson as well as that of his painter brother Marc Anderson and their ceramist brother Peter Anderson. The November Peter Anderson Arts & Crafts Festival is one of the highlights of Ocean Springs's annual arts calendar.

Besides being the venue for top-name entertainment booked into casino showrooms, Biloxi is also the home of the Gulf Coast Symphony, which performs at the Saenger Theatre in New Orleans, and the Gulf Coast Opera Theatre, which uses the same venue. Biloxi Little Theatre presents its performances at Center Stage, mixing new works and standards into what is a year-round season.

Essentials

Visual Arts Venues

Walter Anderson Museum of Art (510 Washington Avenue, Ocean Springs; 228/872-3164) Dedicated to the legacy of an American art legend.

Shearwater Pottery (102 Shearwater Drive, Ocean Springs; 228/875-7320; www.walteringlisanderson.com) Ceramics studio founded by Peter Anderson and his famous brothers Walter and Marc.

Ohr–O'Keefe Museum (136 Ohr Street; 228/374-5547; www.georgeohr.org) Frank Gehry–designed museum with a national exhibitions focus.

Performing Arts & Events

George Ohr Fall Festival of the Arts (Ohr-O'Keefe Museum, 136 Ohr Street; 228/374-5547; www.georgeohr.org) Outdoor arts festival in early October on the Biloxi town green.

Art Talk

Marilyn Lyons, executive director of the Walter Anderson Museum of Art.
I've been here for two-and-a-half years, starting as a volunteer. In that time we've organized a show that traveled to the Smithsonian in D.C., and we've moved to become a fully accredited museum. Our physical space has stayed the same since it was built 13 years ago. We have exhibitions and educational programs for children and adults year-round, plus a summer theatre camp. The local school district is an organization we work with very closely. We collect and display the work of Walter Anderson and his brothers, and some other artists from time to time, such as regional artists who use Anderson's motifs in their work. His art was very close to nature, and we try to emphasize that focus in our exhibitions.

Art Talk

Marjie Gowdy, executive director of the Ohr–O'Keefe Museum.
We primarily, since 1994, have collected and displayed the work of George Ohr, and we've taught pottery classes and have sponsored lectures about pottery as part of that mission. We're also dedicated to exhibiting the work of historic and contemporary African American artists from this region and are very supportive of emerging artists through our exhibitions and programs. We're in the process of developing a 25,000-square-foot, six-building complex in a cultural campus concept developed by Frank Gehry. Our $20-million capital campaign to fund the project started in the mid-1990s and has allowed us to build on a waterfront site, surrounded by oak trees.

Biloxi Little Theatre (220 Lee Street; 228/432-8543) Community theatre company with an intriguing focus on new material.

Gulf Coast Symphony (P.O. Box 542; 228/435-9800; www.gulf coastsymphony.net) Four-concert season presented in the restored Saenger Theatre.

Wine & Dine

Beau Rivage Casino & Resort (875 Beach Boulevard; 228/386-7111; www.beaurivageresort.com) Seafood, Japanese, French, Italian, a brewpub, and barbecue, all under one roof.

Dock of the Bay (119 Beach Boulevard; 228/467-9940; www.dock-of-the-bay.com) Bayside dining with live music and lots of local style.

Java Joe's (834 Howard Avenue; 228/435-9900) The coast's favorite buzz shop.

Accommodations

Casino Magic (195 Beach Boulevard; 228/386-4600; www.casino magic-biloxi.com) Enormous resort with a comedy club, roulette, and breakfast all night long.

Green Oaks B&B (580 Beach Boulevard; 228/436-6257) Quiet, comfortable rooms on the Gulf Coast.

Biloxi Travel Inn (2010 Beach Boulevard; 228-388-5531) Affordable, with room for families.

Information

Biloxi Chamber of Commerce: 1048 Beach Boulevard; 228/374-2717; www.biloxi.org

Population: 50,600

Oxford, Mississippi

ike many of the nation's great college towns, the north Mississippi community of Oxford has an arts scene whose youthful edge infuses this friendly place with a year-round flow of exhibitions and events. It's an energy level that for decades has presented many mid-career artists working in various disciplines with an attractive alternative to life in nearby Memphis, about an hour's drive north. That's a main reason, despite their small size, places like Chapel Hill, North Carolina, Lawrence, Kansas, and Bellingham, Washington, benefit from university-driven arts scenes whose impacts far exceed what these Art Towns could manage on their own.

"Ole Miss," known to others as the University of Mississippi, is located on a sprawling and historic campus filled with Southern Colonial–style structures and shaded by stands of magnolias. Its economic impact, from the pizzas served at Dino's to the faculty positions held by painters and sculptors with national reputations, extends throughout Oxford's life. Conscious of their traditions, Ole Miss and Oxford try to walk a path that's not weighted down by them. Until the end of time, fall football Saturdays will always turn this town on its collective ear, but that hasn't prevented the university from completing its gleaming, new Ford Center for the Performing Arts, a 1,250-seat venue capable of handling everything from touring Broadway shows to world music concerts.

Life in Oxford is strongly influenced by the legacy of William Faulkner, who lived here and wrote about the eclectic characters found throughout the small-town South. Every July, the Faulkner & Yoknapatawpha Conference draws hundreds of writers, historians, playwrights, and literary world luminaries into Oxford, a process that's repeated the following April when the Conference for the Book draws an even glitzier crowd of agents, writers, and publishers. It's no mere coincidence that one of the nation's premier bookstores, the legendary Square Books, occupies a spot in the regional creative conscious that's both physically and metaphorically at the heart of Oxford. Many a literary deal has been struck and many an advance has been negotiated over cappuccinos and croissants in the Square Books Café, an aspect of Oxford cultural life that's rare to find in Art Towns of any size.

Arts Scene

With the completion of the Powerhouse Community Arts & Cultural Center, the Yoknapatawpha Arts Council realized its vision of a multi-purpose visual arts, education, and performance venue whose 160-seat auditorium was much needed by local theatre companies and musicians. The center is also the Oxford Film Festival's main screening site. The premier regional visual arts venue is the University Museums on the Ole Miss campus. The museums, comprised of the historic Mary Buie Museum and the Walton-Young House, is eventually slated to include a William Faulkner wing. National touring exhibitions are showcased here, and the facility is also the site of a summer arts camp for local kids. Bryant Hall Gallery, which is also on the Ole Miss campus, exhibits student and faculty work. Southside Gallery on Courthouse Square is Oxford's leading commercial gallery, exhibiting regional and national artists in all media, and staging monthly opening receptions for its shows. The Double Decker Arts Festival, an April event that includes live music performed on stages set up around Courthouse Square, food booths and an outdoor arts fair with more than 100 artists booths, is Oxford's biggest yearly arts bash. In December the Artists' Studio Tour attracts hundreds of art lovers on its weekend-long, self-guided trek through the work environments of Oxford and the surrounding area.

While the Ford Center for the Performing Arts is a showcase for touring national and international musicians and actors, it's also used by the university's Theatre Arts Department for some of its mainstage plays, though Fulton Chapel is the traditional on-campus venue for live theatre. Paris-Yates Chapel is used by the music department for recitals and concerts. The Grove, a stretch of green lawn on the Ole Miss campus, is the venue for summer's L.O.U. Sunset Series of blues and gospel concerts. Oxford is also the home of a number of national rock and alternative bands who got their start playing the local bars until they were ready for the stage at Proud Larry's, a top venue for touring national and regional bands.

Essentials

Visual Arts Venues

The University Museums (5th & University; 662/915-7073; www.olemiss.edu) Touring national shows and historical exhibits.

Powerhouse Community Arts & Cultural Center (University Avenue & S. 14th Street; 662/236-6429; www.oxfordarts.com) Renovated building housing gallery, performance, and classroom space.

Southside Gallery (150 Courthouse Square; 662/234-9090; www.south sideoxford.com) Representing the top artists of the region.

Performing Arts & Events

Double Decker Arts Festival (Yoknapatawpha Arts Council; 662/236-6429; www.oxfordarts.com) Spring event featuring music and a large outdoor arts show.

The Faulkner & Yoknapatawpha Conference (Center for the Study of Southern Culture; 662/915-5993; www.olemiss.edu) Annual event in July celebrating the legacy of Oxford's most famous resident.

Ford Center for the Performing Arts (100 University Avenue; 662/915-2787; www.olemiss.edu) Multipurpose venue with main-stage and black box facilities.

Art Talk

Elaine Abadie, executive director of the Yoknapatawpha Arts Council.
We moved into the Powerhouse Arts Center in the summer of 2004. It has a theatre, plus gallery, studio, and classroom space in a multiphase process stretching out across several years. It's an old electrical and water utilities structure that was built in the early 1900s from brick, concrete, and wood, so the renovation wasn't too complicated. It's finally given Oxford's local artists the type of venue they needed to have, without relying on the university for a facility. Our local art scene is just exploding. We're compared to places like Boulder and Chapel Hill for our live-music scene, and our Double Decker Arts Festival attracts 65,000 visitors. Our studio tour has grown to more than 20 sites, and the artists are making lots of sales.

Art Talk

Kara Giles, director of Southside Gallery.

I've lived here since 1999 and the visual arts scene has grown a lot since then. The university's arts programs have been vastly improved, and the arts council has moved ahead on its Powerhouse project. We specialize in Southeastern regional art and represent top names in painting, sculpture, and photography. There are lots of people moving into Oxford to retire or build second homes, and they're important buyers of the artists we represent. Our downstairs gallery shows work from two or three artists at a time, while our upstairs gallery is used for solo shows. We open a new exhibition every six weeks and sell lots of art to the football crowd, to our great surprise.

Wine & Dine

Proud Larry's (211 South Lamar Boulevard; 662/236-0050; www.proudlarrys.com) Live-music club with great pastas, subs, and brews.

City Grocery (152 Courthouse Square; 662/232-8080; www.city groceryoxford.com) New southern cuisine, and great wine list.

Bottletree Bakery (923 Van Buren Avenue; 662/236-5000) Favorite local buzz shop and an arts venue.

Accommodations

The Tree House B&B (53 County Road 321; 662/513-6354) Comfortable and quiet, just a short distance from Courthouse Square.

Ole Miss Motel (1517 E. University Avenue; 662/234-2424) Affordable, with lots of room for families.

Days Inn (1101 Frontage Road; 662/234-9500; www.daysinn.com) Modern place, with a swimming pool.

Information

Oxford-Lafayette County Chamber of Commerce: 299 W. Jackson Avenue; 662/234-4651; www.oxfordms.com

Population: 11,800

Asheville, North Carolina

estled into the Appalachian Mountains of western North Carolina, the bucolic community of Asheville is part history exhibit, part college town, and part urban-renaissance showcase. Asheville has retained the walkable, neighborhood type of environment that defines the local lifestyle as something lived on a human scale, rather than as an existence defined by amalgams of gated communities, condo developments, and big box shopping centers. Downtown Asheville's an extremely pleasant place to spend time: The sidewalks are filled with outdoor cafés, and many of the commercial buildings have renovated their upper floors to accommodate housing for the constant stream of relocating East Coast– lifestyle refugees who come here seeking a higher quality of life. Coffee bars (many of which are independently owned and exhibit local art) abound for the caffeine addicted, there's a public produce market on the street level of the Grove Arcade building, and a constant stream of street buskers, Phish fans, camera-slinging tourists, and the occasional mountain mamma and her half-dozen tow-headed kids all wander around downtown Asheville, keeping the street-watching scene fresh and rewarding.

Asheville's economy was founded on the interests of two enterprises, the lumber industry and the health spa business. For most of the 19th and 20th centuries, it was natural resources industries that ruled the region's economic roost, and much of the historic infrastructure that today is Asheville's pride and joy was built with forestry family fortunes. Fortunately, there was also a great deal of local interest in the architecture and design vernaculars developed during the Arts

& Crafts movement of the early 20th century, which is why parts of today's Asheville have more in common stylistically with Pasadena, California, than they do with Raleigh, North Carolina. In 1930, Asheville gained access to what's still its most outstanding architectural treasure when the Biltmore Estate, a Xanadu-like castle built by George Vanderbilt in 1895, opened its towering gates to the public. The 8,000-acre facility, now home to riding trails, gardens, a winery, summer outdoor concerts, and gourmet dining festivals, is one of Asheville's best places to relax and revel in western Carolina's amazing natural beauty. During the summer months, another popular summer hangout is McCormick Field, the 70-year-old ballpark that's home to the Asheville Tourists, a farm club of the major leagues. On a more year-round basis, many mountain residents seem to catch their fever at Cherokee Casino, a gleaming 15-story, Vegas-style fantasia just a short drive from town.

Arts Scene

Unlike communities that embraced a hostile attitude toward their downtowns, allowing locally owned businesses to be replaced by national chain stores, Asheville took a much smarter path. Concerned citizen activists united about Asheville's future and held the power of the voting booth over the heads of local politicos, forcing the issue. In 1992 they were rewarded with the opening of Pack Square Education, Arts & Science Center, which today is Asheville's downtown focal point. Home to the Asheville Museum of Art, the YMI Cultural Center, the Colburn Gem & Mineral Museum, the Health Adventure, and the Diane Wortham Theatre, Pack Square is now used year-round as the region's cultural center. Downtown Asheville is home to the region's largest concentration of art galleries outside of Charleston, South Carolina. Many of these spaces focus on contemporary art and fine crafts, especially the international-caliber glass, art created by artists in the nearby Penland arts colony. Art collectors and dealers from across the nation, aware of the key role Asheville's artists play in feeding the creative supply chain, now make regular sweeps through the local arts fairs, scouting for talent. More than two dozen of downtown's visual arts venues take part in the City Center Art Walks, a Friday-evening event staged monthly from April through October. Pack Square is also home to a very popular summer music series called Downtown After Five, featuring many of the region's bluegrass and folk music talents.

The premier visual arts venue in the region is the Asheville Art Museum, an exhibiting institution with a permanent collection that hosts touring national and regional exhibitions. The museum is also home to a year-round series of art workshops and lectures by art experts and artists, as well as a summer art camp for kids. A short drive from downtown, one of the nation's most innovative artist-oriented programs, the Folk Art Center and Allanstand Craft Shop, represents the sophisticated creations of members of the Southern Highland Craft Guild, which also sponsors year-round artist workshops at the center. Woodturners, dulcimer makers, textiles artists, and ceramicists are among the members of the guild, whose artists are drawn from nine southern states. Through its three galleries there are also exhibitions from the center's permanent collection, themed exhibitions, and one-artist shows.

As is the case in many of the best Art Towns, Asheville's calendar is filled with community festivals celebrating the region's wealth of creative talent. During the summer months there's a weekly Arts and Herbs market in West Asheville. The University of North Carolina at Asheville presents its free Concerts on the Quad series of performances during spring and summer, while Shindig on the Green, featuring regional music and dance, takes place on summer evenings at the City County Plaza. For top-name entertainment in a gorgeous setting nothing beats the Biltmore Estate's Summer Evening Concerts on the south terrace of Biltmore House. These shows are in many ways an Asheville family affair and are ideal places to spread out a blanket, open a bottle of local wine, and stare at the stars.

Asheville is home to an outstanding and energetic live theatre community. North Carolina Stage Company, a new arrival on the scene, presents its performances in the Earth Guild Building, which is across the street from Malaprops Bookstore, one of the nation's top independent booksellers. North Carolina Stage Company's material is mainly drawn from new, off-Broadway plays. Asheville Community Theatre uses its own playhouse on downtown's Walnut Street in presenting its mainstage season of musicals, comedies, and dramas and fills a 45-seat black box for its 35 Below season of experimental and new material. Highland Repertory Theatre's season of dramas and comedies is staged at the Diana Wortham Theatre, a 600-seat venue that's also home to the theatre's own Mainstage Series, which brings touring national and international performers to Asheville. Asheville Symphony uses the Civic Center for its September to April season of masterworks and pops concerts.

Art Talk

Frank Thomson, curator of the Asheville Art Museum.

I came aboard in 1989, and since that time we've moved from the basement of the Civic Center, where we had no visible presence, to Pack Square in downtown Asheville, which is the cultural focus of this community. Our exhibitions' focus has moved from 20th-century American art to an interest in arts of the Southeast as well as art from western North Carolina. The Penland School of Crafts is just 40 miles from here, and many of the artists who live and work in the Penland area are exhibiting in galleries in New York or London or Santa Fe but probably have not had their work shown in North Carolina, so one of the things we now do is present these artists with a venue for exhibiting locally.

Essentials

Visual Arts Venues

Asheville Art Museum (2 S. Pack Place; 828/253-3227; www.asheville art.org) Downtown's center for national and regional visual arts. Exhibitions, lectures, and film.

Folk Art Center (Blue Ridge Parkway; 828/298-7928; www.southernhighlandguild.org) Rotating exhibits in three galleries, featuring top fine crafts talents.

Blue Spiral 1 (38 Biltmore Avenue; 828/251-0202; www.bluespiral1.com) Contemporary gallery representing the premier regional and national talents.

Performing Arts & Events

Heritage Weekend (Folk Art Center, Blue Ridge Parkway; 828/298-7928; www.southernhighlandguild.org) Three-day celebration in September of traditional crafts, music, and storytelling.

City Center Art Walks (Asheville Area Arts Council; 11 Biltmore Avenue; 828/258-0710; www.ashevillearts.com) Monthly First Friday, downtown event from April through October.

Bele Chere (College Street 828/259-5800; www.belechere.com) Late-July outdoor arts festival in uptown Asheville with artists, food, and music.

Wine & Dine

Gold Hill Espresso & Teas (64 Haywood Street; 828/254-3800) Favorite buzz shop with local art exhibitions.

Laughing Seed Café (40 Wall Street; 828/252-3445) Asian-fusion vegetarian in the middle of downtown.

Tupelo Honey Café (12 College Street; 828/255-4863; www.tupelo honeycafe.com) Southern home cooking with a Charleston twist and legendary fresh-baked biscuits.

Accommodations

Abbington Green (46 Cumberland Circle; 828/251-2454; www.abbingtongreen.com) Quiet B&B close to downtown.

The Grove Park Inn (290 Macon Avenue; 800/438-5800; www.grove parkinn.com) Classic, luxurious hotel with turn of the century charm.

Haywood Park Hotel (1 Battery Park Avenue; 828/252-2522; www.haywoodparkhotel.com) Located in the heart of downtown in a former department store.

Information

Asheville Area Chamber of Commerce: 151 Haywood Street; 828/258-6101; www.ashevillechamber.org

Population: 71,600

Art Talk

John Cram, owner of Blue Spiral 1.

I have three galleries in this area, including Blue Spiral 1 in downtown Asheville, a 14,000-square-foot exhibition space that was the first significant private art-related investment in downtown. What attracted me here years ago was the region's outstanding arts tradition, which lends the community a sense of art appreciation. We didn't have a lot of urban renewal here in the 1960s, so Asheville's architectural integrity was largely retained. The local arts scene has experienced something of a roller-coaster-snowball effect where waves of galleries have started through the years only to be reversed by Asheville's cyclical economy. It's been local entrepreneurship that's put together most of the art infrastructure that's here today.

Carrboro, North Carolina

This former textile mill town had for decades been viewed as the poor relative of adjacent Chapel Hill, the gleaming home of the University of North Carolina. But things have changed considerably in the past decade, and Carrboro is suddenly the community of choice for this region's creative sector. The two towns are connected by Franklin Street, an eminently walkable commercial route whose plethora of locally owned businesses and innovative shops reflects the retail mix along Massachusetts Street in Lawrence, Kansas. But while Chapel Hill may indeed be tonier than Carrboro, it's also become one of the most expensive places to live in the Mid-Atlantic region. As a result, Carrboro's evolved into the preferred home to many of the region's artists, musicians, and actors. Not only can they afford to buy a home in Carrboro, but here they can also take advantage of recently developed arts infrastructure that has taken over substantial swaths of what was once the town's underutilized commercial district. Studio space is still affordable, and a number of artists have elected to open their own studio/galleries along Carrboro's side streets. With each passing year, more and more of the area's creative community is electing to sink its roots into Carrboro's red-clay soil.

One of the more recent developments that has enhanced life in Carrboro has been the establishment of a significant Hispanic population. Mexican families, many of whom hail from the southern state of Oaxaca, have migrated here to perform the daily tasks that arise in a fast-growing economy. Like America's immigrants have always done, the Oaxaquenos have started working their way up the economic ladder by establishing businesses, such as El Chilango, a Carrboro restaurant that does double duty as the area's Hispanic Cultural Center. Today one of Carrboro's most popular cultural festivals is the annual La Fiesta del Pueblo, a September weekend event held at Chapel Hill High School to celebrate Mexico's Independence Day.

Carrboro is home to one of the region's largest natural foods stores as well as the year-round sculpture displays along West Weaver Street. From April through November the Saturday Farmers' Market in the Town Commons is one of the community's favorite gathering spots, while the Carrboro Sunday Market uses the same grounds for its twice-monthly outdoor arts fair of local painters, sculptors, and craftspeople. During the year's warmer months the Weaver Street Market presents its Thursday After Hours Concerts series on the lawn of Carr Mill Center.

Arts Scene

With the opening of Century Center, Carrboro gained an important, newly renovated venue for its burgeoning arts and cultural scene. This converted church in the middle of town has the ideal, maple aerobics floor that's much in demand by the region's thriving dance community, and its lobby gallery features rotating exhibitions by local artists. The town's primary arts facility is the ArtsCenter, an important venue for visual, performing, and music arts, as well as an educational facility sponsoring multidisciplinary art classes for the community's adults and kids on a year-round basis. the ArtsCenter's stage is home to many of the region's theatre companies, including the Transactors Improv Company, which uses the ArtsCenter for its presentations of short- and long-form improvisational theatre. The facility also hosts film festivals and performances by traveling national and international entertainers. Its gallery space is used for local and regional one-artist shows as well as juried invitational exhibitions.

There are a half-dozen art galleries in Carrboro's compact downtown, and numerous alternative venues such as the Spotted Dog restaurant and the Open Eye Café use their walls for rotating shows by local artists. There's a monthly Second Friday Art Walk that serves to coordinate the galleries' opening receptions for new shows, and an Open Studios Tour every November includes several dozen artists' homes for a weekend of shows and sales. One of the South's top live-music venues, the Cat's Cradle, occupies a strip mall location in downtown

Art Talk

Jon Wilner, executive director of the ArtsCenter.

We were founded 30 years ago with a single art class, and now we offer 300 art classes a year and serve about 50,000 users a year. We have successfully adapted to this fast-growing community's needs, and we now serve a lot of working mothers and their children through an after-school arts immersion program. We're an art center, so we have all sorts of artists coming in here, including the two-week residency programs we offer in local schools. We have a thriving concert and theatre program as well as a gallery serving the community. There's a major university just down the street, and that gives us an opportunity to play off the university's art strengths by partnering with the university on performances and exhibitions.

Carrboro. The venue is one of the must-do's on many bands' list of nightclubs, and from one end of the year to the other Cat's Cradle presents the freshest in national and international talent. A second venue, Go Rehearsals, features shows by emerging talent on the music scene. Between these two venues, it's little wonder that Carrboro is considered one of the hotbeds of the South's music scene.

Essentials

Visual Arts Venues

The ArtsCenter (300-G E. Main Street; 919/929-2787; www.artscenter live.com) Popular venue for all the arts, plus a strong education program.

Carrboro Century Center (100 N. Greensboro Street; 919/918-7365; www.carrboro.com) Community cultural center with a lobby gallery for local artists.

Sizl Gallery (405 East Main Street; 919/960-0098; www.sizlgallery.com) Contemporary visual arts and locally made fine crafts.

Performing Arts & Events

Cat's Cradle (300 E. Main Street; 919/967-9053; www.catscradle .com) Top national music venue for established and emerging acts.

Playmakers Repertory Company (Paul Green Theater, UNC Campus; 919/962-7529; www.playmakersrep.org) Innovative and risk-taking theatre organization on the University of North Carolina campus.

Carrboro Music Festival (see Chamber of Commerce below, or visit www.carrboromusicfestival.com) Daylong, free live music at 20 Carrboro venues on a September Sunday.

Wine & Dine

Open Eye Café (100-C E. Main Street; 919/968-9410; www.openeye cafe.com) Favorite local buzz shop and an art-exhibiting venue.

Spotted Dog (111 E. Main Street; 919/933-1117) Great wine list, organic and other foods, plus local art shows.

Tyler's Taproom (102 E. Main Street; 919/929-6881; www.tylerstaproom .com) One of the best places to relax and enjoy the Carrboro scenery.

Accommodations

The Carolina Inn (211 Pittsboro Street, Chapel Hill; 919/933-2001; www.carolinainn.com) Historic hotel next to the UNC campus.

Days Inn (1312 N. Fordham Boulevard, Chapel Hill; 919/929-3090; www.daysinn.com) Affordable for families, with a pool.

Sparrow Farm (1224 Old Lystra Road, Chapel Hill; 919/960-6707) Quiet, comfortable inn, with fresh flowers and gourmet breakfasts.

Information

Chapel Hill–Carrboro Chamber of Commerce: 104 S. Estes Drive, 919/967-7075; www.carolinachamber.org

Population: 16,800

Art Talk

Mary Ruth, theatre arts instructor and administrator.

Here in Orange County the interest in arts education has expanded exponentially. What started up, after Playmakers, were community theatre companies that now have grown into large theatre companies, and we now have a large, semiprofessional theatre community. We're at a point where there's not enough of an audience for all the theatre companies that are active in this area, which means that some companies are beginning to struggle. There's a level of brilliance that applies to the music community here, but in theatre we're seeing a less than stupendous commitment to the theatre art form. What we're especially lacking in is directors with impressive vision that extends beyond shallow artistry.

Wilmington, North Carolina

A historic community in the southeast tip of North Carolina, Wilmington is an Art Town as well as one of the East Coast's premier college towns, a place whose lifestyle bonus includes miles of unspoiled beaches tossed in for good measure. For college students, Wilmington has the good-times, lay-on-the-beach vibe of Art Towns like La Jolla, California, Galveston, Texas, and Portsmouth, New Hampshire. For artists, the community's plethora of historic structures translates into easy-to-find, affordable places for setting up the warehouse studio of one's dreams, as well as the availability of reasonably priced residences. Wilmington's past as a seaport has endowed its downtown with dozens of historic commercial buildings. Several are already serving as live/work studio and gallery spaces housing restaurants, design firms, and independent retail shops.

In the 1980s the film industry discovered Wilmington as a location for feature films. Dozens of movies have been shot among downtown's collection of commercial structures and on soundstages built by Hollywood studios. There's a large group of technicians and film industry people who now live here, and their support for Wilmington's arts community has been important to its vitality and growth. Many of the film-industry types can be found at arts events such as the Cinematique Series of foreign, independent, and art flicks screened weekly at the Thalian Hall Center for Performing Arts, downtown Wilmington's top venue for film, theatre, and music.

With its historic architecture, vibrant film and arts scenes, front-door access to spectacular beaches, and relaxed nature, it's no wonder that Wilmington has also attracted substantial numbers of relocating northerners who want as much access to sandy beaches as they do to art galleries, live theatre, and jazz clubs. Wilmington offers all of the above, along with a wealth of great restaurants, an airport with easy connections to metropolitan areas, and a year-round flow of free-spending tourists.

Arts Scene

Wilmington has a lively gallery scene as well as a downtown loaded with working-artist studios and alternative venues in the form of restaurants, bars, and coffee bars. The monthly Fourth Friday Gallery Night is a downtown event coordinating opening receptions among more than a dozen gallery, studio, and alternative venues, while the East Side Gallery Nights is a similar event focused on a gallery stroll during the second Friday of each month for a half-dozen galleries in the Wrightsville Beach area, a short drive from downtown Wilmington. Acme Art Studios, home of the No Boundaries Art Colony, is an 18,000-square-foot complex of working-artist studios in downtown. The Racine Center for the Arts is a community arts facility that combines visual arts exhibitions and education space with two galleries representing the work of local and regional talents, as well as occasional traveling exhibitions. The Glory Academy of Dance Arts also performs at the center.

In recent years one of the most important developments on Wilmington's arts scene has been the opening of the Louise Wells Cameron Art Museum, a state-of-the-art facility whose former identity as the St. John's Museum of Art was closely associated with its being home to a notable collection of works by American master artist Mary Cassatt. The Cameron has incorporated the St. John's permanent collection into its exhibition programs and has vastly expanded the institution's reach by focusing its energies on exhibiting and collecting the works of North Carolina artists, especially contemporary artists. The Cameron uses its 10 galleries for an energetic, year-round exhibitions program that includes traveling regional, national, and international shows, lectures, and film.

Art Talk

Mike Golonka, director of the Racine Center for the Arts.

We're a three-year-old organization and serve as the community's arts education center. We offer classes in painting, ceramics, drama, and dance, and we have a gallery, an arts café, and a gift shop. We have 23,000 square feet of new construction and are privately funded. We host a lot of events as a way of raising money for our programs. Ninety percent of the work in our gallery is from local artists, and we tend to exhibit contemporary work. Wilmington's is a cyclical economy, and being an artist here means being in a competitive environment where lots of people consider themselves artists.

Not surprising in a community whose creative sector makes a substantial share of its living from the film industry, several theatre organizations thrive in Wilmington's arts-supportive climate. These include Stageworks, which has a focus on new works and uses the Inkmate Thalian Studio Theatre for its productions; Opera House Theatre, which uses Thalian Hall for its offbeat and edgy season of musicals, dramas, and comedies; the Thalian Association, which stages off-Broadway dramas, comedies, and musicals, and Big Dawg Productions, which also uses Thalian Hall for its season of presentations. There are several annual concerts by the North Carolina Symphony in Kenan Hall on the campus of the University of North Carolina at Wilmington, and the Wilmington Symphony Orchestra uses that same venue for its six-concert season.

Essentials

Visual Art Venues

Cameron Art Museum (3201 17th Street; 910/395-5999; www.cameronartmuseum.com) State-of-the-art museum with a focus on North Carolina contemporary artists.

Racine Center for the Arts (203 Racine Drive; 910/452-2073; www.racinecenter.com) Community arts center exhibiting local, regional, and national work.

Acme Art Studios (711 N. 5th Avenue; 910/763-8010; www.acmeartstudios.com) Artist complex with monthly events.

Performing Arts & Events

Cape Fear Blues Festival (P.O. Box 1487; 910/350-8822; www.capefearblues.com) Four-day blast of indoor and outdoor shows in late July.

Fourth Friday (see Wilmington Chamber of Commerce below) Coordinated monthly gallery openings.

Big Dawg Productions (see Wilmington Chamber of Commerce below) Produces year-round comedies, dramas, and musicals.

Wine & Dine

The Forks (Cameron Art Museum, 3201 17th Street; 910/395-5999; www.cameronartmuseum.com) Nice wine list, inventive foods, great atmosphere.

El Agave (3809 Oleander Drive; 910/791-9277) Seafood served Mexican style; *mucho* chile and guacamole.

Elijah's (2 Ann Street; 910/343-1448) Elegant spot, with great waterfront views.

Art Talk

Ren Brown, director of the Cameron Art Museum.

I've been here 19 years and feel wonderful about the successes of this museum. We've gone from 13,000 square feet to a new building with 44,000 square feet, and it has been great for us and great for Wilmington. The city's grown dramatically, and throughout North Carolina there's this awareness of the arts scene in Wilmington. When we started our expansion project in 1997 we were in a building that lacked climate control and only had room for showing 10 percent of our permanent collection. We had an endowment to back us up, a board that supported our mission, and a community hungry for a bigger and better art museum.

Accommodations

Benson's Landing (801 Carolina Beach Avenue, Carolina Beach; 910/458-5886; www.bensonslanding.com) Large hotel on the beach.

AmeriHost Inn & Suites (5600 Carolina Beach Road; 800/961-7829) Near the beaches, with room for RVs.

The Greentree Inn (5025 Market Street; 910/799-6001) Affordable place, with a pool.

Information

Wilmington Chamber of Commerce: 1 Estell Lee Place; 910/762-2611; www.wilmingtonchamber.org

Population: 77,500

Beaufort, South Carolina

historic seaport community in the South Carolina Lowcountry, Beaufort is a laid-back and engaging place whose economy once relied upon plantation production of the commodities of rice, cotton, and indigo. Today, after two decades of rapid growth, some areas outside the historic district of Beaufort have been given over to golf course development and pricey homes. Despite the region's population boom, Beaufort's downtown remains one of the most engagingly beautiful spots on the southeast Atlantic Coast. Officially declared a National Historic Landmark District, this compact community center is home to a visual feast of mansions, early-20th-century commercial buildings, and even a military arsenal whose oldest sections were erected in 1798.

This corner of South Carolina is home to Gullah culture, a unique ethnic blend of African, Creole, and Caribbean influences whose roots can be traced back to shipwrecked and freed slaves and an emancipated population that flourished on neighboring St. Helena Island. Nearly a century passed before the island was connected to the mainland by a bridge, but to this day Gullah culture survives as a vivid reminder of the Lowcountry's rich past. On St. Helena it's not uncommon for Gullah descendants to still use their unique blending of Elizabethan and Creole syntax while chatting with each other. The Penn Center, a former schoolhouse for Gullah children that's now a community cultural center and art museum, works year-round to maintain the integrity of the island's treasured cultural foundations.

Beaufort and its surrounding communities are also home to three military facilities, making this a premier spot for military service retirees who enjoy easy access to the base exchanges and medical centers. The multicultural composition of Beaufort also appeals to relocating northerners, and the community's tidy neighborhoods are filled with a sublime blend of families, older folks, and Lowcountry natives.

Arts Scene

Beaufort and the neighboring town of Port Royal are home to an energetic and innovative local arts agency. The Arts Council of Beaufort County does everything from present chamber music performances in a Festival Series staged in the school's performing-arts center (which is also home to the Rafael Sabatin Players theatre company), to staging downtown Beaufort sidewalk shows of the fiberglass Chicago cows and Cincinnati pigs. While it would be advantageous for the Lowcountry's artists to have the arts council develop a fiberglass-creature campaign of its own form (flying oysters, perhaps?), this intriguing blend of local interest and national savvy has helped the regional arts community grow by leaps and bounds. The Beaufort Art Association's gallery on Port Royal Street in downtown is the community's year-round center for visual arts exhibitions as well as art-crowd socializing. The exhibits here from photography to sculpture, and their focus on the local arts community helps give Beaufort's artists a high profile in an important sales venue. Downtown Beaufort is home to nearly a dozen commercial galleries as well as several artists' studios on the upper floors of commercial buildings.

The Beaufort Repertory Company uses the Port Royal Playhouse, a converted church, for its season of plays, while the nearby Shed Center for the Arts serves as a visual arts exhibition and education facility as well as an occasional venue for the performing arts. The Byrne Miller Dance Theatre is a presenter of national performing-arts talents as well as the organizing force behind Beaufort's thriving dance community, using the Battle Creek High School Theatre for its touring national and regional shows. The Penn Center, located among towering oaks draped with Spanish moss, is home to the York W. Bailey Museum, a facility used for exhibitions of work by leading regional and national African American artists as well as events such as the Annual Quilt Show, which showcases local fine crafts talents. The center is also home to a film series as well as a lecture series for nationally respected authors. Ibile Indigo

Art Talk

Kristine Cox, director of public relations for the Beaufort Art Association.

We're a warm, friendly, and open place that presents lots of exhibitions for its member artists at our own gallery and our eight satellite gallery locations. We also offer lots of free and nearly free educational opportunities to the community. We offer adult art classes in the afternoons and evenings and do lectures in our town library. First Fridays are very popular downtown, with lots of businesses staying open until 8 PM and artists here in the gallery doing live demonstrations. Attracting new artists to this area is one of the most important things we can do. Some of our members feel we should be a more exclusive type of group, but with nearly 500 members it's a little too late to turn back that clock.

House, also on St. Helena Island, uses the region's history as an indigo dye center as the focal point for its workshops on indigo production and creating clothing and crafts objects that use the dye.

Essentials

Visual Arts Venues

The Penn Center (38 Penn Center Circle West; 843/838-2432; www.penncenter.org) Unique cultural center and art museum dedicated to the region's Gullah heritage.

Arts Council of Beaufort County (1815A Boundary Street; 843/379-2787; www.beaufortarts.com) Presents performing-arts and visual arts exhibitions at several venues.

Beaufort Art Association (905 Port Republic; 843/379-2222) Local artist exhibitions in a downtown space.

Performing Arts & Events

Arts on the River (see Beaufort Chamber of Commerce below) Mid-May outdoor arts fair in Waterfront Park.

Beaufort Orchestra (P.O. Box 504; 843/521-4144; www.beaufort orchestra.org) November to April series of classical music concerts in the USCB Performing Arts Center.

Penn Center Annual Quilt Show and Sale (38 Penn Center Circle West; 843/838-2432; www.penncenter.com) March event showcasing the best in regional textile arts.

Wine & Dine

Dockside (11th Street West; Port Royal; 843/524-7433) Great seafood and a view of the water.

The Bank (926 Bay Street; 843/522-8831; www.thebankgrillandbar.com) Popular bar and gourmet seafood.

Blackstone's Café (205 Scott Street; 843/524-4330; www.blackstones cafe.com) Favorite breakfast spot, famous for its stone-ground yellow grits.

Accommodations

Rhett House Inn (1009 Craven Street; 843/524-9030; www.rhett houseinn.com) Splendor, style, and luxury in a historic, downtown mansion.

The Beaufort Inn (809 Port Republic Street; 843/521-9000; www.beaufort inn.com) Gourmet dining and historic quarters in downtown.

Comfort Inn (2227 Boundary Street; 843/525-9366; www.choicehotels .com) Affordable, with swimming pool.

Information

Beaufort Chamber of Commerce: 1106 Carteret Street; 843/524-3163; www.beaufortsc.org

Population: 13,400

Art Talk

Annette Teasdell, director of history and culture at the Penn Center Museum. We present art exhibitions and organize events like our three-day celebration of Gullah history in mid-November, with performances and outdoor art booths. The museum, which welcomes visitors year-round, is home to many performances by musicians like the Sea Island Singers and other Lowcountry artists and entertainers. The Penn Center has been in existence for more than 140 years, first as a school and now as a place celebrating the art, history, and culture of this area. Art here can be defined as basketry, boatbuilding, quilting, storytelling, or whatever else it takes to help our people get a clearer idea of their heritage.

Hilton Head,
South Carolina

This fast-growing town on the South Carolina coast is home to a world-class tourism industry that's successfully developed an international reputation as a golf and tennis resort. But there's a lot more to Hilton Head Island than country club–style recreation. This is still home to a sizable number of Gullah people, the descendants of freed African slaves who developed a thriving culture along the barrier islands of the South Carolina Lowcountry and the Georgia Sea Islands. Gullah's distinct dialect remains very much alive in the homes of some island families, and its rich culture is celebrated year-round in the exhibitions and programs presented at the Low Country Artists' Guild.

Since even the former Northerners who occupy vast swaths of Hilton Head's former farmlands cannot tolerate a year-round calendar of activities that only involve swinging a golf club or tennis racket, the island has developed a surprisingly strong arts scene. Not too long ago, the art scene in Hilton Head hadn't progressed much past the stage of an occasional shopping mall show of seascape watercolors. Today, action happens year-round in the form of music, theatre, and a range of visual art exhibitions. As is the case with many Art Towns that were established as resort communities, real-estate prices have soared skyward in recent years, and this means many folks who otherwise would have liked to have brought their creative talents here have been priced out of the market. This has been a bonus to nearby communities such as Bluffton, a coastal town about 10 miles west of Hilton Head that's loaded up on resident artists in the past few years. It's also directed a steady stream of artists toward the Art Town of Beaufort, about an hour's drive north along the coast.

Arts Scene

There's a year-round arts scene on Hilton Head serving the increasing numbers of residents who have either retired here full time or have figured out a way to run their businesses from this tropical paradise. About a dozen commercial art galleries are sharing local and regional artists with a like number of artist studio/galleries open on a catch-as-catch-can basis. The two most prominent visual arts exhibition facilities are operated by the Arts Center of Coastal Carolina and the Hilton Head Art League. The Art League's gallery in Pineland Station showcases the work of its members, and many of these artists also are instructors who teach adult and kids' art classes in the Arts Center of Coastal Carolina's Disney Studios.

Each May the League also sponsors a national invitational exhibition, the Island of the Arts, in the Walter Greer Gallery. The Art League's facility is also home to the Low Country Artists' Guild, which exhibits the work of the island's Gullah and African-American residents.

The Arts Center of Coastal Carolina is a multifaceted community arts facility whose programs cover visual and performing arts as well as music. The space is used for rotating exhibitions of local and regional art, with an emphasis on work that deals with the region's rich history and culture. The center is also used as a performance venue for a range of events including the concerts of Hilton Head Island's own Hallelujah Singers and performances by touring national entertainers, with larger acts booked into the Elizabeth Wallace Theatre. The center's year-round stage series presents five musicals that each run for three weeks' duration.

During the summer months Hilton Head's Sea Pines Resort stages a national entertainers concert series, while during the rest of the year one of the nation's top jazz clubs, the Jazz Corner, serves as a venue for not only the island's surprisingly large group of musicians and jazz lovers but also as a very popular venue for touring national acts. The Hilton Head Jazz Society stages its monthly concerts at the Folley Beach Tennis Resort. Hilton Head is also home to the Coastal Discovery Museum, a science and environmental center with year-round

Art Talk

Kyle Wallace, director of public relations for the Arts Center of Coastal Carolina.

What we have is five program areas: theatre, a presenting series, visual arts with year-round gallery programs, community outreach—like our Gullah Arts Festival in February—and educational programs through school-based classes and children's theatre performances. We're located in a 45,000-square-foot facility with a 350-seat theatre, a 100-seat black box, and a 2,000-square-foot art gallery. Our gallery manager organizes our exhibition programs, working with local and national organizations. Twice a year we exhibit work by members of the Hilton Head Art League, and we do an annual exhibition of art by the Gullah community. It's a diverse exhibitions program that brings in work by local, regional, and national artists.

programs on island history and ecology. South Carolina Repertory Company stages its season in an 80-seat black box theatre on Beach City Road, while the Hilton Head Dance Theatre presents local and regional artists throughout the year. Hilton Head Orchestra stages its 10-concert Master Series at the Elizabeth Wallace Theatre and also oversees the Hilton Head Youth Orchestra, which uses First Presbyterian Church for its concert series.

Essentials

Visual Arts Venues

Arts Center of Coastal Carolina (14 Shelter Cove Lane; 843/686-3945; www.artscenter-hhi.org) Regional, local, and national visual arts shows.

Hilton Head Art League (Pineland Station, Highway 278; 843/681-5060; www.hiltonheadartleague.org) Members' exhibitions and other programs.

Low Country Artists' Guild (Pineland Station, Highway 278; 843/681-5060; www.gullah geechie.com) Celebrates Gullah culture and African American artists.

Performing Arts & Events

Arts Center of Coastal Carolina (14 Shelter Cove Lane; 843/686-3945; www.artscenter-hhi.org) Presenter of year-round theatre and music programs.

South Carolina Repertory Company (136B Beach City Road; 843/681-5194; www.hiltonheadtheatre.com) Dramas and comedies a year in an 80-seat venue.

Hilton Head Orchestra

(P.O. Drawer 5757; 843/842-2055; www.hhorchestra.org) Ten-concert season from September to May.

Wine & Dine

The Jazz Corner (The Village at Wexford; 843/842-8620; www.thejazz corner.com) Great jazz venue with wonderful food. Try the Oysters Gillespie.

Kingfisher Seafood & Steakhouse (Shelter Cove Harbor; 843/842-6400; www.kingfisherseafood.com) Live music and delicious crab legs.

Rendezvous Café (Greenwood Drive, Gallery of Shops; 843/785-5070; www.gaslightrestaurant.com) French cuisine and live music.

Accommodations

Quality Inn (200 Museum Street; 843/681-3655; www.choice hotels.com) Large hotel, with facilities for families.

Residence Inn (12 Park Lane; 843/686-5700; www.residence innhhi.com) Comfy suites, with a pool.

Holiday Inn Oceanfront (1 S. Forest Beach Drive; 843/785-5126; www.hiholidayinn.com) Great beach location.

Information

Hilton Head Island–Bluffton Chamber of Commerce: 843/785-3673; www.hiltonheadisland.org

Population: 34,500

Art Talk

Hank Haskell, cofounder of the South Carolina Repertory Company.
We're a non-Equity, professional company, founded in 1992, which specializes in new, edgy work. My wife and I wanted to start a theatre company where we could direct and produce our own shows, with me running the business end and her running the artistic side. We've grown from nothing into a company with its own 80-seat theatre that we use for plays running up to three weeks, and we do four or five plays a year. Our audience is made up of a lot of senior citizens, many who originally came here from the Northeast or Atlanta, and they tend to be very knowledgeable of theatre and are interested in seeing new stage work. We do small cast pieces like "Talley's Folly," "Wit," and "Proof"—shows that other island companies aren't doing.

Galveston, Texas

Located on a Gulf Coast island 50 miles south of Houston, Galveston is a place that revels in both its historic past and its miles of beachfront. Spanish explorers and the pirate Jean Lafitte made their homes in Galveston at various points in the island's past, and to this day more than 1,500 historic homes are sprinkled around Galveston's historic neighborhoods, including the Strand, a National Historic Landmark District filled with gorgeous Victorian commercial structures and towering palm trees. Nearby, the East End National Historic Landmark District encompasses 20 square blocks of historic residences and commercial structures. A 17-foot-tall seawall extending for more than ten miles protects Galveston from the hurricanes that rip across this region every few years, and when its not in use as a storm barrier the seawall is Galveston's favorite place for jogging, rollerblading, and plain old, Texas Gulf Coast–style lollygagging.

A hundred years ago, much of Galveston was wrecked in a hurricane that claimed more than 6,000 lives. The city quickly rebuilt itself, and to this day much of that redeveloped infrastructure remains standing. Downtown Galveston reflects the relentless local interest in historic preservation and revitalization of the dozens of commercial structures built by the city's forefathers, and it's this same infrastructure that's now become a magnet for artists from across Texas, Louisiana, and Oklahoma who enjoy living in this corner of the South, and who want to live close to the ocean. Go upstairs in most any of the old office buildings along Post Office Street, a vibrant neighborhood loaded with sleek restaurants, European-style coffee bars, clothing stores, and art galleries, and filled with artist studios, architects' offices, and graphic designers working on projects for clients flung far and wide.

Galveston is home to the Kemp Ridley Sea Turtle Research Center, one of the nation's foremost programs aimed at the preservation of this endangered species, which uses the island's beaches for nesting and reproducing. There's a madcap Mardi Gras weekend every February, a Charles Dickens festival in the Strand every December, and the year-round programming of the Moody Gardens, one of the nation's foremost botanical gardens and the site of an IMAX theatre, a tropical beach, and endless educational programs for children and families curious about the workings of the world's environment.

Arts Scene

The local visual arts scene relies on a promising arts center, the interests of a few galleries with a contemporary arts focus and an unusually well-developed group of alternative venues that run major shows through the city's coffee bars and artists' studios. The Galveston Arts Center, located on the Strand, has the potential to develop into a larger, multidisciplinary arts center, but for now it does a great job of using its storefront facility to exhibit the work of highly regarded local, national, and regional visual artists. One venue in particular, the E Street Gallery & Coffee Haus, has dedicated a significant amount of energy and expertise toward developing a first-rate visual arts exhibition program. The MOD Café uses its two-story space on Post Office Street for visual arts exhibitions as well as films and a meeting space for local arts groups, while Java 213 on 23rd Street is another of the local buzz shops that takes seriously its role as an alternative visual arts venue.

Perhaps because it's located at a point along the axis connecting Austin and New Orleans, Galveston has a nightlife and live-music scene that cities many times its size should envy. The bars along Post Office Street and elsewhere are always jumping on weekends, fueled by the island's traditional, two-day influx of party animals from Houston and the city's very tolerant, New Orleans–style open-container policy for alcohol. The East End Theatre Company uses its venue on Post Office Street for a year-round slate of edgy and interesting stage works, while the Strand Theatre presents more mainstream works in its 200-seat

Art Talk

Kathy Buchanan, owner of Buchanan Gallery.

I've had the gallery since the mid-1990s, and it's always had a contemporary arts emphasis. The majority of my buyers are from Houston, but there's a dedicated group of collectors here on the island who buy both locally and in Houston. Most of the artists I represent are from Texas, and I enjoy showing their work in the setting of a smaller community where I can have an impact and be a lightning rod for developments in the regional arts scene. Post Office Street's an eclectic kind of place that used to be just shoe stores and beauty shops, but lately has undergone an exciting transition.

playhouse. During the summer months, Galveston Island Outdoor Musicals stages a trio of campy, overblown productions aimed at the tourist side of the theatre crowd, while Galveston's most prominent performing-arts venue, the Grand 1894 Opera House, is the community's year-round venue for touring Broadway shows, world music, jazz, and the season's concerts of the Galveston Symphony Orchestra.

Essentials

Visual Arts Venues

Galveston Arts Center (2127 The Strand; 409/763-2403) The region's contemporary arts headquarters.

Leslie Gallery (2208 Post Office Street; 409/763-6370) Wide range of work by local and national artists.

Buchanan Gallery (2120 Post Office Street; 409/763-8683; www.buchanangallery.com) Exhibits a range of realist and contemporary work.

Performing Arts & Events

Galveston Art Walk (see Galveston Arts Center above) Monthly exhibiting and networking event for the island's arts community.

East End Theatre Company (2001 Post Office Street; 409/762-3556) Intimate venue staging new and interesting works.

ARToberfest (see Galveston Island Visitors Center below) Downtown's annual outdoor arts fair in mid-October.

Wine & Dine

E Street Gallery & Coffee Haus (2219 Post Office Street; 409/762-4122) The Boss would approve of this hipsters' hangout with its local art and smooth cappuccinos.

Fisherman's Wharf (Pier 22 & Harborside Drive; 409/765-5708) Classy seafood spot close to downtown. Try the flounder.

Gaido's Famous Seafood Restaurant (3900 Seawall; 409/762-9625; www.gaidosofgalveston.com) Ocean views and the best oysters on the seawall.

Accommodations

Grace Manor (1702 Post Office Street; 409/621-1662; www.grace manor-galveston.com) Victorian splendor in a B&B close to all the downtown attractions.

The Commodore on the Beach (3618 Seawall; 409/763-2375; www.commodoreonthebeach.com) Reasonable rates in this great spot on the gulf.

Art Talk

Clint Willour, executive director of the Galveston Arts Center.

Our focus is on regional artists, especially artists from Texas, and on arts education. With our location on the Strand, we're basically here to serve visitors, but we have eight satellite locations around Galveston and also work extensively within the school district. We try to cover all the bases through our mix of one-artist and group shows, 24 a year all told, and we're the center for the Galveston Art Walk. There's a young, happening arts scene in Galveston, with a lot of artists exhibiting year-round. Artists here love the cheap studio rents, the beach, and the town's walkability.

Gaido's Seaside Inn (3802 Seawall; 409/762-9625; www.gaidosof galveston.com) Clean, affordable, and family friendly, with a swimming pool.

Information

Galveston Island Visitors Center: 2215 The Strand; 888/425-4753; www.galvestoncvb.com

Population: 57,500

Kerrville, Texas

Kerrville, a vacation spot on the Guadalupe River, is one of the nation's top breeding grounds for professional rodeo stars, and its local arts scene has long reflected an intimate attachment to the culture of the West. Nearby Fredericksburg, separated by 22 miles of two-lane blacktop northeast of Kerrville, is a German-flavored place that seems to take its creative cues from the artists and entertainers populating Austin. Kerrville and Fredericksburg have vastly different personalities, yet they share a common bond of appreciation and support for the arts.

Kerrville is actively engaged in attempts to restore and revitalize its historic downtown. Its typical tourist tends to be more toward the boot-wearing type of westerner, which means that the shops and restaurants cater to folks whose idea of weekend relaxation includes rare prime rib, bull riding, and a turn or two on the dance floor. Today, Kerrville's cultural side has come completely to terms with its cowboy side, and together they've helped place this once-deteriorating community back on the path of creative expression.

Fredericksburg's been discovered by a wave of lifestyle refugees attracted by the town's architectural style, new restaurants, interior design community, and the occasional presence of film stars. Long timers tend to look upon these newcomers fondly, realizing that anything that drives up the value of their acres of peach trees is probably a good thing. At its heart, Fredericksburg hasn't lost touch with its unique combination of rodeo traditions, German cuisine, Hill Country style, and friendliness. It's just that now there's a ton of money to be made on weekends selling stuff to the visitors coming here for a taste of what Fredericksburg offers. While Fredericksburg has several highly regarded art galleries and a German Community Chorus, its strongest art card is the Fredericksburg Theatre Company, which presents a half-dozen productions during its year-round season.

Arts Scene

The three pillars of Kerrville's arts community are the National Center for American Western Art, a facility that once was known as the Cowboy Artists of America Museum, the Hill Country Arts Foundation, and the Kerr Arts & Cultural Center. The National Center's site, on a hillside overlooking much of Kerrville's scenic terrain, is a modern facility whose programming concentrates on art by Western realist painters and sculptors. Also known as "cowboy art," this style of imagery presents a picture of the West's frontier past, as well as scenes of today's ranching culture. The Arts Foundation's facility, located on the banks of the Guadalupe River, encompasses a 722-seat outdoor amphitheatre that's home to a summer series of concerts and plays and an indoor, 140-seat black box used for winter productions, readings, and rehearsals. The foundation also operates the Duncan-McAshan Visual Arts Center, which offers year-round classes for mid-career artists as well as a highly regarded exhibition program in its art gallery. Downtown's art deco-style post office is now home to the Cultural Center, a facility offering everything from rotating monthly exhibitions to art classes for adults and kids, artist lectures, dance lessons, and yoga classes.

The Arcadia Theatre, a restoration work in progress that's taken more than a decade to complete, is home to the Western Movie Center, dedicated to screening cowboy shoot 'em ups. Playhouse 2000, a performing-arts school and dance company, uses the renovated civic center for its year-round productions. Kerrville Performing Arts Society uses Louise Hays Park and the Trinity Baptist Church for its performances of touring classical and folk musicians. On the second Saturday of each month, more than a dozen visual arts spaces scattered across Kerrville and neighboring Ingram participate in the successful Art in the Hills tour, which keeps the galleries open late for opening receptions and assorted festivities. During the two weeks surrounding Memorial Day, the Kerrville Folk Festival draws thousands of music lovers as well as top bands from across the nation to the Quiet Valley Ranch just a short drive south of

Art Talk

Nelwyn Moser, president of the Hill Country Arts Foundation.
We're sustaining a visual and performing-arts center that serves these disciplines on a 16-acre campus in a program that was started 45 years ago by some folks from Houston who took an interest in the art traditions of the Kerrville area. Our visual arts gallery is 1,700 square feet, and it's used for local, regional, and national shows. We also have an arts workshop program that attracts professional artists and art students from across the country. There's a true sense of momentum in this community, and I think that comes from the increasing number of people who come here to retire, and who choose to start new pursuits as artists.

town. And over Labor Day weekend the same venue hosts the Kerrville Wine & Music Festival, an event with more than a dozen years under its belt, and a more condensed group of entertainers than those featured during Memorial Day.

Essentials

Visual Arts Venues

Kerr Arts & Cultural Center (228 Earl Garrett; 830/895-2911; www.kacckerrville.com) Exhibition and educational facility in downtown's former Post Office.

Hill Country Arts Foundation (507 State Highway 39, Ingram; 830/367-5120; www.hcaf.com) One of the Southwest's premier art workshops, located on the river just west of town.

National Center for American Western Art (1550 Bandera Highway; 830/896-2443) Home to one of the nation's top exhibition venues for Western art.

Performing Arts & Events

Kerrville Folk Festival (Quiet Valley Ranch; 830/257-3600; www.kerrvillefolkfestival.com) Two weeks of great music and fun around Memorial Day, as well as a Labor Day music and wine bash.

Art in the Hills (see Kerrville Area Chamber of Commerce below) More than a dozen galleries stay open late on the second Saturday of each month for this self-guided tour.

Summer Serenade (see Kerrville Area Chamber of Commerce below) Popular, outdoor, summer concert series.

Wine & Dine

Acapulco (1718 Sidney Baker N.; 830/257-6222) Tex-Mex to the max.

Chili's on the River (1185 Junction Highway; 830/895-2445) Best burgers in the county.

Big Earl's Texas BBQ (401 Sidney Baker S.; 830/896-5656) Best brisket in the county.

Accommodations

Y.O. Ranch Resort Hotel (2033 Sidney Baker S.; 830/257-4440; www.yoresort.com) Big, Texas-style lodge with all the amenities.

Budget Inn (1804 Sidney Baker N.; 830/896-8200; www.budgetinn.com) Affordable, with a pool and room for RVs.

Cottage by the River (149 Francisco Lemos Street; 830/895-5515) Restored home with charming guest suites.

Information

Kerrville Area Chamber of Commerce: 1700 Sidney Baker N., 830/896-1155; www.kerrvilletx.com

Population: 20,500

Art Talk

Jim Derby, president of the Kerr Arts & Cultural Center.

A lot of us have moved to Kerrville because of its strong arts situation. Besides, it's cooler and dryer here than in other parts of Texas, and San Antonio is really convenient. We were formed in 1996 by a group of local artists who wanted a venue to show their work, and in 2000 we bought the 1933 Post Office Building, which has given us about 8,000 square feet of gallery space and about 20,000 casual visitors walking through our building each year. Now we have 13 artists' groups and more than 900 members, with changing exhibits every four to six weeks. In the next few years we'll be renovating our building to make new entrances, expand our classroom space, and give us the room we need to start an annual cultural festival.

Marfa, Texas

amed after a character in a Dostoyevsky novel and made famous when James Dean and Rock Hudson arrived in West Texas in 1955 to film *Giant*, tiny Marfa is also famous for its longstanding appeal to UFO theorists who venture here for a glimpse of what's known as the Marfa Lights. Marfa's old-fashioned town square is dominated by an 1886 courthouse and a recently restored, Spanish colonial–style hotel, a vivid reminder that the region's first European settlers were Spanish missionaries who arrived here in the late 1600s on a quest to save souls. Around 1911 the local citizenry became jittery over the revolutionary turmoil taking place in Mexico, just 60 miles south, that a detachment of soldiers was sent to Marfa from El Paso, about 200 miles west. They set up camp south of Marfa in a place that eventually became known as Fort D. A. Russell, a twist of fate that eventually sealed Marfa's role as a place enshrined in the annals of the contemporary art world.

This ranching community's art renaissance began in 1979 when Donald Judd, a minimalist artist best known for precise, elegant aluminum structures that transcend the limits of gravity and geometry, discovered that Fort's 340 acres were on the real-estate market. Using his own money along with substantial support from the Dia Foundation, Judd acquired the fort's barracks, gymnasium, ammunition sheds, and airfield . . . all 340 acres' worth. His vision was as wildly unlikely as it was brilliant, and by 1986 he had reopened the old army outpost as the Chinati Foundation, a living stage for contemporary art, named after a rugged mountain range separating Marfa from the western reaches of Big Bend National Park. Today a new group of contemporary art adherents, from Texas socialites rubbing elbows with Chinati's resident artists to the dozens of painters, sculptors, and writers who have moved here in search of a new and better life, are laboring to make Judd's West Texas art fantasia a reality.

Even though Judd, who was particularly adept at flashing streaks of his New York City–honed temper during his Marfa years, passed away suddenly in 1994, the Chinati Foundation has made significant progress toward achieving Judd's vision. His vision for converting Fort D.A. Russell into a contemporary arts facility has been taken up by a wave of new Chinati residents, and today the fort's grounds are home to permanent and changing exhibitions of international contemporary arts masters. Several structures in downtown Marfa, including Judd's studio and residential compound, the town's former cold-storage facility, as well as the old mohair warehouse, have been turned into exhibition sites for Judd's art and artifacts as well as the work of other artists such as former Santa Fe, New Mexico, resident John Chamberlain, Dan Flavin, and Claes Oldenburg.

Among those who have found themselves drawn along Judd's pathway is the Lannan Foundation, an internationally respected literary and visual arts funding organization that in recent years has relocated its staff and programs to both Santa Fe and Marfa. Lannan has purchased and renovated several of Marfa's unassuming neighborhood residences, converting them into places where a rotating group of resident writers and authors can sequester themselves while they work on projects the foundation has determined worthy of support. Marfa's also home to what's undoubtedly the first ever West Texas incarnation of an independent bookstore, art gallery, coffee house, and wine bar. Through the Marfa Book Company, the Lannan's resident authors and its administrators no longer have to drive an hour south to the shaded comfort of La Estancia in the border town of Ojinaga, Chihuahua, to find a suitable place for knocking down cold brews and proselytizing about the state of American fiction writing.

Arts Scene

When it comes to the arts, there seems to be little that's not possible in Marfa and the several nearby communities that define the Big Bend region. Marfa's Masonic Lodge has been turned into a performing-arts venue for presentations by some of the big-name, heavy-hitter contemporary artists and musicians who have either bought homes here or have decided to make an out-of-their-way pilgrimage to this ranching community in Presidio County. Creativity seems to be bubbling over, and places like the Marfa Theatre have been reenergized into venues for not just Hollywood flicks but for independent films, as well as the stagecraft of the Marfa Theatre Company. Make no mistake, the cowboy way is still alive and well in the Big Bend country, but today it's settled into a comfortable partnership with the arts.

The presence of Marfa's newly arrived contemporary arts community is being felt in many ways. There's the Marfa Studio of Arts, a nonprofit exhibition and education facility occupying what had once been a service station. Art dealer Eugene Binder has opened an art gallery, as has the Dallas-based Highland Photography Gallery. The Marfa Book Company's gallery has become one of the region's most respected venues for its changing slate of top-notch shows by local and national artists. For its part, the Chinati Foundation has become a major tourism draw for its amazingly diverse schedule of exhibitions by visiting artists, its free summer arts camp for local kids, and Chinati's annual Open House, a four-day bash that attracts contemporary arts luminaries and would-be luminaries to Marfa for a series of exhibitions, cookouts, and the kind of parties that Judd established as a way for artists to build stronger connections to the local community.

In the context of West Texas's wide-open spaces, places that are within an hour's drive easily qualify as being nearby. So towns like Marathon, a mere 56 miles east, are considered neighbors of Marfa, drawing the Chisos Gallery and the studio of photographer James Evans into the local arts loop. Same goes for Terlingua, the former mercury-mining town 120 miles away at the edge of Big Bend National Park. Here's where you'll find the Terlingua Trading Post, a combination art gallery and souvenir shop, as well as the Starlight Theatre, a saloon, restaurant, and live-music venue. Twenty miles farther into the National Park is Lajitas, home to noted author and historian Clay Henry III, who in the 1990s served as the region's Republican representative to the Texas State Legislature. Alpine, just 26 miles east of Marfa, is home to the Kiowa Gallery and Sul Ross State University. The school's Kokernot Amphitheatre is the site of the summertime Theatre of the Big Bend. During the academic year the Museum of the Big Bend, also on the Sul Ross campus, exhibits work by local and regional artists as well as its large collection of historic artifacts. Several venues on campus are used for classical music performance and theatre, while the Sul Ross Art Gallery exhibits regional work in addition to its student and faculty shows.

Essentials

Visual Arts Venues

The Chinati Foundation (1 Cavalry Row; 432/729-4362; www.chinati.org) Top-tier contemporary arts on a former army base; guided tours year-round, and a public celebration in October.

Marfa Studio of the Arts (106 East San Antonio; 432/729-4616) Community visual arts exhibition and education center.

Kiowa Gallery (105 E. Holland, Alpine; 432/837-3067; www.kiowa gallery.com) Represents many of the region's best artists and craftspeople.

Performing Arts & Events

Marfa Theatre
(98 S. Austin Street; 432/729-3436; www.marfatheatre.org) Home of the Marfa Theatre Company.

Chinati Open House
(1 Cavalry Row; 432/729-4362; www.chinati.org) October gathering of the local and national contemporary arts tribe.

Marfa Lights Festival (see Marfa Chamber of Commerce below) Celebrates Marfa's spooky side every Labor Day.

Wine & Dine

Marfa Book Company (105 S. Highland; 432/729-3906; www.marfa bkco.com) Bookstore, art gallery, a fine coffee shop, great restaurant, and a wine bar. Did we miss something?

Borunda's Bar & Grill (113 S. Russell Street; 432/729-8163) Great Mexican food and cold brews.

Maiya's (103 N. Highland Avenue; 432/729-4410) New spot with local art, wine list, and innovative dishes.

Art Talk

Keri Artzt, owner of Kiowa Gallery.
We're definitely getting better known as an art region, but there's been a line drawn in the dirt here. Alpine and its galleries are all about the art of the Big Bend, where Marfa's about minimalism, Chinati and Don Judd. To me it's all good, because more is always better, no matter how that looks. What's happening now is that the people drawn to Marfa tend to stay in Marfa, whereas people drawn to Alpine tend to be traveling all over the Big Bend. We're a diverse art community, with glass-blowers, painters, sculptors, and photographers. Lots of Austin and Dallas collectors come into the galleries, and we now have 35 locations open for our monthly Gallery Night.

Art Talk

Lynn Goode, owner of Marfa Book Company.

We moved here seven years ago when the town was dead and people were saying "You're crazy to do that". Well, the store isn't exactly a cash cow yet, but it's surviving on its own. I have a small gallery in the back of the bookstore that I intended to use to show art by some of the friends I made during the years I had my art gallery in Houston. It's unbelievable that artists from New York now are approaching me, wanting to have shows in my bookstore. It's a little gallery space and I hate saying no to people, so now we're just posting an announcement on our Web site that we do not accept solicitations. Marfa's now full of big-name artists, and has become an interesting place to live.

Accommodations

Hotel Paisano (207 N. Highland Avenue; 866/729-3669; www.hotel paisano.com) Renovated, historic hotel in the heart of Marfa.

The Arcon Inn (215 N. Austin Street; 432/729-4826) Affordable rooms and adobe style.

Cibolo Creek Ranch (P.O. Box 44; Shafter; 432/229-3737; www.cibolo creekranch.com) 25,000-acre ranch with guesthouses.

Information

Marfa Chamber of Commerce: 207 N. Highland Avenue; 432/729-4942; www.marfachamberofcommerce.com

Population: 2,200

Charlottesville, Virginia

ome to the University of Virginia, this historic community in the
Blue Ridge Mountain foothills is also where several founding members of American democracy planted their roots and built their
sprawling estates. Foremost among Charlottesville's prime tourist draws
are the homes of Thomas Jefferson, James Madison, and James Monroe,
all of which now serve as historical museums and provide windows into
the region's glorious past. Since the early 1980s, Charlottesville's proximity to Washington, D.C., has led to an influx of lifestyle refugees. As
is the case in Art Towns like Oxford, Mississippi, and Hot Springs,
Arkansas, these same urban castaways are the folks whose spending
drives the growth of the local arts market. It all works to the regional
art economy's advantage.

Downtown Charlottesville has not been overly gussied up in a
developer-driven effort to lure national retail chains. In many ways,
downtown is a blend of laid-back, Southern charm, along with the
vitality of a college town. In other words, Charlottesville is still a somewhat contradictory place, which is why it's possible to find buildings
where studio rents are low and its per-capita ratio of artists is high.
Another plus for painters, sculptors, and craftspeople is this community's Mid-Atlantic location, which places it within easy driving range
of both the Northeast's and Southeast's arts markets. In Charlottesville
musicians can find cheap rehearsal space in the commercial buildings
near the community's Downtown Mall. It is not a shopping mall in
the traditional sense of the word, but rather, an attractive pedestrian

area much like the Lincoln Road Mall in Miami Beach . . . a wonderful place to hang out, grab a latte, watch the streetlife sashay past, and pass an hour or two before heading out for sushi and sake.

Arts Scene

Because Charlottesville's galleries tend to have mixed success staying in business, what fills the region's venue vacuum for visual arts are two art museums, a university art gallery, and one of the South's premier artist-studio complexes. The Kluge-Ruhe Aboriginal Art Collection on the University of Virginia campus is one of the world's most important collecting and exhibiting institutions for Australian Aboriginal Art and has placed Charlottesville on the international art map. Established in 1997 by a media executive who also is one of the region's premier wine producers, the collection provides year-round exhibitions, lectures, and performing-arts programs featuring the world's leading authorities on the art of Australia's native people. The University of Virginia Art Museum keeps the focus of its year-round exhibitions and programs on a decidedly contemporary level, bringing touring exhibitions into Charlottesville as well as originating its own national shows. Local and regional artists as well as the university's postgraduate students and its faculty are featured in the Fayerweather Gallery's exhibitions, located on campus next to the art museum.

In many ways the creative heart and soul of Charlottesville's arts community is expressed in the exhibitions presented at the McGuffey Art Center, an exemplary artist-studio complex. At the McGuffey, a group of more than three dozen mid-career resident artists work in converted classrooms, creating art that's shipped to galleries across the nation, and the former schoolhouse's hallways serve as galleries for work created not only by McGuffey artists but by artists from across the region. The McGuffey also organizes year-round art classes for adults and kids. Second Street Gallery, one of the powerhouse contemporary arts galleries in the Mid-Atlantic region, is located a few blocks away at the City Center for Contemporary Arts. Second Street Gallery's exhibitions survey the best of Virginia's creative community and play a key role in advancing Charlottesville's artists' careers toward national recognition.

The City Center for Contemporary Arts, a new, $4-million building just off the Downtown Mall on East Water Street, is a major addition to the regional arts scene. Home to Live Arts theatre company as well as the Second Street Gallery and Light House, a film and video arts center, the center serves as a creative working and performance space for a broad cross-section of the arts community.

Several theatre companies are based in Charlottesville, including the Heritage Repertory Theatre, which is supported by the university and uses Culbreth Theatre for an extensive season of dramas and comedies. The Virginia Players, the university's drama department company, also uses Culbreth Theatre for its four annual productions. ACT 1, which performs at the Municipal Art Center, has a focus extending toward community theatre. One of the annual highlights of the region's cultural calendar is the Ash Lawn Opera Festival, which produces two operas on the grounds of James Madison's estate.

Essentials

Visual Arts Venues

McGuffey Art Center (201 Second Street; 434/295-7973;) Vibrant complex of working-artist studios.

University of Virginia Art Museum (155 Rugby Road; 434/924-3592; www.virginia.edu) Influential art museum with notable exhibitions of regional, national, and international art.

Kluge-Ruhe Aboriginal Art Collection (400 Worrell Drive; 434/244-0234; www.virginia.edu) The largest collection of Australian Aboriginal art in North America.

Performing Arts & Events

Ash Lawn Opera Festival (1941 James Monroe Parkway; 434/293-4500; www.ashlawnopera.org) Summer outdoor performances in Boxwood Garden.

Art Talk

Rosamond Casey, bookbinder, painter, and mixed-media artist at the McGuffey Art Center.

The key to our success is affordability. We don't focus on community artwork as much as we do on the creations of the working artists who rent studios at the McGuffey and use them as places for artistic growth and experimentation. There's a great balance here, and we work hard at keeping the McGuffey a vital, interesting place that this community values. We artists watch out for and support one another, sharing everything from technical advice to art supplies and names of art dealers. We've started a first-floor, performing-arts space for three dance companies. We're very open to the idea of giving a break to a young artist who is working with a sense of urgency and integrity and who needs a studio to continue that work.

Art Talk

John Gibson, artistic director and CEO of the City Center for Contemporary Arts.

Opening this new building was the end of a seven-year, very exciting process. We've captured a sense of this community's very high energy and creativity level in developing a new venue for theatre, music, dance, performance, and visual arts. Our space is run democratically and is open to all, embracing the community in a way that says art is one of the central points of Charlottesville's quality of life. We're also a community theatre whose work involves reinventing that venerable institution in a way that's relevant to the next millennium. We insist on excellence and work with the most sophisticated repertory possible.

City Center for Contemporary Arts (123 E. Water Street; 434/977-4177; www.c3arts.org) Home of Live Arts, Second Street Gallery, and Light House.

Fridays After 5 (see Charlottesville-Albemarle County Convention & Visitors Bureau below) April to October free concert series on the Downtown Mall.

Wine & Dine

Albemarle Baking Company (418 West Main Street; 434/293-6456) Artisan breads and luscious pastries.

C & O Restaurant (515 East Water Street; 434/971-7044; www.cando restaurant.com) Great wine list and contemporary American-fusion cuisine.

Everyday Café (240 Rolkin Court; 434/295-1344) Pizza by the slice, homemade gelato, free Internet access, and local art.

Accommodations

The Lafayette Hotel (146 Main Street, Stanardsville; 434/985-6345; www.thelafayette.com) Historic hotel built in 1840.

Econolodge (400 Emmett Street; 434/296-2104; www.econo lodge.com) Within walking distance to the university.

The Inn at Monticello (1188 Scottsville Road; 434/979-3593; www.innatmonticello.com) Country inn B&B close to town, with gourmet cuisine.

Information

Charlottesville-Albemarle County Convention & Visitors Bureau: 600 College Drive; 434/977-1783; www.charlottesville tourism.org

Population: 45,000

The Midwest

Lawrence, Kansas

This vibrant university town, home to one of the prettiest main streets in the nation as well as a widely acclaimed music scene, has long appealed to artists, and it's not hard to understand why. Perched among the rolling hills of the prairie and nestled alongside creeks and wooded boulevards, Lawrence is an eminently livable community with affordable homes and a well-educated population, all within an hour's drive of the art museums and pro sports stadiums of Kansas City.

Like many of the best college towns, Lawrence is a place that's constantly changing in response to the cutting-edge trends brought here by the community's large numbers of residents in their 20s and 30s. It doesn't take long for a fashion or a cocktail or a handbag or a band that's making waves on either coast to quickly find its way here, where it shows up on Massachusetts Street or onstage at one of the clubs that draws music-savvy crowds. In other words, it's entirely possible to live in Lawrence and feel plugged in to the national psyche instead of isolated in a windswept corner of a largely conservative state. Getting a blast of urban hippness is as simple as making the haul east to Kansas City or the much longer trip westward to Denver.

Many of Lawrence's neighborhoods are built along the classic lines of early-20th-century bungalow architecture. In the same manner that Chapel Hill's undulating terrain serves to largely conceal the massive infrastructure of UNC, so does the rolling prairie serve to make KU's complex of structures seems less overwhelming than it actually is. Mall development has been ushered away from the town's core, so instead

167

of a downtown disconnected by massive parking lots, Lawrence's streets are filled with quiet neighborhoods, small shopping districts, landscaped approaches to KU, and well-tended parks.

Because of the university's presence, Lawrence enjoys ready access to cultural amenities that much larger cities would envy. As one would imagine, Jayhawks sports are tremendously popular and the town comes alive on frenzied autumn Saturdays as well as winter nights when the highly regarded hoopsters are rolling. There's also the well-funded Spencer Museum of Art, a place with a top-notch permanent collection that includes many works by modern American masters, the Museum of Anthropology and its changing exhibits about the region's Native American culture, the 2,000-seat Lied Center and its intimate, black box performance space, both of which are programmed year-round with everything from touring Broadway shows to world music concerts, classical music, and experimental plays. Also on campus is the University Theatre, which uses the Crafton-Preyer Theater for its presentations of stage standards and new material.

Perhaps most important of all, Lawrence is the kind of place that's proud of its arts conscience. Many of the town's restaurants display local artists' work on their walls, and many neighborhoods are home to not only artists and their families but to their professionally operated studios. Hundreds of national arts careers have been launched from Lawrence's arts-nurturing environment. There's a lot of creative integrity underlying the local arts scene, making Lawrence an attractive place for artists to live and work.

Arts Scene

The backbone of the local arts scene is the Lawrence Arts Center, located in a new, downtown facility. Home to everything from an arts-based preschool to theatre performances and visual arts exhibitions from local, regional, and national artists, the center serves as this community's central contact for all things creative and cultural. The center coordinates many community-wide arts activities such as a summer arts camp for schoolkids, year-round arts workshops in creative disciplines ranging from dance to watercolor painting, an annual Native American art show in September, and the year-round performances of Seem-to-be-Players, a children's theatre company. The community's largest artists' organization is the Lawrence Art Guild, a group of nearly 200 members that organizes several annual events such as May's Art in the Park outdoor show in South Park that attracts more than 100 regional artists, an annual members exhibition at the Lawrence Arts Center in February, and a Holiday Art Fair in early December. There are monthly art walks among downtown's galleries and alternative visual arts venues, as well as the annual Lawrence ArtWalk in October, an event that links together more than 70 artists' studios and exhibiting venues. A public sculpture exhibition lasting several months takes place annually along downtown's commercial streets, and a wealth of spontaneous, artist-driven events are organized by the younger members of Lawrence's arts community.

The Lawrence Community Theatre, which stages its season of mainstage productions in a converted church, focuses its material on comedies and musicals. For more experimental works, the Lied Center's black box as well as the University Theatre are more into American theatre's contemporary side. West Side Folk, a Lawrence presenter of everything from Cuban salsa bands to traveling musicians from Appalachia, uses a variety of local venues such as the Unity Church, the Lawrence Arts Center, and St. Margaret's Episcopal Church for its slate of concerts. During the middle of September, Haskell Indian Nations University, a four-year college dedicated to the education of Native American students, stages its annual Haskell Indian Market, an outdoor exhibition of more than 100 painters, sculptors, and jewelers. During the rest of the academic year, the Haskell Cultural Center & Museum exhibits student and faculty work, as well as shows by nationally prominent artists.

The Lied Center has delivered a tremendous shot in the arm to Lawrence's arts scene in the form of presentations covering the worlds of music, dance, and theatre. Through its Concert Series, the Lied brings opera, dance, and symphony orchestras to Lawrence, while the center's Swarthout Series focuses on chamber musicians. The New Directions Series brings in modern interpreters of dance and opera,

Art Talk

Ann Evans, executive director of the Lawrence Arts Center.

We're now in a 40,000-square-foot building with two galleries, a 300-seat theatre, a gift shop, two classrooms, two dance studios, seven art studios, and facilities for printmaking, ceramics, and writing. It's allowed us to attract a whole new visitor who had never come into our old art center. The new building has helped us improve the quality of our art programs by keeping everything we do under one roof. The $7 million we raised for this building was a public/private partnership and the largest, local capital campaign ever done in Lawrence. One of the most helpful things that's happened here is the local newspaper's fine arts coverage, which comes out weekly and takes very seriously all the great arts events happening in the Lawrence area.

Art Talk

Andrea Norris, director and chief curator of the Spencer Museum of Art. We were created as a place serving all art disciplines, so our collection is used as both an exhibition and educational tool by teachers within the university system. We're the most comprehensive art museum in the state and have a number of important works in our permanent collection. Our exhibitions are typically focused on scholarly concerns, or on community programs, or on issues connected to the historic backdrop of our region. We also have themed exhibitions such as contemporary Cuban art, and we collect some works of contemporary art. On Thursday evenings we have an extensive series of lectures, videos, concerts, and films, and we've done many collaborative programs with the university's music department in our central courtyard.

while the Broadway & Beyond series presents many of the big-name shows barnstorming on national tours. The Lied Family Series brings in traveling children's shows, while its World Series draws in everything from taiko drummers to Scottish bagpipers.

The Spencer Museum of Art is an institution with a national reputation for its exhibitions covering everything from masterworks to the experimental edge of the international arts scene. Many of the art world's top painters and sculptors have added Spencer exhibitions to their résumés, and the local arts scene's integrity is greatly enhanced by the museum's presence. Art films, artist lectures, and children's art-appreciation classes are a small part of the museum's programs, which include the occasional chamber music concert, well-attended opening receptions for the art community's social set, and exhibitions dedicated to the local and regional arts community.

Essentials

Visual Arts Venues

Spencer Museum of Art (1301 Mississippi Street; 785/864-4710; www.ku.edu) Broadly focused institution with year-round exhibitions and extensive public programs.

Lawrence Arts Center (940 New Hampshire Avenue; 785/843-2787; www.lawrenceartscenter.com) Multidisciplinary arts center in the middle of downtown.

Fields Gallery (712 Massachusetts Street; 785/842-7187; www.fieldsgallery.com) Lawrence's oldest commercial gallery, representing dozens of local artists.

Performing Arts & Events

Haskell Indian Art Market (155 Indian Avenue; 785/749-8404; www.haskell.edu) September outdoor arts fair with top Native American artists.

Lied Center (Corner of 16th Street & Iowa Street; 785/864-2787; www.ku.edu) Modern performing-arts center presenting plays, classical music, dance, and Broadway productions.

Lawrence Community Theatre (1501 New Hampshire Street; 785/843-7469; www.community.lawrence.com) Year-round comedies, dramas, and musicals.

Wine & Dine

La Prima Tazza (638 Massachusetts Street; 785/832-2233) Lawrence's best buzz shop and an artists' favorite.

Teller's (746 Massachusetts Street; 785/843-4111) Fine Italian dining in a historic bank building.

Salty Iguana (4931 W. 6th Street; 785/312-8100) Best margaritas and fajitas in town.

Accommodations

Halcyon House B&B (1000 Ohio Street; 785/841-0314; www.the halcyonhouse.com) Nine-room, historic inn close to downtown.

Eldridge Hotel (701 Massachusetts Street; 785/749-5011; www.eldridgehotel.com) Grand hotel with classic 1940s style.

Days Inn (23009 Iowa Street; 785/843-9100; www.daysinn.com) Large, affordable hotel, with swimming pool.

Information

Lawrence Convention & Visitors Bureau: 402 N. 2nd Street; 888/529-5267; www.visitlawrence.com

Population: 82,500

Marquette, Michigan

far removed from the closest big city, the Upper Peninsula Art Town of Marquette has developed a strong, self-contained arts scene whose diversity in no small part is the result of the programs and opportunities offered at Northern Michigan University (NMU), the town's economic lifeblood. In many ways, the classic backdrop for Art Town development exists in Marquette. Once a prosperous iron-mining community ringed by small towns dependent on extractive industry cash flows, Marquette grew fat and happy when the times were good. Fortunately, its downtown has retained much of the turn-of-the-century, historic infrastructure built with mining's profits, and its neighborhoods are filled with Victorian mansions once occupied by the engineers, administrators, and union bosses who kept the local economy running in high gear.

As the shifting sands of global economic interests started Marquette's mines on their decline, much of the community's economic potential was vastly curtailed. Today, this remains the kind of place where the affordability of pieces of Marquette's historic past, especially the large homes that once housed its aristocracy, serve as powerful inducements for a new generation of artists and fine craftspeople willing to take the plunge and move here. What they find is a classic, American town that's become adept at diversifying its local economy while maintaining a strong sense of civic pride. Marquette is safe, supportive, and affordable, which are attractive inducements for the self-contained businesses that artists manage and grow. For artists whose economic lifeblood isn't dependent on selling locally, this town is a great place to live, work, and bond with the U.P.S. guy who ships art to distant markets.

Marquette's location on Lake Superior means this community enjoys spectacular summers and frigid winters. Marquette Mountain Ski Area's 22 trails are within easy reach, as are miles of mountain biking trails that are accessible from anywhere in Marquette, long stretches of wilderness at Painted Rocks National Seashore, and nearly a dozen parks with sandy beaches. Wintertime around here means either packing the Winnebago and heading to South Padre Island for six months of turtle watching or learning how to drill fishing holes in the lake's mantle of ice.

Arts Scene

Downtown Marquette is home to a half-dozen art galleries representing local work as well as several alternative venues such as coffee shops and restaurants that rotate local art shows on their walls. The community's highest profile venues for visual art are the Marquette Arts and Culture Center and the University Art Museum on the NMU campus. The arts center, located downtown, features local, regional, and national invitational as well as one-artist exhibitions in varied media such as painting, fine crafts, and jewelry. The center also offers year-round art classes for adults and kids, coordinates the Children's Theatre Project, and is home to the Cinearts Film Club's monthly presentations of art flicks and foreign films. The University Art Museum, which also oversees the on-campus University Sculpture Walk, offers fifteen exhibitions annually that include local and national artists as well as an annual faculty and student show. The most important regional art event is Art on the Rocks, an annual, outdoor exhibition that takes place in July in Presque Isle Park and features nearly 200 artists' booths.

During the summer months, the Marquette City Band presents its free Thursday-evening concerts in the Presque Isle Park's bandshell. Summer is also when the Pine Mountain Music Festival presents its series of classical music concerts and recitals in various local venues such as St. Peter Cathedral and the arts center. The Marquette Symphony Orchestra's season series of four concerts is presented at Kaufman Auditorium. Lake Superior Theatre's summer season of three, locally flavored plays is presented in the Frazier Historic Boat House on the lakefront. The region's premier venue for performing arts is the Forest

Art Talk

Wayne Francis, director of the University Art Museum.

We're part of the department of art and design at Northern Michigan University, and we're also a community art museum. So that makes us a lab for our students and an exhibition venue for the locals. We offer year-round programming with our biggest shows happening from September to May, and in summer there's a local children's art exhibition, a local art association show, and a regional invitational. We get a lot of summer traffic, and that's always growing, as more and more visitors are looking for a place with an undeveloped, rugged coastline. Artists here are doing a lot more than just painting the lake and lighthouses. We have a number of artists working in very contemporary styles and pursuing national careers who like our remoteness and low cost of living.

Roberts Theatre on the NMU campus. Its season of plays, which range from musicals to drama, takes place during the academic year. Downtown's 1920s-era vaudeville house, the Vista Theatre, is the home venue for the Peninsula Arts Appreciation Council's year-long series of community theatre classics.

Essentials

Visual Arts Venues

Marquette Arts and Culture Center (300 W. Baraga Avenue; 906/228-0472; www.mqtcty.org) Downtown venue for visual arts, film, and a children's summer arts camp.

University Art Museum (1401 Presque Isle Avenue; 906/227-1481; www.nmu.edu) National and regional exhibitions year-round.

Oasis Gallery (227 Washington Street; 906/225-1377) Contemporary artists from the region.

Performing Arts & Events

Art on the Rocks (see Marquette Chamber of Commerce below) This July outdoor exhibition attracts a national group of artists.

Lake Superior Theatre (300 W. Baraga Avenue; 906/227-7625; www.lakesuperiortheatre.com) Summer theatre with a local flavor.

Peninsula Art Appreciation Council (218 Iron Street; 906/475-7188; www.vistatheater.org) Downtown's community theatre company.

Wine & Dine

Sweet Basil Deli (603 N. 3rd Street; 906/226-9718; www.sweetbasil deli.com) Popular downtown lunch spot.

Border Grill (180 S. McClellan; 906/228-5228; www.bordergrill.net) Fine Tex-Mex with a healthy twist.

Casa Calabria (1106 N. Third Street; 906/228-5012; www.thecasa.us) Scaloppini, parmigiano, ravioli, barbera, cannoli.

Accommodations

Blueberry Ridge B&B (18 Oakridge Drive; 906/249-9246) Quiet inn, with famous blueberry pancakes.

Birchmont Motel (2090 U.S. 41 S.; 906/228-7538) Affordable rooms plus swimming pool.

Landmark Inn (230 N. Front Street; 906/228-2580; www.thelandmark inn.com) Elegant hotel in downtown Marquette.

Art Talk

Reatha Tweedie, director of arts and culture for the City of Marquette.

The city runs its arts center in a renovated library, with about 7,000 square feet used for a gallery, a gift shop, and workshop spaces, plus a small stage. I've been here since the 1970s, and since that time the region's arts scene has become much more organized and cooperative. We've even started a symphony orchestra that's been successful over time. Our monthly gallery walks get about 20 participating spaces from working studios to the art museum, and I think this also shows how there has been an increasing amount of downtown economic impact from the local arts community. Our affordability and natural beauty is an important asset for artists who choose to live here.

Information

Marquette Chamber of Commerce: 501 S. Front Street; 906/226-6591; www.marquette.org

Population: 19,800

Saugatuck, Michigan

Nestled among Lake Michigan sand dunes and bordered by the Kalamazoo River, Saugatuck is a beautifully preserved Victorian-era community that's attracted artists since the early 1900s. Home to the stern wheeler *Star of Saugatuck* and the S.S. *Keewatin* maritime museum, the Saugatuck of today is a popular second-home destination for weekending Chicagoans who come here for the town's shopping as well as its nearly 30 art galleries and artist-run studio/galleries.

The main attraction of Saugatuck has always been its miles of sandy beaches, and from one end of the calendar to the other, the town's busy marina is loaded with yachts and sailboats used by urbanites for jaunts out onto the lake's blue waters. Saugatuck and its neighboring community of Douglas are fringed by family-owned farms and orchards that raise some of the best fruit crops in the nation. In recent years several wineries have been carved out of some orchard lands, allowing places like Fenn Valley Vineyards to not only develop a new taste of what life here is all about but to also offer local residents a Sunday-afternoon live-music series in the summer.

Arts Scene

Known as the Art Coast of Michigan, the Saugatuck area is home to nearly 30 art spaces representing work ranging from sculpture and jewelry to contemporary art and lakeshore landscapes. Because of the community's year-round flow of visitors, it's possible for artists to make a living selling through local galleries as well as annual exhibitions such as the Clothesline Art Show during the Heritage Festival in September, the Waterfront Invitational in Cook Park in July, the Blue Coast Artists Studio Tour in October, and the Saugatuck Arts & Crafts Festival in June. While Saugatuck's visual arts scene is quite strong, one of the key pieces missing in the local arts puzzle is the focal point of a community arts center. A group of local residents has developed a capital campaign to fund what's hoped to be the Lakeshore Center for the Arts, a multipurpose facility to be built on the grounds of what had once been a pie factory. The 22,000-square-foot center will include a 600-seat auditorium as well as much needed, noncommercial visual arts exhibition space and classrooms.

As is the case in similarly positioned Art Towns, such as Ephraim, Wisconsin, and Grand Marais, Minnesota, performing arts play a key role in the community's cultural scene. Red Barn Playhouse, a summer professional theatre company whose crowd-pleasing Broadway shows are presented from early June through September, also stages several children's plays during its season. Mason Street Warehouse, a new, live-theatre company, produces its July and August season of newer material in a downtown Saugatuck venue. Established in 1999, the Waterfront Film Festival in June uses venues such as the American Legion Hall and the Saugatuck High School for its screenings of 60 feature-length and short films.

From March through October, the Lakeshore Jazz Connection uses the Saugatuck Women's Club for its monthly series of jazz concerts featuring top talents from Chicago and Detroit. The same venue is used in July and August as the setting for the concerts and recitals of the Chamber Music Festival of Saugatuck, an event that features 12 public performances by nationally renowned musicians.

The fundamental reason that visual artists have flocked to Saugatuck for nearly a century is the presence of Ox-Bow, a summer visual arts institute established in 1910, which is now affiliated with the School of the Art Institute of Chicago. Ox-Bow's summer faculty is drawn from a national group of established artists, while its students attend seminars in disciplines ranging from ceramics to sculpture, glass, painting, and creative writing. Ox-Bow's Friday Night Open Studios Series invites the public onto the Ox-Bow campus for a summer-long series of studio shows during its 10-week sessions.

Art Talk

Marcia Leben, manager of Good Goods.

We represent local and out-of-area artists, and we also have a large number of local furniture makers. There's a great deal of creativity here, with writers, artists, actors, jewelers, and craftsmen all over the place. There's an annual influx of young people who come for the Ox-Bow programs, and that's been a really good thing. The local schools also pay a lot of attention to the arts, and the students seem to be aware of the possibilities of having careers in the arts. Realism is the most popular painting style here, and a number of artists working in this style have opened their own galleries. If you've got talent, good ideas, and know how to run a business, you can get it done here.

Essentials

Visual Arts Venues

Ox-Bow (3435 Rupprecht Way; 269/857-5811; www.ox-bow.org) Summer arts program affiliated with the School of the Art Institute of Chicago.

Good Goods (106 Mason Street; 269/857-1557; www.goodgoods.com) Fine crafts and visual arts from regional artists.

Tuscan Pot Studio & Gallery (321 Water Street; 269/857-5550; www.tuscanpot.com) Italian Majolica pottery and tiles.

Performing Arts & Events

Ox-Bow Summer Art Auction (3435 Rupprecht Way; 269/857-5811; www.ox-bow.org) July event held on the Ox-Bow campus in its teaching studios.

Waterfront Film Festival (see Saugatuck/Douglas Convention & Visitors Bureau below) June screening of nearly 60 films.

Mason Street Warehouse (Lakeshore Community Arts Pavilion; 269/857-4898; www.masonstreetwarehouse.org) New and innovative theatre company.

Wine & Dine

Uncommon Grounds (127 Hoffman Street; 269/857-3333; www.uncommongroundscafe.com) Favorite buzz shop.

Blue Moon Bar & Grille (310 Blue Star Highway; 269/857-8686) Local ingredients, great atmosphere, and a strong wine list.

Chequers (220 Culver Street; 269/857-1868) Best Guinness on the lake.

Accommodations

Bentley Suites (326 Water Street; 269/857-5416) Luxury rooms in the middle of town.

Suncatcher Inn (131 Griffith Street; 269/857-4249;www.suncatcher inn.com) Affordable rooms, within walking distance of everything.

Saugette Motel (6541 Blue Star Highway; 269/857-1039) Affordable rooms on the edge of town.

Information

Saugatuck/Douglas Convention & Visitors Bureau: 2902 Blue Star Highway; 269/857-1701; www.saugatuck.com

Population: 1,100

Art Talk

June Bowman, executive director of Ox-Bow.

We were founded as a summer program, and it's been that way for 94 years. There's been an affiliation with the Art Institute of Chicago since our beginning, as we've used that relationship to evolve from being only an art school to more of a residential program that offers classes into the fall and early spring. Students from the institute can come here and take classes for credit, so we maintain our studios up to the institute's standards. It tends to be a very professional place, but we do get students from all over the country who are coming here at different skill levels. We have 115 acres on a lagoon next to the sand dunes. It's isolated, beautiful, and serene.

Traverse City, Michigan

Known nationally for the bounty of its fruit industry, Traverse City and the nearby Leelanau Peninsula have in recent years developed an arts scene as well as a thriving vineyard industry and a gourmet food culture. The welcome results have made this northwest corner of Michigan's Lower Peninsula a substantially more attractive place to live, especially for the independent art-business owners who have relocated here to take advantage of the region's superb summer climate and its affordable housing prices.

The traffic jams of Detroit are a four-hour drive south of Traverse City, making this isolated spot well suited for the entrepreneurialism of a new wave of artists who now call the region home. Galleries have sprung up like chanterelles after a late-summer rain, and from downtown Traverse City to the peninsula communities of Suttons Bay, Northport, Leland, and Glen Arbor, clusters of art galleries, artist studios, and seasonal arts festivals celebrate the area's creative spirit. In much the same way that artists have settled themselves into the culture of Washington's San Juan Islands, so has a new generation of former city dwellers found this part of Michigan to be a perfect place to live, work, and thoroughly enjoy the region's natural beauty.

There are spectacular beaches around practically every bend along the drive from Traverse City's taverns to the Grand Traverse Lighthouse at the tip of Leelanau Peninsula. To its west there's the 35 miles of shoreline wilderness in Sleeping Bear Dunes National Lakeshore, whose white sand dunes tower 400 feet above Lake Michigan. To the east there's yet another spit of land, the Old Mission Peninsula, separating the Grand Traverse Bay's west and east shores. Throughout the region are dozens of cherry orchards, blueberry farms, vineyards, and family-run vegetable farms, and the annual Cherry Festival in early July is a can't-miss hit on the entertainment calendar. The festival's blowout week of partying includes a solid week's worth of top-name entertainment on an outdoor stage along the Traverse City waterfront. Another favorite summer event, the free, weekly Jazz at Sunset concert series, takes place on the grounds of the Chateau Chantal winery in nearby Mapleton, while the weekend live-music shows and weekly poetry readings at Horizon Books in Traverse City are year-round gathering points for the region's creative community.

Arts Scene

One of the nation's most highly regarded summer series of concerts, lectures, and art workshops takes place at the Interlochen Center for the Arts, whose 3,900-seat Kresge Auditorium is used by the Interlochen Arts Festival for its June through August series of performances ranging from classical and world music to rock and pop. Throughout the rest of the year, Interlochen's Corson Auditorium is used for a less star-filled series of performances, including those of the Traverse Symphony Orchestra. Interlochen is also the home to a year-round arts academy as well as a summer arts camp, and its educational programs serve all levels of students throughout the Grand Traverse region.

Art Center Traverse City, operated by the Northwestern Michigan League of Artists & Craftsmen, organizes the annual Traverse Bay Outdoor Art Fair in July on the grounds of Northwestern Michigan College. Throughout the year, its facility on South Elmwood is used for regional and national exhibitions as well as art workshops conducted by its members. Just a short drive north of town, the Northport Community Arts Center presents a year-round series of classical, world, and jazz music performances in its 447-seat facility. Yet another nearby venue, the Glen Arbor Art Center, uses its space for exhibitions, classes, and the Manitou Music Festival's July and August series of chamber music concerts. The region's premier visual arts venue is the Dennos Museum Center on the NMC campus. In addition to its 367-seat Milliken Auditorium, the Dennos has three visual arts galleries that are used for traveling national exhibitions as well as student, faculty, and regional shows. In Northport a cluster of six art galleries represents

Art Talk

Pat Ford, president of Art Center Traverse City.

A lot of our town's arts conscience comes through the support this community gives to the arts. The city does what it can, but it's the community that really makes a difference. We're a summer resort area with many galleries. Here at the art center we're primarily a teaching organization, but we also do outdoor art fairs and exhibitions. There's a local and a national group of artists in this area, many of whom first came here to teach at Interlochen. Traverse City seems to have this groundswell of arts-related development, which has helped the art center become more of a year-round facility that serves both the visitors and our local residents.

mainly local and regional artists, while spaces like the Gallery 544 in Traverse City and the Michigan Artists Gallery in Suttons Bay have a decidedly contemporary focus.

Stage Door Theatre Company uses Milliken Auditorium for its productions, while Traverse City Children's Theatre uses the Old Town Playhouse, a converted church with a 375-seat main stage and a 100-seat black box studio. The playhouse is also used by the Traverse City Civic Players, a long-standing community theatre group whose productions are presented year-round.

Essentials

Visual Arts Venues

Art Center Traverse City (720 S. Elmwood Street; 231/941-9488; (www.traversearts.org/organizations.php) Revolving exhibits and year-round classes.

Dennos Museum Center (1701 E. Front Street; 231/995-1055; www.dennosmuseum.org) Several galleries plus year-round programs.

Michigan Artists Gallery (309 St. Josephs Street; 231/271-4922) Represents regional and local contemporary artists.

Performing Arts & Events

Interlochen Arts Festival (P.O. Box 199, Interlochen; 800/681-5920; www.interlochen.org) Year-round art institute's expansive, summer performing-artists series.

Old Town Playhouse (148 East Eighth Street; 231/947-2443; www.oldtownplayhouse.com) Year-round community theatre.

Traverse Jazz Festival (see Traverse City Convention & Visitors Bureau below) Weeklong event in various local venues.

Wine & Dine

Amical (229 E. Front Street; 231/941-8888; www.amical.com) Innovative cuisine using local ingredients, plus a great wine list.

Auntie's Pasta Café (2030 S. Airport Road; 231/941-8147) Chicken picatta and Zio's pub.

J & S Hamburg (302 W. Front Street; 231/947-6409) Best burgers on the bay, plus a view.

Accommodations

Linden Lea on Long Lake B&B (279 S. Long Lake Road; 231/943-9182; www.lindenleabb.com) Small, quiet B&B on a lake.

The Grainery B&B (2951 Hartman Road; 231/946-8325) Close to Interlochen and lakeshore beaches.

Cherry Tree Inn on the Beach (2345 U.S. 31 N.; 231/938-8888; www.cherrytreeinn.com) Large hotel on the lakefront.

Information

Traverse City Convention & Visitors Bureau: 101 W. Grandview Parkway; 231/947-1120; www.mytraversecity.com

Population: 14,700

Art Talk

Sue Ann Round, owner of the Michigan Artists Gallery.

I've made this place a contemporary gallery with an eclectic mix of artists and artwork, and so far, the feedback has been good. Traverse City has been getting itself on the country's art map, and we're seeing a lot more national visitors coming into town for Interlochen and then into the art centers and galleries to buy local art. All of my artists are from this area, either full-time residents or instructors at the college. There are lots of people moving into this area who are building very large homes and want local art on their walls. Because we're a successful gallery, I have to keep a list of artists who I'd want to show here, if any of my existing artists were ever to leave.

Grand Marais, Minnesota

With its spectacular harbor on the shores of Lake Superior, its miles of national forestlands, hundreds of lakes and streams, and Sawtooth Mountains views stretching 40 miles north into Canada, it's no wonder this Art Town has long been favored by Minnesota artists as an ideal summer retreat. In the mid-1940s the first wave of painters, sculptors, and fine craftsmen established the Grand Marais Art Colony, which has evolved from its original, informal status into its present role as one of the Midwest's best-regarded summer art-workshop programs.

From that early beginning Grand Marais has grown to become "A North Shore Work of Art." Summer homes abound, filled with part-time residents each May and shuttered in early October before the winter hits. While many artists, especially painters and furniture makers, choose to live here year-round, the majority of them arrive after the ice melts, bringing with them an expanded summer season of visual arts shows, music performances, live theatre, and community arts festivals. Winters, though long and hard, are something people cope with through outdoor activities such as ice fishing on the lakes, snowmobiling on the many miles of trails that fan out across the Superior National Forest, and downhill skiing at nearby Lutsen Mountain. Those in need of a dose of warmer weather make the two-hour drive down to Duluth, where they can catch a flight to Tampa.

Arts Scene

While the Grand Marais Art Colony provides a historic anchor for this community's visual arts scene, the convergence of large numbers of artists, second-home owners, and culturally attuned tourists that pour into Grand Marais during its warmer months has led to a steady growth in the community's visual arts scene. The premier exhibition venue is the Johnson Heritage Post Art Gallery, which has rotating displays of work by local and regional artists whose imagery reflects the region's culture and heritage. Several commercial galleries, such as Silverstone Gallery, Waters of Superior, and Lake Superior Trading Post, represent locally created art. The mid-July Grand Marais Art Festival, an outdoor event held on the streets surrounding the harbor, attracts more than 100 artists' booths for its juried, weekend-long run. A highlight of the festival is its annual staging of a Greek theatre piece on the harbor's rocky shoreline.

Arrowhead Center for the Arts, a multidisciplinary facility that houses the Grand Marais Art Colony's programs as well as the performance space used by the Grand Marais Playhouse and the North Shore Music Association, is a recent addition to the town's arts infrastructure. The center's 300-seat theatre is used year-round for everything from the recitals of Sterling Dance Company to the weeklong Grand Marais Jazz Festival, an April event that signals the arrival of spring's warmth with performances by top national jazz musicians. North Shore Music Association works year-round to bring noted jazz, world, and rock musicians into Grand Marais. Its performances are typically sold-out affairs that are also highlights of the town's social calendar.

Grand Marais Playhouse, another of the year-round arts organizations active here, has earned a solid reputation for its innovative selection of classic and new material. Its "Ten Minute Plays Festival" in April is a premier showcase for the state's top playwrights, and its two-week

Art Talk

Jane Johnson, administrator of the Grand Marais Art Colony.

We're connected to the Minneapolis College of Art and Design through a number of instructors who come up here to teach during the summer, but we're an independent organization and most of our instructors come from across the state. We have an outstanding, 50-plus-year reputation as a place with good instructors and 24/7 studio access for our students. It's one big studio inside an old church, and it's an energetic, creative environment. Having the art colony in Grand Marais has been an asset for all of the region's artists because it has given them a chance to develop, come in for a class or a lecture, and move their careers forward.

Art Talk

JoAnn Krause, director of the Johnson Heritage Post Gallery.

We promote local and regional artists through eight shows a year selected by a screening committee. We want to feature art that raises the awareness of the region's heritage, and we have a permanent collection of regional art in our harborside, log building. We have two galleries in our building, plus space for lectures and art workshops. More artists are moving into this area, and quite a few want to exhibit their work here. Our shows really mix it up, with lots of fine crafts, fiber art, paintings, and sculpture, and collectors come here knowing they'll find art that's about the area.

Shakespeare Festival, staged in late June and early July, is the type of top-notch event that elevates Grand Marais's arts scene far above what's typically found in communities this size.

Essentials

Visual Arts Venues

Johnson Heritage Post Art Gallery (115 Wisconsin Street; 218/387-2314) Primarily exhibits regional and traditional work.

Grand Marais Art Colony (P.O. Box 626; 218/387-2737; www.grand maraisartcolony.org) Long-standing arts organization offering summer art workshops.

Arrowhead Center for the Arts (11 W. 5th Street; 218/387-1284; www.northshorearts.org) Grand Marais's center for exhibitions and performances.

Performing Arts & Events

Grand Marais Arts Festival (see Grand Marais Art Colony above) July outdoor arts festival.

Grand Marais Playhouse (P.O. Box 996; 218/387-1284; www.grandmaraisplayhouse.com) Year-round theatre, plus summer Shakespeare.

Grand Marais Jazz Festival (see Greater Grand Marais Chamber of Commerce below) April event, with national performers.

Wine & Dine

Gun Flint Tavern (111 Wisconsin Street; 218/387-1563; www.gunflinttavern.com) Coldest draft beer on the North Shore.

Blue Water Café (3719 W. Highway 61; 218/387-1597; www.blue watercafe.com) Legendary breakfasts.

World's Best Donuts (1806 County Road 7; 218/387-1345) Krispy Kreme Doughnuts, watch out!

Accommodations

Gunflint Motel (101 West 5th Avenue; 218/387-1454; www.gunflintmotel.com) Affordable rooms, within walking distance of town.

Sawtooth Cabins & Motel (510 W 2nd Street; 218/387-1522) Cabins, plus room for RV parking.

Super 8 Motel (1711 W. Highway 61; 218/387-2448) Affordable family motel.

Information

Greater Grand Marais Chamber of Commerce: 13 N. Broadway; 218/387-9112; www.grandmaraismn.com

Population: 1,300

Lanesboro, Minnesota

$\int$trange bedfellows occasionally provide the impetus for unexpected and unusual developments in an Art Town. That's certainly the case in the southeast-Minnesota community of Lanesboro, once the center for a thriving forest-products industry but whose latest infusion of vitality arrived courtesy of two entities: bicycling and the arts.

Decades ago, when millions of board feet of lumber made their way from Lanesboro's loading docks to nearby Rochester, about an hour's drive north by today's standards, they did so on the flatbed cars of a railroad whose pathway followed the contours of the Root River. In the early 1990s, those railbeds were converted into one of the nation's first Rails-to-Trails projects, and, in an especially fortuitous stroke of luck, enough money was allocated to provide asphalt paving for most of the Root River Trail's course. Once word got out about the miles of narrow, vehicle-free blacktop that wound its way through some of the upper Midwest's prettiest scenery, hordes of weekending bicyclers, roller bladers, stroller pushers, and families on cross-country treks started pouring into Lanesboro, looking for a cold drink, a good hot dog, and something interesting to do with their spare time.

They were not disappointed. B&Bs soon popped up all over town, and today more than 60 miles of an expanded Root River Trail winds its way through the scenic bluffs connecting Lanesboro, the trail's hub, to neighboring communities such as Harmony and Preston. During winter, the trail becomes a magnet for cross-country skiers. The B&Bs

have been joined by more than a dozen restaurants, including the inimitable Das Wurst Haus, where the owner not only makes his own hot dogs but also plays his tuba to entertain diners.

Arts Scene

Lanesboro's reputation as an Art Town is built on the foundation of two astute local arts organizations, the Commonweal Theatre Company and the Cornucopia Art Center. Through their year-round activities they provide a constant flow of creative ideas that keep the arts at the forefront of what Lanesboro offers its visitors and residents.

There are other aspects to the local arts scene, such as the summer Cool Breeze concerts in Sylvan Park's gazebo, the barn dances in the Sons of Norway Hall, the annual Bluff Country Artists Studio Tour in mid-April, exhibitions at the Clover Gallery in Harmony, June's Art in the Park weekend at Sylvan Park, and the annual Buffalo Bill Days blowout in August. There's even been a public art trail developed along Lanesboro's streets.

Cornucopia Art Center, located in a two-story commercial building in the heart of town, is an ambitious, multidimensional arts center whose programs and exhibitions are carried out at a consistently high level of quality. The center's monthly visual arts shows include one-artist exhibitions for the region's best painters, sculptors, and craftspeople, as well as invitational juried shows that attract attention from artists throughout Minnesota and the Midwest. The center's sales gallery is a powerful marketing tool for Lanesboro's artists, and its Meet the Artist lecture series has gone a long ways toward introducing the town's residents to the new generation of artists who trickle in each year. Its year-round art classes, geared toward all levels of proficiency, have proved to be a powerful networking tool for the regional arts community, and its Jerome Foundation Residency Program brings emerging artists from

Art Talk

Holly McDonough, executive director of Cornucopia Art Center. We have a contemporary arts focus, and in our 10 years of existence we've tried to define our exhibitions as a forum to broaden and expand upon the art available in our juried sales gallery. Most of our artists are drawn from the southern part of Minnesota and seem to know how to put together art shows that will raise people's awareness about art and start a conversation. Our educational role has expanded in recent years with new classes targeted toward artists in various media, and our teachers always seem to want to come back and teach again. We have a 2- to 4-week residency program for national artists where they engage the community in some sort of project.

Art Talk

Hal Cropp, founder and artistic director of the Commonweal Theatre Company.

Two new things about us are our Ibsen Festival, which is taking on a national type of significance, and our more comprehensive development of new plays that's the result of our relationship with the Guthrie Theater. We've partnered with Cornucopia on many of our programs, and this has helped us attract more than 1,500 people to our Ibsen Festival's opening weekend. We even have an invited playwright residency program that will result in our staging five new plays over the next five years. We have eleven full-time employees and seven college interns, and we're all focused on building our audiences and programs in preparation for our next phase of development, which will turn the old cheese factory into a new home for the Cornucopia and Commonweal, with a 180-seat facility for us and a new gallery space for Cornucopia. We're looking at a $3.5 million capital campaign that will get us in there by 2006.

across the region into Lanesboro for short-term residencies.

A few years ago, the founder of the Great American Think-Off, an event staged in New York Mills, Minnesota (profiled in previous editions of this book), packed up his Airstream motor home and relocated to Lanesboro. John Davis had no sooner planted his legs on local soil before developing the Kids Philosophy Slam, an international philosophy competition now staged in Lanesboro during the spring months. The City of Philosophy project, another of Davis's visions for Lanesboro's future, has the potential to widen this community's stature in international intellectual circles

Founded in the late 1980s, Commonweal Theatre Company presents six plays in a year-round schedule. The great strength of Commonweal is its willingness to stage new and decidedly nonmainstream material along with the occasional, crowd-pleasing classic. The company also offers a summer theatre camp for local kids, student matinees of plays staged during the school year, and a semester-in-residence program for university theatre majors. The St. Mane Theater, a 225-seat playhouse on Lanesboro's main street, is also the site for Commonweal's May through August live-radio program "Over the Back Fence," a slice of broadcast Americana that would do Garrison Keillor proud.

Essentials

Visual Arts Venues

Cornucopia Art Center (103 Parkway Avenue N.; 507/467-2446; www.lanesboroarts.org) Local, regional, and national visual arts exhibitions, and year-round art workshops.

Frank Wright Studio (106 Coffee Street; 507/467-3376) Master carver of spoons and utensils.

Clover Gallery (25 Center Street E., Harmony; 507/886-3313) Large art space representing dozens of local and regional artists.

Performing Arts & Events

Commonweal Theatre Company (206 Parkway Avenue N.; 507/467-2525; www.commonwealtheatre.org) Year-round presentations of classics and new material.

Kids Philosophy Slam (507/467-0107; www.philosophyslam.org) Unique event involving debates about issues of global importance.

Art in the Park (see Lanesboro Visitors Center below) June art event in Sylvan Park.

Wine & Dine

Old Village Hall (111 Coffee Street; 507/467-2962; www.oldvillage hall.com) Great steaks and a nice wine list.

Das Wurst Haus (117 Parkway Avenue N.; 507/467-2902) Homemade brats and a lot of fun.

Chat & Chew (701 Parkway Avenue S.; 507/467-3444) Burgers, with a view of the river.

Accommodations

Habberstad House (706 Fillmore Avenue S.; 507/467-3560; www.habberstadhouse.com) Historic B&B, within walking distance of the art center.

Stone Mill Suites (100 Beacon Street; 507/467-8663; www.stone millsuites.com) Spacious rooms in a restored grain mill.

The Old Barn Resort (Rt. 3, Box 57, Preston; 507/467-2512; www.barnresort.com) Luxurious spot, with a golf course and pool.

Information

Lanesboro Visitors Center: 100 Milwaukee Road; 507/467-2696; www.lanesboro.com

Population: 800

Fargo, North Dakota

The national reputation of this Art Town a four-hour drive west of Minneapolis has largely been sealed through the filmmaking imagination of Hollywood's Coen brothers. But while Fargo and its neighboring community of Moorhead certainly are frozen and windswept for part of the year, they're not quite loaded with the rotating cast of lunatics that played so well in the movie. This college town on the banks of the Red River is extremely supportive of its arts community, ensuring that its two art museums, opera company, symphony orchestra, renovated performing-arts theatre, community stage company, art galleries, and alternative visual arts venues are recognized for the year-round contributions they make to Fargo's quality of life.

Added to these elements of arts infrastructure are the performing-arts programs and exhibition venues on the campuses of North Dakota State University and the Minnesota State University at Moorhead, as well as two folk arts centers whose programs celebrate the area's Scandinavian heritage. Folks living here have a range of arts-oriented entertainment options that far exceed those of cities much larger than Fargo.

The low cost of living and extensive arts infrastructure this place offers its visual artists, musicians, and actors has molded Fargo into a talent-loaded incubator for creative field professionals. After their educational tenure here, many of these individuals can forge a living from their art skills, soldiering on until their careers reach the point where they can be self-sustaining in the Twin Cities and points beyond. For those who choose to make Fargo their permanent home, the colleges offer numerous opportunities for jobs as instructors in their arts departments, and there is also a range of positions available in the local museums and performing-arts groups.

Arts Scene

The leading edge of Fargo's arts scene and one of the nation's most innovatively programmed art institutions is the Plains Art Museum, whose 9,000 square feet of exhibition space is located in a historic, renovated warehouse. Everything about the museum, from the noontime music presentations in its Café Muse to its aggressive pursuit of cutting-edge artists from New York and Los Angeles for its Schlossman Gallery contemporary arts exhibition series, is exemplary. Through its ArtView series the museum uses three alternative gallery spaces to give local and regional artists the exhibition opportunities necessary to incubate their promising careers, while its Rolling Plains Art Gallery is an 18-wheeler that hauls exhibitions and materials to rural communities across North Dakota and Minnesota. Year-round, the Plains Museum is the region's focal point for artist lectures, films, workshops, and fundraising events. The Rourke Art Museum in Moorhead is dedicated to exhibiting and preserving the permanent collection of Orland Rourke and also mounts exhibitions of local and regional artists with ties to the area's culture and heritage.

While there are several gallery and café exhibition venues in Fargo, the more prominent sites for visual arts are those on the NDSU campus. The Memorial Union Gallery exhibits regional and national artists, while Reineke Visual Arts Gallery is dedicated to student and faculty work, as is the President's Gallery in Old Main. During the academic year several campus venues are used to stage the Lively Arts Series, which brings touring performers into town for much-needed relief from winter's chill.

The Fargo Theatre, a 1926 masterpiece of art deco style, is used for everything from the Fargo Film Festival's screenings of documentaries to year-round children's theatre performances. While the Straw Hat Players are a highly regarded summer theatre company based in Moorhead at MSUM's Hansen Theatre, the region's premier stage company is Fargo-Moorhead Community Theatre, which presents an interesting array of drama, musicals, comedies, and children's theatre in its own, 300-seat playhouse. The company also produces an After Hours series of cutting-edge plays for adult audiences. The Fargo-Moorhead Symphony, which uses NDSU's Festival Concert Hall for its September

Art Talk

Rusty Freeman, vice president of curatorial and educational programs at the Plains Art Museum.

On a practical note, we serve people living within a 150-mile radius of Fargo. We've recognized the need to be supportive of our regional artists as well as national contemporary artists in our exhibitions program, and it's not always been easy to do this. But over time, as we've pushed the envelope, we've found a surprising amount of local and regional support for challenging types of art. That's one of the main reasons why we're excited about the development of the next generation of artists from this area. We're located in what once was an International Harvester warehouse in downtown Fargo. It looks old on its outside but is completely renovated and modern on its inside. We're just below the radar in terms of national recognition, but the Midwest is aware of our reputation for showing challenging, new work.

through March series of performances, also offers local audiences a chamber music series, a pop-concert series, and family concerts. Fargo-Moorhead Opera uses the same venue for its two annual productions, both classic standards, which are presented in the fall and spring.

Essentials

Visual Arts Venues

Plains Art Museum (704 1st Avenue N.; 701/232-3821; www.plainsart.org) Broadly focused art museum with strong exhibits of local, regional, and national artists.

Memorial Union Gallery (1401 Administration Avenue; 701/231-7900; www.ndsu.nodak.edu) Offers rotating shows of local and national artists.

Gallery 4 (118 Broadway; 701/237-6867) Artist cooperative representing top regional talents since the mid-1970s.

Performing Arts & Events

Red River Street Fair (701/241-1570; www.fmdowntown.com) Major summer art show with more than 100 outdoor booths.

Taste of the Valley (Heritage Hjemkomst Interpretive Center; 201 First Avenue N; 218/299-5511) Summer kicks off with this June restaurant event and an accompanying art show.

Fargo-Moorhead Community Theatre (333 4th Street S.; 701/235-1901; www.fmct.org) The community's year-round theatre company presenting a wide range of adult and children's materials.

Wine & Dine

Atomic Coffee (15 4th Street S.; 218/299-6161) Hip hangout for the local arts community.

Babb's Coffee House (315 Broadway; 701/271-0222) Live music, Snickers cheesecake, and pepperoni pizza.

Gecko's Grill & Bar (1515 42nd Street, SW; 701/293-6369) Best Southwest-style foods in North Dakota.

Accommodations

C'Mon Inn (4338 20th Avenue SW; 701/277-9944) Upscale place with year-round swimming pool.

Kelly Inn (4207 13th Avenue, SW; 701/277-8821) Affordable rooms, swimming pool, and parking for RVs.

Wingate Inn (4429 19th Avenue, SW; 701/281-9133; www.wingate inns.com) Business hotel with an indoor pool.

Information

Fargo-Moorhead Convention & Visitors Bureau: 2001 44th Street SW; 701/282-3653; www.fargomoorhead.org

Population: 90,000

Art Talk

Dean Sather, executive director of the Heritage Hjemkomst Interpretive Center. Our core mission is to present the heritage of the Red River Valley. Not just the immigrant experience of 120 years ago, but its ongoing growth and its local flavor. Local folk art traditions are an important part of that heritage, especially as we move away from being nearly all Scandinavian to becoming more of a multicultural area with Mexican migrant families and refugee families from across the globe. Our building in downtown Moorhead is owned by the city and houses several organizations. We get about 25,000 college students moving into Fargo and Moorhead each year, and they're adding their own take on culture to the societies that are already established here.

Bayfield, Wisconsin

Bordered by the Apostle Islands National Lakeshore, this town on the northernmost tip of Wisconsin has long been favored as an ideal summer haven, a place where blueberry fields and apple orchards frame a forested landscape filled with mountains, streams, and spectacular views of Lake Superior. Bayfield, which is connected to nearby Madeline Island by a seasonal ferry service, has a quirky, Northwoods flavor that's balanced by the year-round presence of artists, the summertime presence of cash-laden tourists, and an incredibly beautiful environment.

Living here means adjusting for the pleasures of each season. When it's warm, there's no better place to be than out on the lake, which is why Bayfield's charming harbor is loaded with sailboats, impressive yachts, and the powerboats favored by locals for fishing, water skiing, and romantic evenings under the stars. Summertime also means that the hundreds of cabins scattered around Madeline Island spring to life with vacationing families from Chicago, Duluth, and Milwaukee, turning the island into a three-month celebration of all things artistic and authentically crazy.

Artists have been filtering into Bayfield for the better part of the past few decades, seeking a better life in a place that offers minimal distractions. And once the warm summer breezes head south, that description certainly fits Bayfield. Winter, as they say, arrives early and usually overstays its welcome. Hunkered down in their homes, Bayfield's artists use those frigid months to create works of art that will either be shipped to galleries in Minneapolis and Chicago, or stored until the next summer's flood of tourists starts showing up in mid-May, or get hauled out of town in the back of a van by those who hit the summer outdoor arts fair circuit.

Arts Scene

Bayfield is one of those places where the arts flourish despite the lack of a community arts center. There's lots of talent at all levels of arts disciplines in this region, but without a place to exhibit art, schedule instructional workshops, build sets, rehearse concerts, and coalesce the various local interests working on behalf of the arts, the community-wide impact that the arts are capable of leveraging never gets fully realized. Nonetheless, as is the case in places such as Bigfork, Montana, and Prescott, Arizona, the local arts scene's development is capably carried on the backs of talented, dedicated individuals who have one foot planted

Art Talk

Mary Gardner, owner of Water Music Jewelry & Art.

Since I moved here in 1997, Bayfield's changed a little. There are more artists, more galleries, and even a new art-supplies store. I think more people are coming here looking for art and for our August arts festival, so we're trying to highlight the arts community more than what's been done in the past. It's tough running a business in a smalltown that relies on seasonal visitors, so we've combined the gallery with a workshop and have a Web site to try to increase our sales. Each year brings a bit more business into town, and we're even starting to see more activity during the winter season. We need an art center in Bayfield, a place for art classes and a venue for improving the exposure of our artists.

in the realities of making a living from their creative output and the other foot dangling in the sometimes chilly waters of civic-minded arts activism. The LaPointe Center on Madeline Island, a compact facility in the town shopping center, uses its tiny quarters for seasonal exhibitions, films, and artist lectures.

While Madeline Island is a quirky, seasonal place whose artists have the common sense to board up their storefronts and head for Oaxaca, Mexico, when the trees start losing their leaves, Bayfield's creative community exhibits a more rooted type of personality that tilts itself into the force of winter's mightly gales and soldiers on. Several art galleries selling local and regional work are scattered around the town's very walkable streets, and it's not at all difficult for local artists to find a downtown location for starting the studio /gallery of their dreams. The best time to get a look at the Chequamegon Bay area's artists is during the annual Bayfield Festival of the Arts, whose main events take place in the town's Waterfront Park on the first weekend of August. Set against the jewel-like backdrop of the lake's sparkling blue waters, every artist in a hundred-mile radius seems to have a presence at this show. The second-best time to scope out the arts scene is during the Bayfield Apple Festival, an early-October weekend of parades, mayhem, and events featuring the consumption of ungodly amounts of apple cider, apple bratwurst, apple dumplings, and (of course) beer.

While Holy Family Catholic Church is the preferred venue for choir performances, the Bayfield Schubert Festival, which was started in the mid-1990s, sets up for its July and August performances at the Christ Episcopal Church and also stages a free performance during the annual Blessing of the Fleet in June. Many of the musicians featured in the Schubert Festival also teach at the Madeline Island Summer Music Camp, whose Sunday concerts are staged on the island from mid-June through July.

The jewel in Bayfield's arts scene is the summer music festival of Lake Superior Big Top Chautauqua. Staged from May into September in a 780-seat tent set up on the grounds of Mt. Ashwabay Ski Area, the festival is the best place to see and be seen (outside of the midnight crowds at Tom's Burned Down Tavern on Madeline Island). The festival draws top-tier international music talent into Chequamegon Bay for 70 nights of acts that range from cowboy musicians from Austin to the Delta bluesmen of Mississippi and the staging of musicals spoofing Northwoods culture.

Essentials

Visual Arts Venues

La Pointe Center (103 Lakeview Place; Madeline Island; 715/747-3321) Summer arts exhibitions, lectures, and films.

Kerr Studio & Gallery
(21 Front Street; 715/779-5790; www.kerrart.com) Sculpture and glass.

Water Music Jewelry & Art
(13 S. Second Street; 715/779-5262; www.watermusicjewelry.com) Multifaceted gallery making innovative types of wearable art.

Performing Arts & Events

Bayfield Festival of the Arts (see Bayfield Chamber of Commerce below) Early August event with outdoor shows, art auction, and special exhibits in alternative venues.

Lake Superior Big Top Chautauqua (Mt. Ashwabay Ski Area, Washburn; 715/373-5552; www.bigtop.org) Summer-long festival of music and theatre under a huge tent at the base of a ski area.

Bayfield Schubert Festival (125 N. 3rd Street; 715/779-3401; www.bayfieldschubertfestival.org) June, July, and August concerts staged in a historic church.

Wine & Dine

Tom's Burned Down Café (1 Middle Road, Madeline Island; 715/747-6100; www.tomsburneddown cafe.com) Outdoor bar, poetry readings, the exhibitions of Phoenix Gallery, and reggae under the stars.

Art Talk

Brian Kerr, owner of Kerr Studio & Gallery.

I've lived in Bayfield since 1978, and have been a full-time artist since 1981. My medium is metal, from sculpture to jewelry. It's direct metal fabrication through welding, forming, and hammering. I work in a small studio space in a converted house that my father remodeled. When I got here in 1978 this place was vastly different from what it is now. I'm right on the waterfront and can see the lake from my driveway, which is a problem in the summer because it makes me cut out of work early to go sailing. For me it's the outdoor accessibility of Bayfield that keeps me here. I'm more interested in having quality personal time than I am in working long hours just to increase my income.

The Egg Toss (41 Manypenny Avenue; 715/779-5181; www.eggtoss-bayfield.com) Best omelets in the Northwoods.

Wild Rice (84860 Old San Road; 715/779-9881; www.wildrice restaurant.com) Upscale, regional cuisine with a good wine list.

Accommodations

Island Inn (852 Main Street; Madeline Island; 715/747-2000; www.ontheisland.com) Affordable rooms near the ferry dock.

Harbors Edge Motel (33 N. Front Street; 715/779-3962; www.harborsedgemotel.com) Rooms with great views right in town.

The Bayfield Inn (20 Rittenhouse Avenue; 715/779-3363; www.thebayfieldinn.com) Lake-view rooms with a touch of luxury.

Information

Bayfield Chamber of Commerce: 42 S. Broad Street; 800/447-4094; www.bayfield.org

Population: 610

Ephraim, Wisconsin

The reasons why this Art Town on the Door Peninsula has such a diverse and sophisticated arts scene are the same reasons why places such as Brattleboro, Vermont, Prescott, Arizona, and Idyllwild, Calififornia, are such outstanding Art Towns. They're all in locations with lots of natural beauty and are also places that combined their long-standing reputations as towns that welcome artists with an infusion of urban seasonal residents, resulting in new life as arts-powered retreats.

In Ephraim's case the summer visitors come from Milwaukee, about a three-hour drive south, and especially Chicago, nearly five hours distant. For more than a century, the small towns along the Door Peninsula have offered city dwellers a perfect place to leave their urban concerns behind and enter an idyllic, summer haven speckled with fruit orchards, swimming holes, natural harbors, and miles of rolling, wooded hillsides. As time marched forward, so did the peninsula's population. It came to include a number of artists, actors, and musicians who first arrived as summer visitors and who eventually were converted into year-rounders.

Today, while there's art activity practically around every bend in the roads winding along the peninsula, the small-town of Ephraim has come to symbolize the area's center of arts activity. While the arts are present here year-round, they're especially active from Memorial Day through mid-October, when winter turns the peninsula back into a windswept finger of frozen land. Ephraim has turned out to be an ideal town for artists who want to live someplace where there's a tidal wave of activity part of the year but peaceful the rest of the year. They know that the art they create during winter will sell to the surge of visitors who hit the peninsula in summer, looking to haul homeward a tangible piece of evidence that, once upon a time, they really did take a vacation to Door County.

Arts Scene

Founded as a Moravian religious retreat in 1853, Ephraim stays in touch with its past through the exhibits at the Anderson Barn Museum, the Anderson Store Museum, and carefully preserved historic structures such as the Svalhus, the Pioneer School, and the Hillside Hotel. The community's creative past and present are preserved and celebrated through year-round exhibitions and programs offered by the Francis Hardy Center for the Arts, which operates the seasonal Dockside Gallery and the Uptown Gallery. Named after local artist Francis Hardy, the center uses both of its galleries for juried and invitational group exhibitions. It also organizes a summer studio tour that takes place on Tuesday afternoons from June through September, an artist lecture series held at the Uptown Gallery, a summer arts camp for kids, and the Festival of the Arts in early August in downtown Ephraim.

Artist studios and artist-run galleries are a common sight along the Door Peninsula, with the densest concentrations found in places such as Ephraim, Fish Creek, Sisters Bay, and Bailey's Harbor. The Peninsula Art School in Fish Creek offers workshops in various arts disciplines throughout the year, as well as innovative, one-artist and group exhibitions in its Guenzel Gallery. The William S. Fairfield Museum in nearby Sturgeon Bay features a permanent collection of works by Henry Moore and exhibitions surveying year-round contemporary themes as well as eras in art history.

Partnering with this strong visual arts scene is an equally strong performing-arts scene. Niches filled by organizations such as the Wisconsin Theatre Game Center in Bailey's Harbor, whose workshops attract a nationwide roster of students, and mainstream venues such as the Door Community Auditorium, a 750-seat venue whose summer calendar ranges from the Milwaukee Symphony to Neil Sedaka and contemporary dance companies. The Peninsula Players, whose performing-arts pavilion, the Theatre in a Garden, is located outside of Fish Creek along the shores of Green Bay, presents a season of comedies, dramas, and musicals that runs from June to mid-October. The

Third Avenue Playhouse in Sturgeon Bay is the peninsula's year-round community theatre company, while American Folklore Theatre presents its summer season of madcap comedies in the Peninsula State Park Amphitheatre outside of Ephraim. Birch Creek Music Performance Center in nearby Egg Harbor offers a summer series of workshops and classical music concerts from June to August, while Midsummer Music Festival's May through June season showcases top national chamber music talents in venues all along the peninsula, including Village Hall and the Uptown Gallery in Ephraim.

Essentials

Visual Arts Venues

Francis Hardy Center for the Arts (Anderson Lane; 920/854-2210; www.thehardy.org) Two gallery venues displaying top local and regional artists.

Guenzel Gallery (3900 County F, Fish Creek; 920/868-3455; www.peninsulaartschool.com) Part of the Peninsula Art School, the Guenzel exhibits contemporary work from local, regional, and national artists.

William S. Fairfield Art Museum (242 Michigan Street, Sturgeon Bay; 920/746-0001; www.fairfieldartmuseum.com) Small but powerful art museum with an outstanding permanent collection and well-designed national and regional exhibitions.

Performing Arts & Events

Festival of the Arts (Francis Hardy Center for the Arts; 920/854-2210; www.thehardy.org) This August outdoor arts fair fills Ephraim's streets with more than 100 artists' booths.

Art Talk

Lena Negly, curator of the William S. Fairfield Art Museum.

We're defining ourselves as a museum promoting both local artists and artists of international fame. Our niche is to bring art to Door County that would normally go to larger cities. It's difficult to get our message out in a place that's so swamped with tourists. Our visitor numbers quadruple in the summer, so during the winter season our focus shifts to regional exhibitions and children's art shows. We have a five-story, 100-year-old sandstone building with a modernist design. We have an excellent collection of works on paper, including many prints by Henry Moore, and our high-season shows tend to have a works-on-paper focus.

Art Talk

Janet Comstock, director of the Francis Hardy Center for the Arts. We're the home of the Peninsula Art Association, which is Door County's mother arts organization. We've had a historic pattern of Chicago tourism, which is our main audience for the local nonprofits and the commercial galleries. Our founder's mission is to provide a central location for the artists of this community, so we're a showcase for regional artwork. Lots of our artists live here year-round. Our summer arts festival in August draws a huge crowd, and we're always trying to catch up with the expanding numbers of artists who want to be in the show and the visitors coming here to see their work.

American Folklore Theatre (Peninsula State Park, Fish Creek; 920/854-6117; www.folklore theatre.com) A true slice of Wisconsin under the stars.

Peninsula Players (Peninsula Players Road, Fish Creek; 920/868-3287; www.peninsulaplayers.com) Summer outdoor theatre on the shores of Green Bay.

Wine & Dine

Bubba Burgers (9922 Water Street; 920/854-9092) Double cheeseburgers, anyone?

Good Eggs (9820 Brookside Lane; 920/854-6621) Legendary breakfast omelets.

Old Post Office (10040 Water Street; 920/854-4034) Authentic fish boils and lakefront dining.

Accommodations

The Ephraim Inn (9994 Pioneer Lane; 920/854-4515; www.theephraiminn.com) Historic inn on the lakefront.

Trollhaugen Lodge (10176 Highway 42; 920/854-2713; www.troll haugenlodge.com) In the heart of Ephraim, a hop from the bay.

The Ephraim Motel (10407 Highway 42; 920/854-5959; www.ephraimmotel.com) Affordable rooms on the lakefront.

Information

Door County Chamber of Commerce: 1015 Green Bay Road; 920/743-4456; www.doorcountyvacations.com

Population: 420

The Rocky Mountains/ Southwest

Bisbee, Arizona

Even though it's located just a few miles from the Mexican border, Bisbee's nearly one-mile-high elevation lends this small Art Town in the Mule Mountains a much more moderate climate than one would normally expect from a desert community southeast of Tucson. A classic example of a former mining town that found new life as an artists' community, Bisbee and its now-closed Copper Queen Mine left behind a legacy that lives on in the form of a beautifully preserved, early-1900s downtown that's wedged into a series of narrow canyons. Among these is Brewery Gulch, which for a century has served as Bisbee's favorite place for unwinding and partying in a series of what once were rough-and-tumble miners' bars. Today, even though it's taken on a more genteel flavor as home to several restaurants, as well as a continual flow of converts to its unique take on desert living, Bisbee has managed to retain the spirit of its wilder past.

To enjoy Bisbee, you've got to park your car and trek up and down its wickedly steep, confusingly terraced, and alarmingly narrow streets. Concrete stairways that were built a century ago by mining engineers still interlace the town's front yards, back alleyways, and commercial streets, making the process of walking around here about as confusing as finding one's way from Jardin de la Union to the feet of El Pipila in the Mexican mining town of Guanajuato several hundred miles to the south. After much of Bisbee burned down in a 1908 fire, it was rebuilt in a gorgeous, neo-classical style using generous amounts of hand-carved stone. That's one of the main reasons why artists started moving here shortly after the mine shut down its operations in 1975. Cheap cabins notched into Bisbee's hillsides that in the 1970s sold for $10,000 now cost 10 times as much, but studio space is still plentiful and affordable due to the two- and three-story architecture used along downtown's Main Street and Subway Street.

Arts Scene

Bisbee is one of those places that's small enough, friendly enough, and funky enough to enjoy a high degree of participation in most aspects of its public life. The Cochise County Center for the Arts, an arts organization that stages and presents productions in its own downtown playhouse, has a rotating cast of characters and supporters that seems to include half the town. The same goes for the Bisbee Community Chorus and for Dance Matrix, the community's education and performance company for contemporary dance.

One of the town's pride and joys is the Bisbee Mining & Historical Museum, located in front of the Victorian-era elegance of the Copper Queen Hotel in a building that once was the mining company's headquarters. It has great exhibits on the town's old gambling halls, miners, and lawmen, as well as mountains of geodes and ore samples. A former grade school has been converted into the Central School Project, a complex of studios that's also home to a film series and an annual studio tour. Another old schoolhouse, the Lincoln School, is being used by the Southwestern Institute for Culture & Arts as a venue for year-round art-education workshops for adults and kids, as well as visual arts exhibitions and even a fiber arts workshop. Every October the Bisbee Fiber Arts Festival attracts weavers from across the continent to Bisbee for a week of workshops and exhibitions.

One of the town's most popular events is the weekly Farmers' Market on Saturday in Vista Park, which takes place from May through October. There are Sunday movies in the Earwig Factory, a popular venue that serves as a live-music hall for regional bands. Bisbee's Public Library is another venue for films, but to catch a new Hollywood release you've got to drive a half hour to a Sierra Vista mall. Many of the town's businesses serve as important venues for visual artists, and the well-known Café Roka is not only an alternative exhibition venue but also a performance spot for the town's enthusiastic jazz community.

Among the many reasons why Bisbee became an Art Town is the large numbers of artists who have settled here from places such as

Phoenix, Los Angeles, Tucson, Dallas, and Denver. There are as many as 10 venues serving as galleries or studio/galleries. Primarily local work is exhibited and sold in Bisbee's galleries, though for Bisbee's artists, tapping in to the regional arts markets and selling outside of Arizona is crucial to surviving on an artist's income.

Essentials

Visual Arts Venues

Southwestern Institute for Culture & Art (536 Tombstone Canyon; 520/432-4200; www.southwestern institute.org) Dedicated to multidisciplinary arts education and exhibitions.

Tang Gallery (32 Main Street; 520/432-5824; www.minatangkan .com) Exhibiting regional, national, and international artists.

Belleza Fine Art Gallery (29 Main Street; 520/432-5877) An ongoing project of a women's arts group.

Art Talk

D. K. Kiser, artistic director of the Cochise County Center for the Arts. We've picked up where the old Bisbee Repertory Theatre left off, using their facility and equipment to produce and present the kind of entertainment Bisbee craves. We've become a civic venue for all the performing arts and have expanded our scope to include a café and music. I came here a year ago to produce a play I had written, and it ended up running for nearly eight weeks, so I decided to stay and see what other sorts of surprises Bisbee had in store for me. I've been amazed at the kind of talented, experienced, and educated people who live here. People with top-level professional experience in theatre, film, and music now live here, and they're the ones who come through the art center's door, volunteering their services and time to help make our plays a success.

Performing Arts & Events

Cochise County Center for the Arts (94 Main Street; 520/432-6065) Community theatre and music presented in a former church.

Bisbee Fiber Arts Festival (see Bisbee Chamber of Commerce below) Mid-October gathering of the nation's top weavers.

Brewery Gulch Daze (see Bisbee Chamber of Commerce below) Early September celebration of Bisbee's wild side.

Wine & Dine

Café Roka (35 Main Street; 520/432-5153; www.caferoka.com) Gourmet spot, with great art, cool jazz, and fine wines.

Art Talk

Mina Tang, artist and gallery owner.
My work is mainly abstract, and you wouldn't think art like that would sell in a small town like Bisbee, but since I opened my gallery in 2001 I've discovered that all sorts of people from all over the world come here, and they buy the kind of art I make. Bisbee gets this very cosmopolitan type of visitor who comes here during the winter months and knows what they like. It also attracts a lot of artists who want to live in a small, tightly connected town that's laid out like a hillside Italian village. I've been able to establish my gallery as a place selling half locally created work and half work from outside the area, and all of it seems to sell. Paintings of the regional landscape always sell best, but we have a surprising number of people coming through here who are interested in figurative work and photography.

Old Bisbee Roasters (2 Copper Queen Plaza; 866/432-5063) Town's favorite artist hangout and buzz shop.

Bisbee Grille (6 Copper Queen Plaza; 520/432-6788) High-style chop house.

Accommodations

Copper Queen Hotel (11 Howell Avenue; 520/432-2216; www.copper queen.com) Elegant hotel from the turn of the 20th century.

School House Inn (818 Tombstone canyon; 520/432-2996) Bisbee's old elementary school, now a B&B.

The Shady Dell (1 Douglas Road; 520/432-3567; www.theshady dell.com) Airstream trailers and deluxe retro style.

Information

Bisbee Chamber of Commerce: 31 Subway Street; 866/224-7233; www.bisbeearizona.com

Population: 6,100

Flagstaff, Arizona

The words "alpine" and "Arizona" are mutually exclusive, right? In general, the answer's affirmative, but Flagstaff is an exception to the conventional wisdom. Laid out at the 7,000-foot level of the San Francisco Peaks' foothills, this historic college town close to both the Grand Canyon and the Navajo and Hopi Reservations is a place where cool climes and tall pines have for decades attracted summer refugees from the sweltering, low deserts of Phoenix, a three-hour drive south. During its long winters, Flag, as it's known, gets a big dose of snowy days and frigid nights, and the ski area called Arizona Snowbowl at the edge of town becomes a snowboarder's paradise.

Home to Northern Arizona University, a four-year institution whose fine arts department has evolved into an outstanding training ground for a new generation of contemporary painters, sculptors, and printmakers, Flagstaff retains much of its early-20th-century architecture and its aesthetic appeal as a Route 66 crossroads. For nearly a century, this was where transcontinental trains would disgorge passengers bound for the Grand Canyon and where dude ranches lured easterners with promises of cowboy coffee, Navajo blankets, and saddle sores. Its downtown is one of the Southwest's best surviving examples of sensible design, a place laced with walkable streets, stone courthouses, and wood-frame commercial structures that look as if they were lifted from the back lot of the TV's *Gunsmoke*.

Flag's downtown neighborhoods are filled with both unassuming commercial structures as well as a large number of Victorian mansions that have survived the past century in surprisingly great condition. The town's outskirts are a mix of the familiar Arizona sprawl along with gated communities selling fantasies of western living to retirees. There are a number of employment opportunities for artists on the NAU campus, though the vast majority of local artists are self-employed studio masters whose creative output is sold through galleries in Sedona, Scottsdale, and Santa Fe. There's a surprisingly high sense of cohesion in Flagstaff's artist community, and many of the town's restaurants serve as alternative exhibition venues for local painters. On any given morning, dozens of artists can be found wandering around Macy's European Coffee and La Bellavia, two hangouts on South Beaver Street connecting downtown Flag to the NAU campus.

Arts Scene

The leading arts institution in Flagstaff is the Museum of Northern Arizona, whose historic facility on the community's northern outskirts is home to a broadly focused exhibitions program and a festivals calendar with an ethnographic and Southwestern cultural emphasis. Every summer, MNA is the setting for arts and cultural celebrations of Hispanic, Hopi, Zuni, Navajo, and Pai societies, while through the rest of the year it offers a full slate of arts education programs.

NAU's Old Main Gallery is Flagstaff's premier exhibition venue for local and regional contemporary artists, as well as for the students enrolled in graduate art programs. The Coconino Center for the Arts, which has finally emerged from several years of hibernation, is a performance and exhibition space with a grassroots focus. Its 200-seat theatre and 4,000-square-foot exhibition hall are available for rent to outside presenters. Beaver Street Gallery, a recent arrival on the local gallery scene, is the premier commercial gallery representing contemporary art, while the Artists Gallery, a cooperative space in downtown Flag, is the community's best venue for local jewelers, landscape painters, and fine craftspeople. All told, there are a half-dozen art galleries spread around downtown, though Brandy's Bakery serves as the town's most prominent alternative venue, featuring monthly rotating exhibitions of local artists' work.

While downtown's art galleries have organized a very unpopular First Fridays ArtWalk, the most prominent annual event on Flagstaff's visual arts calendar is the Flagstaff Open Studios tour in September, a weekend featuring more than 100 self-guided stops. Wheeler Park is the favored venue for outdoor summer arts fairs. Like most college towns,

Flagstaff has a music scene capable of sustaining several nightclubs. The Orpheum Theatre is downtown's favored venue for touring national acts. The Flagstaff Symphony Orchestra presents its eight-concert season in the 1,500-seat Ardrey Auditorium on the NAU campus, while the Flagstaff Light Opera Company presents two productions annually. Theatrikos Theatre Company stages its year-round slate of six plays at the Flagstaff Community Playhouse.

Essentials

Visual Arts Venues

Museum of Northern Arizona (3101 N. Fort Valley Road; 928/774-5213; www.musnaz.org) Focused on the arts and cultures of the Colorado Plateau and the Southwest.

The Artists Gallery (17 N. San Francisco Street; 928/773-0958; www.theartistsgallery.net) Well-run artists cooperative in a prominent downtown location.

Old Main Gallery (Northern Arizona University; 928/523-3479; www.nau.edu) Elegant, contemporary arts space in a historic campus building.

Performing Arts & Events

Flagstaff Open Studios (Artists Coalition of Flagstaff; 2532 N. 4th Street; www.flagstaffopenstudios.com) Premier autumn arts event with more thanl 100 participating artists.

Festival of Arts & Crafts (see Flagstaff Convention & Visitors Bureau below) Large, outdoor show in July with national artists.

Art Talk

Roberta Rogers, painter.
I came here 34 years ago to go to Northern Arizona University and decided to stay when I got a job at the library to help students with their research projects. I had always been painting, and in 1977 the library ended up giving me my first show. The arts community back then was very small. A barn had been converted into an art center, and the art you found here was either crafts or landscape or art made by artists from the Hopi and Navajo reservations. Things started to change after downtown went into a slide. In the early 1990s a group of artists got together, found an empty downtown space in what had once been a hardware store. We started a cooperative gallery that was willing to show contemporary arts and it was immediately successful. We've been there more than 13 years and represent more than 40 artists from Flagstaff. Today we're one of the most important tourist attractions in downtown.

Art Talk

Joel Wolfson, photographer.

I came here in 1995 after living in the Midwest. I had been looking for a community that was into arts and culture, with the diversity of a university town. Flagstaff impressed me as a place with a strong, local arts scene. The university and the arts center present a lot of interesting shows throughout the year, and there's been growth in the local gallery scene. Downtown's First Friday gallery walk has really taken off, and there's around 20 venues participating. I've been able to exhibit my work in three downtown venues, and selling locally has been a new experience. I travel throughout the Southwest for my photography, I sell my work nationally, and Flagstaff is very convenient to this region's mountains, deserts, and coastline. I think Flagstaff has reached that point of critical mass where people want to be part of the arts revival that's taking place here, and that's a great thing for this community.

Flagstaff Light Opera Company (see Flagstaff Convention & Visitors Bureau below) Musical theatre organization staging two yearly productions on the NAU campus.

Wine & Dine

Brandy's Bakery (1500 E. Cedar Avenue; 928/779-2187) Popular café with great hotcakes and hot arts exhibitions.

Macy's European Coffee (14 South Beaver Street; 928/774-2243) The best coffee in town is at this artists' hangout.

Pesto Brothers (34 S. San Francisco Street; 928/913-0775; www.pesto brothers.com) Superb bruschetta and a smartly selected wine list.

Accommodations

Inn at 410 (410 N. Leroux Street; 928/774-0088; www.inn410.com) Historic B&B close to downtown.

Hotel Monte Vista (100 N. San Francisco Street; 928/779-6971; www.hotelmontevista.com) Affordable, downtown spot with a live-music club.

Weatherford Hotel (23 N. Leroux Street; 928/779-1919; www.weatherfordhotel.com) Traditional-style hotel with a gourmet restaurant in downtown.

Information

Flagstaff Convention & Visitors Bureau: Santa Fe Railroad Depot; 800/217-2367; www.flagstaffarizona.org

Population: 53,000

Prescott, Arizona

Arizona's stereotypical image as a desert overrun by scorpions is turned on its head in this picturesque, high-altitude community. Set in a mountainous landscape and shaded by tall pines, Prescott is just a 90-minute drive north of Phoenix but a world away in its weather patterns. Cool evenings and sunny days are Prescott's summer calling card, while its winters are filled with chilly nights and even some snowy weekends.

Though its fast-growing outer regions are reflective of the sprawl that Arizona's economy has feasted upon for decades, Prescott's lovely and historic central district has more in common with places like Durango, Colorado, and Ashland, Oregon, than it does with Phoenix and Tucson. Built before the turn of the 20th century as a mining town and territorial capital, Prescott has retained much of its prosperous, Victorian-era charm, which is why its residential streets and its gorgeous plaza look as welcoming as any Hollywood vision of small-town America.

Like many other places in Arizona, Prescott takes a certain pleasure in celebrating its wilder (a.k.a. "Zonie") side. No place in Yavapai County better demonstrates this tendency than Whiskey Row, a string of bars whose appearance and reputation ranges from seedy to rough and tumble, alongside one or two somewhat more upscale places, all lining one street bordering the lovely Plaza. On most weekends these watering holes are packed shoulder to shoulder with a wild assortment of Harley riders, college students, Vietnam veterans, ranch hands, tourists, and singles looking for fast hookups. The action starts around 10 AM on Friday and doesn't let up until sundown on Sunday. It's one of those must-see Arizona rituals that embodies this overheated state's wacky sense of how to have a good time.

Arts Scene

Like many of the nation's best Art Towns, Prescott's arts scene is strong because it's diverse. Much of the reason for this diversity comes from the creative input flowing from the arts departments of nearby Prescott College and Yavapai College, while another reason emanates from the influx of creative-minded individuals moving here from Phoenix, California, the Pacific Northwest and points east. A group of established artists has joined forces with environmentalists and outdoor recreation enthusiasts in forming the core identity of the local arts community, and they've been joined by recently arrived sculptors, musicians, and performers, all attracted here by the town's Victorian architecture and affordability.

Because of its proximity to Phoenix, Prescott has promoted a dense schedule of weekend arts festivals and events as an effective means for developing its arts scene. Summer movies on the town plaza are a tradition here, as are events such as Tsunami on the Square, a June weekend of jugglers, fire dancers, stilt walkers, and acrobats. Prescott's Saturday-morning Farmers' Market is one of the state's best, while its active schedule of Art in the Park shows around the historic plaza fills the middle of town with artists' booths.

Throughout the year there are music performances presented at both the Yavapai College Performance Hall and at the Elks Opera House in downtown Prescott. Though the town has several art galleries, sustaining a commercial visual arts space here can be difficult, which is why two of the town's best art galleries are the cooperative, artist-run spaces on Whiskey Row. Many artists choose to stay home and work in their studios, sending their paintings, sculpture, glass, and jewelry to galleries in Sedona, Scottsdale, and Santa Fe, which is why the wonderfully diverse Arizona Designer Craftsmen Open Studio Tour in late November is a must-do Prescott weekend for serious art collectors.

Trinity Presbyterian Church is Prescott's favorite venue for chamber music performances, while Granite Creek Park is the place for September's Arizona Shakespeare Festival shows. Prescott Fine Arts Association uses a former church building for its visual arts exhibitions, theatre performances, and concerts. There's a highly regarded visual arts gallery at Yavapai College, which also presents a year-round slate of touring national musicians and entertainers, and a promising gallery cluster along McCormick Street close to the Plaza. In August the Prescott Jazz Summit moves into local venues for several days' worth of cool tunes.

One of the most outstanding aspects of Prescott's arts scene is its capacity to support three art museums. The Phippen Art Museum has its focus set on living and deceased artists of the West, regularly mounting shows featuring the region's top landscape and figurative painters. The Smoki Museum mounts exhibits and sponsors programs on the West's cultural heritage and its connections to Native American peoples, staging its annual Native American Festival in September. Sharlot Hall Museum, founded by a poet in 1928, looks at the West's human and natural history, offering a year-round lecture series on Western culture, exhibits about the West, drama performances in its Blue Rose History Theatre, a summer youth program, and festivals such as the Prescott Indian Art Market in July and a Folk Music Festival in October.

Art Talk

Dave Newman, artist.

We'd been visiting Sedona for 15 years before moving here from southern California. We wanted a quiet, scenic community and didn't need to make our living from the local arts market, so Prescott seemed ideal. It has a real western flavor and a nice variety of weather. It's also convenient to Phoenix, which is important to me because I travel quite a bit from that airport. To our surprise, Prescott has turned out to be a strong market for my art. We opened up a small art gallery, and it's done very well, selling mainly to people from Phoenix who come up here during the summer to get out of the desert's heat. There's been a lot of growth here in the second-home market, and the tastes of these new homeowners has made it possible for more galleries selling contemporary art to survive.

Essentials

Visual Arts Venues

Phippen Art Museum (4701 Highway 89 North; 928/778-1385; www.phippenartmuseum.org) One of the state's top art museums, the Phippen features exhibits about the West's artists and culture.

Arts Prescott Gallery (134 S. Montezuma Street; 928/776-7717; www.artsprescott.com) The oldest of Prescott's artist-owned cooperative galleries.

Art Talk

Marthe Early, jeweler.

I moved to Prescott after a family member moved to Arizona and I came here on an afternoon visit. It looked like the perfect place, so I quit my job and moved here to learn ceramics in a Prescott business. The job was great, and I learned a lot about painting ceramics and the high-end ceramics business. Eventually I started taking jewelry classes at the community college, which was a great experience from the start. In two years I went out on my own, and now I have representation in 75 art galleries, fine crafts shops, and jewelry stores. Prescott's summer arts fairs taught me a lot about how to do business directly with the public, and while I don't do those shows anymore I now have five national shows on my yearly calendar. Prescott's historic and beautiful. It's a classic American community with lots of independently owned businesses filled with artists who like being in Arizona but don't want to live in the desert.

Van Gogh's Ear (156 S. Montezuma Street; 928/776-1080) The newer of Prescott's artist-owned cooperative galleries.

Performing Arts & Events

Arizona Designer Craftsmen Open Studio Tour (see Prescott Chamber of Commerce below) This late-November event is the best time to see where and how Prescott's artists live and work.

Prescott Fine Arts Association (208 N. Marina Street; 928/445-3286; www.pfaa.net) The town's leading presenter of theatre and music.

Blue Rose History Theatre (Sharlot Hall Museum; 115 S. McCormick Street; 928/445-3122; www.sharlot .org) Music and historical theatre in a lovely setting.

Wine & Dine

Bird Cage Saloon (148 S. Montezuma Street; 928/778-9921) Historic watering hole on Whiskey Row.

Murphy's Restaurant (201 N. Cortez Street; 928/445-4044) Friendly, two-story pub and restaurant, with a busy bar scene and great steaks.

Zuma's Woodfired Café (124 N. Montezuma Street; 928/541-1400) Popular place with a bar, outdoor patio, and great salads.

Accommodations

Hassayampa Inn (122 E. Gurley Street; 800/322-1927; www.hassayampainn.com) Historic hotel in pristine shape with a classy bar.

Hotel St. Michael (205 W. Gurley Street; 800/678-3757) Affordable rooms close to the downtown plaza.

Hotel Vendome (230 S. Cortez Street; 928/776-0900; www.vendome hotel.com) Lovely B&B in a classic, brick building.

Information

Prescott Chamber of Commerce: 117 W. Goodman Street; 928/445-2000; www.prescott.org

Population: 34,500

Sedona, Arizona

There's a darn good reason why this Art Town in central Arizona is considered the continent's most beautiful place. It's all about the breathtaking majesty of Sedona's Red Rock canyons, a series of towering, sheer-walled geologic formations that lend this new-age haven the appearance of a distant planet. Perhaps this explains Sedona's never-ending fascination with UFOs, energy vortexes, channeled spirits, and mystic healers. Add a high desert climate to that amazing natural scenery, one that delivers snowfall during the winter and 100-degree days in summer, and you end up with an ideal place to live and work as an artist.

Painters working in Western realist and transcendentalist visionary styles first started calling Sedona home during the mid-1950s. While the transcendentalist movement never gained much traction with art collectors, the town's Western realist arts community continues to be the guiding force for the local arts scene. From sculptors creating bronze monuments of Rocky Mountain wildlife, to painters recreating the Wild West's past, to landscape masters enamored with the Southwest's timeless beauty, Sedona's environment has made it a magnet for Western artists.

Like many of the region's Art Towns, Sedona has built its economy on the profitable pillars of tourism and real-estate development. Many of its weekend visitors come from Phoenix, a two-hour drive south; others are so attracted by Sedona that they make it their new home, relocating their lives and careers here from Los Angeles,

Oklahoma City, and points east. Sedona's neighborhoods are filled with an eclectic mix of architecture ranging from traditional adobe homes to two-story ranchettes. Spectacular views are common, and while the town's main streets are hectic during the summer months, from October through May the community's quiet enough to make curbside bicycle riding a non-life-threatening experience.

Arts Scene

The Sedona Arts Center, established in 1958, carries on as the central focus of this town's creative spirit. Many of Sedona's best artists choose to sell their work through the Center's gallery, which represents its member artists. The Center's exhibition space is small but imaginatively run, mounting painting, sculpture, and fine crafts exhibitions year-round that have both a regional and national scope, with juried shows centered on locally relevant themes. The Center is also one of the state's major art-education facilities, using its classrooms as a venue for year-round instruction in pottery, jewelry, painting, and sculpture.

While rubber tomahawk shops have overrun some of Sedona's uptown retail territory, several clusters of aesthetic sanity do exist here. One is the beautiful shopping district of Tlaquepaque, a place designed along the architectural lines of a Mexican Colonial village; the other is Hillside Sedona, a more modern place that's home to several art galleries and a great wine shop. In nearby Cottonwood and the old mining town of Jerome are a few other art galleries and alternative venues representing many of the region's best contemporary artists and craftspeople.

Art Talk

Robert Siracusa, sculptor.

I lived in Sedona for several years before moving down the road to Cottonwood, which is less expensive and not so crowded. For me, there's no greater luxury that having an outdoor studio where I can work year-round without worrying about getting frostbite. Of course, there are summer months when you need to be in an air-conditioned studio, but I prefer that to dealing with winter's cold. To me, Cottonwood is a charming place where the possibilities are wide open. People here have a live-and-let-live attitude about life, but they're also very friendly and supportive of what I do as an artist. I think of Sedona as a great place to live, but not an especially great place for contemporary artists to try and sell their work. Art about the West, and especially art about Sedona's landscape, does best here. If you're creating something different then you need to get gallery representation somewhere else.

Art Talk

Karen Ely, executive director of the Sedona Arts Center.

We offer about 270 art classes a year for artists from beginning levels to accomplished, and in the past five years these programs have attracted an increasingly national group of students as well as instructors. Our outreach programs go into Sedona's schools, and our adult-education program offers low-cost art classes for many Sedona residents. Our juried gallery and store are mainly showing work by Sedona artists, with preferences given to our member artists and those enrolled in our classes. We're in the process of converting our old theatre space into more classroom and exhibition areas for our visual arts programs, eventually giving us five fully equipped classrooms. Sedona keeps attracting artists and visitors who care about art because of its physical beauty. For 60 years this has been a quiet, supportive place where artists teach and inspire each other.

Canyon Moon Theatre Company presents a season of innovative works through its Mainstage and Splinter Series, performed in a former Sedona retail space. In late May the Sedona Chamber Music Festival brings its roster of national talents to St. John Vianney Church. There's the still-small annual Sedona International Film Festival in March and the outdoor Sedona Arts Festival each October, as well as the Shakespeare in Sedona Festival every July and early August. In recent years the Sedona Cultural Park's outdoor concert series has developed into one of Arizona's premier summer festivals of blues, jazz, rock, and world music. Its performers take to the summer stage of a 5,000-seat amphitheatre with drop-dead views of Boynton Canyon.

Essentials

Visual Arts Venues

Sedona Arts Center (15 Art Barn Road; 928/282-3809; www.sedonaarts center.com) Innovative facility, with great exhibitions and extensive workshops.

Lanning Gallery (431 Highway 179; 928/282-6865; www.lanning gallery.com) Sedona's leading contemporary art gallery.

Jerome Artists Cooperative (502 N. Main Street, Jerome; 928/639-4276) One of Arizona's best artist-run spaces.

Performing Arts & Events

Sedona Arts Festival (P.O. Box 2729; 928/204-9456; www.sedona artsfestival.org) Quality outdoor show in October drawing artists from across the Rocky Mountain West.

Shakespeare Sedona Festival (see Sedona–Oak Creek Chamber of Commerce below) Three weeks of the Bard in Red Rock country at the height of summer.

Sedona Jazz on the Rocks (1487 Highway 89A; 928/282-1986; www.sedonajazz.com) Late-September outdoor music festival drawing top national and international talent.

Wine & Dine

Thai Spices (2986 W. Highway 89A; 928/282-0599) After a day of hiking the Red Rock canyons, nothing hits the spot like a dish of shrimp pad Thai.

Oaxaca (321 W. Highway 89A; 928/282-6291; www.oaxaca restaurant.com) Best huevos rancheros north of Bank One Ballpark.

Ravenheart of Sedona (315 W. Highway 89A; 928/282-5777) Shade-grown coffee is the forte of Sedona's best buzz shop.

Accommodations

Best Western Arroyo Roble Hotel & Creekside Villas (400 W. Highway 89A; 928/282-4001; www.bestwesternsedona.com) Affordable. with swimming pool.

Sedona Village Lodge (78 Bell Rock Boulevard; 928/284-3626; www.sedonalodge.com) Budget rooms, convenient to everything.

A Territorial House (65 Piki Drive; 928/204-2737; www.territorial housebb.com) Quiet, wooded place on the edge of Sedona.

Information

Sedona–Oak Creek Chamber of Commerce: 331 Forest Road; 928/282-7722; www.sedonachamber.com

Population: 10,350

Tubac, Arizona

This Art Town just 30 miles north of the Mexico border has come a long way since it was included in this book's first edition. There has been a significant upgrading of the local gallery scene through an effort led by an innovative arts center whose influence extends not only to the visual arts community but also to local performing arts, music, and festivals. Artist Dale Nichols started an art school here in 1948, and soon his artist friend Ross Stefan joined him. From that modest start, Tubac has grown to a place with three dozen art galleries and studios, a coffee bar, an arts center, and a flow of tourists that slows down to a trickle during summer.

Established as a Spanish *presidio* (fort) in 1752, Tubac and its concentration of artists' studios and galleries is located on the grounds of what once had been a frontier garrison guarding Jesuits and farmers in the Santa Cruz Valley. What remains of the Spaniards' presence is preserved in the Tubac Presidio State Park, a short stroll from the town's gallery and restaurant district. The nearby town of San Xavier del Bac is home to a gleaming, white mission church established by Padre Kino in the late 1600s. To live here is to realize that the difficulties encountered by these first European settlers didn't stop when the indigenous Apache residents were deterred from their practice of raiding cattle ranches. Today, instead of being an administrative center for priests seeking souls to convert to Catholicism, Tubac seeks buyers for its artists' creations.

Nearby communities such as Patagonia and Sonoita have also evolved into attractive places for artists and other creative field entrepreneurs, with Sonoita becoming the center of Arizona's small but promising wine industry. In Patagonia, a former silver-mining town that's a roundabout drive from Tubac, a new generation of artist pioneers is settling in and changing things for the better through the establishment of several art galleries and a fall arts festival on the grounds of an old railroad depot.

Arts Scene

Tubac's art galleries have, in part, developed through the community's proximity to Tucson, which is less than an hour's drive north. Tubac's become a place where lower overheads and a steady flow of visitors have translated into art sales. Galleries from out of town have noticed this trend, which is why Tubac is attracting some of the high-end galleries that would in years past have located to Tucson. Monthly Tubac Under the Stars art walks on Saturday evenings have helped get the word out about the vibrant gallery activity here, as have well-publicized events such as the Tubac Festival of the Arts in February and An Art Experience plein air painting festival in mid-November. In Patagonia, the Fall Festival of Music and Arts is an October event attracting more than 150 artists to this cozy community's tree-shaded public park.

Tubac's is a diverse gallery scene, one where the emphasis is placed on artist-operated studio/galleries that maintain a friendly and casual air. There's a strong representation of fine crafts as well as some contemporary art, but the motifs that carry the day are Western realism, Southwestern expressionism, and Native American. A more diverse approach is followed at the Tubac Center for the Arts. Its 3,500 square feet of exhibition space is given over to national and regional invitational exhibitions as well as exhibitions focused on individual artists of southern Arizona. From September through May the center presents a performance series that features both national and regional

Art Talk

Nicholas Wilson, sculptor and painter.

I enjoy Tubac's proximity to the Santa Rita Mountains, which I paint in my landscapes. There are a lot of people living here who know a great deal about art, so another of the things I enjoy about Tubac is that it's possible to have an intelligent conversation about art with someone you just run into at the post office. Tubac has this wonderful, small village environment that makes it a quiet and comfortable place to live. When I'm working on a sculpture I just go out into my backyard, no matter what time of year it is, and start work. The climate here is perfect for much of the year, but things really slow down in summer when the tourists are in other parts of the country. We moved here three years ago from Wisconsin and have no regrets.

Art Talk

Michael Gibbons, painter.

We came down here from Oregon in 1996 and immediately fell in love with Tubac's architecture and its sense of history. We bought an old adobe from the 1700s and fixed it up, then bought the place next door, which was built in the 1800s, and restored that place as well. Now I've got the perfect studio environment that's quiet, isolated, historic, and beautiful. Tubac is surrounded by this wonderful setting of mountains and valleys, and we have the Santa Cruz River running just two blocks from our house. It was difficult at first to get acclimated to the desert environment, but since I love doing outdoor painting and learning how the sunlight changes my perceptions of the landscape, the weather was something I just got used to. Tubac attracts the kind of visitor whose ideas about art run more toward the decorative side of things than they do toward the serious side of art, which is why the art you find in most galleries is priced inexpensively.

entertainers as well as the concerts of the Tubac Singers. When it's not staging a performance, the art center is home to a comprehensive art-education program focusing on workshops for adults and kids. There's a kids' summer arts camp in July as well as monthly meetings of the local painting society, which critiques its members' work, shares business contacts, and helps unify the creative spirit that's grown Tubac's arts scene. Patagonia Creative Arts is another of the area's important art-education centers, with its Tin Shed Theatre serving as a 100-seat venue dedicated to local drama productions as well as touring music performances.

Essentials

Visual Arts Venues

Tubac Center for the Arts (9 Plaza Road; 520/398-2371; www.tubacarts.org) Diverse programs have made this mid-size facility one of the state's leading community arts centers.

Mesquite Grove Gallery (371 W. McKeown Avenue, Patagonia; 520/394-2358) Representing the best in local and regional work.

Cobalt Fine Arts Gallery (5 Camino Otero; 520/398-1200; www.cobaltfinearts.com) Contemporary glass, ceramics, painting, and sculpture.

Performing Arts & Events

Tubac Festival of the Arts (Tubac Visitors Center; 520/398-2704; www.tubacaz.com) For more than 40 years this been the premier showcase for local, national, and regional artists.

An Art Experience (Tubac Visitors Center; 520/398-2704; www.tubacaz.com) This November event is dedicated to painting in the clear, dry climate of Arizona's spectacular winter.

Patagonia Fall Festival of Music & Arts (P.O. Box 241; 520/394-2823; www.patagoniaaz.com) October outdoor arts fair with more than 150 artists' booths.

Wine & Dine

Tubac Deli & Coffee (6 Plaza Road; 520/398-3330) The town's leading buzz shop.

Tubac Jack's (7 Plaza Road; 520/398-3161) The oldest restaurant in Tubac is justifiably famous for its burgers and ribs.

Velvet Elvis Pizza Company (292 Naugle Avenue, Patagonia; 520/394-2102; www.velvetelvispizza.com) Calzone, pizza, and pictures of the King. Hubba hubba, who needs more?

Accommodations

Stage Stop Inn (303 W. McKeown Avenue, Patagonia; 520/394-2211) Affordable rooms with space for RVs.

Tubac Country Inn (13 Burruel Street; 520/398-3178) Comfortable B&B with private baths.

Tubac Secret Garden Inn (13 Placita de Anza; 520/398-9371) Spanish Colonial–style accommodations in the historic district.

Information

Tubac Visitors Center: 520/398-2704; www.tubacaz.com

Population: 950

Aspen, Colorado

This legendary ski town in the middle of the Rockies, which until the 1960s was still a place where a down-on-his-luck miner could run up a tab at local bars, has evolved into a year-round, international arts center. Surrounded by massive peaks like the 14,433-foot Mt. Elbert and the 14,092-foot Snowmass Mountain, natural assets are the reason why this place was first able to attract hard-rock miners in the late 1800s and in more recent times has successfully lured an unending procession of A-list celebrities, corporate leaders, and their entourages.

Most visitors still come here to ski through the champagne powder for which Aspen's justifiably famous, or perhaps they're in search of that perfectly cozy, $12-million, ski-in, ski-out lodge on a snow-blanketed hillside. Some are paparazzi lurking outside of nightclubs, hoping to steal a snapshot of a vacationing celebrity trying to quietly sneak into the night with a swimsuit model. But look hard enough and you'll also spot the legions of Spanish-speaking cooks, maids, and security guards from Michoacan who are paid better-than-average wages to man the hotel and restaurant battle stations and tend to Aspen's unglamorous chores. For them, Aspen is a dream come true of a different sort.

Aspen is a community loaded with contradictions, an amazingly beautiful place that's constantly at war with one billionaire or another with plans to build yet another mansion on a ridge overlooking the Roaring Fork Valley. Of course, it's used for exactly two months a year to host oil industry executives from Houston. Aspen is a place where the merely rich have nearly been run out of town by the wealthy, and where a community long ago learned not to blink when newcomers waxed on about the seven-figure sums they paid for their vacation lodges in gated communities with fluky names like Condor Wisdom.

In many parts of the Rocky Mountain West, public officials refer to the slippery slope of "Aspenization" when discussing the pitfalls communities should avoid as they wrestle with rapid growth. To be fair, there's another operative term in these discussions, the phrase "Santa Fe-ification." Both phrases have come to mean that the people who live in the most desirable parts of the Rocky Mountain West should not allow their communities to be taken over by a real-estate-development complex whose ultimate goal is to devour every trace of normal living and convert the community into a theme park vision. In the eyes of many long-term residents of the Roaring Fork Valley, the Aspen they once knew has disappeared forever.

But look beyond the Hollywood producers lunching in downtown's cafés, and you'll find there are still traces of the true Aspen for those willing to hunt for it. Parts of old Aspen are visible in the coffee and bagel shops where ski instructors and cops slam down carbs before heading out on one of Aspen's crystal-clear, mid-February days. Many locals get their fun fix at down-valley joints like the Woody Creek Tavern and Steve's Guitars in Carbondale. Late at night, other parts of the old Aspen can be glimpsed at places like the Cooper Street Pier or at the Double Diamond when it features local bands on its G-Spot stage.

Aspen's working-class folks have been resettled down valley in places like Carbondale, Basalt, Glenwood Springs, and even Rifle. This exodus has had an interesting, positive impact on the quality of life in many of these places, as artists and other talented individuals with connections to Aspen's arts scene have brought their studios, galleries, and arts events with them. But the lion's share of the region's arts action remains in Aspen, where the galleries do quite well, where the restaurants are crowded most of the year, and where plenty of tickets can be sold for concerts at the Aspen Music Festival.

Arts Scene

Aspen's diverse and balanced arts scene allows hundreds of Colorado artists the opportunity to make their living as performers, visual artists, musicians, actors, and presenters. Summers here explode with outdoor events that take advantage of the region's amazing climate, while the winter months are prime time for indoor pursuits in the visual arts, dance, and theatre.

The Anderson Ranch Arts Center and the Aspen Art Museum provide the bookends for a local visual arts scene that flourishes year-round, with more than two dozen Aspen art galleries as well as a dozen or more visual arts venues scattered down valley. Located in a historic building, the Aspen Art Museum has established itself as a place willing to take a chance on exhibitions by top, established, and emerging names in national and international contemporary arts circles. The museum also provides artists from the Roaring Fork Valley and the rest of Colorado with an important and accessible exhibitions venue. The museum's educational activities, from its members' tours of top North American art exhibitions to lectures by leading figures in the art world, as well as its year-round slate of outreach programs, serves as a great example of how an innovative and energetic arts institution can raise the art standards of a region.

When established artists from across the Rocky Mountain West discuss the places where they most enjoy teaching and working on special projects, more often than not the Anderson Ranch Arts Center is at the top of their list. This historic property in Snowmass Village has evolved from its 1960s roots as a hippiesque collaboration of artists studios in old barns to its current position as a multi-disciplinary arts center offering more than 130 workshops each summer to more than 1,200 visitors drawn here from across the globe. They come for the opportunity to work closely with some of the world's top photographers, sculptors, painters, jewelers, and furniture craftspeople. The arts center also offers outstanding programs for children, as well as a nonstop series of free artist lectures and artist exhibitions that embellish the lives of many Aspen and Roaring Fork Valley residents. While the ranch is busiest during summer, there's activity here throughout the year. Its public programs are set on a low simmer during winter months, though one glaring exception to this is Wintersculpt, the mid-January ice- and snow-carving competition that draws artists from across the state to compete for cash prizes.

Perhaps the best internationally known of all Aspen arts events is the Aspen Music Festival, a June to August gathering of the classical music world's top performers and its most promising music students for a series of performances and workshops in various local venues including the Wheeler Opera House, Harris Concert Hall, and the Benedict Music Tent. During the winter months the Aspen Music Festival tours a scaled-down version of itself through many Colorado communities, inspiring the development of tomorrow's generation of music talents.

Aspen's also known for its mid-winter Comedy Fest, a gathering of top comedy pros and emerging talents who, for an entire week, turn venues such as the Wheeler Opera House into comedy clubs. The Aspen/Santa Fe Ballet is based here, providing a two-city solution to the age-old question of how best to support the cash-intensive performing-arts form of classical dance in a cultural environment where limited numbers of individuals attend ballet's carefully staged performances. Another of the community's gems is Aspen Theatre in the Park, an effort of the former Aspen Theatre Company that's grown to the point where it stages four outdoor plays as well as a very highly regarded play-reading series during its summer season. The festival has also provided the impetus to renovate parts of Rio Grande Park. During the winter months another established organization, Aspen Stage, presents its series of plays and readings.

Many of the best Art Towns offer a range of art opportunities, and while Aspen has this in spades, it also has something less common in Art Towns: a bona fide nightlife. Instead of the usual live-music joint or two presenting reggae for the ski crowd or blues for the boomer audience, Aspen revels in a live-music scene and nightclubs that would be the envy of many large cities. Not only do a number of top-name music talents call this place home (at least part of the time), but entrepreneurs who have learned the music business's ropes have developed superb, new venues and upgraded existing ones. The Double Diamond is where top-names like Lyle Lovett, Sheryl Crow, and Bruce Hornsby appear onstage, while Cooper Street Pier and Ute City Bar & Grill are favored venues for regional and local acts. Club Chelsea is another popular live-music venue for rock, while Syzygy is the local jazz club. Hannibal Browns is another live-music venue, while at night the places to see and be seen include the J-Bar, Whiskey Rocks, and the Greenhouse.

Even bluegrass music has carved out a space for itself in this busy town, with the Beyond Bluegrass festival taking place each March and the summer months highlighted by Bluegrass Sundays atop Aspen Mountain. Jazz is alive and well in Aspen, roaring to life each June during the acclaimed Jazz Aspen Snowmass festival, an event that not only brings top acts to venues such as the Hotel Jerome Ballroom and Aspen Art Park but also sets up a stage on Cooper Avenue mall near Wagner Park for a series of free, afternoon and evening performances. Another free, summer concert series, which extends through mid-August, takes place on Fanny Hill in Snowmass Village. And on Labor Day weekend there's a traditional summer wrap-up when the Janus Jazz Festival

Art Talk

Dean Sobel, director of the Aspen Art Museum.

We have a national and international outlook, a tradition that dates back to the 1940s and '50s, when the first generation of Aspen's arts organizations started laying the foundation for an arts scene that doesn't limit itself regionally. Over the years, a number of people have come to Aspen, either as full-time or part-time residents, who have been involved at the top levels of art museums, symphonies, operas, and arts organizations, either as administrators or board members, and so the arts groups active in this town tend to program themselves to meet those peoples' expectations. We're not a collecting institution, so our staff is able to stay focused on our exhibition and education programs. We have about eight shows a year in our two visual arts galleries, with our higher profile exhibitions scheduled during the summer and winter tourist seasons, and local artist exhibitions during the shoulder seasons. Our exhibition's focus for our larger shows is on contemporary art created over the past 50 years.

moves into Snowmass Town Park. Aspen Filmfest stages its weeklong soiree in late September as well as sponsoring a festival of short films in April, and the Aspen Literary Festival brings top authors, agents, and publishers to town for a weeklong conclave in June.

Essentials

Visual Arts Venues

Aspen Art Museum (590 N. Mill Street; 970/925-8050; www.aspenart museum.org) Small, influential contemporary arts museum with active community programs.

Anderson Ranch Arts Center (5363 Owl Creek Road; 970/923-3181; www.andersonranch.org) Year-round facility with artist residencies, summer workshops, and artist lectures.

Basalt Gallery (200 Basalt Center Circle; 970/927-9668; www.basalt gallery.com) This first-rate art space down the valley features outstanding regional artists.

Performing Arts & Events

Aspen/Santa Fe Ballet (245 Sage Way; 970/925-7175; www.aspen santafeballet.com) Exemplary dance company with a regional and national following.

Aspen Music Festival (2 Music School Road; 970/925-3254; www.aspenmusicfestival.com) One of the classical music world's top summer festivals, running from June through late August.

Aspen Theatre in the Park (110 E. Hallman; 970/925-9313; www.aspen tip.org) Three-month outdoor theatre festival in Rio Grande Park.

Wine & Dine

The Red Onion (420 E. Cooper; 970/925-9043) Great place for local flavor, burgers, and brews.

Popcorn Wagon (305 S. Mill Street) Gyros, hot dogs, and popcorn.

Aspen Bagel Bites (300 Puppy Smith Street; 970/920-3489) Fantastic bagels and a great patio.

Accommodations

Christmas Inn (232 West Main Street; 970/925-3822; www.christmas inn.com) Family-owned spot close to the center of town.

Hotel Jerome (330 East Main Street; 970/920-1000; www.hoteljerome.com) Favored spot for visiting elites.

Sky Hotel (709 East Durant Avenue; 970/925-6760; www.theskyhotel.com) Retro 1950s hotel and hipster bar close to the ski lifts.

Information

Aspen Chamber Resort Association: 425 Rio Grande Place; 800/670-0792; www.aspenchamber.org

Population: 7,500

Art Talk

James Baker, executive director of the Anderson Ranch Arts Center.

We work quite hard at doing what we do, for an audience that's becoming increasingly international. We invite artists and instructors who are the best in their fields to come here, do their work, and teach art-making as a vehicle for achieving growth in one's life. We serve beginning to advanced artists, and we believe in the power of the human need to express one's creative spirit. Our teachers, in addition to being great artists, are also expected to be mentors and guides. We see art-making as a vehicle as well as an end in itself, and many of our students use art-making as a key influence in the process of deciding what their life is about and how they are going to develop a richer and fuller life. We have a resident group of professional artists who in many cases live here year-round. A third of our students are beginners, a third are professional artists looking to improve their skills, and a third are trying to determine the role art is going to play in their lives and careers.

Boulder, Colorado

Their names roll off the tongue like a list of fabled destinations: Lawrence, Kansas, Bellingham, Washington, Chico, California, Flagstaff, Arizona, Charlottesville, Vitginia, Oxford, Mississippi, and Burlington, Vermont. They're all Art Towns, and they are also home to major universities. Hotbeds of creativity, these towns enjoy healthy nightclub scenes, downtowns filled with historic buildings offering emerging artists affordable (if somewhat dingy) studio and rehearsal space, and yearly calendars filled with a wealth of theatre festivals, concerts, arts fairs, and studio tours.

Boulder, located among the breathtakingly beautiful flatirons rock formations on the Rocky Mountains' Front Range, is another of these places. Less than an hour's drive outside of Denver, this bustling, prosperous, and creative place is not only home to the University of Colorado but also the favored weekend destination for fun-loving folks across Colorado. Many come here for events tied to the university, such as the Buffaloes' football games on October afternoons.

But for others the attraction is Boulder itself. Not long ago, this eclectic college town was known as a hippie haven, a place filled with panhandlers, couples living in Volkswagen vans, and would-be flower children searching for remnants of the Summer of Love. Today, this community retains much of its flavor as a place where alternative viewpoints and lifestyles are encouraged and nurtured, if not exactly given government handouts. The pedestrian paradise of Pearl Street still has its share of street buskers strumming on guitars or juggling a few bowl-

234

ing pins. But it doesn't take much strolling time before one realizes that Pearl Street's coffee bars, brewpubs, and sidewalk cafés have evolved to fit into a more upscale concept of what's appropriate in a community's public space.

What's changed is that many independent types, from business owners to chefs running trendy restaurants, to fashionistas selling designer Italian clothes, to a tidal wave of baristas who have left Starbucks to start buzz shops of their own, have flocked here in recent years to pursue their dreams. Boulder has its share of big box and national chain retailers and restaurants on the community's outskirts. But the activist nature of this town's local government has bent over backward to nurture an innovative, home-grown type of entrepreneurial venture, and the results are evident on Pearl Street and its surrounding neighborhoods.

Arts Scene

Boulder's arts scene is diverse, well supported, and highly respected in national arts circles. One example is the exceptionally well-produced and professional Colorado Shakespeare Festival, one of North America's most acclaimed summer Shakespeare festivals. It's an event that's logged nearly 50 seasons in the Greek-style Mary Rippon Outdoor Theatre and the proscenium stage of University Theatre, both on the University of Colorado campus. The festival's July and August season draws more than 40,000 Bardophiles to its four, full-scale productions and brings nearly 100 actors and techies into Boulder to produce a season's performances.

Nomad Theatre Company presents its professional season of mainstream comedies and new works from November through June at its playhouse on Quince Avenue, and the community even supports a children's theatre company, the Peanut Butter Players, which stages plays year-round and conducts a summer theatre camp for kids. Upstart Crow Theatre Company, an alternative troupe presenting original and contemporary work, conducts its season at the Dairy Center for the Arts. The Boulder Philharmonic Orchestra and Boulder Ballet perform at Mackey Auditorium on the CU campus, which is also home to the Artist Series, a nine-month slate of performing-arts presentations by international musicians, dancers, and thespians. The chill of winter's months is warmed up by the performances of the Boulder Bach Festival and the Boulder Chorale, and for an entirely different take on performing arts there's Naropa Institute's slate of Buddhist-inspired music and dance presentations.

While Boulder is considered to be one of the nation's most enthusiastically outdoor-recreation-focused communities, its visual arts scene is vigorous, diverse, and constantly in search of the new. It all starts with the Boulder Museum of Contemporary Art, an institution whose reputation for staging exhibitions by some of the best national and international contemporary arts talents is well deserved. BMoCA, as it's commonly known, offers a year-round slate of lectures, films, performances, and workshops to the community, and many of these are coordinated with the institution's energetic slate of changing exhibitions by local, national, and international talents. Art along more traditional lines is the specialty of the Leanin' Tree Museum of Western Art, a corporate-sponsored yet publicly accessible collection of landscape and figurative works. On the university campus there's the CU Art Galleries, located in the Fine Arts building and focused on presenting cutting-edge contemporary work.

Another of the greatest assets of Boulder's arts scene is the Dairy Center for the Arts, a massive complex now filled with visual arts galleries, performance spaces, and offices for many of the community's art-oriented nonprofits. This former ice-cream and yogurt factory uses its space year-round, and its art galleries exhibit a wide range of contemporary work. Several arts nonprofits are headquartered here, including dance companies, community-access cable television, and theatre companies.

Downtown Boulder supports more than a dozen art galleries, many of which are located along the tree-shaded Pearl Street pedestrian mall. It's all here, from new age mysticism to cowboy romanticism. There's also art displayed on the walls of local restaurants, coffee bars, and music stores. One of the premier art experiences on Pearl Street is a walk through the Boulder Arts & Crafts Cooperative, an artist-founded venture that's endured more than 30 years of up-and-down economic cycles. Owned and operated by its 45-member artists, the cooperative is a great place to get a sense of the creative integrity that's helped Boulder's arts scene to flourish.

As is the case in most Art Towns with influential universities, Boulder's the home to a dynamic and well-patronized live-music and nightclub scene. Venues such as the Boulder and Fox Theatres book the latest and greatest in touring national acts, while more than a dozen clubs give local and regional jazz musicians, rockers, DJs, and hip-hop acts the venues they need to hone their acts and reach their audiences. And anyone looking to bump into some of Boulder's artists, musicians, and entertainers during daylight hours should probably take a look inside the Boulder Dushanbe Teahouse, a gift to the city from its sister city of Dushanbe, Tajikistan. Tajik craftsmen built this structure and shipped it piecemeal to Boulder. It now serves teas from across the globe and hosts the Rocky Mountain Tea Festival in August.

Essentials

Visual Arts Venues

Boulder Museum of Contemporary Art (1750 13th Street; 303/443-2122; www.bmoca.org) Innovatively programmed and focused on presenting top examples of work from established, emerging, and regional artists.

Boulder Arts & Crafts Cooperative (1421 Pearl Street; 303/443-3683; www.boulderartsandcrafts.com) Representing top regional artisans working in a range of media.

The Dairy Gallery (2590 Walnut Street; 303/440-7826; www.thedairy .org) Known for great exhibitions, including those of its Community Curator program, which presents innovative voices from the region's contemporary arts community.

Performing Arts & Events

Colorado Shakespeare Festival (303/492-0554; www.colorado shakes.org) Presents its award-winning performances on the CU campus in both indoor and outdoor venues.

Kinetic Conveyance Race (303/444-5226; www.kbco.com) This annual, early-May gathering of artists at Boulder Reservoir draws 40,000 sun lovers to witness various craft attempting to float and race across the reservoir's waters.

Art Talk

Charmain Schuh, program director for the Dairy Center for the Arts. We moved into an old, 40,000-square-foot-dairy building that was scheduled to be torn down, after convincing the city that the arts groups in Boulder would flourish in a low-cost environment like this. We turned the dairy's huge refrigerated rooms into studios for dance and visual arts, took out the old railroad tracks, turned the loading docks into a 250-seat theatre, which has added to our 150-seat theatre-in-the-round and our 78-seat, black box space. We're busy all the time because Boulder has so many groups that need performance space. Our three visual arts spaces are run individually. In one we have our Community Curator program for local or statewide artists, in another we have our In Focus gallery, dedicated to photography, and then we have our Polly Addison space in the main lobby area, which shows work by local and regional artists.

Art Talk

Richard Devin, artistic director of the Colorado Shakespeare Festival.
Our audiences average from 36,000 to 42,000 yearly, and it's certainly an advantage for us being just 26 miles from Denver, a city that provides us with 70 percent of our summer audience. We're the largest arts organization in Boulder County and employ about 200 people for 90 days each summer. We're not like other Shakespeare festivals that are in themselves an arts destination for people on a three-day visit. Our audience comes here after work with a picnic dinner to enjoy a night of Shakespeare under the stars. We're the second-oldest Shakespeare festival in the nation, and we use a 1,000-seat, Greek theatre as our main stage and a 450-seat proscenium theatre for our other plays. We also organize 14 different outreach programs around the state as well as a Shakespeare summer youth camp.

Boulder Art Fair (303/449-3774; www.boulderdowntown.com) This mid-July exhibition along Pearl Street Mall attracts more than 150 artists, and thousands of buyers from across the state's Front Range.

Wine & Dine

The Boulder Dushanbe Teahouse (1770 13th Street; 303/442-4993; www.boulderteahouse.com) Teas from around the world in an authentic, central Asian environment.

Hapa Sushi Grill (1117 Pearl Street; 303/473-4730) Live music and local art to go along with your spicy tuna roll.

Mountain Sun Brewery (1535 Pearl Street; 303/546-0886) Great pub grub and cold draft brews.

Accommodations

Briar Rose B&B (2151 Arapahoe Avenue; 303/442-3007; www.briarrosebb.com) Victorian charm in the middle of town.

The Hotel Boulderado (2115 13th Street; 303/442-4344) Classic, grand hotel in a 1909 structure.

Boulder Creek Quality Inn (2020 Arapahoe Avenue; 303/449-7550; www.qualityinn.com) Modern hotel, with a pool.

Information

Boulder Colorado Convention & Visitors Bureau: 2440 Pearl Street; 303/442-2911; www.bouldercoloradousa.com

Population: 95,000

Creede, Colorado

The highest of North America's Art Towns, Creede is located at the 8,900-foot level of the San Juan Mountains in south-central Colorado. Surrounded by national forests and public lands, this former mining community in a spectacular box canyon once housed 10,000 miners searching for mother lodes of silver ore. Today there's still a search on for wealth, but it's coming from a new source: vacation homes that are popping up around this scenic area like columbines after a summer rain.

The Rio Grande's headwaters flow from alpine meadows just west of Creede, and by the time those clear waters hit the town's southern flank they're a swift-running trout stream that from May through October lures thousands of anglers. The 12,000-foot peaks surrounding Creede still harbor a few hardy prospectors and small mines, though the fortunes of legendary sites such as the Holy Moses Mine have long since dried up. Being a boomtown that time forgot, Creede was able to hang on to much of its 19th-century architectural legacy, which is why the entire town has now been declared a National Historic District.

The great outdoors is at Creede's instant disposal, which is why living here means being swept up in everything from mountain biking to ice climbing, bow hunting, cross-country skiing, and high-altitude gardening. Fixing up one's historic home is a favorite local pastime, especially in order to prepare for Creede's legendarily long and brutal winters. Tourist season hereabouts slams to a hard stop in early

Art Talk

Julie Jackson, outreach director for Creede Repertory Theatre.

We're the town's largest employer, and as an arts organization we're also its biggest tourist attraction. Last year our season attracted more that 17,000 ticket buyers in a town of 400, so you can understand why the town loves us. We were founded in 1966 by some people from the University of Kansas theatre department who came here to revive Creede's old movie theatre, and it all started with 12 individuals. We now present a varied season of plays and events. Our main stage is used for two musicals and a comedy, and our 87-seat black box is where we do children's plays, dramas, and new material. Creede itself seems to be attracting a new generation of younger residents, people moving here to make a life change. They're either very artistic, or they come here to start some specific type of business, including lots of on-line businesses.

November and roars to life each May. Outside of summer's warm months, many locals get themselves out of here during winter, settling in among Tucson's palm trees while hundreds of inches of snow pile up against their Creede homes.

Arts Scene

Many of the classic, Victorian-era structures along Creede's historic Main Street now house galleries on their first levels and artists' studios on their upper levels. Some of the artists are living and working here year-round, and enough stick it out through winter to lend this community a decidedly artsy flavor throughout the year. Nearly a dozen storefronts along Main Street serve as galleries, which is more than enough fodder for the town's monthly Art Walk as well as a series of tourist-luring events that entice the art-hunting hordes. The very active Creede Arts Council organizes special exhibitions in the Creede Repertory Theatre's lobby gallery and also uses the theatre's stages to present summer concerts by touring national acts.

The biggest arts attraction in Creede, and one of the most locally influential of any Art Town arts organizations, is the Creede Repertory Theatre. Founded by an adventurous group of University of Kansas drama professors and students in the 1960s, this presenting and producing organization has developed into one of the Rocky Mountain West's premier summer playhouses. Thousands of tickets are sold for Creede Rep's short but action-packed May to September season. The theatre draws visitors from across the nation, especially Denverites making their 265-mile trek. Its main stage productions are geared toward crowd pleasers, with plays such as *A Tuna Christmas* and *Forever Plaid* packing them in. Less mainstream material is presented in the third-floor black box space. Creede Rep also offers a children's theatre season each summer, as well as a wide-ranging outreach program that tours its productions far outside the boundaries of Mineral County.

Essentials

Visual Arts Venues

The Art Park (105 N. Main Street) This outdoor space is administered by the Creede Arts Council and exhibits a rotating slate of locally made sculpture and fine crafts.

Rare Things (106 N. Main Street; 719/658-2376; www.rarethings gallery.com) Home to braided horsehair and jewelry, this gallery and home-furnishings store also exhibits work by local and regional artists.

Quiller Gallery (110 N Main Street; 719/658-2741; www.quillergallery .com) Studio/gallery base of landscape painter Stephen Quiller, who has painted the region for more than two decades.

Art Talk

Jenny Inge, jeweler and gallery owner. Creede has an incredible, naturally beautiful setting with access to remote wilderness. It's a place where you find people who are both interesting and friendly, and artists who prefer to work in an environment that has a minimal number of distractions. I moved here in 1974 when there were virtually no art buyers coming into Creede. Over the years that's turned around, and now the buildings in town have been renovated and filled with tenants. A number of people move into this area with the idea that they're going to live in a cabin and be completely self-contained, but if you want to participate in the life of Creede the locals are more than happy to invite you in. I run a business that survives on the strength of its main sales season, which is our short and hectic summer. That's how you have to be to make a life here, and you have to work hard to do that. Now I employ 22 people, and I live in a town that understands how important the arts are to its future.

Performing Arts & Events

Creede Repertory Theatre
(124 Main Street; 719/658-2540; www.creederep.com) This highly regarded summer theatre festival features mainstream and new material during its four-month season.

Taste of Creede (see Creede & Mineral County Chamber of Commerce below) This traditional, late-May kickoff to Creede's summer arts season features exhibition openings in all of the town's galleries, plus food booths along Main Street.

The Woodcarvers' Rendezvous (see Creek & Mineral County Chamber of Commerce below) July gathering and outdoor arts show featuring top carvers and knife makers from across the Rockies.

Wine & Dine

Café Olé (112 N. Main Street; 719/658-2880) Downtown spot for coffee, breakfast burritos, and bagels.

Creede Hotel & Restaurant
(120 N. Main Street; 719/658-2608; www.creedehotel.com) Historic inn, with a gourmet café and great breakfasts.

Tommyknocker's Tavern (101 N. Main Street; 719/658-0138) Best burgers and brews in the county.

Accommodations

Creede Hotel & Restaurant (120 N. Main Street; 719/658-2608; www.creedehotel.com). Comfortable, affordable rooms in Old-style Colorado surroundings.

The Old Firehouse B&B (123 N. Main Street; 719/658-0212) Large rooms in a converted fire station.

Blessings Inn (422 S. Main Street; 719/658-0215) Hot tubs and a spa just south of town.

Information

Creede & Mineral County Chamber of Commerce: 1207 N. Main Street; 719/658-2374; www.creede.com

Population: 377

Durango, Colorado

photographer friend of mine came up with a great way to describe this historic town in southwest Colorado. He calls the place "Base Camp Durango," as it seemed to him that at least half the town was perpetually engaged in some strenuous outdoor activity involving mountains, rivers, bicycles, or skis . . . and sometimes all of these in just one day. Established in 1881 as a frontier mining town on the Animas River, Durango has retained much of its historic Victorian-era architecture in both its downtown commercial district and in the tree-lined neighborhoods fanning out from the beautifully maintained depot of the Durango & Silverton Narrow Gauge Railroad. This masterpiece of civil engineering provides a daily link to the artsy and equally outdoorsy town of Silverton, another former mining community, located at the 9,300-foot level of the San Juan Mountains.

Its location is one of the best things Durango has going for it. Just 36 miles west of here is Mesa Verde National Park, a treasure trove of ancient Anaasází cliff dwellings. Also nearby are Hovenweep National Monument and the Glen Canyon National Recreation Area, one of the West's premier sites for houseboating. To the north of downtown is the Durango Mountain Resort ski area, and just a roundabout, two-hour drive northwest of here is the Art Town of Telluride. The La Plata and Animas Rivers are two of the best trout-fishing rivers in the Southwest. Some anglers prefer those sections of the rivers running across the Southern Ute Indian Reservation. The tribe's very successful Sky Ute Casino has spawned two major additions to the region's quality of life:

the Southern Ute Indian Cultural Center and the annual Rally in the Rockies, a September biker gathering and concert series.

Durango is also home to Fort Lewis College, a four-year institution that attracts thousands of nightclub-going, free-spending, low-wage-earning college students. That's why Durango is able to support a respectable nightlife and live-music scene, and it's also why this community has an above-average number of tattoo shops, music stores, and bicycle-repair specialists.

Arts Scene

Durango's dozen or so downtown art galleries represent an intriguing range of art. There are influences from both the Native American and Hispanic cultures of the Southwest, as well as a growing importance attached to contemporary arts. Some of the artists working here have representation in New Mexico's high-powered arts scene as well as a presence in Colorado's contemporary arts scene. There's a strong presence of traditional Western cowboy art and regional landscape painting.

What Durango is short on isn't local arts talent or the presence of art dealers willing to promote strong regional work. A scarcity of collectors has prevented this community's visual arts scene from exploding into a powerhouse, which is why an expansion of cultural tourist numbers is critical to the long-term economic viability of Durango's arts sector.

The highlight of the year for visual artists comes when tens of thousands of art lovers show up downtown each August for the Main Street Arts Festival, an outdoor show that features more than 100 artists' booths. There's no understating the critical role the Durango Arts Center, located downtown in a former car dealership, plays in shaping and promoting the region's visual and performing-arts scenes, as well as the Main Street Arts Festival. Its year-round gallery exhibits, lectures, films, performances, and arts community meetings are the glue that binds local artists and arts groups to one another. The region's other major visual arts venues are the Southern Ute Indian Cultural Center and the Fort Lewis College Art Gallery, which features an innovative mix of regional and local talent in its one-artist and group exhibitions.

The Community Concert Hall at Fort Lewis College is Durango's premier venue for touring dance, theatre, and music talent. It's also the home of the San Juan Symphony and one of several venues used by Music in the Mountains, a highly regarded July and August series of classical music concerts, recitals, and workshops in a large tent at the base of the ski area. Every April the Durango Bluegrass Meltdown kicks the summer arts season into gear, and by the time the Silverton Jubilee Folk Music Festival roars to life in late June, Durango's arts scene is cranking at full speed. Summer drama from Silverton's A Theatre Group, which performs its five-play season at the Miners Union Theatre, is a local tradition, as is the Diamond Circle Melodrama at the Strater Hotel in downtown Durango. Trimble Hot Springs, a natural mineral spring on Durango's northern flank, presents its free summer concert series on Sunday afternoons, while the Durango Film Festival in March showcases independent American and international filmmakers. Every Labor Day, Durango closes out its summer with classic rock's head bangers showcased at the Rally in the Rockies, a massive biker fest on the Southern Ute Reservation.

Essentials

Visual Arts Venues

Durango Arts Center
(802 E. 2nd Avenue; 970/259-2606; www.durangoarts.org) Downtown arts center with year-round exhibitions, performances, and events.

The Fort Lewis College Art Gallery (1000 Rim Drive; 970/247-7167; www.fortlewis.edu) Durango's premier space for touring and regional shows.

Art Talk

Laurie Dickson, photographer and author.

This place's beauty and majesty, as well as the idea of living so close to wilderness, is what inspires and compels many artists to move to Durango. For those who come, Durango turns out to be an important piece in the puzzle of how you live in order to create the kind of art that you want to do. The first time I came here was in 1977, and it immediately felt like home. I moved here full time in 1989 and haven't regretted a minute of it. Back in those early years, this was a quiet and economically depressed place with a very small art center and a large creative community. Now our economy, especially the real-estate end of it, is moving along quite well, and Durango has one of Colorado's best art centers. There's been an overall improvement to the quality of art that's created here, and Durango's artists now have a sense of professionalism and depth that used to be the exception to the rule. We have a large number of artists who live here but aren't represented by galleries here. They just love living in this amazing place.

Art Talk

Brian Wagner, musician and executive director of the Durango Arts Center.

We're an arts center with three distinct functions, operating in a 17,000-square-foot facility with two art galleries, a gallery shop, a theatre, offices for arts nonprofits, a children's museum, a workshop/classroom, a library, and a conference room. We're the quasi-official local arts agency for LaPlata County. Our exhibitions program is divided among juried shows, shows based upon our Four Corners' regional landscape, nonjuried exhibitions of our members' work, and a series of exhibitions that feature three regional artists in four shows each year. Our college tends to attract a very talented, artistic type of student, and many of those graduating from the college find ways to stay on in town. We offer a lot of year-round art classes for adults and children, and we collaborate with Ft. Lewis College in efforts to bring strength to the local performing-arts groups, especially in areas such as dance. Durango has become a destination for retirees, and they've brought a tremendous amount of talent and energy to the arts center and its programs.

Southern Ute Indian Cultural Center (Highway 172, Ignacio; 970/563-9583; www.southernute museum.org) Exhibits top Native American artists from the Southwest.

Performing Arts & Events

San Juan Symphony (970/247-7657; www.sanjuan symphony.com) This classical music organization presents its season at the Fort Lewis College Community Concert Hall.

Silverton Jubilee Folk Music Festival (800/752-4494) June outdoor festival with national acts performing in a 9,300-foot-high meadow.

Rally in the Rockies (see Durango Area Tourism Office below) Labor Day motorcycle festival on the Southern Ute Reservation with rock concerts, an outdoor arts fair, and lots of beer.

Wine & Dine

Club Scoot n' Blues (900 Main Avenue; 970/259-1400; www.scootn blues.com) Durango's favorite spot for live music.

Lady Falconburgh's Barley Exchange (640 Main Avenue; 970/382-9664; www.ladyfalconburgh .com) Huge sandwiches, 150 brews, and a great selection of scotches.

Farquahrts Restaurant (725 Main Avenue; 970/247-4427; www.farquahrts.com) Classic American food in the historic downtown.

Accommodations

Grand Imperial Hotel (1219 Green Street; 800/341-3340; www.grandimperialhotel.com) Victorian-era hotel with 40 rooms, located in Silverton.

Durango Lodge (150 East 5th Street; 970/247-0955; www.durango lodge.com) Affordable rooms, with a swimming pool, in downtown Durango.

Dollar Inn (2391 Main Avenue; 970/247-0593) Great value and tidy rooms close to downtown.

Information

Durango Area Tourism Office: 111 S. Camino del Rio; 800/525-8855; www.durango.org

Population: 13,900

Loveland, Colorado

Located about an hour's drive north of Denver, Loveland has not only revitalized itself through the presence of art and artists but has harnessed growth opportunities through the arts. Not long ago, this place was stuck on the roller-coaster cycles of an agricultural-based economy and the national attention it drew around Valentine's Day (a.k.a. Love Land). Otherwise, Loveland was the kind of place where retirees found quiet streets and where kids dreamed of escaping to Denver. Fortunately, much of Loveland's unpretentious, middle-class charm remains. Its neighborhoods are tidy and still quiet, while its downtown reflects as much all-American charm as does any Art Town.

Loveland's blessed with a year-round abundance of water flowing from 12,000-foot Rocky Mountain front range peaks, an hour's drive from downtown's Benson Park. This means that during the summer months Lovelanders can enjoy water skiing and sailing on the 1,700 acres of Boyd Lake State Park, while during winter the powdery slopes of family-friendly Loveland Ski Area are within easy reach.

Loveland provided the inspiration for this book's original version. I came through here in the early 1990s after a Santa Fe friend told me about a summer arts festival that was attracting many of the Rocky Mountain West's best sculptors. To my delight, what I found was a place absolutely excited about three-dimensional art. Foundries had moved into town to serve a community of several dozen artists who were working in bronze, realist sculpture. Soon, artists from other parts of the country who were having their work sized, molded, cast, and patinaed in Loveland's foundries had decided to move here on a part-time basis. Over the years, increasing numbers of artists calculated that the travel time spent between their homes and the Colorado foundries creating their work could be better invested while working in a Loveland home studio.

Accompanying these sculptors was a wave of craftspeople and arts specialists engaged in everything from building crates for shipping completed sculptures to technicians who crafted marble bases for sculpture, and dozens of studio assistants recently graduated from university arts departments. Today several hundred Loveland families now rely on the sculpture business's revenues to keep their mortgages paid. Home values have risen in recent years as more and more sculptors from across the nation have decided that living in a place where they're surrounded by other sculptors, and where well-trained studio assistants, suppliers, and foundries are readily available, simply makes good business sense.

The City of Loveland has developed one of the most successful public arts programs in North America. Monumental scale bronze sculpture is installed across the community, most especially at the city's entrances, the bucolic setting of City Hall and at Benson Park, a lovely retreat surrounded by sprawling gardens and lush lawns. To live here is to reside in a place where the economic potential and the aesthetic influence of art are evident around practically every corner. From bronze turtles crawling through a public garden to a soaring, Native American warrior sculpture at the town's north gateway, the message that sculpture communicates to Loveland's visitors and residents is crystal clear: Welcome to the town where sculpture is king.

Arts Scene

The decision to institute Colorado's first Art in Public Places program, which from its beginning in 1985 set aside 1 percent or slightly more of every publicly funded, capital improvement project of $50,000 or greater for a public art purchase fund, has resulted in Loveland's having a public art collection valued at several million dollars. Some of the early success of this effort was the result of the local impact of Art Castings of Colorado, a 25,000-square-foot foundry established in the early 1970s. While Loveland now is home to several foundries, the spearhead role that Art Castings played in elevating Loveland's arts conscience is part of local legend. Its expertise attracted the first members of what's evolved into a national sculpture community with big-time clout in the local economy.

There's so much sculpture being created here that when one meets someone who describes him- or herself as an artist, the safe assumption to make is that they mean they're a sculptor. Among Loveland's arts community, painters are categorized as "flatworkers," and are quick to describe their expertise as "two-dimensional art." Oh well, if wood turners ruled the world I'm sure things would be equally odd.

The highlight of Loveland's yearly arts calendar takes place in early August when two massive outdoor sculpture exhibitions take place across the street from one another. Sculpture in the Park, the older and more tightly juried of these two shows, fills up the better part of Benson Park with its enormous tents and upscale evening events, attracting artists from across the continent. While the exhibition's emphasis is on realism, the show has expanded to include a balanced representation of ethnographic, contemporary, and abstract art. During this three-day event, standing alongside their work, sculptors chat with the curious while seeking out potential collectors.

Just across Taft Avenue, on that same August weekend, the Loveland Sculpture Invitational takes place on the grounds of Loveland High School. This equally large outdoor show tends to include more Western-style realism and has developed a reputation as a great venue for emerging art talents. The combined impact of both these shows has proved irresistible to art collectors and gallery owners. And as if those two shows weren't enough activity, on that same weekend there's also the annual Art in the Park, a juried crafts show that takes place on the shores of Lake Loveland, just a stone's toss from the sculpture exhibitions.

While there are a dozen art galleries scattered throughout Loveland's pretty downtown, the focus of the community's visual arts scene takes place at the Loveland Museum/Gallery. Its exhibits typically cover local history and a wide range of visual arts, with an emphasis on sculpture, fine crafts, and ethnographic objects, as well as painting by local, national, and international talents. The facility also offers a year-round, performing-arts series and lectures, as well as art workshops for adults and kids, and a summer art camp.

The Loveland Academy of Fine Arts, established in the early 1990s, attracts mid-career artists from across the nation to its classes in sculpture, painting, and fine crafts. Loveland is just down the road from Ft. Collins, a larger community that's home to Colorado State University, which presents a top-notch performing-arts series and maintains several on-campus galleries. Ft. Collins is also home to a significant number of artists as well as the nationally famous Walnut Street Gallery, one of the top places to find visual arts and photography by well-known names in the rock music business.

Loveland's Rialto Theatre, a 1919 vaudeville palace that's been restored to its full, architectural glory, is now a 450-seat performing-arts venue used for everything from touring children's theatre to plays presented by the Loveland Stage Company. The theatre is also used as a venue for classic movies, film festivals, touring national music acts, and classical music concerts.

Essentials

Visual Arts Venues

Loveland Museum/Gallery (503 N. Lincoln Avenue; 970/962-2410; www.ciloveland.co.us) Multidimensional art space used for exhibitions, performances, and arts education.

Gallery East (229 E. 10th Street; 970/667-6520; www.galleryeast.com) Established art space representing sculptors, painters, and fine crafts artists.

Columbine Gallery (2683 N. Taft Avenue; 970/667-2015) Loveland's top sculpture gallery.

Performing Arts & Events

Rialto Theatre (228 E. 4th Street; 970/962-2120) This historic, downtown Loveland venue is the community's favorite spot for movies, music, and live theatre.

Loveland Sculpture Invitational (970/663-7467; www.loveland sculpturegroup.org) August exhibition that emphasizes

Art Talk

Travis Erion, painter.

Loveland's loaded with painters, but you'd never know it from the huge number of sculptors living here. I grew up here and have always thought of Loveland as a great place to make art and to learn how to make art. When I was in high school I had a part-time job as an apprentice in Fritz White's studio, just helping him on things. He gave me the freedom to draw out parts of his sculptures and work alongside him on building the different parts of a piece. Artists in Loveland are still working this way, still taking on apprentices and teaching kids not just how to be an artist, but how to survive in the art business. This town is a very supportive place to be an artist, with lots of facilities artists need and lots of places where artists can network. You give up a little in terms of local sales when you live here, but from what you gain back in lifestyle and being part of a community, it's worth the sacrifices.

Art Talk

Linda Prokop, sculptor.

I've lived here for 20 years, and the relationships I established back then are still important to my life. I was a printmaker at first, but after moving here I got a job in a sculptor's studio just doing the backroom work. I loved it, and I learned something new every day but had to quit for several years when I started my family. Then, once the kids got old enough, I started thinking of ways I could get back into sculpture, but doing my own thing. So I formed this idea for a certain working style and got a part-time job helping out a friend in her sculpture studio. After saving up some cash and getting my technique up to speed, I bought some clay and started working on sculptures in my laundry room. After I got them to where I wanted them, I had the pieces cast and they immediately started selling. Now I'm doing shows all over the country, and several galleries represent my work. It's been an amazing career, and I think it all happened because I live in Loveland.

contemporary arts, Western realism, and architectural works and is a great place to find new talents.

Sculpture in the Park (P.O. Box 7006; 970/663-2940; www.sculptureinthe park.org) Loveland's oldest sculpture show is filled with top artists and national collectors.

Wine & Dine

The Breakfast Club (1451 N. Boise Avenue; 970/461-1261) Popular morning hangout for artists.

Heartland Café (301 E. 4th Street; 970/669-7774) Straightforward and reasonably priced, with an all-American menu.

Braddy's Downtown Restaurant (160 W. Oak; 970/498-0873) This Ft. Collins spot has local art on its walls and a great wine list.

Accommodations

Cattail Creek Inn (2665 Abarr Drive; 970/667-7600; www.cattailcreek inn.com) Comfortable, on a golf course, close to Benson Park.

Rose Bud Motel (660 E. Eisenhower Boulevard; 970/669-9430) Plenty of room for RVs at this quaint spot.

Comfort Inn (1500 N. Cheyenne Avenue; 970/593-0100; www.choicehotels.com) Great place for families, and it has a pool.

Information

Loveland Chamber of Commerce: 5400 Stone Creek Circle; 970/667-6311; www.loveland.org

Population: 52,000

Paonia, Colorado

framed by 10,000-foot peaks and surrounded by eight mesas, this Art Town in the heart of Colorado's prime fruit-growing country has many natural assets, not the least of which is an endless supply of crystal-clear water. With its rich soil and 5,645-foot elevation, this corner of Delta County is famous for its early springs and long, warm autumns . . . conditions that are perfect for producing some of the nation's premier apples, peaches, cherries, and grapes.

This politically and environmentally progressive region is home to three natural resources protection groups, a national newspaper *(High Country News)* that tracks environmental and community development issues, and a top-notch public radio station (KVNF) whose programming somehow manages to appeal to this surprisingly diverse area's eclectic mix of hard-working farmers, studio artists, and recently arrived retirees.

Like in many of the West's Art Towns, life in Paonia is embellished by its proximity to breathtaking natural beauty. The Gunnison River flows nearby, and its Black Canyon has recently been designated as a national park. The river is an ideal place for white-water rafting and trout fishing. The mesas surrounding Paonia are filled with lakes, mountain-bike trails, and two-lane ribbons of blacktop ideal for long bicycle treks. There are several wineries in the area, and while their vines are still young their early releases look promising, which is why there's a great deal of local interest in the prospect of the area someday becoming a Western Slope counterpart to Yakima and Napa Valleys.

Arts Scene

Historic downtown Paonia, which is compact and well preserved, is the home of the Blue Sage Center for the Arts, located in the Curtis Building, a two-story Victorian-era structure. A combination community center, visual arts exhibition space, performance hall, dance studio, and theatre, Blue Sage is an arts center that's positioned itself at the core of this community's social life. The facility is used year-round for classes ranging from yoga to fencing, as well as music, art, and dance instruction.

One of the most active users of the Blue Sage is the Colorado West School of Performing Arts, an organization based in Delta County. The school's very active Amadeus Music Society is one of the region's leading philanthropic concerns, and its performances range from piano recitals to chamber music concerts and youth symphony.

Paonia's the kind of place that's most attractive to artists who have established their commercial gallery representation in places such as Aspen, which is slightly more than two hour's drive distant. They choose to live here because of the region's affordable real estate as well as its quiet and safe lifestyle. In Paonia, one can find a home and studio on ten acres of apple orchards and enjoy easy access to outdoor recreation magnets like Powderhorn Ski Area. The town's biggest arts event is the annual Mountain Harvest Festival, a three-day weekend in September when artists' booths are set up along Grand Avenue, special shows take place in many venues, and performances are scheduled back to back at the Blue Sage. In late August the Black Canyon Music Festival brings national bluegrass and folk music's top names to the Delta County Fairgrounds, while the annual Render the Rock arts festival in nearby Crawford draws many local artists to town for the express purpose of painting the Needle Rock pinnacle. There are several art galleries in the nearby town of Cedaredge, which seems to also be the county's top spot for fine crafts.

Essentials

Visual Arts Venues

Blue Sage Center for the Arts (228 Grand Avenue; 970/527-7243; www.bluesagecenter.org) A very active arts space, the Blue Sage offers year-round classes, exhibitions, and performances.

Daphna Russell Studio (250
S. Grand Mesa Drive, Cedaredge;
970/856-7005) Studio and gallery
operated by a prominent sculptor.

Lincoln Fox Studio & Gallery (P.O.
Box 178; Crawford; 970/527-6677;
www.lincolnfox.com) Studio and
gallery operated by one of the
nation's premier realist sculptors.

Performing Arts & Events

Mountain Harvest Festival (see
Paonia Chamber of Commerce below)
This three-day event in late
September includes an art walk, stu-
dio tour, and special exhibitions at
the Blue Sage Center for the Arts,
Lofty Perch Gallery, and Expressions
Bookstore, as well as music perform-
ances in the Blue Sage, Paradise
Theatre, and Lamborn Building.

**Colorado West School of
Performing Arts** (P.O. Box 792;
970/527-7407; www.cwestart.com)
This Paonia-based concert presenter
and music education organization
keeps classical music strong in Delta
County.

Art Talk

Thomas Smith, executive director of
the Blue Sage Center for the Arts.
We're located in a historic, 1902 hardware
store that we purchased in 1999. It's a
two-story building, and we use the
upstairs for gallery and event space and
the downstairs for classrooms, lectures,
exhibitions, and music. Other regional arts
organizations also use this facility, which
has 2,200 square feet on each floor. We
deal with promoting the arts and humanities in the North Fork area, which includes
the towns of Paonia, Hotchkiss, and
Crawford. Our art exhibitions program is
run through a committee, and we're in the
process of ramping up from our current
schedule of four shows a year. This area
has become home to a significant number
of artists in the past few years. I see them
walking through the art center's door, and
many of them seem to be coming here
based on Paonia's word-of-mouth reputation as an arts-friendly place.

Paonia Cherry Days (see Paonia Chamber of Commerce below) This
early-July festival kicks off Paonia's summer arts season.

Wine & Dine

Pizza My Heart (202 Grand Avenue; 970/527-3265) Favorite dinner
spot for the local arts community.

Butch's Café (1478 Highway 133; 970/527-6801) Great breakfasts.

Coal Train Coffee House (328 W. Bridge Street, Hotchkiss; 970/872-
5282) County's busiest buzz shop.

Art Talk

Linda Myers Bialobroda,
oil painter.

My subject matter has changed since I moved here, when I started painting the landscape. I live about a mile outside of Paonia on a quiet mesa surrounded by mountains and orchards. This is the largest organic growing region in the state, and during the spring and summer you'd swear you were living in Eden, there's so much fruit and vegetables grown here. I moved here from New Mexico, looking for a small town that was still living on a human scale, a place with great light, pure air, affordable land, and mild temperatures. I'm inspired by the soft, almost feminine landscape of this area. Artists here tend to be on the reclusive side. They live here, work here, and look to other places for selling their work.

Accommodations

Bross Hotel (312 Onarga Street; 970/527-6776; www.paoniainn.com) Historic, 1906 hotel in the middle of town.

Pitkin Mesa B&B (39594 Pitkin Road; 970/527-7576) Rural accommodations close to nature.

Whistling Acres Guest Ranch (P.O. Box 88; 970/527-4560; www.whistling acres.com) Horses, riding trails, snowmobiles, log cabins, and more.

Information

Paonia Chamber of Commerce: P.O. Box 366; 970/527-3886; www.paonia chamber.com

Population: 1,500

Salida, Colorado

Surrounded by mountain peaks soaring more than 14,000 feet high (The Fourteeners), this Art Town along the Arkansas River's headwaters offers an outstanding treasure trove of outdoor recreation opportunities. The Arkansas River's year-round white-water crashes right through downtown Salida, rolling under the concrete F Street Bridge, which happens to overlook a large section of the kayak racecourse used during each June's FIBArk Whitewater Festival, one of the continent's top gathering of pro white-water racers.

In a happy accident of 1980s civic planning, the historic structures of downtown Salida were spared destruction when the Highway 50 road-building project elected to bypass downtown in favor of what then were vacant farmlands. Today, box stores, malls, and chain motels line the highway's route. But Salida's downtown, which the local gentry once derided as too old fashioned to be worth considering for restoration, was turned over to artists, river runners, bed and breakfast operators, and coffee shop owners. That's why in today's prosperous Salida, this same downtown's coalition of progressive and creative interests controls a big chunk of Chaffee County's economic and political power base.

Like many of the best Art Towns, Salida is an affordable place whose older neighborhoods are tidy, safe, and filled with small homes with detached garages perfect for working environments. Downtown Salida is loaded with two- and three-story, turn-of-the-century commercial buildings whose upper floors offer inexpensive, light-filled working quarters. The historic Salida Hot Springs Aquatic Center pipes in naturally heated mineral water from a source 5 miles distant, providing year-round relief for artists with aching, or just cold and tired, bones. Though it's surrounded by towering mountains of both the Sawatch Ranges and the Sangre de Cristo Range, Salida itself is blessed with a much warmer than average micro climate that allows folks living here the pleasure of a long gardening season.

Arts Scene

In recent years Salida's developed a healthy downtown gallery scene that's been effectively promoted in nearby population centers such as Denver and Colorado Springs. There's a wealth of fine crafts created here, and the galleries are diverse enough to support everything from contemporary painting to the realist bronze sculpture more commonly associated with Loveland's arts community. There are a dozen or so art galleries making a go of things in Salida, and while there's some turnover, this is the kind of place that attracts so many talented artists and entrepreneurial art-business people that the visual arts scene has the critical mass necessary to renew and redefine itself year after year.

The premier event on Salida's visual arts calendar is the annual Salida Art Walk, a late-June affair that attracts several thousand art buyers into the historic downtown. More than 40 venues participate in the Art Walk, which does a great job of inspiring the region's artists to hook up with not just the galleries but alternative venues such as coffee bars, restaurants, and outdoor recreation equipment stores. Another big event for Salida's visual artists is the Buena Vista Gallery Walk in June, organized by the Arkansas Valley Arts Center and utilizing the 1883 Courthouse Gallery in nearby Buena Vista as a central exhibition facility.

Salida's performing arts are showcased at the Salida Steam Plant, a historic, power-generating station on the banks of the Arkansas River. The facility is also home to visual arts shows, while a sculpture garden on its west side provides the region's three-dimensional artists with a much-needed public exhibition space. Stage Left Theatre Company uses the Steam Plant's renovated environs for its year-round slate of plays and readings, while regional music promoters regularly tour blues and folk acts through the Steam Plant. This is also the main venue for the new Guitars on the River Festival in mid-September.

Essentials

Visual Arts Venues

Salida Steam Plant Theatre (Sackett & G Street; 719/530-0933; www.steam plant.org) Combined performing- and visual arts venue in an old powerhouse.

Articulation Gallery (131 E. 1st Street; 719/539-0600) Cooperative space representing two dozen artists.

Chivvis & Lovell (148 N. F Street; 719/539-4001) Contemporary works by local artists.

Performing Arts & Events

Salida Art Walk (877-772-5432; www.salidaartwalk.org) More than 40 art spaces on display in this June arts celebration.

Stage Left Theatre Company (see Heart of the Rockies Chamber of Commerce below) Local, year-round community theatre presented at the Steam Plant.

Art Talk

Greg West, artistic director of Stage Left Theatre Company.

The Steam Plant has been renovated into a great, 200-seat space with good acoustics and lighting. It's a perfect venue for our smaller shows, but it's not a space especially well suited to plays that call for larger sets. Our newer works do quite well in front of the local audience, and we've found that people here are interested in more than mainstream classics. I've been in Salida just over three years and established the company to enhance the profile of theatre in this community, to give it more than the occasional musical. We have brought newer works of American theatre onto the local stage and have participated in events like the annual Art Walk. I can see this company growing into a drama training organization teaching acting, design, and directing.

Salida-Aspen Concert Series (see Heart of the Rockies Chamber of Commerce below) This July event stages chamber music performances at Salida High School and First Baptist Church.

Wine & Dine

Cornucopia Bakery & Café (216 N. F Street; 719/539-2531) Downtown buzz shop.

Victoria Tavern (143 N. F Street; 719/539-9003) Live music and cold beer in a historic pub.

Dakota's Bistro (122 N. F Street; 719/530-9909) Innovative cuisine with regional influences and a great wine list.

Art Talk

Jack Chivvis, sculptor.

I've been in the art business here for 23 years, starting with an antiques store and then evolving into more of a gallery when my wife and I combined our shops after getting married. For the past five years I've focused on doing my art. Salida's a great place to be an artist if you're willing to stick it out during the ups and downs. The town has a great lifestyle, and having the arts scene take off in the past few years has been more than a lot of us artists could ever have hoped for. Now, the artists and galleries are widely recognized as the main reason more and more tourists are coming into Salida, and that if it weren't for us the downtown would be empty. Our main visitors are weekend folks coming here from Denver, and they're also the ones buying the most art, as long as the prices are kept in that $500 and under range.

Accommodations

Circle R Motel (304 E. Highway 50; 719/539-6296) Casual, affordable motel on the bypass. Room for families and RVs.

Gazebo Country Inn (507 E. Third; 719/539-7806; www.gazebocountry inn.com) Comfortable B&B in Salida's historic downtown.

Aspen Leaf Lodge (7350 W. Highway 50; 719/539-6733) Affordable accommodations, with room for campers.

Information

Heart of the Rockies Chamber of Commerce: 406 W. Highway 50; 719/539-2068; www.salida chamber.org

Population: 5,700

Steamboat Springs, Colorado

Tucked away in a spectacular alpine valley in northern Colorado, Steamboat Springs is a one-time ranching community that has evolved into one of the continent's top alpine sports towns after chairlifts began shuttling skiers uphill in 1963. Today, Steamboat Springs's six mountains and 142 downhill trails are the primary reason why not only tourists are attracted here in the winter, but also why many professional skiers choose to make this funky and somewhat affordable place their full-time home.

Outside of ski season this community serves as a scenic gateway into high-altitude corners of Colorado and southern Wyoming. Denver is 160 miles southeast of here, and Art Towns such as Boulder and Loveland lie across high-altitude mountain passes. Outdoor recreation is a main summer activity for Steamboat residents, with fly fishing and river rafting rating high on local lists, along with mountain biking and hiking.

In this corner of the state there's no denying Colorado's historic heritage as a mecca for cowboys and ranchers. Each Fourth of July weekend, one of the West's oldest rodeos, Cowboys Roundup Days, draws many of the nation's top pro rodeo hands into town for a celebration of ridin', ropin', and bronc bustin' at Romick Arena. There's a gala rodeo parade, a community pancake breakfast, cowboy poetry readings, and live western music on the courthouse steps.

As the ski resort's fortunes began to develop, Steamboat Springs underwent a growth spurt that's not unfamiliar to many Rocky Mountain communities. But perhaps due to its remoteness, the development crisis that completely turned Art Towns such as Aspen, Colorado, Jackson, Wyoming, and Sun Valley, Idaho, on their heads was tempered a bit in Steamboat's case. That's why the Steamboat of today, and especially the small communities nearby, remain places where working families can establish a toehold. This is still a great, down-to-earth place to live, especially for artists who love the outdoors.

Arts Scene

The heart of this town's arts scene is the Steamboat Springs Arts Depot, a station built in 1909 for the Denver & Rio Grande Western Railroad and renovated to include the Baggage Room performance space, the Eleanor Bliss Center for the Arts, and the Small Works Gallery. Larger shows are staged in the Eleanor Bliss space, while more contemporary works, such as an exhibition spotlighting the graphics designs used by local snowboard and skateboard manufacturers, are mounted in the Small Works Gallery. While there are a half-dozen or so art galleries in downtown Steamboat, many local businesses and restaurants are exhibiting regionally created art. The recently developed ArtThursdays program links together nearly three dozen downtown alternative exhibition and studio sites with music performances.

Among the places to see locally created art are City Hall, which houses the Centennial Hall Collection, the Artisans Market, a 20-year-old business representing Colorado artists, and Torian Plum Plaza, whose Thursday-afternoon ArtWalk brings out some of the best and funkiest of Steamboat's artists in a flea market atmosphere. The River Art Studio offers a year-round series of visiting artist workshops. During three weekends spread across July and August the ski area hosts Art on the Mountain, an outdoor show in Gondola Square.

In the summer months, State Bridge Lodge is Steamboat's favorite venue for outdoor concerts by touring national acts. From early June through August the Torian Plum Plaza at the base of Mt. Werner becomes the home of the Strings in the Mountains Festival of Music, a series of Saturday-evening concerts under a large tent, featuring acts ranging from chamber musicians to Celtic singers and cowboy fiddlers. The festival also presents the free Music on the Green concerts on summer Thursdays in Yampa River Botanic Park, a six-acre refuge featuring 35 gardens and many places to stretch out, relax, and soak in nature's beauty. Emerald City Opera presents one full-length production each summer at the Steamboat Springs High School Auditorium, while the Steamboat Community Players uses the 7th Street Playhouse to present its year-round productions and readings. Steamboat is home to the Perry-Mansfield Performing Arts School, which presents dance and drama events as well as its New Noises Festival live artist demonstrations during the summer months.

Essentials

Visual Arts Venues

Steamboat Springs Arts Depot (1001 13th Street; 970/879-9008; www.steamboatspringsarts.com) Multidisciplinary arts center in downtown's old train station.

River Art Studio (430 Yampa Street; 970/846-0791) Working artist studio with workshops by visiting artists.

Two Rivers Gallery (56 9th Street; 970/879-0044; www.tworivers gallery.com) Carries traditional and contemporary art of the West.

Art Talk

Jean Perry, painter.

I moved here in 1980 from Denver because this community impressed me as being a well-balanced place. I had always been an artist, and when I moved here I began painting realism. It was mostly the landscape of mountains, lakes, barns, ranches; and the community immediately took to my work and adopted me as a local artist. In a small town like this you feel certain responsibilities toward the community, so I became very involved in placing my art wherever people wanted to see it, as a way to let people know Steamboat Springs had its own artists. Today, there's a much larger presence of art in this town, and the artists have a lot of contact with each other. We may meet over at the Art Depot to talk about art, or we may get together to go out and paint somewhere. My career now takes me all over the country, but it's Steamboat's environment that influences me and my work the most.

Performing Arts & Events

Strings in the Mountains Festival of Music (1875 Ski Time Square Drive; 970/879-5056; www.stringsinthemountains.org) This summer music festival at the base of the ski area brings in a variety of performers, with a classical music emphasis.

ArtThursdays (see Steamboat Springs Art Depot above) Weekly event turning the focus onto dozens of art sites around town, with a shuttle bus service.

Art Talk

Nancy Kramer, executive director of the Steamboat Springs Art Depot.

We've been in our building since the early 1970s, after the last passenger trains went through here in 1968. The old Rio Grande Railroad used to run loads of hunters and skiers up through here. In 1980 we completed an extensive rehabilitation of this structure, and in 1994 we converted the old baggage area into a performing-arts space. That's now used for community events like plays, concerts, films, and meetings. Our front gallery is an 800-square-foot space that still looks like a train station waiting area. We select shows that change every month and run them through the year, mixing our exhibitions between juried invitationals, themed shows, and one-artist exhibitions. We have a prolific and inventive arts community living here. There's lots of art shown in alternative venues, and there's a sense of momentum building in Steamboat's studio scene.

Art on the Mountains (see Steamboat Visitors Center below) This outdoor arts-and-crafts event takes place three weekends in July and August, drawing local artists.

Wine & Dine

Café Diva (Torian Plum Plaza; 970/871-0508; www.cafediva.com) New American cuisine in a mountain setting, with a great wine list.

Geek's Garage Internet Café (730 Lincoln Avenue; 970/879-2976) Live music, good food, and affordable prices at this artists' hangout.

Mocha Molly's Coffee Saloon (635 Lincoln Avenue; 970/879-0587; www.mochamollys.com) Steamboat's best buzz shop and gossip station.

Accommodations

Steamboat Bed & Breakfast (442 Pine Street; 877/335-4321; www.steamboatb-b.com) Affordable rooms in the center of town.

Bunk House Lodge (3155 S. Lincoln Avenue; 877/245-6343; www.steamboatbunkhouse.com) Quiet place outside of town with affordable rooms.

Rabbit Ears Motel (201 S. Lincoln Avenue; 970/879-1150; www.rabbitearsmotel.com) Close to downtown and across the street from the Steamboat Recreation Center.

Information

Steamboat Visitors Center: 1255 Lincoln Avenue; 970/879-0880; www.steamboatchamber.com

Population: 9,800

Telluride, Colorado

Tucked into a narrow box canyon in southwest Colorado's San Juan Mountains, this historic community was once filled with miners who scoured underneath mountain slopes in search of silver and gold. But since 1972, when the first ski runs were cut into the sides of those hills, Telluride's idea about what constituted a "mother lode" has evolved by leaps and bounds. Today, it's skiers, snowboarders, and ice climbers, and the gold mined from their pockets, has replaced the yellow stuff that once came from the ground. Telluride has also successfully positioned itself as one of the nation's premier destinations for festival-goers, people who travel here from across the globe to celebrate everything from bluegrass music to mountain films to chanterelle mushrooms and Côtes du Rhône wines.

The older parts of Telluride are a treasure trove of historic, lovingly preserved, Victorian splendor. From the unassuming miners' cabins that line its steep-pitched residential streets to the majesty of century-old commercial structures such as the New Sheridan Hotel, Bank of Telluride, Pekkarine Building, and the San Miguel County Courthouse, the older parts of Telluride are almost as breathtaking as the mountains surrounding it. Over the past two decades, increasingly expensive residential development has pushed real-estate values toward stratospheric heights, forcing many long-term residents to move into neighboring communities such as Ridgeway, Rico, and Placerville. Today, homes owned by weekend visiting urbanites intrude upon some of Telluride's majestic views, and many Telluride conversations seem forever focused on the booming real-estate values.

Arts Scene

The strength of Telluride's diverse arts scene lies in its incredible capacity to put on a show . . . a really, really big show that fills hotel rooms for miles around, jams the town's parking lots and streets, makes a windfall for tow truck operators, and loads buckets of tips into the pockets of local restaurant workers. What started years ago as the slightly whacked-out notion of using aging jazz musicians and wandering bluegrass pickers as a lure to fill the huge gap in Telluride's summer tourism calendar has evolved to the point where near-pandemonium reigns across most of the warmer months' weekends. Telluride Jazz Celebration used to be a casual, fun way to pass an August weekend at Town Park. Now it's a dog-eat-dog battle for hotel and dinner reservations, as half of the state feels obligated to be here. Almost the same can be said of June's Bluegrass Festival and September Blues & Brews Festival. Three film festivals also highlight Telluride's calendar, bringing the best of mountain films, independent flicks, and mainstream productions here during the summer. By tradition, the festival season wraps up with the Telluride Mushroom Festival in late August.

Telluride Repertory Theatre Company stages most of its productions in the 1895 Sheridan Opera House, as well as presenting one classic play each summer in Town Park. The company, founded in 1990, presents an intriguing mix of new material as well as crowd-pleasing favorites. Telluride Chamber Music Festival presents its two-week season in mid-August, while Dance in Telluride serves as both a presenter of nationally known dance companies and the force behind a local dance academy.

The community's 10 or so art galleries need to navigate the fickle tastes of Telluride's visitors and second-home owners, which for local artists means there are not as many opportunities to sell their work in Telluride as they would want. To survive here as an artist you've got to be represented in Art Towns like Santa Fe, New Mexico, and Aspen, Colorado, or just hit the road and sell in crafts fairs. The Ah Haa School for the Arts, a long-standing and stabilizing presence on Telluride's arts scene, serves the region's artists as an exhibition space, education center, and performance venue. One of the Ah Haa's strengths is its year-round programs for writers, which range from presenting lectures by visiting authors to regular meetings of the region's literary community, as well as workshops to help local authors hone their marketing skills.

Essentials

Visual Arts Venues

Ah Haa School for the Arts
(135 S. Spruce Street; 970/728-3886;
www.ahhaa.org) Multidisciplinary arts
center with a strong educational
focus.

Lucas Gallery (151 S. Pine Street;
970/728-1345) Exhibits an innovative
mix of contemporary visual arts and
fine crafts.

Scott White Contemporary Art (127
W. Colorado Avenue; 970/369-0073;
www.scottwhiteart.com) Telluride
branch of an established La Jolla
gallery exhibiting top contemporary
works.

Performing Arts & Events

Beaux Arts Ball (P.O. Box 152;
970/728-3930; www.telluridearts.com)
This February event is the leading
fundraiser for Telluride's arts scene.

**The Telluride Repertory Theatre
Company** (P.O. Box 2469; 970/728-
4539; www.telluridetheatre.com)
Highly regarded community theatre
that stages new and classic works.

Art Talk

Judy Kohin, mixed-media sculptor and
executive director of the Ah Haa School
for the Arts.

We're a vibrant organization that's supportive of the arts needs of local residents by working with children and adults and by offering well-equipped workshop space for painters, photographers, and ceramists. We work hard at staying in the forefront of what our residents tell us they want, which is why we organize things like cooking classes and have started an internationally recognized institute in the study of leather bookbinding. Our children's art classes are usually full and have waiting lists. Our local exhibitions take place three times a year and generate huge amounts of interest. We also do themed invitational shows and one-artist exhibitions in all types of media for artists living within a 50-mile radius of Telluride. We have space in two historic buildings and own both of them, which is an indication of how strongly our supporters feel about the need to sustain an institution like this.

Telluride Jazz Celebration (see Telluride Reservations Center below)
This August bash brings top international music talents to Telluride
for a week of performances and workshops.

Wine & Dine

Baked in Telluride (127 South Fir; 970/728-4775) This bagel and
sandwich shop is a favorite place for skiers, musicians, and pet
lovers.

Art Talk

Kandee DeGraw, actor/director and board member of the Telluride Repertory Theatre Company.

In a small town like this the community-theatre people tend to wear lots of hats. We rope in new people with the lure of acting roles, and then gradually get them to accept more and more responsibilities until one day they wake up and find themselves on our board of directors. We present three productions a year, including our spring musical, our classic play in the town park, and a Shakespeare in the Schools production that tours the regional schools. Education is a large part of our mission, and we work at recruiting young people to take part in our shows, both onstage and behind the scenes. Our summer audience is at least half tourists, so in a way we have to compete with the festivals for attention. Telluride is very supportive of its arts organizations, and it's common for different groups to share their resources and expertise in an effort to make sure that everyone does the best job possible.

Blue Point Grill & Noir Bar (123 S. Oak; 970/728-8862) Seafood spot with a popular bar.

Honga's Lotus Petal (133 S. Oak; 970/728-5134) Sushi and sake.

Accommodations

Bear Creek Inn (221 E. Colorado Avenue; 970/728-6681; www.bear creektelluride.com) Friendly spot with European flair on the sunny side of town.

New Sheridan Hotel (231 West Colorado Avenue; 800/200-1891; www.newsheridan.com) Upscale and historic accommodations in the middle of everything.

Telluride Mountainside Inn (333 S. Davis Street; 888/728-1950; www.telluridemountainlodging.com) Affordable, comfortable rooms in the middle of town.

Information

Telluride Reservations Center: 888/376-9770; www.telluride.com

Population: 2,300

Moscow, Idaho

s the creative hub of a region extending from Lewiston, Idaho, to the middle of Idaho's panhandle, Moscow has become a destination for artists from accross the Pacific Northwest. Its older neighborhoods resemble the classic, tree-lined streets found in Seattle and Portland, while on the community's outskirts there's plenty of evidence that agriculture still drives the parts of the local economy that aren't tied into the University of Idaho (UI). Moscow's the kind of place that's somewhat remote, which seems to suit its 21,000 residents just fine. The closest city is Spokane, about 80 miles north across a stunning landscape of wheat fields and small farming communities. What artists love about this Art Town is its serenity and affordability, as well as its fingertip access to the cultural programming brought into the region by UI and Washington State University (WSU), which is located just 15 miles west in the considerably less scenic community of Pullman.

While the UI Art Department and its counterpart at WSU are able to provide jobs for more than a hundred visual artists, classical musicians, drama instructors, and sculpture teachers, for most Moscow artists living here means working industriously and incessantly while developing gallery representation that's independent of the local economy. To be sure, a certain amount of art and fine crafts made by local artists manages to find buyers at one of Moscow's art galleries, or at the Saturday Farmers' Market in Friendship Square or at one of the region's summer arts festivals. But to really survive here as an artist you've got to be making sales in Seattle, Portland, Sun Valley, and even on the road.

Arts Scene

Downtown Moscow, which is a short walk from the University of Idaho campus, is home to a collection of classic, small-town commercial buildings. Scattered around downtown are literally dozens of perfect artist loft and studio spaces, but in this Art Town home-based studio space is affordable and plentiful. The Prichard Art Gallery, a large and sophisticated gem of a space, is located right on the mid-point of Main Street and attracts local art lovers to its year-round series of exhibitions by local, regional, national, and international artists. An outreach venture of the UI Art Department, the Prichard is one of the nation's most successful, university-based efforts at employing visual arts as part of an Art Town's downtown revitalization. The Moscow Arts Commission, an energetic and influential organization whose roles include supervising Moscow's extraordinarily successful Saturday Farmers' Market just off Main Street, operates its Third Street Gallery on the second and third floors of the community's restored, turn-of-the-20th-century City Hall. Another of the community's cultural stalwarts is the Moscow Food Co-op, which not only serves as Moscow's favorite meeting point for local artists but also operates an impressive visual arts gallery whose focus is the emerging and mid-career talent. On campus, the Ridenbaugh Gallery serves as a showcase for art created by UI graduates and post-graduates.

The Kenworthy Performing Arts Center, a renovated movie theatre on Main Street, is home to a year-round series of films, plays, and concerts, while the Beasley Coliseum at WSU is the region's top venue for major rock concerts and the occasional touring Broadway play. During late February the UI campus honors the legacy of Lionel Hampton, an American jazz pioneer, with its five-day Lionel Hampton Jazz Festival, while in the summer months Idaho Repertory Theatre presents its four-play season on both the expansive lawns of the UI campus and at Hartung Theatre. Throughout the year the university's music department presents a series of faculty and visiting artist classical music concerts, while a student-run foreign film series brings first-run flicks to the Idaho Commons. There are free community concerts at East City Park in the summer months, a Mardi Gras each March, the Rendezvous in the Park outdoor music festival in June, and a constant flow of Pacific Northwest rock bands, contemporary folk musicians, and DJs coming into Moscow and Pullman nightclubs to serve the region's nearly 30,000-strong community of college students. The Renaissance Fair, which takes place the first weekend of May in East City Park, is a top venue for the Northwest's fine crafts artists, with nearly 150 artists' booths as well as musical stages set up in the park for this three-day event.

Essentials

Visual Arts Venues

Moscow Food Co-op Gallery (221 E. Third Street; 208/882-8537; www.moscowfoodcoop.com) Popular marketplace that's not only a favorite meeting spot for local artists but also a visual arts venue for regional talents.

Prichard Art Gallery (414 S. Main Street; 208/885-3586; www.uidaho.edu) Sophisticated art space operated by the UI art department and located in the heart of downtown Moscow. Exhibits note-worthy regional and national artists.

Third Street Gallery (Moscow City Hall, 206 E. Third Street; 208/883-7036; www.ci.moscow.id.us) A two-story exhibition space inside the city hall, exhibiting a wide range of local painting and photography.

Art Talk

Deena Heath, director of the Moscow Arts Commission.

We're a presenter of arts-focused educational programs, and we run an art gallery in City Hall that has rotating shows throughout the year. Another of our functions is to coordinate the 26-week Farmers' Market, which includes 70 vendors in a downtown park, with a mix of 40 percent farmers, 40 percent arts and crafts, and 20 percent food vendors. It's the community's social event of the week and attracts as many as 3,000 people. Not only does the Farmers' Market give artists a chance to sell their work directly, it also allows the commission to support Moscow's music scene by hiring performers each weekend for the market. A lot of the university's art department graduates choose to stay in Moscow and pursue their art, usually by working a full-time job, then devoting themselves to their work in their spare time.

Performing Arts & Events

Moscow Renaissance Fair (see Moscow Chamber of Commerce below) One of the top Pacific Northwest arts fairs, this May celebration of visual and performing arts attracts nearly 150 artists, crafts-people, and sculptors to East City Park.

Rendezvous in the Park (see Moscow Chamber of Commerce below) A July festival in East City Park featuring three days performances by musicians from across the globe.

Idaho Repertory Theatre (UI Hartung Theatre; 208/885-5182; www.uitheatre.com) Summer stage festival organized by UI theatre

Art Talk

Gail Siegel, painter.

I live about 25 miles outside of town in a place where I can enjoy the peace and quiet of nature. In my studio I'm concerned with painting my immediate world, creating images of abstracted landscapes and small animals. My home environment plays a large role in my work, and the rural setting of my studio is a perfect place to find inspiration. Moscow has an amazing concentration of artists and arts supporters, and all the arts are very much visible throughout the community. Opening receptions at the Prichard will attract as many as 400 people. Artists here tend to have the mind-set that they're part of a supportive community, so we see lots of opportunities for networking, communicating, and sharing advice among artists. Exhibitions at the Prichard tend to be very focused on the work of Moscow's younger generation of artists, as well as on important national and international figures in the contemporary arts world. It's a place that aims high and achieves lots in terms of solidifying the arts presence in downtown.

department featuring outdoor performances.

Wine & Dine

Moscow Food Co-op (221 E. Third Street; 208/882-8537; www.moscowfoodcoop.com) Espresso bar, sandwiches, local arts and a vegetarian menu.

Wheatberries Bake Shop (531 Main Street; 208/882-4618) Fresh breads, sandwich wraps, and coffee.

CJ's (112 N. Main Street, 208/883-3147; www.cadillac jacks.com) Large nightclub and sports bar in downtown Moscow featuring live bands and DJs.

Accommodations

University Inn (1516 Pullman Road; 208/882-0550; www.uinn moscow.com) Large, full-service hotel, with a swimming pool and RV parking.

Peacock Hill B&B (1015 Joyce Road; 208/882-1423) Located on a tall hillside, this family run inn features peacocks and emus wandering on its grounds.

Palouse Inn (101 Baker Street; 208/882-5511; www.palouseinn.com) Economical choice in downtown, pets OK.

Information

Moscow Chamber of Commerce: 411 S. Main Street; 208/882-1800; www.moscowchamber.com

Population: 21,000

Sun Valley, Idaho

The Sun Valley area includes nearby communities such as the town of Ketchum and the artsy surrounding areas of Hailey, a short drive down the Wood River Valley and a growing hub for restaurants, galleries, design shops, and mountain homes. Living here means being surrounded in a year-round flow of cultural and outdoor recreation activities. The cultural end is largely the result of programs offered through the Sun Valley Center for the Arts, one of the West's best small-town art centers, as well as the opening receptions and artist lectures offered by the dozen-plus art galleries in Ketchum and Hailey.

In 1936, the 9,150-foot Bald Mountain became home to Sun Valley Lodge, and by 1939 Sonja Henie had come to town to film *Sun Valley Serenade*. Hollywood soon adopted the place as its unofficial winter wonderland, and a spurt of growth was started that continues to this day in the form of a real-estate-development boom that's pushed down the valley into places like Bellevue, Gannett, and Magic City.

While skiing, ice skating, and snowboarding dominate the area's winter activities, summers provide its own explosion of alpine recreation opportunities. Wildflower hikes along the Harriman Trail attract scores of visitors, while others hit the rugged backcountry in Sawtooth National Recreation Area for everything from single-track mountain biking to rock climbing and mountaineering. A 60-mile drive north leads to the high-country town of Stanley, one of the continent's premier destinations for white-water river rafting on the Payette, Salmon, and Sawtooth Rivers.

Art Talk

David Blampied, actor and producing artistic director of the New Theatre Company.

I lived as an actor in New York City for a number of years, but when I found out about the formation of this theatre company I moved back to Idaho to help develop a strong theatre presence in this community. New Theatre Company has strong roots in this region, dating back to 1994 when we started by presenting new and interesting work, which is still our identity today. We're the place to go for provocative, American stage work, and one of our programs focuses on new works by Idaho playwrights. Sun Valley is a resort town, and all the local arts organizations program to some degree around the mainstream tastes of the tourists. We've had to work very hard to develop a strong base of local support for our company's productions, and we do that by touring some plays across the state and by offering a number of in-school theatre programs.

Arts Scene

Like many Art Towns that are also resort communities, Sun Valley is top-heavy with art galleries tailored toward the upscale tastes of its high-season visitors and vacation homeowners. There's everything here from realistic bronze sculpture made in the studios of top artists in Loveland and Santa Fe to the studio-glass art crafted in hot shops sprinkled around the Puget Sound region. Sun Valley's galleries for the most part are focused on artists with national reputations and well-developed groups of collectors, which narrows the scope of opportunities available to local artists.

The exhibitions offered by the Sun Valley Center for the Arts, a multidisciplinary exhibition, performance, and education facility that's been bringing national talent to the Wood River Valley for better than 30 years, are important opportunities for local and regional artists. The center's extensive, year-round art workshops combine the best of the region's creative talents with shows by visiting national artists and classes for adults and kids. There's a highly active music component to the center's programming that covers everything from classical to blues, and its summer arts and crafts show is one of the Rocky Mountain West's premier outdoor events.

The New Theatre Company, the region's oldest thespian organization, stages a half-dozen productions annually, as does the Company of Fools, an organization with a year-round arts-education program in local schools. From July to August the Sun Valley Summer Symphony presents a dozen free concerts as well as a chamber music series in a large tent set up on the Sun Valley Lodge Esplanade.

Essentials

Visual Arts Venues

Sun Valley Center for the Arts
(191 Fifth Street E.; 208/726-9491;
www.sunvalleycenter.org) Diverse and
very active arts center with year-
round exhibitions and programs ranging from jewelry classes to an
acclaimed wine auction.

Kneeland Gallery (271 First Avenue
North; 208/726-5512; www.kneeland
gallery.com) Represents many of the
West's top painters and sculptors.

Friesen Gallery (320 First Avenue
North; 208/726-4174; www.friesen
gallery.com) Seattle-based gallery carrying contemporary works by many
national and Northwest artists.

Performing Arts & Events

Sun Valley Arts & Crafts Festival
(see Sun Valley/Ketchum Chamber &
Visitors Bureau below) National artists
have made this a must-stop on the
West's summer arts circuit. Taking
place in August, this outdoor show
draws thousands of well-heeled buyers.

Chamber Artist Series (Sun Valley
Center for the Arts; 208/726-9491)
This winter series of concerts draws
international classical and chamber
music talents to Sun Valley for presentations of the best new and
traditional music.

Art Talk

Sam Gappmayer, executive director
of the **Sun Valley Center for the Arts.**
We're a highly arts-conscious community,
from the year-round events at the art center to all the arts groups working to serve
the creative needs of the residents of the
Wood River Valley [the region that
includes Sun Valley, Hailey, Ketchum, and
Bellevue]. We've been around as an arts
center for more than 30 years, and we
take a lot of pride in knowing that many of
the region's arts organizations have their
roots in the arts center. We've moved programs like our summer concert series to
venues such as Hailey in our continuing
effort to reach the valley's full-time population with our cultural programming. We
also have the opportunity to work with a
seasonal population that tends to be quite
generous to the arts center, which challenges us as an institution serving two very
different constituencies. Our summer arts
and crafts show is an incredible success
and has a reputation for exhibiting top-
quality arts and fine crafts, and our wine
auction raises more than $100,000 each
year for our programs.

The New Theatre Company (see Sun Valley/Ketchum Chamber &
Visitors Bureau below) This drama company presents an intriguing

mix of primarily contemporary material throughout the year at its nexStage Theatre facility in Ketchum.

Wine & Dine

Sushi on Second (Second & Main Streets; 208/726-5181) The best place for yellowtail and octopus in Idaho. Try the Idaho trout sashimi.

Chester & Jake's (110 Main Street, Bellevue; 208/788-4722) Flown in daily, the seafood here is top-notch.

Big Wood Bread (270 Northwood Way; 208/726-2034) Great bakery and a local's favorite for breakfast and lunch.

Accommodations

Knob Hill Inn (960 N. Main Street; 208/726-8010) Luxury hotel, with all the amenities in the middle of town.

High Country Motel (765 S. Main Street, Bellevue; 208/788-2050) Affordable motel; great for backpackers and families on a budget.

Wood River Inn (603 N. Main Street, Hailey; 208/578-0600) Reasonable rates in a quiet setting.

Information

Sun Valley/Ketchum Chamber & Visitors Bureau: 800/634-3347; www.visitsunvalley.com

Population: 1,500

Bigfork, Montana

Waterfront real estate, 8,000-foot alpine peaks, legendary trout fishing, and a treasure of the national parks system are what make Bigfork's lifestyle the envy of many. Add to it a roaring summer tourism industry, a healthy and year-round arts scene, and access to some of the continent's best skiing and hiking, not to overlook the area's affordable real estate, and it's easy to see why this Art Town in northwest Montana continues to attract both artists and the art lovers who support their efforts.

Bigfork's jewel-like setting at the mouth of the Swan River on the eastern shore of Flathead Lake has infused this community with a resort atmosphere. Marinas and spectacular homes dot the shoreline, giving local residents easy access to 180 miles of coves, inlets, and bays spread across Flathead Lake's clear waters. The Swan Range's peaks define Bigfork's east boundary, and their snowmelt runoff irrigates hundreds of acres of nearby cherry orchards. Their early-summer harvest makes this community's Fourth of July celebrations one gigantic festival of cherry-eating pleasure in all imaginable forms.

Part of the tourism-focused Flathead Valley region, Bigfork's neighboring communities of Kalispell and Whitefish have respectable arts scenes of their own, though local residents tend to lump all three communities' activities together when considering where to go, what to do, and how to entertain oneself. The biggest tourism draw is the area's spectacular natural environment, especially inside the boundaries of

Art Talk

Eric Thorsen, sculptor.

I enjoy the process of making and selling my own art, which is why I have a studio and gallery in downtown Bigfork. You can do those kinds of things here, and it helps if you have the spirit to do all of that in front of people, while they're asking you questions. In the 15 years I've been here there's been a huge change in Bigfork, which is starting to get its national identity developed as place that has charm and an awareness about the arts. This town has a number of artists who work in their own galleries and who prefer being in a social environment instead of just working in their studios. This is an inspiring, fantastic place filled with interesting people. It's a small town where everybody seems to know everybody else.

Glacier National Park. Home to moose and grizzly bears, the park sprawls across the US–Canada border, sheltering vast mountain ranges, lakes, and valleys. Living in Bigfork means having easy access to the park's treasures, as well as to places such as Big Mountain Ski Resort in Whitefish, the Mission Mountain Wilderness, and the National Bison Range, both located a short distance south of here.

Arts Scene

The leading venue in Bigfork's arts scene is the Bigfork Summer Playhouse, a professional theatre company that springs to life every May and continues its superb productions through the middle of September, which is around the same time that eagles begin gathering in Glacier National Park for the annual salmon run. Productions are staged at the 430-seat Bigfork Center for the Performing Arts, a modern facility located in the middle of the community's very walkable downtown. Some members of the regional theatre group have also managed to establish themselves as the Whitefish Theatre Company, whose brief summer season is supplemented by a series of concerts by national acts in the O'Shaughnessy Center. The Whitefish Company's main season runs from September through May. Both groups maintain strong summer programs for children. Bigfork Summer Playhouse offers up a season of fairly standard musicals and light material, while Whitefish Theatre Company gets a bit deeper into contemporary stagecrafts.

One of the state's oldest outdoor arts fairs, the Bigfork Festival of the Arts, takes over downtown's streets on an early-August weekend, drawing thousands into town to prowl through more than a hundred artists' booths. A larger and more tightly juried outdoor show, Arts in the Park, takes place in Kalispell's Depot Park in late July. The Kalispell show's organizer, the Hockaday Art Museum, is the region's top visual arts exhibition facility and uses its historic building, a former Carnegie library, to stage an innovative, year-round series of exhibitions of both contemporary and traditional arts. While Kalispell and Whitefish both have several art galleries in their downtowns as well as Whitefish's wonderful Stumptown Art Studio, the biggest concentration of art galleries is in Bigfork, where a dozen or so art spaces represent everything from contemporary work to traditional landscape painting and realist bronze sculpture. There are monthly ArtWalks during the summer season, and in Sliter Park the popular Riverbend Concerts in an open-air amphitheatre bring bluegrass and folk music to town each week.

Essentials

Visual Arts Venues

Hockaday Art Museum (302 Second Avenue; 406/755-5268; www.hockadaymuseum.org) This highly regarded visual arts center presents year-round exhibitions, lectures, films, and programs.

Kootenai Galleries (573 Electric Avenue; 406/837-4848; www.kootenaigalleries.com) Large gallery representing top regional and national artists.

Eric Thorsen Gallery (547 Electric Avenue; 406/837-4366) Realist bronze-sculpture studio and gallery in downtown Bigfork.

Performing Arts & Events

Bigfork Summer Playhouse (546 Electric Avenue; 406/837-4886; www.bigforksummerplayhouse.com) This popular summer company stages light drama and musicals in a downtown theatre.

Bigfork Festival of the Arts (406/881-4636; www.bigforkfestivalofthearts.com) Downtown street festival in August with food, entertainment, and more than 100 artists' booths.

Art Talk

Brett Thuma, painter.

Bigfork's the kind of place where I can own my own business and just paint. There's a certain amount of advantage an artist gains in terms of control over your time and income when you have your own gallery. It's difficult to survive here in the winter, and you really need to sell your work out of town and on the Internet. I paint nature in general, wildlife, songbirds, landscapes, and fly-fishing scenes. Most of my subject matter comes from this region, so being in Bigfork is very important to my art. The quality of light here, the mountains, and the wildlife are all part of my work. The second-home owners moving in here are an increasingly important part of my business, and they tend to be buying the higher end of what I'm making.

Whitefish Theatre Company

(1 Central Avenue; 406/862-5371; www.whitefishtheatreco.org)
Presents contemporary American material during its nine-month
season.

Wine & Dine

La Provence (408 Bridge Street; 406/837-2923) Traditional French
cuisine with an outstanding wine list.

Champs Grill at Marina Cay (180 Vista Lane; 406/837-5861)
Lakeside dining and a popular spot in summer.

Bigfork Inn (604 Electric Avenue; 406/837-6680) Great cuisine, with
live music on weekends.

Accommodations

Pine Lodge (920 Spokane Avenue; 406/862-7600) Great views of the
river.

Bayview Resort & Marina (543 Yenne Point Road; 406/837-4843;
www.bayviewrm.com) Lakeside cabins and boat moorage.

Beardance Inn & Cabins (135 Bay Drive; 406/837-4551) Cabins
right on the bay.

Information

Bigfork Area Chamber of Commerce: Old Towne Center;
406/837-5888; www.bigfork.org

Population: 1,400

Bozeman, Montana

A fast-growing college town north of Yellowstone National Park, Bozeman in recent years has become one of the nation's top places for both second-home owners wanting a getaway in the Rockies and for self-contained artists and entrepreneurs seeking a place with the services of a city but tempered by the friendliness of an Art Town.

Like most of this spectacular region's communities, Bozeman promotes itself as a gateway to Yellowstone National Park. Tourism provides an important underpinning to the local economy, which has been broadened by the growth of nearby communities such as the ski resort town of Big Sky to Bozeman's south and Livingston to the east. Both of these communities have developed respectable art scenes of their own and have expanded the market for all of the region's visual and performing artists.

Bozeman's growth curve has been both a blessing and a curse to long-time residents. On the downside, growth has pushed real-estate prices to heights that those tied to the local economy have difficulty when looking for a place of their own. It's also led to the development of mini-ranches that sprawl away from Bozeman's core neighborhoods like ants in search of picnic tables. In itself this wouldn't be so bad, were it not for the inappropriate (that is, faux Santa Fe–style) architectural motifs used by some of the region's homebuilders.

What sets Bozeman apart from other, similarly sized communities is the presence of Montana State University. This progressive institution,

Art Talk

Jeane Alm, executive director of the Emerson Center for the Arts & Culture. On all levels, Bozeman's a growing and changing place, and our new cultural council is working to coordinate the mass of artists and arts organizations that are competing for attention. The Emerson is a truly unique facility, and we've recently remodeled our gym into a more functional conference, performance, and exhibition space. We have a tenant mix of working artists, creative field businesses, and arts educators. You can come here in the morning for piano lessons and in the afternoon for Japanese lessons. Our usual occupancy rate is 97 percent, and we keep a waiting list of artists who want to rent studio space in our building. Our mission is to provide low-cost studio and workshop space for people engaged in some aspect of the arts. Montana State University's art department has started to run our visual art exhibition space, and it has been a real asset to have their shows taking place here.

which supports its intercollegiate rodeo and downhill skiing programs as much as it does intercollegiate football, has a diverse arts department whose programs in visual and performing arts as well as music embellish the quality of life for all of the Bozeman region's residents.

Arts Scene

One of the nation's most outstanding examples of incubating Art Town creativity takes place inside the Emerson Center for the Arts & Culture, located in a 70,000-square-foot, former middle school in downtown Bozeman. This two-story structure reflects and supports the diversity and cooperative nature of the region's artists as well as those working in creative field businesses. It's the kind of place that gives artists, photographers, actors, musicians, designers, jewelers, and authors a place to congregate, while offering them an affordable climate for moving their careers toward sustainability. There's also a performance space that's used by local theatre companies for plays and rehearsals, several art galleries, as well as a frame shop, cafés exhibiting local arts, architects' offices, music classrooms, graphic design studios, and offices for environmental groups.

Bozeman's the kind of place where most art galleries tend to have short lives, but in the current cluster of a half-dozen or so art spaces scattered across downtown, one longtime exception is the Montana Trails Gallery, an art space exhibiting Western realism and landscape work. Contemporary arts have a strong presence at the Emerson's gallery and lobby exhibitions, and it's also the favored genre for exhibitions at the Helen Copeland Gallery in Haynes Hall on the Montana State University campus, as well as in the Bealle Park Art Center. Just

east of here, in the very western surroundings of Livingston, there's a cluster of galleries exhibiting primarily
Western realism and landscape art.
Livingston's also home to the Depot
Center, a performance venue and
visual arts exhibition facility whose
exhibitions showcase the regional arts
community.

Montana State University's fine arts
departments have had an enormous
impact on Bozeman's performing-
arts and music scenes. Faculty members provide the punch behind the
Bozeman Symphony Orchestra, as well
as the InterMountain Opera Company,
which presents its productions at
Willson Auditorium. Through the academic year the MSU Lively Arts Series
presents a strong slate of touring
national theatre, popular music, and
dance performances, while local drama
companies such as Vigilante Theatre
and Equinox Theatre stage their plays
at the Emerson. During the summer
months one of the main local attractions is Music in the Mountains, an
outdoor concert series at Big Sky.

Art Talk

JoAnn Brekhus, executive director of
the Sweet Pea Festival.

We're a volunteer-driven event that draws
an audience of more than 10,000 people
for our annual festival during the first
week of August. We organize a week's
worth of events leading up to a three-day
arts festival, and it includes things like a
street painting contest, a costume ball, live
music, the Bite of Bozeman culinary festival, and lots of things for children. We also
organize an open and juried art show that
takes place at various venues, and most of
the artists we work with come from this
region. We award prizes to our artists and
aren't restrictive as to media or content.
We call ourselves the Sweet Pea Festival
because this once was an agricultural
region that shipped peas to all over the
country, so in 1979 when a group of artists
got together to start the festival they
decided to honor our historic traditions by
naming the festival after a carnival that
had been in Bozeman from 1908 to 1916.

Essentials

Visual Arts Venues

The Emerson Center for the Arts & Culture (111 South Grand
Avenue; 406/587-9797; www.theemerson.org) This multidisciplinary
arts center is the heart and soul of Bozeman's arts community.

Montana Trails Gallery (219 East Main Street; 406/586-2166;
www.mountaintrails.com) One of the top Western realism galleries.

Livingston Depot Center (200 Park Avenue; 406-222-2300)
Livingston's busy arts center presents everything from live music
and theatre to film and visual arts.

Performing Arts & Events

Music in the Mountains (P.O. Box 160038; 877/995-2742; www.bigskyarts.org) This July through August outdoor music festival at Big Sky features top national acts.

Equinox Theatre Company (2304 N. 7th Street; 406/587-0737; www.equinoxtheatre.com) Year-round, professional drama company presenting adult and children's material.

Sweet Pea Festival (111 South Grand Avenue; 406/586-4003) This early-August event is Bozeman's premier outdoor summer arts fair.

Wine & Dine

Johnny Carino's (2159 Burke Street; 406/556-1332) Famous for its 12-layer lasagna.

Café Internationale (111 South Grand Avenue; 406/586-4242) Located inside the Emerson Center, this popular spot features local art on its walls.

Azteca Cantina (505 W. Aspen; 406/586-0030) The region's best place for green chile burritos.

Accommodations

Lindley House B&B (202 Lindley Place; 406/587-8403; www.lindley -house.com) 1889 Victorian mansion close to the Emerson Center.

Wingate Inn (2305 Catron; 406/582-4995; www.wingateinns.com) Reasonably priced hotel with accommodations for families.

Fox Hollow B&B (545 Mary Road; 406/582-8440) Affordable inn close to downtown.

Information

Bozeman Area Chamber of Commerce: 2000 Commerce Way; 406/586-5421; www.bozemanchamber.com

Population: 28,000

Helena, Montana

There's a dynamic quality to life in the West's state capitals. The smaller ones, such as Santa Fe, New Mexico, Olympia, Washington, Salem, Oregon, and Carson City, Nevada, are home to surprisingly strong arts scenes that over the past 30 or so years (make that 400 years in Santa Fe's case) have evolved into full-fledged, year-round celebrations of their unique mix of talent and culture. Helena, located in the foothills of the Rocky Mountains, is a place where locals know they enjoy a great quality of life as a result of the thousands of well-paid local jobs connected to state and federal government. These same folks provide the crucial base of ticket-buying and art-collecting support that sustains a wide range of cultural amenities, from foreign film screenings at the Myrna Loy Center to the holiday season performances of two Helena-based theatre companies to the Helena Symphony's concerts.

Built with the enormous wealth generated by Montana's forestry and mining industries, much of Helena is an elegantly preserved example of Victorian splendor. Its compact downtown is one of the prettiest anywhere, and the neighborhoods close to the center of town are a treasure trove of restored mansions whose lineages date back to the 19th century.

To live here is to be engaged with the tremendous natural beauty surrounding this corner of the West. It's all about winter skiing at Great Divide and summer water-skiing on Canyon Ferry Lake. It's hiking along the far reaches of Gates of the Mountains Wilderness, and it's white-water rafting on the turbulent waters of the Dearborn River. This is what passes for day-to-day living in a close-knit community whose reputation for friendliness and creative integrity is more than an advertising pitch.

Arts Scene

One of the best medium-sized art museums in the West, the Holter Museum of Art is the jewel in Helena's visual arts crown. This modern facility on the edge of downtown's historic district is known for its year-round presentation of exhibitions, educational workshops, art films, lectures, and performances, and it has recently expanded its facility by 6,500 square feet. National, regional, and local artists are included in the Holter's comprehensive exhibitions calendar, and its Artworks Gallery in the museum's store is a superb place to find examples of work from Helena's top emerging talents.

While there are several commercial art galleries in downtown Helena, the Archie Bray Foundation for the Ceramic Arts has in large part developed much of the talented foundation for Helena's arts scene. Located on the grounds of what once was a commercial brickyard, the Archie Bray is internationally respected as one of the most forward-looking ceramics centers on the continent. The center's artist residency programs attract some of the world's top teaching talents, and its year-round classes and workshops help local artists keep abreast of the latest trends in international ceramics art circles. Much of the ceramics art created here is marketed through the Bray Gallery and its online sales venue. The Bray's year-round exhibitions of work created by its resident and visiting artists are among the highlights of Helena's arts calendar.

Downtown Helena, a place filled with cafés, coffee bars, pubs, bakeries, and sports bars, is the region's favored destination for arts festivals such as the Sidewalk ArtMart in June, the summer-long Alive @ Five series of music performances, the weekly Farmers' Market on Fuller Avenue, and the Last Chance Bluegrass Festival in July. During the summer months Montana Shakespeare uses Performance Square for its outdoor productions, while during the rest of the year the Myrna Loy Center for the Performing & Media Arts is the community's favored venue for everything from weekend foreign films to the year-round Mondays at the Myrna series of live music, theatre, and dance performances by touring regional and national talents. The Myrna Loy is also home to an ambitious, media arts program that covers areas such as video editing and cable television production. The Helena Civic

Center and the Covenant United Methodist Church are used by the Helena Symphony for its eight-month concert season.

Helena has two resident theatre companies: Grandstreet Theatre and Toadstone Theatre. Grandstreet, which performs its season in a converted church structure, also operates a theatre arts school for local youth. Its season of drama, musicals, and comedies runs year-round. Toadstone Theatre, which spends much of its year touring productions throughout Montana, stages adult and family shows, ranging from classics to comedies as well as original works.

Essentials

Visual Arts Venues

Holter Museum of Art (12 E. Lawrence; 406/442-6400; www.holter museum.org) Contemporary arts museum with regional, national, and intercultural exhibitions.

Archie Bray Foundation for the Ceramic Arts (2915 Country Club Avenue; 406/443-3502; www.archiebray.org) Residencies, workshops, and exhibitions of ceramic arts.

Upper Missouri River Artists Gallery (7 N. Last Chance Gulch; 406/457-8240) Cooperative arts space representing more than a dozen local artists.

Performing Arts & Events

Sidewalk ArtMart (see Helena Chamber of Commerce below) June weekend arts fair with more than 100 artists' booths.

Art Talk

Mary Evelynn Sorrell, executive director and senior curator of the Holter Museum of Art.

We're very focused on contemporary art, both in our exhibitions programs and in our permanent collection. Montana's a sparsely populated state, so we collect work by artists from the state as well as from across the Northwest, which is consistent with how people in this part of Montana relate to the larger region. With our recently completed expansion, which doubled our exhibitions space and added two new classrooms for our education programs, we were also able to add a gallery exclusively for exhibiting the work of younger and emerging artists. This gallery has proved very popular with the local arts community, which is loaded with young, well-trained talent. The Archie Bray Foundation has been a huge influence for the regional arts community, and Helena's now home to a tremendously talented group of contemporary ceramics artists.

Art Talk

Josh DeWeese, ceramist and resident director of the Archie Bray Foundation. The Archie Bray is one of the regional organizations that works to put Helena's arts scene on the map. We still have to work hard to maintain the strength of our ties to the local arts community, because many of our students, teachers, and programs are oriented toward national and international ceramics artists. We've developed more events and exhibitions geared toward the local arts community, sponsoring things like a lecture series and our Mother's Day open house, and year-round education programs. We're building the Shaner Studio Building, which will give us state-of-the-art facilities for ten resident artists as well as a new kiln building and a "clean room." Contemporary ceramics is a very competitive field, and this building helps us keep up with the latest developments in our field.

Myrna Loy Center for the Performing Arts (15 N. Ewing; 406/443-0287; www.myrnaloy center.com) Historic jailhouse turned into a multipurpose performing-arts venue and education center.

Grandstreet Theatre (325 N. Park Avenue; 406/442-4270; www.grand street.net) Year-round community theatre.

Wine & Dine

The Stonehouse (120 Reeders Alley; 406/449-2552; www.stonehouse helena.com) Superb American cuisine in a historic home.

Miller's Crossing (52 S. Park Avenue; 406/442-3290; www.millers crossing.biz) Favorite local brewpub with live music.

Flicker's Coffeehouse (101 N. Last Chance Gulch; 406/443-5567) Local art, live music, great espresso.

Accommodations

The Sanders B&B (328 N. Ewing; 406/442-3309; www.sandersbb.com) Victorian inn close to downtown.

Fairfield Inn (2150 11th Avenue; 406/449-9944; www.marriott.com) Large motel, with a pool.

Lamplighter Motel (1006 Madison Street; 406/442-9200) Affordable rooms close to downtown.

Information

Helena Chamber of Commerce: 225 Cruse Avenue; 406/447-1530; www.helenachamber.com

Population: 25,800

Missoula, Montana

Political activism is alive and well in this Pacific Northwest college town. An eminently outdoorsy place whose downtown is bordered by three rivers and the edges of Lolo National Forest, Missoula is the kind of town where year-round activities such as skiing, kayaking, hiking, camping, and mountain biking are just a few of the attractions local folks revel in.

When they're not shooting the rapids on a churning stretch of the Bitterroot River or cutting through fresh powder at Big Mountain Ski Resort, Missoulians are plugged into the social life of a funky college town that's large enough to support a range of ethnic restaurants, live-music venues, bars aplenty, and the typical tattoo parlors and used-record shops. Winters are long stretches of surprisingly mild days followed by nights when the bottom drops out of thermometers, but summers are spectacular, especially when the student population has temporarily exited town and you can actually find parking spaces.

While there's a fair amount of historic architecture scattered throughout this community, the more recent additions to Missoula's infrastructure tend toward structures whose design cues seem cribbed from shopping malls. An exception to this is the campus of the University of Montana (UofM), a bucolic place connected by foot-bridges crossing the Clark Fork River. As is the case in places such as Spokane and Boise, the town's most desirable residential addresses are streets whose Victorian structures were erected a century ago. Here in Missoula, these grand dames are carefully restored masterpieces occupied in many cases by the university's faculty.

Arts Scene

While Missoula is a favorite place for artists seeking an affordable, supportive community in which to raise families and pursue studio-based careers, its visual arts scene is led by the university's galleries and museum, as well as the local, regional, and national exhibitions at the Art Museum of Missoula. On campus, the Montana Museum of Art & Culture is mostly concerned with historical art, while the Gallery of Visual Arts has risen to the forefront of Missoula's contemporary arts scene with a balanced exhibition slate of local and national shows. The Art Museum of Missoula has two changing galleries offering exhibitions of contemporary arts, fine crafts, and photography, as well as year-round arts-education classes for the community, and a kids' summer arts camp.

As seems fitting for a community whose downtown claim to fame is an elegant, 19th-century-style carousel in Caras Park along the Clark Fork River, and whose Crystal Theatre movie house offers independent and foreign films, Missoula's performing-arts scene is as solid as a rock. Leading the way is the Missoula Children's Theatre, a nationally touring theatre company whose new performing-arts center gleams like an arts jewel. MCT not only produces its own year-round plays in its state-of-the-art theatre, it also employs legions of locals in putting together the 30 teams of entertainers who venture out from Missoula to stage children's theatre across the globe.

The University Theatre on the U of M campus presents an inspired slate of touring music, theatre, dance, and classical music during the academic year, while the school of music's recital hall offers a full calendar of chamber concerts. Montana Repertory Theatre, which tours nationally, is based here and presents a year-round slate of challenging and original material. The Missoula Folklore Society, which presents national and international acts at the Crystal Theatre, is also where contra dancers can hook up at weekly gatherings. During the summer months, the Fort Missoula Amphitheater presents the musical drama *Charlie Russell's Montana* as well as a great slate of outdoor concerts and even a Shakespeare play or two.

Essentials

Visual Arts Venues

Montana Museum of Art & Culture (University of Montana Campus; 406/243-2019; www.umt.edu) This multidisciplinary

|institution now has a historical focus as well as showcasing visual arts exhibitions.

Art Museum of Missoula (335 N. Pattee; 406/728-0447; www.art missoula.org) This center for traditional and contemporary arts serves the local and regional arts community.

The Montana Craft Connection (www.mtcraftconnection.com) Great on-line gallery for finding the best contemporary and traditional crafts made by regional artists.

Performing Arts & Events

Missoula Children's Theatre (200 N. Adams Street; 406/728-1911; www.mctinc.org) The nation's premier children's theatre company, MCT offers a year-round slate of local performances.

Montana Repertory Theatre (University of Montana; 406/243-6809; www.montanarep.org) This professional company tours nationally and presents local performances of new material.

Art Talk

Laura Millin, executive director of the Art Museum of Missoula.

A lot of our programming centers around the local arts community and the way this area's artists express their concerns about issues such as the environment and local history. Our collection is drawn from artists living and working in the western states, with an emphasis on Montana artists, as well as Native American artists. We've been in a Carnegie library building since the 1970s, running an ambitious program of year-round exhibitions and events. We've decided to renovate our structure to add a modest amount of space, update the look of our galleries, add classroom space, and improve our handicapped access. We're quite dedicated to contemporary arts, which provide the focus for many of our programs.

Fort Missoula Ampitheater (Highway 93 South; 406/728-3476) Missoula's favorite venue for summer concerts under the stars.

Wine & Dine

The Bridge Bistro (515 S. Higgins; 406/542-0638; www.bridge bistro.com) Great pizza and crabcakes in this longtime locals' favorite.

The Mustard Seed Asian Café (Southgate Mall; 406/542-7333) Pan-Asian restaurant serving everything from Sushi to Kung Pao Chicken.

Art Talk

Michael McGill, music director and production department head for the Missoula Children's Theatre.

When I started here we had five touring teams and were heavily invested in presenting community theatre. Now we have 30 touring teams and we still maintain that sense of dedication to presenting community theatre for Missoula. We've evolved into a fixture of what Missoula has come to expect for its entertainment and arts education, and we have an extensive, locally oriented performance and education program that involves the region's schools in our efforts to evolve the theatre company's works in progress as well as reach out to the community's schoolchildren. We present a season of community theatre and bring in professional actors for our productions. It's a family-oriented program comprised of straight shows and musicals. We have a history of developing the idea in children's minds that theatre is one of the many career possibilities that exists in their lives.

Viva Mexico (2221 South Avenue; 406/549-3651) Best Mexican food and cervezas in the Bitterroots.

Accommodations

Gibson Mansion (823 39th Street; 406/251-1345; www.gibson mansion.com) Victorian B&B in downtown Missoula with huge rooms.

Holiday Inn Parkside (200 S. Pattee Street; 406/721-8550; www.himissoula.com) Located on the Clark Fork River in downtown and convenient to the university campus.

Foxglove Cottage B&B (2331 Gilbert Avenue; 406/543-2927; www.foxglove cottage.net) A cozy, 100-year-old house with a garden, near downtown, UofM, and Rattlesnake Wilderness Area.

Information

Missoula Chamber of Commerce: 825 E. Front Street; 406/543-6623; www.missoulachamber.com

Population: 57,500

Red Lodge, Montana

D rive 60 miles northeast of Yellowstone National Park, a route that traverses an 11,000-foot mountain pass along the Beartooth Highway, and you'll wind up in this authentically western community. Even though Red Lodge has a population of less than 3,000, this south-central Montana Art Town has acquired a national reputation for its freestyle form of living, incredible outdoor recreation opportunities, and the part-time presence of movie stars and corporate giants living on ranches scattered across Carbon County's verdant valleys.

While hundreds of artists working in various media call Red Lodge home, they all have in common a love of the outdoors and an appreciation for this supportive community's spirit. Red Lodge is the kind of town that's developed a track record of steadily improving both its quality of life and its range of opportunities for locals and newcomers. Much of the community shells out for annual passes to Red Lodge Mountain Resort, a family-oriented ski area whose 69 trails are just a few miles from Red Lodge's well-preserved, downtown. Snowmobiling and cross-country skiing are other favorite pursuits during the notoriously long and cold winters, whose final weeks are marked by annual Ski-Joring races featuring horses pulling beer-sodden skiers around a snow-covered meadow.

Established in the late 19th century as a mining town, Red Lodge celebrates its multiethnic heritage during August's Festival of Nations. This is also a place where angling for bass, walleye, and trout lures fishermen from far and wide to the banks of the Stillwater and Clarks Fork

Art Talk

Deborah Kline, executive director of the Carbon County Art Guild & Depot Gallery.

We're a nonprofit arts organization that provides artists with a place to show their work and that offers year-round art classes to the residents of Carbon County. We use local, professional artists to teach our classes, and we supplement the art instruction that takes place once a week in our local schools. Usually, but not always, our exhibitions focus on work by local artists as well as artists from across Montana. During the summer months we get a lot of tourists coming through the gallery, and we get a lot of artists who come here to participate in our arts festivals. It's not uncommon to see artists set up around town, doing plein air painting, and more than 200 local residents are either full- or part-time artists. We're far out of the way, but a number of artists are choosing to live here because of that same remoteness. Red Lodge is supportive of its arts community, and if you can get over the challenges of living here and develop outside channels for selling your work, then this is a great place to live.

Rivers. Some locals enjoy sailing on the placid waters of Cooney Reservoir, Wild Bill Lake, and Greenough Lake. Red Lodge Books, an independent bookseller, offers a year-round slate of author book-signings and lectures that help keep the arts community in contact with each other, while the Roman Theater, the town's movie palace, keeps a steady flow of independent films pouring into town. In late July, an annual mountain-man rendezvous at Howell's Encampment celebrates the region's historic connection to hunters and trappers. Also in July there's the Iron Horse Rodeo for Harley riders, as well as the Home of Champions Rodeo for those preferring their rodeo action on four hooves instead of two wheels.

Arts Scene

While there are several art galleries in downtown Red Lodge, the center of the region's visual arts scene is the Carbon County Arts Guild & Depot Gallery, located in the former Burlington Northern train station, right next to the community's historic Carnegie Library. Its three galleries exhibit local and regional work as well as Native American and Western art. Every summer, the Art Guild organizes its Flamboyant Furniture Festival during Iron Horse Rodeo weekend. The event features furniture reconditioned and reconstructed into funky masterpieces by many of Red Lodge's leading artists. One of the nation's premier Native American painters, Kevin Red Star, lives in the area and maintains a gallery in the neighboring town of Roberts.

Red Lodge has a surprisingly active summer music scene that kicks off in early June with the Red Lodge Music Festival, a student-focused music camp featuring nine glorious days of recitals and concerts led by members of symphony orchestras from across the continent. In late June there's the annual Mountain Music Fest, an outdoor rock concert at the Home of Champions Rodeo Grounds. The following weekend, those with leftover energy strive to complete the high-altitude Beartooth Run on the switchbacks of Beartooth Highway. In July and August, national touring acts such as Willie Nelson are featured at the rodeo grounds, while in late July the Montana State Fiddle Championship moves into town for a week of fiddlin' around.

The summer months are a whirlwind of action at the Round Barn Restaurant & Theater, located just outside of town on Highway 212. This buffet-style restaurant, located in a former dairy, has a 125-seat theatre that's used for everything from the slapstick comedies of Bozeman-based Vigilante Theatre Company to touring country & western bands, and even the occasional Elvis impersonator.

Art Talk

Merida Red Star, gallery director. We run a national art gallery out of Roberts, and we used to be in Red Lodge but moved out of town when a big, perfect building came on the market. This place has everything we need, room for exhibitions, studio space, storage, and room for visiting artists. Ten years ago this was a very different county than it is today. There's been a major expansion of the local arts scene, and there are many more opportunities for artists to sell their work. A number of artists move here because of the easy access to the ski area, and then they decide to stay on in Red Lodge because of its friendliness and solitude. I moved here from Santa Fe, and it was tough for me to make that adjustment. But things have changed in Red Lodge over the years. It's become a more open-minded place, a more knowledgeable place, and a better place to live.

Essentials

Visual Arts Venues

Carbon County Art Guild & Depot Gallery (11 West 8th Street; 406/446-1370) This historic train station uses its three galleries year-round for exhibitions of local and regional art.

Kevin Red Star Gallery (103 S. Main Street, Roberts; 406/445-2211) Nationally respected artist collected by many top North American art museums.

Coleman Gallery & Studio (223 S. Broadway; 406/446-1228; www.colemangallery.biz) Photographer famed for Yellowstone National Park images.

Performing Arts & Events

The Round Barn Restaurant & Theatre (Highway 212; 406/446-1197) Dinner house and performance space with great food and live entertainment.

Red Lodge Music Festival (Red Lodge Civic Center; 406/252-4599; www.redlodgemusicfestival.org) Early-June music camp for students featuring recitals and performances by several of the nation's top classical musicians.

Mountain Music Fest (see Red Lodge Area Chamber of Commerce below) Red Lodge's traditional, mid-June kickoff for its rock n' roll summer.

Wine & Dine

Bear Creek Saloon & Steakhouse (Highway 308; 406/446-3481) Best steakhouse in the county, and headquarters for the Bear Creek Downs Pig Races.

Red Lodge Pizza Company (115 S. Broadway; 406/446-3333) Best place in town for chicken parmesan.

The Pollard (2 N. Broadway; 406/446-0001; www.pollardhotel.com) Innovative, new American cuisine.

Accommodations

The Pollard (2 N. Broadway; 406/446-0001; www.pollardhotel.com) Small, historic hotel that's hosted outlaws and Hollywood stars.

Chateau Rouge (1505 S. Broadway; 406/446-1601) A-frame style motel with reasonably priced rooms.

Rock Creek Resort (Box 3500; 800/667-1119; www.rockcreek resort.com) High-style resort with its own restaurant just outside of town on Highway 212.

Information

Red Lodge Area Chamber of Commerce: 601 N. Broadway; 406/446-1718; www.redlodge.com

Population: 2,250

Mesilla, New Mexico

The historic, 1-square-mile Art Town of Mesilla sits directly south of Las Cruces, New Mexico's second-largest city. Much of Mesilla was built in the 1800s, when this was a frontier outpost where the Camino Real connected Santa Fe to Zacatecas, Mexico. Mesilla also intersected with the Butterfield stagecoach line's San Francisco to Kansas City transportation network. Most of Mesilla's frontier beauty has been preserved, and the place looks much like it did when Billy the Kid spent a night or two in the local hoosegow before staging one of his most legendary jailbreaks.

Known throughout New Mexico for having what's arguably the prettiest town plaza in the state (some say Santa Fe, others Mesilla), this community about an hour's drive north of El Paso looks out onto the spectacular, ruggedly beautiful Organ Mountains, a series of 9,000-foot peaks separating the lush and fertile Mesilla Valley from the vast desert of White Sands. To live in Mesilla is be in constant contact with Las Cruces, itself a former frontier town and now best known as home to New Mexico State University (NMSU). To the north of here, around the town of Hatch, the state's premier agricultural crop, chile peppers, are grown for a worldwide marketplace and are celebrated each year during August's Hatch Chile Festival. As unlikely as it seems, one of the Southwest's premier grape-growing regions lies just south of Mesilla, and its dependably large harvests are shipped to winemakers across Arizona, New Mexico, and Texas.

Because of their proximity to El Paso and Las Cruces, artists living in Mesilla have easy access to a range of cultural offerings, from the

Art Talk

Sharon Bode-Hempton, executive director of the Las Cruces Museum of Fine Art.
We're located in a region whose influence extends down to El Paso, and it's a very active place for a number of artists. Many artists have moved into the region from Taos and Santa Fe, attracted by our warmer weather and lower cost of living. In other parts of the state there are commercial arts scenes that can become very competitive, though that's not the case here, even though many of our local artists are represented in Taos and Santa Fe galleries. We organize our shows around themes, like the southern New Mexico landscape, and we also bring in a number of exhibitions that are relevant to the people and culture of this area. Our museum has 19,000 square feet and two large art galleries. The arts department at New Mexico State University has helped develop a sense of creative integrity among the artists living here, and the department's young artists are a welcome presence in the community.

rock bands brought here for NMSU concerts to the lectures, exhibitions, and presentations organized by the El Paso Art Museum. Regular trips to Santa Fe for a dose of summer opera are a must, as are winter jaunts to Ski Apache's alpine slopes, an hour's drive northeast. Homes are still very affordable, especially in older neighborhoods where the population is divided between descendants of the region's Hispanic settlers and the assortment of newcomers lured here by the area's mild climate, pervasive sense of historic connection, and the laid-back southern New Mexico lifestyle.

Arts Scene

There are a half-dozen galleries scattered around Mesilla's compact, adobe-walled plaza. Some are artist owned and operated, while others carry a mix of imported Mexican crafts and locally created folk art. The region's premier visual arts venue is the Las Cruces Museum of Fine Arts, which is adjacent to the Las Cruces Historical Museum. The art museum presents a year-round series of exhibitions, art workshops, lectures, and films in its 5,000-square-foot facility, giving local and regional artists an opportunity to exhibit alongside national talents. The history museum tends to focus on cultural events such as an October quilters fair, as well as exhibits on the region's frontier past. On the university campus there's another historical museum, though this one maintains a more ethnographic orientation in its exhibitions, while on the outskirts of town the New Mexico Farm & Ranch Heritage Museum exhibits artifacts from the state's past and present. It shows the region as a place where ranchers and farmers, including Hispanics, Native

Americans, and Anglos, helped build this former Spanish outpost into a thriving community. Among the annual events at the Farm & Ranch Museum are Cowboy Days in October and La Fiesta de San Ysidro in May, an event that showcases the talents of the local Ballet Folklorico de la Tierra del Encanto.

Every October, the Mesilla Jazz Happening turns the community's art galleries, restaurants, and plaza into a weekend-long celebration of this American art form. Year-round, the Fountain Theatre, the state's oldest movie house, presents foreign and independent movies in its historic surroundings. No Strings Theatre Company, which presents its season of new plays and classics at the Black Box Theatre, located near the fine arts museum, is one of two local drama companies. The Las Cruces Community Theatre, which stages classics and time-proven crowd pleasers such as *Annie Get Your Gun,* stages its performances in a nearby, downtown Las Cruces venue.

Art Talk

Carolyn Bunch, painter and gallery owner.

I've been in the art business in Mesilla and this area since 1984, and my first gallery was in an 1850s building behind the plaza. We renovated that one and built a much nicer gallery a few blocks away. Since we arrived here Mesilla's developed a strong awareness of the need to protect its unique architecture and its heritage. The community in general now sees its artists as being important to the community's long-term economic health, so there's a type of respect for artists that wasn't necessarily here a few years ago. Representational art sells best in the galleries, though we're seeing more sales of contemporary arts from year to year, and more gallery owners are jumping in and making a go of things here.

Essentials

Visual Arts Venues

Las Cruces Museum of Fine Art (500 N. Water Street; 505/541-2155) The area's premier visual arts venue presents a year-round slate of local and regional exhibitions.

Galeria on the Plaza (2305 Calle de Guadalupe; 505/526-9771) Mesilla's largest gallery is a great place to find work from local artists.

William Bonney Gallery (2000 Calle de Parian; 505/526-8275) Art and artifacts, with a Billy the Kid–sense of whimsy.

Performing Arts & Events

Mesilla Jazz Happening (see Mesilla Visitors Center below) October gathering of top regional musicians performing in several indoor and outdoor venues.

La Fiesta de San Ysidro (New Mexico Farm & Ranch Heritage Museum; 4100 Dripping Springs Road; 505/522-4100) This May event celebrates New Mexico's past as a colony of Spain and its present as a borderland to Mexico.

The Whole Enchilada Festival (see Mesilla Visitors Center below) This weekend of chile and cerveza madness takes over downtown Las Cruces each September, with artists' booths, live music, and performances.

Wine & Dine

Double Eagle (2355 Calle de Guadalupe; 505/523-6700; www.double eagledining.com) Historic building dating back to the late 1800s, featuring a great bar and classy dining.

La Posta de Mesilla (2410 Calle de San Albino; 505/524-3524; www.laposta-de-mesilla.com) Fantastic, southern New Mexican cuisine in an old stagecoach depot.

Old Mesilla Pastry Café (810 S. Valley Drive; 505/525-2636) Favored spot for breakfast burritos.

Accommodations

Lundeen Inn of the Arts (618 S. Alameda Boulevard; 505/526-3326; www.innofthearts.com) Artist-run B&B with rotating exhibitions.

Meson de Mesilla (1803 Avenida de Mesilla; 800/732-6025; www.mesondemesilla.com) Historic spot, with a swimming pool.

Mesilla Valley Inn (100 Motel Boulevard; 505/524-8603; www.best western.com) Large motel, with a pool.

Information

Mesilla Visitors Center: 2340 Avenida de Mesilla; 505/647-9698; www.oldmesilla.org

Population: 2,500

Ruidoso, New Mexico

Alpine climates, Native American culture, and the Mexican border are all evident in the southern New Mexico Art Town of Ruidoso. Located just a two-hour drive north of El Paso, and surrounded by the Sierra Blanca Mountains (whose tallest peak soars above 12,000 feet), Ruidoso is an anomaly of a place whose economy and culture is influenced by year-round tourism, a very large ski area, a thriving casino on the nearby Mescalero Apache reservation, an active arts scene, and a thoroughbred racetrack.

For decades this place has been a favorite summer getaway for Texans and residents of northern Mexico venturing here in search of heat relief. It's also the outdoors recreation outlet for places in southern New Mexico such as Roswell, Las Cruces, and Carlsbad. Over the past 20 years a diverse restaurant and entertainment scene has developed to serve these weekenders, second-home owners, and newly arrived residents. Whereas Ruidoso was once loaded with retirees, in recent years an influx of mid-career professionals has not only lowered the region's gray-haired quotient but has also led to the establishment of a broader year-round range of cultural activities.

Outdoor activities such as horseback riding, fly fishing, golf, and mountain hiking are key components of the Ruidoso lifestyle, and this is also a place that's keenly aware of its historic ties to the region's Wild West, frontier past. Billy the Kid and Sheriff Pat Garrett were regular visitors to the nearby town of Lincoln, and cowboy culture is still very much alive in the small-towns of Lincoln County.

Art Talk

Michael Hurd, artist.

Our last governor forced a four-lane highway through here a few years ago, kicking a lot of doors down without regard for the ways people feel about development in this area. But since he left we've gotten the go-ahead to do a redesign on the project, which is sort of like making lemonade from lemons. I left here to go to school and work, but the Hondo Valley never was far from my mind. This is a beautiful and fragile place that needs to be protected, and I got my sense of land stewardship from my father. My paintings are about the time I live in, and I try to intergrate modern imagery with things that make me think. The place I live in and the environment I work in have a definite influence on my art. This entire area is broadening the diversity of its arts and cultural sectors. People coming here are more interested in having access to the arts than the older residents seem to be.

Arts Scene

Ruidoso's visual arts scene is well supported by the more than three-dozen galleries throughout the community. While there's a certain amount of southwestern and cowboy western imagery created here, that's balanced by an equal amount of sophisticated landscape painting, realist bronze sculpture, and a wealth of fine crafts represented in the galleries. Master artists such as sculptor Dave McGary, Western painter Gordon Snidow, and Hispanic sculptor and painter Luis Jimenez all make their homes in the region, but perhaps the most noted of all the area's artists are the members of the Wyeth family. This American art clan, whose roots are firmly grounded in faraway communities such as the Art Town of Rockland, Maine, operates the Hurd-La Rinconada Gallery in the nearby community of San Patricio, exhibiting historic paintings by the likes of N. C. Wyeth, Peter Hurd, Andrew Wyeth, and Henriette Wyeth. The legacy of the Wyeth family has also led to a presence of Wyeth and Hurd family art in several of the region's art galleries.

The Hubbard Museum of the American West, founded in 1992, is a nationally recognized institution devoted to the preservation and advancement of cowboy culture. Its year-round activities include artist lectures and workshops, programs for families and kids, exhibits about the region's Wild West past, an annual Cowboy Culture Symposium, and exhibits on the history of thoroughbred horse racing. The museum is just a mile away from the Ruidoso Downs Racetrack and Casino, which books top-name acts in Country Western music during its summer concert series.

While one of the big summer music events is the Mountain of Blues Festival, held outdoors in mid-June, the jewel of Ruidoso's arts scene is the Spencer Theatre for the Performing Arts. This $22-million, privately funded, performing-arts center opened in 1997 with a 514-seat auditorium and a year-round slate of touring concerts, plays, symphony performances, and comedy shows. The facility also uses an outdoor configuration that accommodates 1,200 seated on a grass lawn. Everything from jazz shows to the town's July 4 fireworks show happens here, as does children's theatre, Broadway revivals, and the occasional Elvis show. During the summer months there are free concerts in Schoolhouse Park, monthly gallery walks during evening hours, and a very large, outdoor arts fair in late June.

Essentials

Visual Arts Venues

The Hubbard Museum of the American West (841 Highway 70 W; 505/378-4142; www.hubbard museum.org) Well-funded facility with educational programs, festivals, and exhibitions.

Hurd—La Rinconada Gallery (Highway 70 W., San Patricio.; 505/653-4331) Home of master artists from the Wyeth and Hurd families.

McGary Studio (2002 Sudderth Street; 505/257-1000) Sculpture by one of the nation's top realist artists.

Performing Arts & Events

Spencer Theatre for the Performing Arts (Highway 220, Alto; 505/336-4800; www.spencertheater.com) State-of-the-art venue presenting touring shows and concerts year-round.

Ruidoso Art Festival (see Ruidoso Valley Chamber of Commerce below) This June event in Schoolhouse Park attracts more than 125 artists.

Art Talk

Jan and Dave Houser,
photographers.

Jan: We left San Diego and came here when we decided we wanted to live in a more affordable and dramatic place. What inspires us about this area is its openness and its spectacular diversity of landscape. We get over 300 days of sunshine a year, and we love living in a quiet, scenic setting where we never hear our neighbors.

Dave: I think color was invented in New Mexico. This community has a relaxed, respectful, and friendly way of life, and that's important to both of us. Even though we left a big city to come here, our careers gained momentum after making the move. We've been able to find the right people to work with, and we've been able to find the right balance of work and relaxation that we didn't have before. You don't come here for financial gain. You come here for a lifestyle.

Lincoln County Cowboy Symposium (see Ruidoso Valley Chamber of Commerce below) One of the nation's top festivals of the American West, this celebration of cowboy culture takes place in mid-October.

Wine & Dine

Ruidoso Roastery (113 Rio Street; 505/257-3676; www.ruidoso roastery.com) The county's top buzz shop and a favored artist hangout.

Coyote Cantina (2408 Sudderth Drive; 505/257-7522) Local spot for live music and dancing.

Lincoln County Grill (2717 Sudderth Drive; 505/257-7669) Texas-style BBQ restaurant and an outdoor deck.

Accommodations

Black Bear Lodge (428 Main Road; 505/257-1459) Family-owned B&B in the tall pines.

Aspen Lodge (201 Upper Terrace; 505/257-2978) Affordable rooms close to the center of town.

Innsbruck Lodge (601 Sudderth Drive; 505/257-4071; www.inns bruckruidoso.com) Affordable and a skiers' favorite.

Information

Ruidoso Valley Chamber of Commerce: 720 Sudderth Street; 505/257-7395; www.ruidoso.net

Population: 7,800

Santa Fe, New Mexico

ettled by Spanish colonialists in the late 1500s, this corner of the high desert Southwest was first known to its Native American inhabitants as the Dancing Ground of the Sun. The Spaniards, who were protected by the swords of conquistadores and the prayers of priests in their quest for gold and souls, declared this the northern terminus of their Camino Real territories. To this day, Santa Fe remains a largely Hispanic community that considers itself "tri-cultural," a place populated by Hispanics, Native Americans, and Anglos (a catch-all phrase applied to everyone else, including African Americans and Asians). Connecting with today's descendants of Santa Fe's original residents isn't difficult. Simply board one of the shuttle busses that ferry local residents from downtown's historic neighborhoods to the sprawling, Camel Rock Casino located several miles north of town on Tesuque Pueblo tribal land. Chances are better than even that sitting around the casino's blackjack tables or parked up against one of its hundreds of slot machines, there will be more than a few folks who are fluent in Tewa, the original language of several Rio Grande Indian tribes.

As the capital city of a thinly populated state, Santa Fe should have lots in common with similarly situated communities such as Helena, Montana, and Salem, Oregon, Instead, this one-time colonial outpost has developed into one of the continent's leading tourist destinations, a place that's busy year-round catering to the spending patterns of thousands of visitors who venture here for everything from spiritual rejuvenation at one of Santa Fe's many spas and retreats, to cultural stimulation offered during the summer performances at Santa Fe Opera. Santa Fe has evolved into a diverse, sophisticated community whose stunning beauty and seductive architecture continues to attract independent-thinking and creatively motivated individuals from points across the globe.

This isn't an especially affordable place to live (for low housing prices, check out Helena), yet many newcomers are willing to shoulder the burden of Santa Fe's pricey real estate in order to reside in a place that not only embraces the quirky spirit of creativity, it unashamedly celebrates it. From the startling, artistic diversity on display most weekends at the town's two flea markets (one is adjacent to the Santa Fe Opera grounds), to the weeklong, September madness of Fiestas de Santa Fe, a whirlwind celebration of Hispanic heritage that culminates in the destruction of a towering, fireworks-filled puppet, Santa Fe is the kind of place that gains strength from the ready acceptance of its quirky nature. As is the case in most resort communities, Santa Fe wages are painfully low. Many people work two jobs, and raising a family in this Art Town costs substantially more than it does in the state's largest city, Albuquerque, located an hour's drive south. But for thousands of part-time waiters, ski lift operators, tour guides, massage therapists, and retail clerks, it's a sacrifice well worth making. That's because their off-duty hours are religiously spent in their home studios where they paint, sculpt, weld, and polish the components of the art they hope will eventually free them from the need to work a day job in order to support their art habits. In Santa Fe, nearly every artist has his or her dream about being represented in one of the town's leading art galleries and successfully making a living from their art. And a startling number of artists have achieved that goal.

Lots of well-intentioned people move here to start new phases of their lives and become better human beings. Conversely, a number of individuals move here after messing up their lives in some other place, hoping they can get a fresh start in the shadow of the Sangre de Cristo Mountains. You see evidence of this every day, walking around the streets surrounding the plaza, in the form of individuals who are dressed to the hilt in outfits reflecting some interpretation of the elusive "Santa Fe style." But enjoying life in this part of the high desert Southwest involves more than a year-long shopping trip, though it seems that many attempt to beat the odds and try to buy their way to happiness. This is a wonderful place to live for those willing to dig below its shiny surface and find out how Santa Fe functions behind the wizard's curtain. For those unwilling to make that effort, Santa Fe has a way of pointing them toward the egress.

Santa Fe is an amazing place to live. Despite the breakneck pace of its real-estate development, the neighborhoods where many of the town's hard-working artists and Hispanic families live shoulder to shoulder are both beautiful and closely knit. Entrepreneurial new-comers move here to start everything from Italian bakeries to software-consulting firms, and while some of these ventures fizzle in a year or two, enough keep their heads above water to provide a continual flow of new energy and ideas into the region. There are National Forest lands just outside the city limits, as well as an acclaimed children's museum. While the city's parks are few, they're being improved and are much nicer today than they were a decade ago. The historic center of town, the plaza, is a place where arts festivals, political rallies, ice-sculpting contests, summer concerts, dozing tourists, and an endless flow of creative spirit provide an ever-changing window onto the City Different's soul.

Arts Scene

Somewhere in the range of 200 galleries battle for the hearts, minds, and credit cards of Santa Fe's art buyers. While there's some annual turnover in the local gallery and restaurant scene, many new ventures find ways to survive, proving that good ideas combined with solid business practices continue to be rewarded, even in the face of stiff competition from businesses in Art Towns such as Jackson, Wyoming, and Aspen, Colorado. Thousands of artists from across North America strive for Santa Fe gallery representation, trying to get a foot in the door of what they perceive to be a nonstop money train. The reality of the situation is not so simple, as international economic trends have the tendency to significantly cut down on Santa Fe's tourist traffic and art sales. Certainly, there are many established artists who do quite well no matter how the economy is holding up. But for most artists and galleries, even in Santa Fe, tough times are not that unusual.

In recent years contemporary arts have taken the upper hand in Santa Fe's galleries. There's still a market for cowboy art and Western realism, though the niche this style of art occupies continues to shrink. Traditional landscape painting and realist sculpture has moved into the void, and it's now easy to find landscape scenes painted by artists working outside the Rocky Mountain West and the desert Southwest. But it's the contemporary arts that have elevated Santa Fe's visibility on the international arts scene. Large-scale events such as SITE Santa Fe, a biennial contemporary arts show, and ART Santa Fe, an international

Art Talk

Rachel Darnell, painter.

Santa Fe has many art galleries and many ways for an artist to get involved in the art world. I got here in 1996, rented out a studio space, and started working in art galleries to give myself some knowledge about the ways things worked here. Once I got my art into my first gallery, I was able to make a living from my work. Santa Fe is the kind of place that allows you to build an arts career, in comparison to many cities much larger than Santa Fe that lack these access points for younger artists. Here, if you work hard and have talent, you can quickly move your way up the ladder. The buyers coming through here tend to be from large cities, and they have sophisticated, metropolitan tastes. They tend to be the types of collectors who understand the statement an artist is trying to make in her work. This town is filled with creative people, but it's not a frenetic place to try and make your mark as an artist. You can live here and get an accurate picture of the bigger art world that's going on around you.

contemporary arts expo, have helped lead the way for this transition, as have a wave of art galleries representing contemporary artists from across the globe. Serious collectors of contemporary art have placed Santa Fe on their annual itineraries, sometimes making a point of stopping first in the Art Town of Marfa, Texas, before finding their way here for a cruise through the galleries. And as if to prove that the Santa Fe arts scene has forever turned its back on its howling coyote past, there's now a wealth of art galleries addressing serious collector niches such as Japanese basketry, Hispanic devotional art, studio glass, and Native American fashion.

There are eight art museums in Santa Fe: the Georgia O'Keeffe Museum, which is dedicated to the arts legacy of this late New Mexico artist and her contemporaries; the Institute of American Indian Arts Museum, celebrating the contemporary art genius of Native American cultures; the unique Museum of Spanish Colonial Art, dedicated to the fine arts and crafts of Santa Fe's European settlers; the New Mexico Museum of Fine Arts, which exhibits historic and contemporary art from the state's artists as well as national and international artists; the Palace of the Governors, a history museum whose long portal is home to a daily influx of Native American jewelry artists and vendors; the Museum of Indian Arts & Culture, whose exhibits celebrate the traditions of Native American art in addition to its current expressions; the Museum of International Folk Art, home to a world-class fiber art collection; and the Wheelwright Museum of the American Indian, which is focused on Native American creative expressions. There's also El Museo Cultural, an arts center for Hispanic traditional and contemporary art; the Institute of American Indian Arts, a fully-accredited four-year college dedicated to the academic and artistic training of tomorrow's generations of Native American artists; and a community contemporary arts center. The College of Santa Fe has its own contemporary arts and photography,centers, and several organizations offer summer programs in painting, photography, and sculpture. While Santa Fe's major arts festivals include the Hispanic Market in July and the Santa Fe Indian Market in August, there are weekly outdoors arts and crafts shows around the downtown plaza during spring, summer, and fall.

Entertainers of all types call Santa Fe their second home, from Hollywood stars to Latin American recording artists who move here for the town's Spanish-flavored anonymity. Promoters and producers have also flocked here, and there's no better evidence of this than the stunning, world-class Santa Fe Opera, whose two-month, five-opera season is staged in an outdoor pavilion seating 2,128. The opera season is also the height of Santa Fe's performing-arts season, a time when music- and opera-loving art collectors fill Santa Fe's hotels and restaurants in a mad dash for art-guided pleasure. Also taking place during the summer months are the Santa

Art Talk

Jack Parsons, photographer.

I moved here 30 years ago after being sent to Santa Fe from London, where I was living, on a film project. I fell in love with New Mexico's landscape, its weather, its environment, and its culture. This was a great place to develop a photography career because not only did you have all the natural inspiration you could possibly need, but you also had a tight community of photographers who helped each other, and the right kind of labs to get your work done. Since then, Santa Fe's become a haven for photographers. The College of Santa Fe started a photography center, the photography workshops have expanded exponentially, and there are several galleries specializing in photography. Even though Santa Fe's a lot less affordable place than it used to be, it's become a better place to live. The main issue we're facing has to do with water and its impact on the community's growth.

Fe Chamber Music Festival, the season of the Sante Fe Desert Chorale (a professional chamber music chorus), the outdoor productions of Shakespeare in Santa Fe, the innovative performances of Santa Fe Stages, Aspen/Santa Fe Ballet, the international caliber Spanish dance of Maria Benitez and her Teatro Flamenco. All of it comes to a close in September with the staging of the fantastic Santa Fe Wine & Chile Fiesta on the Santa Fe Opera grounds.

The action slows down, but doesn't stop, during the winter months. The Lensic Performing Arts Center, a renovated, Vaudeville-era movie house turned into an 850-seat performing-arts venue, serves as the home of the Santa Fe Symphony and Santa Fe Pro Musica as well as the favored spot for a vibrant slate of touring national musicians and entertainers. There's also a thriving theatre community that stages its works at a host of smaller venues, a film festival, and a performing-arts school.

Essentials

Visual Arts Venues

SITE Santa Fe (1606 Paseo de Peralta; 505/989-1199; www.site santafe.org) Exhibits the best in international, local, and regional contemporary arts.

Museum of Spanish Colonial Art (750 Camino Lejo; 505/982-2226; www.spanishcolonial.org). The nation's premier exhibition and education facility for New Mexico's European-influenced art forms.

Georgia O'Keeffe Museum (217 Johnson Street; 505/995-0785; www.okeeffemuseum.org). This outstanding addition to Santa Fe's arts scene exhibits not only O'Keeffe's work but that of her contemporaries and the artists who influenced them.

Performing Arts & Events

Santa Fe Indian Market (P.O. Box 969; 505/983-5220; www.swaia.org) The nation's premier fine arts event for Native American painters, jewelers, weavers, designers, and sculptors, this late-August event draws more than 100,000 art lovers to the Plaza.

Spanish Market (see Museum of Spanish Colonial Art above). This late-July celebration of Hispanic devotional art features only New Mexican artists in its traditional section.

Las Fiestas de Santa Fe (see Santa Fe Convention & Visitors Bureau below) Post–Labor Day event celebrating the true spirit of Santa Fe and featuring the torching of the original Burning Man, the mighty, 30-foot-tall puppet named Zozobra.

Wine & Dine

Maria's New Mexican Kitchen (555 W. Cordova Road; 505/983-7929) Great margaritas, fajitas, and New Mexican food at its finest.

Downtown Subscription (376 Garcia Street; 505/983-3085) Popular buzz shop, magazine stand, and gossip headquarters near the Canyon Road galleries.

El Farol (808 Canyon Road; 505/983-9912; www.elfarolsf.com) This historic spot in a Canyon Road adobe serves great Spanish tapas and has a bar scene with live music.

Accommodations

El Rey Inn (1862 Cerrillos Road; 800/521-1349; www.elreyinn santafe.com) Affordable and stylish rooms a short drive from the plaza.

Houses of the Moon (3451 Hyde Park Road; 505/992-5003; www.tenthousandwaves.com) Japanese-style complex of cabins on a mountainside, next to a one-of-a-kind spa.

Garrett's Desert Inn (311 Old Santa Fe Trail; 505/982-1851; www.garrettsdesertinn.com) Reasonably priced hotel in the center of town, with a swimming pool.

Information

Santa Fe Convention & Visitors Bureau: 201 W. Marcy Street, 505/955-6200; www.santafe.org

Population: 64,500

Silver City, New Mexico

The southwest corner of New Mexico is a five-hour drive from Santa Fe's turbocharged arts scene, which is precisely why increasing numbers of artists, writers, and musicians who formerly called places like Santa Fe, Taos, and even Tucson home have decided to relocate to this mining community in the Pinos Altos Mountains. Here, there are plenty of living connections to New Mexico's historic past as well as abundant proof that centuries ago this remote corner of the continent was home to prehistoric cultures of the Mimbres and Mogollon peoples.

Though there's still ample evidence of the presence of the mining industry that built modern Silver City, one of the big reasons artists have pinpointed this place is its abundance of affordable real estate. Storefronts along Yankie Street and Broadway that used to cater to the needs of miners have been converted into coffee bars, galleries, fine crafts stores, and cafés, while second-story lofts that once housed dentists offices and insurance agencies are now home to artist studios, loft apartments, and Web-based businesses.

North of here is the Gila Wilderness and the Gila Cliff Dwellings National Monument, a place framed by the Mogollon Mountains' 10,000-foot peaks and housing the architectural remnants of an ancient civilization. The small town of Pinos Altos, which lies between Silver City and the cliff dwellings, is home to the Buckhorn Saloon and Opera House, once a favored hangout of Billy the Kid and now the home of a melodrama theatre in summer and a performing-arts series in winter. Many Silver City artists are influenced by the traditions of the Mimbres culture, and there's a great deal of local interest in the ongoing cultural revival taking place among the Mata Ortiz ceramics community near Casas Grandes, in Chihuahua, Mexico, about a three-hour drive south.

Arts Scene

While there's some yearly turnover in Silver City's galleries, nearly a dozen art spaces seem to make a go of things, along with a few galleries in Pinos Altos. Western New Mexico University, a state-supported school with everything from a football team to a performing-arts series, occupies some prime real estate overlooking Silver City. Its history museum is home to one of the nation's premier collections of pottery and artifacts from the Southwest's prehistoric cultures, especially the Mimbres and Casas Grandes peoples (the museum cooperates on exhibitions with the Centro Cultural Paquime in Casas Grandes), as well as ceramics from the Rio Grande tribes of northern New Mexico. The McCray Gallery, which is also on campus, is the area's premier visual arts venue, exhibiting regional as well as local work. The Silver City Museum in downtown is another place to find exhibits of Mimbres culture, along with shows on the region's cowboy culture, silver mining, and Hispanic heritage. There are lots of alternative arts venues in Silver City, and places such as bank lobbies, coffee bars, and restaurants are popular venues for local artists. Many of these sites feature rotating exhibitions organized by the Mimbres Regional Arts Council and the San Vicente Artists.

Two of the biggest events on the region's arts calendar are the Art Fair in Big Ditch Park, which takes place in Silver City's downtown park,

Art Talk

Cindy Northrup, ceramist and painter.

I create functional pottery and watercolor paintings, and I make my living by selling through the co-op gallery. I moved here about a year ago from Florida, where my work was represented all over the state, but now I'm just here in Silver City, and I also sell over my Web site. There's a ton of wonderful artists living here. We do a lot of networking through the gallery, advising each other on marketing strategies and technical things. Most of the artists living here have moved into Silver City from other parts of the country. This is a small, supportive community with a high sense of awareness about the value of the arts. The cost of living here is affordable, and the local economy has its ups and downs. But the artists survive, mainly because we get a year-round flow of tourists who specifically come here for the galleries and the arts events.

Art Talk

Jim Madsen, coowner of Eklektikas
I & II.

When I decided to move back to the US with my partner, North Johnson, after spending a number of years in San Miguel de Allende, we found Silver City to be the sort of place that straddled the American and Mexican cultures. Ten years ago the arts community wasn't as visible as it is now, and downtown looked pretty sad. Today, we have a situation where more than two dozen sites stay open during our art walk, and where the galleries are doing well showing local and national work. I see artists walking into my gallery all the time who are looking around Silver City to see if it's the right place for them to move to. Some of those artists want to be represented locally, but a number of them are just choosing to live here, and they sell their work in other parts of the country. Our typical Silver City visitor is a tourist who knows art, likes going into galleries, and is very open to the idea of buying something they find interesting.

and the Pinos Altos Art Fair in mid-June. Both events attract more than 50 artists and turn out large crowds of locals and visitors who travel here knowing that many Silver City artists also sell their work in galleries in Santa Fe and Taos. In mid-September, Silver City hosts the Renfaire celebration of the era of knights and damsels, while the Fiesta de las Ollas in mid-July celebrates the region's historic and living cultural connections to pottery as high art. The highly regarded Silver City Blues Festival brings national and regional talents into Gough Park during late May, a cowboy poetry festival rolls into town in September, and the mid-October Weekend at the Galleries signals the climax of Silver City's yearly tourist season.

Essentials

Visual Arts Venues

McCray Gallery (1000 College Avenue; 505/538-6517) Located on the campus of Western New Mexico University, this art space displays regional and local arts.

Eklektikas Gallery (104 W. Yankie Street; 505/538-8081) Innovative gallery exhibiting visual arts and ethnographic work.

Lois Duffy Art (108 W. Yankie Street; 505/534-0822; www.loisduffy.com) Artist-owned studio/gallery.

Performing Arts & Events

Art Fair in Big Ditch Park (see Silver City/Grant County Chamber of Commerce below) Silver City's largest outdoor arts show takes place on Labor Day weekend.

Pinos Altos Melodrama Theatre (Pinos Altos Opera House; 505/388-3848) Corny, funny, and lovable summer comedy in a historic venue.

Silver City Blues Festival (see Silver City/Grant County Chamber of Commerce below) This growing, popular festival in late May brings national music acts into Silver City's park and its nightspots.

Wine & Dine

A.I.R. Coffee Company (112 W. Yankie Street; 866/892-3009; www.aircoffee.biz) Legendary gathering place for local artists.

Buckhorn Saloon (32 Main Street; 505/538-9911) Historic bar in Pinos Altos, where everyone goes to have fun, listen to music, chow on burgers, and dance up a storm.

Vicki's Deli (107 W. Yankie Street; 505/388-5430) Popular, downtown lunch spot with local art on the walls.

Accommodations

Palace Hotel (106 W. Broadway; 505/388-1811) Affordable rooms in a quirky but quaint downtown hotel.

Bear Mountain Lodge (2251 Cottage San Road; 505/538-2538; www.bearmountainlodge.com) Eleven guest rooms in an historic home outside Silver City, operated by The Nature Conservancy.

Casitas de Gila Guesthouse (Rt. 180, Cliff; 505/535-4455; www.galleryatthecasitas.com) Local art abounds in this five-*casita* inn.

Information

Silver City/Grant County Chamber of Commerce: 201 N. Hudson Avenue, 505/538-3785; www.silvercity.org

Population: 10,850

Taos, New Mexico

I t all began nearly a century ago with two wandering artists, one bro-
ken wagon wheel, and a spectacular autumn day in the high-desert
glory of northern New Mexico. That's when Ernest Blumenschein and
Bert Phillips were sidelined here during their journey from Denver to
the city of Chihuahua, Mexico. As the two soon found out, the powerful charm of this ancient place had such an impact that Phillips never
left, and Blumenschein spent his summers here until finally making a
permanent move in 1919. Over the next few years they eventually
talked several of their artist pals into doing the same, and the Taos
Society of Artists was soon born. By the time Mabel Dodge Luhan arrived
on the Taos scene, attracting her coterie of drinking pals that included
D. H. Lawrence, Georgia O'Keeffe, Carl Jung, and Thomas Wolfe, the
die was cast and this sleepy community in the foothills of the Sangre
de Cristo Mountains became known as one of the nation's outposts for
free-spirited, morally independent artists. Wealthy American families
with black sheep sons and daughters who were out of step with mainstream society now had a new place to add to their lists of dumping
grounds for their family problems, aligning Taos with other Art Towns
in this book such as Key West, Florida, Provincetown, Massachusetts,
Carmel, California, and Woodstock, New York.

But the early-20th-century arrival of traditionally trained painters
wasn't the first time Taos had come into contact with creative genius.

316

This one-time frontier outpost, where Kit Carson bought a home in 1843, was first settled by members of the Taos Indian Pueblo in the early years of the millennium. For more than 900 years this Native American culture has thrived as a society with distinct artistic traditions that live on today in the form of pottery, metalwork, basketry, and wood carving. Taos Pueblo's geometric, stacked architectural style is the creative inspiration upon which the entire Southwestern/Pueblo/Adobe design motifs were established, and to this day it's well worth the small fee charged by the Pueblo to each carload of visitors who want to drive onto reservation lands to see this timeless wonder for themselves.

The first European settlers to stake their claim to this corner of the continent were the Spanish colonialists who arrived here more than 400 years ago in caravans protected by the swords of conquistadores. Though their original intent was to track down the ethereal Seven Cities of Gold, their disappointment eventually turned toward the pragmatic business of farming and the conversion of Native American people to Catholicism. Centuries of intermarriage later, the histories of Taos's colonialist settlers and Native American founders have intertwined into one storyline. The Hispanic settlers brought with them classic art traditions, learned in Spain and Mexico, that to this day are followed in the form of Spanish Colonial art created by the region's many *santeros* and *santeras*. An astounding level of furniture craftsmanship is seen in today's Taos style of tables, sofas, chairs, and doors, and the elegant tinwork that adorns the walls of many of the region's churches and public buildings as pure New Mexico artisanship.

Taos remains a place that's subject to divisive passions. On some issues, Native Americans disagree with Hispanics. The following month it will be a real-estate lawsuit pitting an out-of-state corporation against a Taos neighborhood, or maybe it's loggers vs. environmentalists the following month, and river rafters vs. farmers yet another month. Nonetheless, the Taos of today is a major tourism destination whose winters draw skiers and summers draw an international array of art lovers, bikers, truth seekers, and cultural tourists. It's become an expensive place to live, and this economic reality drives many of the community's oldest residents to seek public assistance. For some families, the development of sprawling homes in gated communities overlooking vast stretches of what once were alfalfa fields is an employment opportunity. For others, it's an insult. In any case, Taos remains spectacularly beautiful and blessedly peaceful outside of its winter and summer tourist season peaks.

Arts Scene

Not many Art Towns can boast of having more than 80 art galleries, a vibrant and diverse community arts center, four art museums, and three history museums, all of which explains why Taos is one of the nation's top places for art-motivated tourists and relocating artists. There are artists' studios scattered across the region's rolling landscape. Taos is the kind of place where highly well-known artists maintain part-time residences and studios, quietly slipping in and out of town throughout the year, though their impact is felt mostly in local bars and restaurants.

Taos isn't able to stage as many of the major arts events that high-light the summer arts calendar as Santa Fe, located 75 miles south of here. To be sure, there's a Spring Arts Celebration in May and a Fall Arts Festival in September, as well as the Wool Festival in October, the ZoukFest in July, and the Solar Music Festival in June. The spring and fall arts festivals are well-staged affairs, with dozens of art galleries open-ing new exhibitions and all of the museums staging special shows and programs. Reflecting the breathtaking diversity of the local arts scene, Taos's galleries offer an inspiring array of art ranging from traditional work by many of the top names in the Native American and Hispanic art worlds to cutting-edge contemporary by some of the big-name artists maintaining their homes and studios here. In between there's everything from cowboy realism to captivating landscapes to Southwestern expressionism. There are also substantial amounts of jew-elry as well as textile arts, blown glass, fine crafts, and elegant home furnishings.

The Taos Center for the Arts operates the Stables Gallery and the Taos Community Auditorium, and both of these venues are kept busy throughout the year with exhibitions, films, and performances. Two art schools, the Taos Institute of Arts and the Taos Art School, employ local artists during the summer months and attract a national group of early- and mid-career student artists. The Harwood Museum of Art, operated by the University of New Mexico, offers exhibits of historic and contemporary art as well as regular programs for adults and kids. It's nationally known for its collection to Taos School painters as well as New Mexico's Hispanic and Native American artists. The Millicent Rogers Museum, named after its wealthy late benefactor, is one of the Southwest's top ethnographic institutions, with a special emphasis on Native American and Hispanic work, while the Fechin Institute and

Home celebrates the work of deceased Russian émigré artist Nicolai Fechin (1927–33).

In June the town gears up for the Taos Poetry Circus, a nationwide invitational event, while in late July the community's Hispanic culture is celebrated (loudly, and with lots of tequila) during Fiestas de Taos, a four-day bacchanal that completely ties up traffic in and around the plaza. From mid-June through mid-August the Taos School of Music stages a world-class program of chamber concerts at the Hotel St. Bernard in Taos Ski Valley, and just as the summer season closes there's the Music from Angel Fire's two-week celebration of world-class classical music concerts, recitals, and orchestra presentations in various regional venues, including the Taos Center for the Arts. Taos is home to a substantial number of Hollywood film community actors, producers, and technical specialists. It comes as no surprise, then, that the April Taos Film Festival of the Arts attracts filmgoers to its weeklong series of screenings of all-digital films, lectures, and soirees.

Art Talk

Jean Marquardt, executive director of the Taos Art Association.

We're the designated local arts association for this community, so we support most of the art activities taking place on the visual and performing-arts fronts. We own a theatre and an art gallery, and we help local organizations that want to use these facilities to put on their own programs. We also do our own presenting, from taiko drumming to ballet, and we organize annual shows in our Stables Gallery that showcase the innovation and expertise of this community's many artists. Taos is a community whose arts needs grow in different ways, so we stay flexible in addressing things like the gaps in our schools' arts-education programs.

Essentials

Visual Arts Venues

Taos Center for the Arts (133 Paseo del Norte; 505/758-2052; www.taoscenterforthearts.org) The Stables Gallery features rotating exhibitions covering everything from contemporary arts to ethnographic artifacts.

The Harwood Museum (238 Ledoux Street; 505/758-9826; www.harwoodmuseum.org) One of the Southwest's leading arts institutions, the Harwood showcases traveling shows as well as local arts and works from its permanent collection.

Art Talk

Holly Wilbur, sculptor.

I moved here 10 years ago after studying sculpture in Italy because I like the size of Taos as well as its beauty and quiet. To my eyes, Taos has the look and feel of an Italian village, but one with a very different climate than Pietrasanta's. This is a real artists' community, so it's also a place where it's very easy to meet people. It's also a place that's very aware of and respectful of its Native American heritage, and going to the ceremonies and celebrations at Taos Pueblo is one of the benefits of living here. I have turned to painting as a way to help me work out some of the sculpture problems I come across in my studio. Artist friends have always been there for me, giving advice when I needed it. Most of the people living here realize that in life, you've got to be faithful to doing whatever makes you feel best.

The Millicent Rogers Museum (Millicent Rogers Road; 505/758-2462; www.millicentrogers.org) Historic home, 4 miles north of the Taos Plaza, featuring outstanding exhibitions of regional, national, and ethnographic work.

Performing Arts & Events

Taos Poetry Circus (see Taos County Chamber of Commerce below) Spring event attracting fans and slammers from across North America.

Taos Film Festival of the Arts (P.O. Box 474; 505/751-1654; www.taosfilmfestival.com) Screens the latest in Hollywood digital films.

Taos Solar Music Festival (Kit Carson Park; 505/758-9191; www.solarmusic fest.com) This June, solar-powered weekend of music attracts top national names in rock, blues, and international music.

Wine & Dine

Eske's Brew Pub (106 Des Georges Lane; 505/758-1517; www.eskesbrewpub.com) Friendly spot and a great place for handcrafted brews.

Trading Post Café (4178 Highway 68, Ranchos de Taos; 505/758-5089) Popular with the gourmet crowd, with a great wine list.

Doc Martin's Restaurant (125 Paseo del Pueblo Norte; 505/758-2233) Legendary breakfast spot and watering hole in the Taos Inn.

Accommodations

Taos Inn (125 Paseo del Pueblo Norte; 505/758-2233; www.taos inn.com) Historic hotel with Pueblo-style architecture in the center of town.

The Bavarian Lodge (100 Kachina Road; 505/776-8020; www.the bavarian.com) Luxury for skiers at Taos Ski Valley.

Casa de las Chimeneas (405 Cordoba Road; 505/758-4777) Comfortable B&B close to the plaza.

Information

Taos County Chamber of Commerce: 1139 Paseo del Pueblo Sur; 800/732-8267; www.taoschamber.com

Population: 4,700

Ogden, Utah

L ocated an hour's drive north of Salt Lake City, Ogden is a fast-growing community anchored by a state university. It's within a short drive of the urban center's major league sports, art museums, and international airport. Ogden's east boundary is defined by the towering Wasatch Mountains, home to 9,572-ft. Mt. Ogden and ski areas such as Snowbasin, Nordic Valley, and Powder Mountain, all of which are a short drive from Ogden's well-preserved, turn-of-the-20th-century downtown.

Like most of Utah, Ogden is a place that's family friendly and whose social and political life is strongly influenced by the Mormon Church. What Ogden has going in its favor is an efficiently run civic government that's been able to spearhead a decade-long downtown revival while maintaining the affordable and safe lifestyle for which the community is famous. Ogden's access to some of the continent's most spectacular natural treasures, including a local water system fed by alpine snowmelt, makes this a very attractive community for artists who enjoy the great outdoors. Ogden's family-owned farms and dairies continue to thrive, and what's actually a high-desert community has been turned into a verdant oasis of tree-lined boulevards and gorgeous city parks.

Arts Scene

Because it's home to students attending Weber State University (WSU), Ogden benefits from both the spunky presence of thousands of tattooed college kids as well as the broad range of arts-oriented activities, programs and performances organized by WSU. The university's mountainside campus is just a few miles from downtown, which makes for a smooth integration of the community's and WSU's arts resources.

When it comes to the arts, Ogden's combination of town and gown begins on campus in the Browning Performing Arts Center and its three spaces: Austad Auditorium, Allred Theatre, and Eccles Theatre. These venues are used year-round for performances by everything from touring symphonies to Cuban all-star salsa bands and are the home base of both Utah Symphony and Ballet West. Nearby, the Kimball Visual Arts Center's Mary Shaw Gallery hosts touring national shows as well as faculty and student exhibitions.

WSU's Utah Musical Theatre is staged in the considerably more stylish environs of Peery's Egyptian Theater, an elegantly restored, 1924 movie palace in downtown Ogden that handles audiences of 800. This is also a favored venue for touring national acts representing all niches of contemporary music, as well as the very popular Pharaoh's Film Series and segments of the Sundance Film Festival. Downtown's Historic 25th Street serves as the community's favorite gathering spot and is home to an array of coffee bars, restaurants, and the ubiquitous "private clubs," which are Utah's answer to the widely voiced visitor query of "Hey, where can I get a drink in this town?"

The newly restored Union Station is home to four museums as well as the Gallery at the Station, a venue with rotating monthly shows of local and national art. Those museums are the Browning Arms Museum, Browning Kimball Car Museum, Utah State Railroad Museum, and the Odgen Natural History Museum. Also downtown is the Eccles Community Art Center, a visual arts education and exhibition facility as well a performance space. Located in a beautifully restored, turn-of-the-century Victorian mansion, the Eccles's Main Gallery and Carriage House Gallery are venues for touring exhibitions, while its sculpture garden exhibits a range of contemporary and traditional works. The Gallery Theater, which seats audiences of 50, is home to a community theatre company performing works by local playwrights.

Art Talk

Sandy Havas, executive director of the Eccles Community Art Center.

We have a university in town and many of the art students graduating from there tend to stay in Odgen, so it's one of our missions to provide those artists with a chance to exhibit their work. Our gallery is usually booked three years in advance, and we have no problem organizing our shows around specific themes that the younger artists will use as opportunities to show challenging and confrontational work. We're a private organization that's been around since 1959, so we can afford to take a more progressive stance than we could if we were a government-supported group. Odgen's still developing a sense of itself as a place that's attractive for artists who want to live and work in a supportive, safe community. We're small, family oriented, and scenic, and that's meaning more and more to many of the artists who choose to live here.

Essentials

Visual Arts Venues

Eccles Community Art Center (2580 Jefferson Avenue; 801/392-6935; www.ogden4arts.org) Ogden's very active art center is located in a Victorian-era, sandstone mansion. Its two visual arts spaces are supplemented by arts education classrooms, a community theatre, sculpture garden, gift shops, and offices for local arts groups.

Gallery at the Station (2501 Wall Avenue; 801/629-8446). A 1,500-square-foot art gallery wedged into an oddly shaped space formerly occupied by loading platforms for Union Pacific passenger trains. Built with many high-tech flourishes, Gallery at the Station is a showcase for local arts. The nearby Myra Powell Gallery houses a permanent art collection on the facility's second floor.

Kimball Visual Art Center's Mary Shaw Gallery (Weber State University; 801/626-6420; www.weber.edu) Operated by the university's visual arts department, this exhibition facility features touring, museum-quality exhibitions as well as WSU's annual faculty and student art exhibitions.

Performing Arts & Events

Browning Performing Arts Center (Weber State University; 801/626-7000; www.weber.edu) This three-theatre facility is a showcase for programs offered by the WSU performing-arts department. Music presentations range from symphony to jazz, along with Shakespeare and ballet.

Peery's Egyptian Theater
(2415 Washington Boulevard;
801/395-3200; www.peerys
egyptiantheater.com) This 800-seat,
expertly restored 1924 movie palace is
home to a year-round series of films
and performances presented by both
WSU's performing-arts department
and independent promoters.

The Gallery Theater (2580 Jefferson
Avenue; 801/392-6935; www.ogden4
arts.org) Intimate, 50-seat community
theatre inside the Eccles Community
Art Center focused on productions by
local playwrights.

Wine & Dine

The Athenian Restaurant (252
Historic 25th Street; 801/621-4911)
Serving the best souvlaki in Utah.
Don't miss the belly dancers on
weekends.

Bagels and Buns (2487 Grant
Avenue; 801/394-7142) Great place to
pull up an outdoor patio chair, order
a lox with a schmear, and watch the human parade go by.

The City Club (264 Historic 25th Street; 801/392-4447; www.the
cityclubonline.net) Ogden's most popular nightclub is said to be the
area's best spot for love-seeking singles.

Accommodations

Ben Lomond Historic Suite Hotel (2510 Washington Boulevard;
801/627-1900; www.benlomondhotel.com) This elegant, 1927 hotel
is on the National Historic Register.

Ogden Marriott (247 24th Street; 801/627-1190; www.marriott.com)
Modern hotel in the middle of downtown Odgen. Large swimming
pool and facilities for families.

Art Talk

Scott Knauer, director of the Mary
Shaw Gallery.

Our contemporary arts exhibition program
covers national, regional, and international
shows, with two shows each year set aside
for students, and a faculty exhibition every
two or three years. Many of our students
are interested in what's happening in
Ogden and show their work in places like
Union Station or in the galleries and shops
along 25th Street. The edgiest place in
town for visual arts is our art center's student gallery, where there's no editing of
the statements our art students want to
make about their art. Artists who choose
to live in Ogden are coming here for its
environment. We're just 45 minutes from
Salt Lake City, but to some people that's
a long distance in terms of the local
mind-set.

Ogden Comfort Suites (2250 S. 1200 West; 801/ 621-2545; www.choicehotels.com) Hotel with facilities for campers, RVs, and families.

Information

Ogden and Weber Convention and Visitors Bureau: 2501 Wall Avenue; 866/867-8824; www.ogdencvb.org

Population: 77,300

Park City, Utah

This resort community lies an hour's drive from downtown Salt Lake City yet is a world apart in terms of not only its alpine surroundings but also in its attitude and altitude. Park City is truly the state's playground, a place where nightclubs, Rastafarian skiers, call girls on weekend getaways with their best tippers, and Hollywood stars wanting some anonymity have all managed to carve out niches in this freewheeling refuge that caters to their hedonistic needs.

The key to Park City's success is its bull's-eye location in the midst of some of the best ski terrain on the globe. Long, frosty winters dump dozens of meters of champagne powder on the Wasatch Mountains slopes of nearby Deer Valley, the Canyons, and Park City Mountain ski resorts, luring thousands of second-home owners to their mountain getaways and enticing many more thousands of short-term visitors who spend their vacation dollars in Park City's hotels, restaurants, and art galleries.

While living in Park City is an expensive proposition (which explains why many of the local artists represented in galleries have Salt Lake City zip codes), the town is loaded with so many hangouts and hip coffee bars that hundreds of semi-itinerant artistic, ski-crazed folks find it a hard place to leave. That's why the tattooed woman with blue hair pulling espresso at the coffee bar is willing to scrape together the bucks needed to just break even on the rent in her high-priced studio apartment. Oh, and by the way, she's also a world-class snowboarder training for the 2006 Winter Olympics.

Arts Scene

There are nearly 20 art galleries in Park City, with most of them located along the sloping sidewalks of Main Street, the town's commercial core. Realism in the form of landscape painting, bronze figurative sculpture, and wildlife art does quite well here, though a few galleries have had some success with contemporary arts and fine crafts. Each August, the Park City Arts Festival fills Main Street with more than 200 booths of top artists in one of the nation's premier outdoor summer arts shows. During the show's two-day run, three stages set up at its fringes feature live music by some of the best folk and blues bands in the Rocky Mountain West. Artists who make their way through the festival's tough jurying process are rewarded with strong sales, which is why many national talents come back here year after year.

During July, August, and the first half of September, Mountain Sound Stages presents free afternoon and evening concerts at venues along Main Street. During these same months the Utah Symphony performs a full slate of summer concerts at Deer Valley, and the Park City International Music Festival presents its program of orchestra concerts, recitals, and chamber music performances at various Summit County venues.

Park City is the home of the Sundance Film Festival, which fills the town with actors, film fans, dealmakers, and producers each January. During other parts of the year the Park City Film Series showcases independent films for local audiences whose standards for cinematic arts are as sophisticated as they come. Community theatre is the specialty of the Egyptian Theatre Company, whose plays are presented year-round in the Arabesque surroundings of the Egyptian Theatre on Main Street.

It's hard to understate the impact the Kimball Art Center has had on the development of Park City's visual arts scene. This former car showroom and garage, which Park City Resort founder Bill Kimball turned into a community arts center in the mid-1960s, is the kind of arts facility most small towns dream of having. Well-funded, innovative, multifaceted, and open-minded, the Kimball combines a first-rate visual arts exhibition facility with well-equipped classrooms and a year-round program of lectures, performances, and special events. Exhibitions here tend to be more contemporary than what's shown in Park City's commercial galleries, which is another reason why the regional arts community has such high regard for the Kimball's programs.

The Eccles Center, a lavishly equipped performing-arts center, opened its doors in 1999 and immediately gave Park City its first venue capable of handling touring national and international acts in music, theatre, and dance. The Eccles's programs, which run year-round, range from children's theatre to rock concerts and ballet, performed in the state-of-the-art, 1,259-seat surroundings of Kearns Auditorium.

Essentials

Visual Arts Venues

Meyer Gallery (305 Main Street; 435/649-8160; www.meyergallery.com) This art space features landscape painting and bronze sculpture by many of the region's top talents.

Coda Gallery (804 Main Street; 435/655-3803; www.codagallery.com) A multidisciplinary arts space with a special emphasis on contemporary fine crafts.

Kimball Art Center (638 Park Avenue; 435/649-8882; www.kimball-art.org) Has earned a strong reputation for its contemporary arts exhibitions and educational programs.

Performing Arts & Events

The Park City Arts Festival (638 Park Avenue; 435/649-8882; www.kimball-art.org) This late-summer, outdoor arts show combines booths by more than 200 top, national arts and fine crafts talents with several stages of nonstop, live entertainment.

Last Fridays Arts & Eats Gallery Stroll (638 Park Avenue; 435/649-8882; www.kimball-art.org) Monthly event on the final Friday of each

Art Talk

Susan Jones, owner of Meyer Gallery. It used to be that half the buildings on Park Avenue were boarded up and condemned, but now you can't touch any of them for under a million dollars. For artists, there's been a huge benefit from the past 20 years of Park City's development, and a large part of the credit for what's happened here goes to the Kimball Art Center, which has provided the venue and leadership necessary to move this town forward. Of course, all this development has left Park City's artists in a position where many of them can't afford to live right in town, but Salt Lake City is close enough to be a viable alternative for housing. Developing affordable housing for artists and the people who work in restaurants and ski areas is an ongoing challenge. Visitors to Park City seem most interested in representational styles of art, and the work that's purchased here gets shipped across the world.

Art Talk

Pam Crowe-Weisberg, director of the Kimball Art Center.

The Kimball is well known for its strong exhibition programs and for the year-round art-education programs run through here. We offer local residents a fully equipped ceramics studio, a photography studio, and a painting studio. We also have a children's program, which we're in the process of expanding, and after-school programs. Our teachers are drawn from this area's many talented artists. We present eight art exhibitions a year, with two or three of those being traveling shows and the rest focused on artists of this region, especially the shows that rotate through our smaller gallery space, which is dedicated to local artists' shows. We don't have a performance program, but we do present the annual arts festival, which draws 60,000 visitors in one weekend.

month matching local art galleries with restaurants in presenting a $3 per person gallery walk combining the visual and culinary arts.

Park City International Music Festival (1420 W. Meadowloop Road; 435/649-5309; www.pcmusic festival.com) This mid-June to August classical music festival at the Canyons Resort presents orchestra, chamber, jazz, and solo concerts in many venues.

Wine & Dine

Grappa (151 Main Street; 435/645-0636; www.grapparestaurant.com) Sophisticated, Northern Italian restaurant with an outstanding wine list.

La Casita (710 Main Street; 435/645-9585) Mexico City–style restaurant presenting classic dishes and avoiding Tex-Mex abominations.

Wasatch Brew Pub (250 Main Street; 435/649-0900; www.wasatch beers.com) This award-winning brew-pub is famous for its affordable, innovative menu, featuring delights such as fish & chips and Utah trout.

Accommodations

Old Miners Lodge (615 Woodside Avenue; 435/645-8068; www.oldminerslodge.com) Affordable accommodations in a historic, centrally located lodge.

Goldener Hirsch Inn (7570 Royal Street E.; 435/649-7770; www.goldenerhirschinn.com) European-style luxury hotel with a great restaurant.

Best Western Landmark Inn (6560 N. Landmark Dr.; 435/649-7300) Reasonably priced hotel convenient to highways, with a swimming pool.

Information

Park City Chamber of Commerce and Visitors Center: 800/453-1360; www.parkcityinfo.com

Population: 7,400

St. George, Utah

ounded by a pioneering group of cotton farmers in 1861, by 1862 St. George was also home to enough creative energy that a group was formed to stage southern Utah's first play. It was such a hit that the thespians followed that success by establishing the St. George Lyceum and Dramatic Association a few years later (all that was missing was the announcement of a $5-million capital campaign). In any case, a tradition of local support for the arts was started and nurtured, which explains why the community of St. George is now home to a performing-arts center, an innovatively programmed art and history museum, several art galleries, and a long-standing tradition of outdoor arts festivals.

Located just north of the Arizona state line about an hour's drive outside Las Vegas, St. George is the largest community in a region that includes Cedar City, which itself is home to one of the nation's premier summer Shakespeare festivals, as well as Zion National Park and the small town of Springdale, which has attracted a group of resident photographers and painters.

In the past 20 years St. George has grown considerably, fueled by the real-estate-development business and the cash flows of retirees seeking a place in the sun. What they find here is a community very aware of its Mormon pioneer heritage, which lends the local lifestyle a slightly religious undertone. If St. George's mix of golfing geezers and young, LDS families doesn't crimp one's lifestyle, this community becomes an appealingly affordable and safe place to live.

Arts Scene

The jewel in St. George's arts scene is the St. George Art Museum and the Pioneer Center for the Arts. Located in what had once been a seed warehouse, the facility has year-round exhibitions of local, regional, and national work, and also exhibits ethnographic art and artifacts from the region's Native American cultures. While there are about a half-dozen commercial art galleries in St. George, the region's biggest gallery cluster is in Springdale, a small town at the entrance to Zion National Park. The area's premier visual arts event is the annual St. George Art Festival, an April outdoor exhibition that takes place along the streets of the town's historic district and features more than 120 artists' booths. In March the annual Canyon Country Western Arts Festival in Cedar City attracts visual artists as well as national musicians and entertainers.

Utah's premier performing-arts organization, the Utah Shakespearean Festival, stages its spectacular season of plays, workshops, and readings in Cedar City from June through October and is considered one of the nation's top Shakespeare festivals. Each season the company presents more than a half-dozen works by Shakespeare in two playhouses on the campus of Southern Utah University. The college is also the home to an active theatre studies program that presents numerous productions throughout the academic year.

The Tanner Amphitheatre in Springdale, a 2,000-seat outdoor venue set among the red-rock landscape of Zion National Park, is home to a May to August series of concerts sponsored by Dixie State College. During the academic year the college also presents a Celebrity Concert Series in an indoor, 1,200-seat performing-arts facility that's also used

Art Talk

Beverly Canty Marshall, painter.
I'm a member of the Artists Gallery, which is a cooperative space that got started in 1990 and is now the longest-surviving gallery in St. George. We started out on Ancestors Square and are now about 6 miles from there in a historic building, but the city owns this space and the rent is very reasonable. We have 10 members, with all types of media represented. We offer art classes for adults and kids, and award scholarships for school kids who want to pursue studies in the arts. For me, the attraction of the landscape is what makes me want to live here, and I find the red-rock cliffs to be inspiring. The summer arts show is the best place for local artists to exhibit their work, and the spring arts show tends to have lots of artists from outside southern Utah. In recent years this area has had a large influx of painters, and many of them are artists who are retiring to this part of the country from other places.

Art Talk

Jenny Dawn Stucki, manager and curator of the St. George Art Museum. We do 15 shows a year, bringing in a diverse group of artists who normally wouldn't be able to find a place to exhibit their art locally in the galleries, and works from our permanent collection of local, regional, and national artists. In the nine years I've been here there's been an exciting growth in the visual arts of this community. We started off with a small space in the basement of a city building and now are located in a new building with 3,000 square feet. Our shows bounce around from fantasy art to regional landscapes, and we use a review committee to select our shows. Lots of artists have started moving in to this area, and everyone from painters to metalworkers seems to find this area conducive to pursuing their work.

by the Southwest Symphony for its six concert season. A classical music recital series is staged in the college's Dunford Auditorium. The college's visual arts exhibitions, which include local and regional work, are staged in its North Plaza exhibition space. Tuacahan Center for the Arts in nearby Ivins is home to a series of summer musicals, while the St. George Musical Theatre presents its performances in the St. George Opera House.

Essentials

Visual Arts Venues

St. George Art Museum
(47 East 200 North; 435/634-5942; www.sgcity.org) Regional, local, and national exhibitions in a multipurpose facility.

Dixie State College (225 South 700 East; 435/652-7800 www.dixie.edu) Student, faculty, and traveling shows in North Plaza.

Artists Gallery (100 E. Telegraph, Washington; 435/628-9293) Artist-run cooperative art space.

Performing Arts & Events

Utah Shakespearean Festival (351 W. Center St.; Cedar City; 435/586-7880; www.bard.org) Summer Shakespeare festival staged in two theatres.

St. George Musical Theatre (735 E. Tabernacle; 435/628-8755; www.sgmt.org) Year-round musicals.

St. George Art Festival (see St. George Chamber of Commerce below) April outdoor arts festival.

Wine & Dine

Scaldoni's (929 W. Sunset; 435/674-1300; www.scaldonis.com)
Home-style Italian in the historic district.

Bearpaw Coffee Company (75 N. Main Street; 435/634-0126)
Favorite local buzz shop.

Painted Pony (2 W. St. George Blvd.; 435/634-1700) Fine dining and
a nice wine list.

Accommodations

Green Gate Village Inn (76 W. Tabernacle; 435/628-6999;
www.greengatevillage.com) Historic inn in the middle of town.

Ambassador Inn (1481 S.
Sunland Dr.; 435/673-7900; www.ambassadorinn.net) Affordable
rooms, with a pool.

Travel Inn (316 E. St. George Blvd.; 435/673-3541) Affordable hotel,
with room for families and RVs.

Information

St. George Chamber of Commerce: 97 E. St. George Boulevard;
435/628-1658; www.stgeorgechamber.com

Population: 49,900

Cody, Wyoming

C owboy culture is alive and well in this northwest Wyoming Art
Town, the home to a thriving Western furniture community, a
major art museum devoted to the Wild West's past, and several art
galleries specializing in realist sculpture and landscape painting. Located
an hour's drive from the east entry to Yellowstone National Park, Cody
is a carefully preserved throwback to this region's past as a frontier outpost. Ranching and forestry are major underpinnings of the local economy, though in more recent years the full-bore pursuit of tourism
development has kept the bills paid for increasing numbers of Park
County families.

Living in Cody means being fully engaged with the great outdoors.
Fishing, hunting, skiing, hiking, and horseback riding aren't pigeon-
holed as once-a-year activities . . . they're how many people make use
of the spectacular natural beauty surrounding them. The crystal clear
waters of the Shoshone River slice right through Cody, making this one
of the state's primo destinations for white-water rafters and kayakers.
The Buffalo Bill Reservoir, located just west of town, is a summer magnet for water skiers and even a sailor or two, while the Absaroka
Range's 11,000-foot peaks beckon hikers into some of the continent's
most rugged wilderness.

Year-round jobs in this community of 9,000 are scarce, and low
wages are the norm. That's why it's a good idea to bring your job with
you when you move here, which explains the town's high percentage
of artists, jewelers, craftsmen, clothing designers, and small-business

owners. It's not uncommon to hear stories about families who moved here with the best of intentions to start a new life in this historic, scenic, and safe community, yet who eventually moved away because of the paucity of work and the severity of Cody's winter weather.

During the summer months Cody comes alive when a landslide of tourist spending combines with a flood of local events to create a three-month economic boom. In early July the Buffalo Bill Cody Stampede, one of the West's premier rodeo events, rolls into town with hundreds of dual-axle pickups and a like number of testosterone-overloaded cowboys from Texas, New Mexico, and parts west. From June through August, the Cody Nite Rodeo brings daily ridin', ropin', and barrel racin' action to the fairgrounds, helping to develop Cody's next generation of national rodeo stars.

Arts Scene

With its dozen art galleries, a major art and historical museum, revivalist furniture industry, and hundreds of artists working in home studios, it's little wonder that Cody has developed a healthy arts scene. During the winter months, when the town's tourism flow shuts off, many of these gallery owners and artists head southward to spend the cold months holed up in places like Tucson and Las Vegas, building up a head of creative steam and a large amount of inventory destined to fill the homes of the following summer's tourist hordes.

When they're not windsurfing on the clear waters of the Buffalo Bill Reservoir or tossing their fishing lines into the blue-ribbon trout haven of the North Fork of the Shoshone River, Cody's amazingly talented furniture craftsmen and craftswomen are creating some of the most beautiful, classic Western and contemporary Western home furnishings on the planet. Respected master craftsman Marc Taggart makes his Thomas Molesworth revivalist furniture in Cody, and his success has spawned a small industry that's allowed his protégés to establish successful furniture and home accessories businesses of their own, both in the Molesworth tradition and along other lines of inspiration.

The Cody Country Art League's members exhibit their work inside a lodge that once had been the Buffalo Bill Historical Center. Many of the league's artists aspire to have their creations represented by one of the town's very successful, commercial art galleries. In these venues, Western realism, wildlife painting, landscape painting, and realist bronze sculpture are celebrated as the crème de la crème of the regional creative vernacular. These are serious galleries that would very much

Art Talk

Josie Hedderman, marketing assistant for the Buffalo Bill Historical Center. We're the main tourism draw in Cody. Some of our visitors are surprised to find an institution with five separate museums thriving in a town this size, but we're here because of Buffalo Bill Cody's legacy and were started in 1917 for the purpose of celebrating that man's achievements. As a museum we maintain a hand-in-hand relationship with the community through extensive, year-round programming that appeals to residents of the Bighorn Basin. We have free admission days that attract up to 4,000 local residents, free lectures and films, a Native American seminar, and regional tours. Local artists are brought into the museum to teach art classes, and we regularly exhibit our instructors' art. People in Cody are keenly aware of the strength of its arts community and understand the economic impact of the arts.

be at home in places such as Taos, New Mexico, and Scottsdale, Arizona, and represent many of the West's most famous artists.

One of the nation's top museums celebrating Western culture and lore is the Buffalo Bill Historical Center, located on Sheridan Avenue at the west end of Cody's tree-lined, eminently walkable downtown. Five museums comprise the facility: The Buffalo Bill Museum, which examines the life and legend of W. F. "Wild Bill" Cody; the Whitney Gallery of Western Art, which exhibits classic and contemporary artwork of the West; the Cody Firearms Museum, which exhibits American and European guns; the Plains Indian Museum, which celebrates the region's Native American cultures; and the Draper Museum of Natural History, focused on the Yellowstone region's ecosystem. Throughout the year, the Buffalo Bill Historical Center presents special programs, lectures, and curatorial discussions on various topics in historic and contemporary art circles.

Essentials

Visual Arts Venues

Buffalo Bill Historical Center (720 Sheridan Avenue; 307/587-4771; www.bbhc.org) This broadly focused, multidisciplinary institution is the heart and soul of Cody's creative community. It presents year-round programs such as films and lectures on subjects ranging from cowgirl rodeos to vintage Western architecture.

Big Horn Galleries (1167 Sheridan Avenue; 307/527-7587; www.big horngalleries.com) A top-notch art exhibition facility emphasizing

Western painting, wildlife art, landscape painting, and realist sculpture.

Marc Taggart & Company (307/587-1800; www.marctaggart.com) Elegantly crafted Western furnishings created in the style of the late Thomas Molesworth; sold at shops worldwide, local showroom by appointment.

Performing Arts & Events

Western Design Conference (P.O. Box 1434; 307/587-1357; www.westerndesignconference.com) This September gathering of furniture craftsmen and craftswomen celebrates the latest innovations taking place in home furnishings and fashions inspired by the West's heritage.

Annual Plains Indian Museum Powwow (Buffalo Bill Historical Center, 720 Sheridan Avenue; 307/587-4771; www.bbhc.org) This event draws artists and performers from the region's Arapaho, Crow, Cheyenne, Kiowa, Comanche, Blackfeet, Sioux, Pawnee, Gros Ventre, and Shoshone tribes.

Art Talk

Bob Brown, owner of Big Horn Gallery.

We have galleries both here and in Tubac, [Arizona], with more or less the same artists in each. There's a lot of difference between these two towns, with Tubac just gaining in recognition, and Cody being a well-known place with a changing economy that's moving toward becoming more focused on second homes and tourism. I work with lots of artists who make their homes in the Bighorn Basin, which is a region with 35,000 residents. There's a sophisticated talent base here, and in recent years a number of successful artists have relocated to Cody in pursuit of a better life. Their best work tends to be traditional art or representational work that echoes the art of Wyoming's past. During the summer months Cody attracts a blue-ribbon group of art collectors and tourists, most of whom come here to visit the Buffalo Bill Historical Center.

Annual Yellowstone Jazz Festival (Buffalo Bill Historical Center, 720 Sheridan Avenue; 307/587-4771; www.bbhc.org) Mid-July event at the BBHC presenting national musicians in outdoor concerts on the center's manicured lawns.

Wine & Dine

The Beta Coffeehouse (1132 12th Street; 307/587-7707) Cody's favorite place for a caffeine buzz.

Zapata's (1362 Sheridan Avenue; 307/527-7181) Reasonably priced Mexican standards served alongside potent margaritas.

The Irma Hotel (1192 Sheridan Avenue; 307/587-4221; www.irma-hotel.com) Cody's classic, cowboy-style hotel is a great place to watch the local color parade past, as well as dig into a prime beefsteak.

Accommodations

Rainbow Park Motel (1136 17th Street; 307/587-6251) Reasonably priced rooms, plus a coffee bar, all within a short walk from downtown.

Pawnee Hotel (1032 12th Street; 307/587-2239) Downtown, plus it's a pet-friendly hotel.

Gateway Motel and Campground (203 Yellowstone Avenue; 307/587-2561) Affordable campsites and rooms, plus many with family-friendly facilities.

Information

Cody Country Chamber of Commerce: 836 Sheridan Avenue; 307/587-2777; www.codychamber.org

Population: 8,800

Jackson, Wyoming

ramed by the breathtaking, 13,700-foot summits of the Grand Teton range to its northwest and the formidable, 10,000-foot peaks of the Gros Ventre range to its southeast, its easy to understand why the "hole" referred to in the title Jackson Hole refers to the geographic wonder of a high-altitude river valley coursing between the region's mountain ranges. Jackson's 6,200-foot elevation may not be the continent's highest, but its location in the northwest corner of Wyoming guarantees that this 48-mile-long river valley and its surrounding mountains receive unworldly amounts of champagne powder snow during winter, followed by a summer that's bright, crystal clear, and packed with tourists.

Jackson's year-round residents live in a place where the traditions of the cowboy West have for decades joined forces with the enthusiasm of a vibrant, outdoor recreation community. But both of these entities have been under pressure in recent years, as the combined impacts of vacation-home development and a tourism industry whose growth has been nothing short of exponential, have threatened to turn the Jackson Hole region into an amusement park for those who want to play cowboy and cowgirl, especially during weekend jaunts to the area's restaurants.

The region's proximity to some of North America's greatest natural treasures has made Jackson the state's tourism success story. Grand Teton National Park, Yellowstone National Park, Gros Ventre Wilderness, and Bridger-Teton National Forest are so close that local residents take for granted the year-round access they have to spectacular trout fishing, ice climbing, cross-country skiing, snowmobiling, hiking, hunting, and single-track mountain biking. But like many other Art Towns, the local employment scene is notorious for its skinflint wages, and it's not at all uncommon for locals to hold down two jobs just to make ends meet. The past decade has seen housing prices skyrocket, which has forced many working folks to move across the state border to Driggs, Idaho, in search of affordable housing. The main problem with that is the 8,400-foot Teton Pass separating Jackson from Driggs. Think your commute is tough? Try punching your way across the Grand Tetons on a snowy morning in February, just to make $8 an hour slinging lattes to skiers with snarky attitudes.

Arts Scene

For most of the year, Jackson's art galleries survive by selling to the region's swelling ranks of second-home owners and the steady stream of tourists who come here between Memorial Day and Labor Day on their way to and from the national parks. While art sales during the months falling between ski season and summer tourist season are flat, a huge boost is provided in mid-September by the annual Jackson Hole Fall Arts Festival, a two-week blast combining an outdoor arts fair with dozens of art openings, evening cowboy music concerts and poetry readings, classical music concerts, a film festival, artists' studio tours, and wine tastings. It's a time when many of the nation's top collectors of Western art, landscape painting, and realist bronze sculpture pour into Jackson Hole, hot on the heels of the artists whose creations they value. It's marked in the galleries by huge art sales, great fun, and camaraderie and is one of the nation's top Art Town cultural events.

The Mountain Artists' Rendezvous Art Fair is Jackson's other major summer visual arts event, attracting a juried national group of nearly 150 contemporary painters, sculptors, and craftspeople to its downtown locale in Miller Park for its two, weekend-long runs in July and August. One of the area's top galleries is ArtWest, a nonprofit space operated by the Art Association, an arts education and exhibition organization that's incubated the careers of dozens of northwest Wyoming artists.

When the National Museum of Wildlife Art opened its spectacular facility on the north side of Jackson in the late 1990s, it provided the region with not only a 51,000-square-foot, world-class exhibition facility but also a year-round place for lectures, films, and music performances. Its Cook Auditorium is used as a venue to showcase finalist films from the annual Jackson Hole Wildlife Film Festival, and the museum's main galleries host touring exhibitions from institutions such as the Smithsonian Museum and many of the nation's top Western and wildlife art museums.

Jackson is also the home of the Jackson Hole Playhouse, a Western-theme dinner theatre formerly known as the Pink Garter Theatre. The tone is considerably more upscale at the Grand Teton Music Festival, which operates as a year-round performance and presenting organization delivering top-notch, international classical and chamber music talent to Jackson. The festival presents more than 40 concerts during its action-packed summer season, with an all-star orchestra in residence from mid-June through August, performing in the 740-seat Walk Festival Hall, a mere snowball's toss from the ski lifts at Jackson Hole Mountain Resort.

Essentials

Visual Arts Venues

ArtWest Gallery (260 W. Pearl Street; 307/733-6379; www.art association.org) Jackson's favorite space for local artwork, ArtWest Gallery is known for exhibiting contemporary arts created by top local and regional talents.

Art Talk

Karen Stewart, executive director of ArtWest Gallery.

We're finally under way with the building of a new community arts center, which will have room for the art association, a dance studio, space for local art organizations, an arts education facility, and a new state-of-the-art exhibition space for ArtWest. It's going to be located downtown on land the city owns, and when it's all said and done the project will cost $28 million over a five year period. We're still the premier exhibition facility for contemporary arts in this part of the state, and we'll continue doing this in our new building, just in a bigger and better way. This community is highly aware of the fact that Jackson has a vibrant arts community that exerts a significant economic impact. There's lots of art in the restaurants, coffee bars, and professional buildings. This is an exciting time to be an artist in Jackson.

National Museum of Wildlife Art (2820 Rungius Road; 307/733-5771; www.wildlifeart.org) This sophisticated art museum has lots of exhibition space as well as a sculpture garden and a 200-seat auditorium for lectures, performances, and film.

Trailside Galleries (105 N. Center Street; 307/733-3186; www.trailsidegalleries.com) One of the nation's top galleries for

Art Talk

Francine Carraro, executive director of the National Museum of Wildlife Art.

My personal goal is to help bring credibility to the wildlife art genre and to deal with the perceptions wildlife art has in the public's eye. The museum's mission is to promote wildlife art and develop its stature in the context of humanity's relationship with nature. Wildlife art has a lot to do with the ways artists have come to terms with the American Frontier and the boundless promise of the American West. Our main area of interest is American art, but we do use our exhibitions as opportunities to draw art from collections worldwide. We collect the work of some local artists and work hard at getting artists and their families into the museum for our programs through events like free Sundays, concerts, lectures, films, and family activities.

Western art, Trailside represents many of the region's top painters and sculptors.

Performing Arts & Events

Grand Teton Music Festival (4015 W. Lake Creek Drive; 307/733-3050; www.gtmf.org) This multifaceted classical music festival operates year-round with several winter concerts but really springs to life from June through August when it presents more than 40 concerts, chamber performances, and recitals, including a wildly popular Fourth of July extravaganza.

Jackson Hole Fall Arts Festival (see Jackson Hole Chamber of Commerce below) One of the nation's top Art Town events, this two-week affair attracts hundreds of artists and collectors for a nonstop whirlwind of openings, exhibitions, and lectures.

Mountain Artists Rendezvous Art Fair (The Art Association, 260 W. Pearl Street; 307/733-6379; www.art association.org) Taking place across two summer weekends, this largely contemporary outdoor arts fair draws top artists from Salt Lake City, Denver, and elsewhere.

Wine & Dine

Betty Rock Coffee House (325 W. Pearl Street; 307/733-0747) Jackson's best buzz shop is also the town's top alternative exhibition venue for visual arts.

The Bunnery Bakery (130 N. Cache; 307/733-5474; www.bunnery.com) The most popular breakfast haunt in Jackson is famous for the state's best cinnamon rolls.

Snake River Brewing Company (265 S. Millward; 307-739-2337; www.snakeriverbrewing.com) Great pub, with an Italian kitchen serving calzone, pizza, and pasta.

Accommodations

Bentwood Inn B&B (4250 Raven Haven Rd; 307/739-1411; www.bentwoodinn.com) Sumptuous log cabin inn within an easy walk of downtown.

The Sassy Moose Inn (3895 Miles Road; 307/733-1277; www.sassy moose.com) Comfortable and reasonably priced B&B close to Jackson Hole Mountain Resort.

Days Inn (350 S. Highway 89; 307/733-0033; www.daysinn jacksonhole.com) Spacious hotel, with accommodations for RVs and families.

Information

Jackson Hole Chamber of Commerce: P.O. Box 550; 307/733-3316; www.jacksonholechamber.com

Population: 8,900

The Pacific Region

Homer, Alaska

T here's only one way to drive into Homer—it's via AL 1, which wraps its 200-mile way from Anchorage, down the Kenai Peninsula, past the Kenai National Wildlife Refuge and along the Cook Inlet, petering out just past Homer, an Art Town of hardy souls living in spectacular natural beauty. Once you get here, if you ever want to leave, you've got to go out the way you came in, unless you have wings, a boat, or a ticket on the *Tustumena,* the twice-weekly ferry to Seldovia and Kodiak.

An amazing place surrounded by spectacular natural beauty, Homer is one of those Shangri-La's where the mountains meet the ocean, resulting in a setting loaded with breathtaking, hillside homes as well as tidal flats perfect for long mountain bike rides or walks on the Kachemak Bay's beaches.

This being Alaska, one of the common features of life in the Lower 48 states that locals here have no need for is air-conditioning. Summer temperatures rarely rise into the 80s. Winter is not as brutal as in other parts of Alaska, due to Homer's waterfront location. Average annual snowfall is around five feet, with the January daytime temperatures hovering around 28 degrees. It's little surprise that many of Homer's artists migrate south in November and head back north in April, preferring the trailer parks of sunny Tucson to the steel gray gloom of Alaska's winter.

While Homer operates as a year-round community, the juice that keeps the economic wheels turning is tourism. During those five months when the weather's good, huge cruise ships pull into Homer's deep water harbor, disgorging masses of money-laden, wide-eyed buyers of everything from french fries to hand-stitched quilts. During those same months, the harbor's commercial fleet doubles to nearly 1,500 boats, including everything from yachts owned by dot-com millionaires to commercial fishing craft hunting the region's massive salmon and halibut.

Arts Scene

While there's serious money to be made in Homer's annual Jackpot Halibut Derby, there's also a surprisingly strong local arts scene that's active through events like year-round First Friday art openings and theatre, generating enough opportunity for many talented individuals to make a part-time living from their art.

During the summer months Pier One Theatre, which has logged more than 20 seasons in its quarters on Homer Spit along the Kachemak Bay, presents typical summer repertory fare such as *Nunsense* and *Love Letters*, as well as children's theatre. Occasionally, some more challenging fare such as *The Laramie Project*, *The Search for Odysseus*, and even dance concerts slip onto the Pier One's stage. The Kenai Peninsula Orchestra's Summer String Festival takes place across the early part of August and uses venues throughout the peninsula such as Bunnell Street Gallery and Tutka Bay Lodge. Homer's also home to a thriving literary colony whose local luminary is Tom Bodett, the Motel 6 "Leave the Light on for 'Ya" guy. Writers gather regularly for readings at places like the Pier One Theatre in summer and any open tavern in winter, while the Kachemak Bay Writers Conference takes place in June on the campus of Kenai Peninsula College.

Come winter, the performing-arts action shifts to Homer Mariner Theatre, a state-of-the-art facility at Homer High School, which is also used as a venue for large arts events such as the Shorebird Festival Arts & Crafts Fair in May and the Nutcracker Arts & Crafts Fair in December. The Homer Council on the Arts is a key motivating and organizational force for the local arts scene, staging events such as May's Homer Homes Tour and monthly visual arts exhibitions in the Arts Council Building.

The Pratt Museum, one of Alaska's finest historical museums, is an innovative facility whose exhibits range from ecological examinations of the Exxon *Valdez* oil spill to Homer's early-20th-century Anglo homesteaders (a group led by former New Yorker Homer Pennock), to the

Native Peoples of the Kenai Peninsula. Regional artists are also included in the museum's calendar through its exhibitions and collections programs and through events such as the Ritz Art Exhibition auction each September.

Homer's visual arts scene is centered around the Bunnell Street Gallery, a nonprofit art space located in the Old Inlet Trading Post. Over the years, Bunnell Street has developed a reputation as one of the state's leading innovative forces, traveling its shows throughout the Northwest and holding regular workshops aimed at enhancing the skill and contacts of Homer painters, sculptors, jewelers, and printmakers. While the number of Homer's art galleries and open studios varies from year to year, there are usually about 10 venues operating in any given summer, giving local painters, ceramists, sculptors, and jewelers lots of opportunity to sell into the bustling tourist market.

Art Talk

Janet Bowen, director of the Homer Council on the Arts.

The town and people of Homer place a high value on the arts, which is why we're a growing arts organization. We try to expose local residents to a sense of the opportunity that's available to them through the arts, be it as a career or just as something that enhances their lives. We have seen artists moving in here from across Alaska as well as from the lower states, people who want to be in a beautiful, supportive, and safe community. We're in the process of developing a public art program for Homer, and we need resources like a community photography lab, which will probably happen through an expansion of our building.

Essentials

Visual Arts Venues

Bunnell Street Gallery (106 W. Bunnell Street; 907/235-2662; www.bunnellstreetgallery.org) Long-standing cooperative gallery with monthly exhibitions of local and statewide artists in one-person and juried invitational exhibitions.

The Pratt Museum (3779 Bartlett Street; 907/235-8635; www.prattmuseum.org) Historical, cultural, and regional fine arts exhibitions plus public programs year-round.

Homer Council on the Arts (355 W. Pioneer Avenue; 907/235-4288; www.homerart.org) Year-round exhibitions, performances, and public programs such as the Second Sundays Speaker Series.

Art Talk

Asia Freeman, executive director of the Bunnell Street Gallery.
Our arts scene is becoming more and more organized, with lots of artists moving in from outside Alaska. We're getting more visual artists, musicians, and actors all the time, seeking an innovative and supportive place to live and create. As a gallery we enjoy the challenge of balancing the needs of these newer artists with the responsibilities we have toward our longtime resident artists. We have an adequate number of commercial and alternative venues around Homer for our artists, and there's a serious commitment to excellence coming from Homer's studio arts community.

Performing Arts and Events

Pier One Theatre (P.O. Box 894; 907/235-7333; www.pierone theatre.org) Summer performances of Broadway musicals and comedies.

Kachemak Bay Shorebird Festival (see Homer Chamber of Commerce below) May celebration of the return of migratory birds, plus an arts and crafts fair.

Art-Rageous Weekend (see Homer Council on the Arts above) Early-November weekend with an open-studio tour, performances, and art-gallery openings.

Wine & Dine

Salty Dawg Saloon (Homer Spit; 907/235-6718); Built in 1897 as the town's first post office, this famous hangout on the Homer Spit is a favorite with everyone from tourists to the shot-and-a-beer fishermen crowd.

Alice's Champagne Palace (195 E. Pioneer Avenue; 907/235-7650; www.aliceschampagnepalace.com) Homer's live-music venue of choice, with karaoke, an in-house brewpub, great seafood, and touring bands from Anchorage.

Bear Claw Bakery (177 E. Pioneer Avenue; 907/235-2747); Bagels, pies, donuts, and the strongest cup of java north of Pioneer Square.

Accommodations

Heritage Hotel (147 E. Pioneer Avenue; 907/235-7787; www.alaska heritagehotel.com) A log cabin hotel located within easy walking distance of galleries and restaurants.

Ocean House Inn (1065 Krueth Way; 907/235-3294; www.homer oceanhouse.com) A spacious, cliffside bed & breakfast, with incredible views of Kachemak Bay.

Best Western Bidarka Inn (575 Sterling Highway; 907/235-8148; www.bestwestern.com) A full-service motel, with room for RVs, conventions, and family reunions.

Information

Homer Chamber of Commerce: P.O. Box 541; 907/235-7740; www.homeralaska.org

Population: 4,400

Carmel, California

Set among the spectacular beauty of central California's Pacific coastline, the Art Town of Carmel squeezes its residents and hordes of year-round tourists into 1 square mile of what's arguably the most scenic place on the continent. Located 130 miles south of San Francisco, Carmel has long attracted artists, photographers, writers, and beachcombers to its tidy neighborhoods of cottages and cabins. Edward Weston, one of America's preeminent photographers, called this area home, as did John Steinbeck, who planted himself in the fishing town of Monterey, just a short drive up the Pacific Coast Highway.

Cool, misty mornings are a regular feature of life here, as are the reliable winds that almost always blow that mist away by late morning, revealing yet another glorious day in paradise, a day perfect for walking along the white sands of Carmel Beach or an afternoon run along the Scenic Road. Most of the time it's even OK to gather up some driftwood for a campfire on the beach, provided you douse the fire with seawater when you're done cooking your hot dogs.

Despite its quaint practice of not assigning numbered street addresses, downtown Carmel is one of those ultra-competitive places where high retail overheads have made it difficult for locally oriented galleries to survive. Restaurants seem to have a better-than-average chance at making a go of things, as do boutiques and garden stores catering to the tastes of day-tripping housewives from Bay Area suburbs. For most locals, living here becomes possible only after learning a few key tricks. One is knowing how to avoid weekend traffic jams in and around the commercial center of Ocean Avenue and where to find that rarity of all rarities, the free parking space. The other trick is the simpler one of discovering the lower prices for everything from radishes to roto tillers in nearby Monterey.

Arts Scene

Diverse and loaded with places to go and things to do, Carmel's visual arts scene is primarily oriented toward tourist tastes, while on its performing-arts front there's an emphasis placed on meeting higher standards. The town's oldest gallery is operated by the nonprofit Carmel Art Association, and it happens to be the preferred home of many, highly skilled local artists whose work had been overlooked by the commercial galleries along Ocean Avenue. In fact, finding visual arts created locally has become an increasingly difficult task in Carmel, even though 50-some-odd galleries are in business here. The Center for Photographic Arts, one of the nation's most respected photography galleries, is one exception to this trend, as is the Silver Light Gallery, which is home to many of the present generation of photographers enchanted by the Big Sur's breathtaking beauty.

There's consistency on the community's performing-arts front, which is led in many ways by the Carmel Bach Festival, which takes place during July and August in the Sunset Center Theater. Classical music is so important to this community that it also supports a year-round performing-arts presenter, the Carmel Music Society, which cherry picks top names from the international music world and brings them into town from October through April. These performances, as well as those of the Monterey County Symphony, take place at Sunset Center Theater.

One of Carmel's unique experiences is attending performances of the Pacific Repertory Theatre at the Outdoor Forest Theater, an amphitheatre main stage set up on a beautiful, wooded site close to downtown. Pacific Rep's fare ranges from Shakespeare to Broadway musicals, but if you plan on attending remember to dress warmly. During summer months the theatre is also used for a community concert series and a film series. In mid-October the Carmel Performing Arts Festival takes over more than a dozen local venues for its weeklong flood of national and international music, drama, and dance talents. And ever since Peter Townsend honed his classic, windmill motions, the Monterey Jazz Festival has attracted hordes to its sprawling fairgrounds each September.

Art Talk

Stephen Moorer, artistic director and founder of Pacific Repertory Theatre. Twenty years ago there was no professional theatre on the Monterey Peninsula, but there was a need for a company that paid and supported its actors. We knew that to really make a theatre organization work we would have to be good, we needed to be regional, and we needed to be year-round. Today we're not only running our productions through the year, but we also have an extensive outreach program. Our plays are selected from the world's stages, and we do new works, Shakespeare, and classics by the great playwrights. Becoming an Actors Equity company in 2001 gave us access to the best and newest material, and it opened up the region's best talent pool to our productions. We have an August to October season in our beautiful amphitheatre and use our two indoor stages from January through October.

Essentials

Visual Arts Venues

Carmel Art Association (Dolores Street between 5th & 6th Streets; 831/624-6176; www.carmelart.org) One of the region's best community art galleries, with a roster of sophisticated painters and sculptors.

Center for Photographic Art (San Carlos & 9th Street; 831/625-5181; www.photography.org) An education center and gallery, representing work by the likes of Ansel Adams and Edward Weston.

Silver Light Gallery (San Carlos between Ocean & 6th; 831/624-4589; www.silverlight.com) Great collection of contemporary photographers capturing images of the California coast and the world.

Performing Arts & Events

Carmel Bach Festival (P.O. Box 575; 831/624-1521; www.bach festival.org) Two summer months of world-class chamber music, symphony concerts, and recitals.

Monterey Symphony Orchestra (Sunset Center; 831/624-8511; www.montereysymphony.org) October to June concert series staged at various regional venues, including Sunset Center Theater.

Pacific Repertory Theatre (Monte Verde & 9th; 831/622-0700; www.pacrep.org) Stages its Shakespeare festival each summer on the main stage of Forest Theater and presents community theatre during other parts of the year.

Wine & Dine

5th Avenue Deli (5th Avenue between San Carlos & Dolores; 831/625-2688) The best pastrami sandwich to be found between San Francisco and Santa Monica.

Carmel Valley Coffee Roasting Company (Lincoln & Ocean; 831/626-2913) Popular buzz shop for Carmel's eclectic arts community.

Carmel Chop House (5th & San Carlos; 831/625-1199; www.carmel chophouse.com) Great steaks and a regionally inspired wine list.

Accommodations

Townhouse Lodge (San Carlos & 5th; 831/624-1261; www.best western.com) Central location with easy parking and a pool.

Blue Sky Lodge (10 Flight Road; Carmel Valley; 800/733-2160; www.blueskylodge.com) Secluded, romantic getaway just a 20-minute drive from Carmel.

Art Talk

Susan Klusmire, executive director of the Carmel Art Association.

We were established in 1927 by a group of notable California painters who needed a place to show their work. To this day, that remains central to what we do, exhibiting members' work through new exhibitions that take place year-round and change on the first Wednesday of the month. We show the work of our 120 active members, all of them living within 35 miles of Carmel. We also offer some art classes and have a year-round series of lectures. For local artists there's a great deal of prestige involved in exhibiting their work at the association. It's unfortunate that more of the local galleries aren't interested in showing art created by local artists, and it can be a real challenge finding representation here. We've developed a reputation as the best place in the region to find strong, local work.

Adobe Inn (Dolores & 8th; 831/624-3933; www.adobeinn.com) Luxurious hotel in the heart of Carmel, within walking distance to the beach.

Information

Carmel Visitor & Information Center: San Carlos & 6th Street; 831/624-2522; www.carmelcalifornia.org

Population: 4,000

Chico, California

S ay you wanted to find an Art Town with a dynamic and growing university, the kind of institution you could rely upon for everything from weekend foreign-film festivals to an arts department employing dozens of mid-career professional painters, dancers, actors, and musicians. And say this town had to be somewhere in Northern California and within a reasonable drive of San Francisco and Lake Tahoe, yet close enough to the Sierra Nevada foothills to make afternoon bike rides in Gold Rush Country an easily enjoyed diversion. And, oh yes, this place has to also be affordable for an artist couple.

Welcome to Chico, an unpretentious and increasingly popular release valve for Bay Area artists who are tired of being overcharged for their loft digs . . . artists grateful to find a place that's temperate, safe, and even entertaining, all within a three-hour drive of North Beach's traffic-clogged streets. Nearly 70,000 people live here, and many of them are connected to the town's largest employer, California State University at Chico (CSU), a.k.a. Chico State.

Located in the north end of the Sacramento Valley, Chico is surrounded by some of the world's most fertile farmlands. Everything from almonds to bok choy is commercially grown in the region, which is why the Saturday-morning and Thursday-evening Farmers' Market in downtown Chico is top-heavy with picture-perfect produce, locally harvested honey, sun-dried fruits, and organically grown beef. Of course, this being a college town there's also more than one eclectic group of street buskers performing for spare change while shoppers go about their business.

Living here means having easy access to everything from the public golf courses dotting the Sierra Nevada foothills to water skiing on the accessible waters of Lake Amanour and Lake Oroville. There's alpine hiking nearby on the trails of Lassen Volcanic National Park, and numerous vineyards are nestled among the verdant Sierra foothills. Local residents are as likely to be college professors as they are artists or business owners, or maybe even employees of Chico's homegrown microbrewery, Sierra Nevada Brewing, which operates a popular restaurant and conference center adjacent to its production facility.

Chico's older neighborhoods are tree-shaded enclaves of homes ranging from the modest to the immense, and many were built during the early 20th century. The downtown, built to accommodate the commercial needs of a prosperous agricultural region, reflects a classic, small-town appearance with retail spots filled by independently owned cafés, bars, record stores, musical instruments shops, hardware stores, and beauty shops. Downtown is eminently walkable and has a vibrant street life courtesy of the 10,000-plus college students attending Chico State.

Arts Scene

As is the case with many Art Towns that serve as homes to universities, the arts scene in Chico is greatly enhanced by the presence of Chico State. At CSU there's an emphasis on performing arts and the presentation of national musicians, actors, and entertainers. The campus is home to Laxson Auditorium and a two-theatre performing-arts center, as well as three art galleries. The performing-arts season gets under way in late August and continues with weekly events through June. Everything from children's theatre to world music, drama, classical music, dance, and opera make it onto the CSU stages. The university's visual arts galleries include the Turner Print Gallery, which exhibits works on paper, primarily from its permanent collection but also from CSU students and faculty, as well as the occasional touring exhibition. The University Art Gallery brings in occasional national shows and commissions site-specific installations by artists from the Bay Area. Trinity Hall, which is home to CSU's Humanities Center, has a gallery oriented toward shows of student work as well as themed invitationals open to the entire community.

The community's visual arts scene, which is visible on Chico's streets thanks to a locally funded murals project, is primarily a studio-based effort whose focus is to create work destined for West

Art Talk

Cynthia Scontriano-Schildhauer,

encaustics painter.

Before moving to Chico six years ago
I was living in the Mojave Desert area. At
the time my painting was mostly self-
reflective. In Chico I've found a place that
worked nicely as a town filled with people
from other parts of the country, people
who moved here to do their own dreams.
I entered the MFA program at Chico State
University, which is a great place filled with
experienced teachers and well-equipped
studios. I discovered encaustics there, and
it changed the direction of my life. Now,
I'm selling well in Chico, have gallery representation out of town, and am getting
ready for my first one-person show. This is
a great place to live as an artist. There's a
lot of art expertise in this area, and people
have no problem sharing their knowledge.
This is a progressive community with a
good sense of itself as an arts-supportive
place.

Coast galleries. To live here as an artist is to accept the challenge of running one's life as a business creating art that's largely sold in other places. But there are many artists living here who sell some of their work locally, especially during the annual Open Studios Tour, an autumn event organized in nearly 100 studios throughout Chico as well as in surrounding communities such as Paradise and Magalia. The center of the local visual arts scene is the Chico Art Center, located downtown in a reno- vated railway depot. Home to a large gallery space as well as workshops and a sales gallery, the art center is perpet- ually busy with shows, classes, and entertainment. A small community of professional glass artists with national reputations has established itself in Chico in recent years, which is why hot-shop employment is an option for some students enrolled in CSU's arts department.

Downtown Chico is home to a stu- dio scene that's flourished in the sec- ond stories of several retail buildings housing music stores, tattoo parlors, and coffee bars on their street levels. These studios have been pioneered by an interesting combination of CSU art grads and Bay Area artists who have relocated here for the area's low cost of living and high concen- tration of creative workers. Two full-time galleries are located down- town. The Vagabond Rose is part frame shop, part art gallery, and a good place to find local fine crafts as well as paintings. The 1078 Gallery, an artist-run space, is a decidedly contemporary art gallery, the sort of venue where edgy and experimental art is more than welcome. Many of downtown's restaurants and cafés serve as alternative exhibi- tion venues for local artists, providing important sales opportunities for Chico's up-and-comers.

The Blue Room Theatre is Chico's foremost drama company, pre- senting new and original works. At the Senator Theatre, a restored movie house, the entertainment focus is on performing acts primarily geared to the CSU audience, though an occasional dance company, jazz band, or even a Christmas season performance of the *Messiah* manages to appear onstage from time to time.

Essentials

Visual Arts Venues

Chico Art Center (450 W. Orange Street; 530/895-8726; www.chicoart center.com) Year-round exhibitions, performances, and art workshops.

1078 Gallery (738 W. Fifth Street; 530-343-1973; www.1078gallery.org) Contemporary art space run by artists, showcasing year-round exhibitions of local and regional work.

Turner Print Gallery (Laxson Auditorium at CSU; 530-898-4476; www.csuchico.edu) Features art from a permanent collection as well as shows of works on paper by CSU faculty and students.

Art Talk

Rick Satava, glass artist.
I got here in 1975, specifically for the glass program at Chico State University. I was originally a ceramist but turned to glass because it was a better way to make a living. I bought an old house in downtown Chico and started building a studio in back. I got into some retail stores, so that gave me a steady income. I started doing more shows and getting into sculptural, free-form work, and now have a balanced line of sculptural and functional pieces, with five employees in my shop. Chico's a small community where you feel well connected to the art world outside. Artists here can't depend on the local economy to keep them going. You have to get your work represented across the country if you're going to survive here as an artist. The art that does sell in Chico tends to be the more affordable stuff.

Performing Arts & Events

Open Studios Tour (see Chico Art Center above) Self-guided studio tour of nearly 100 artist spaces in Chico and surrounding communities.

Chico Performances (see Chico Chamber of Commerce below) Energetic, multidisciplinary performing-arts presentations from late August until early June.

The Blue Room Theatre (139 W. 1st; Street; 530-895-3749; www.blueroomtheatre.com) Year-round performances of classics and new works in a second-story playhouse above downtown's streets.

Wine & Dine

Sicilian Café (1020 Main Street; 530-345-2233) Great patio and a regional wine list accompany the foods at this pasta palace.

Red Tavern (1250 The Esplanade; 530-894-3463; www.red tavern.com) Superb wine list and new American cuisine in a former neighborhood storefront.

Moxie's Café & Gallery (128 Broadway; 530-345-0601) Local arts and regional foods combine to make this one of Chico's favorite artist hangouts.

Accommodations

The Grateful Bed B&B (1462 Arcadian Avenue; 530-342-2464) Victorian-era inn, in a quiet, residential neighborhood.

Safari Garden Motel (2352 Esplanade; 530-343-3201) Affordable, old-time motor court in a residential neighborhood.

Days Inn (740 Broadway; 530-343-3286; www.daysinn.com) Large motel, with a swimming pool and great for families.

Information

Chico Chamber of Commerce: 300 Salem Street; 530-891-5556; www.chicochamber.com

Population: 68,500

Eureka, California

I f you think of California living as defined by San Francisco's techies, Los Angeles's aspiring actors, and San Diego's surfers, welcome to the very different Humboldt County. Here, in the Golden State's far northwest corner, about 275 miles north of San Francisco, the lifestyle more closely resembles that of the Pacific Northwest. Artists have been migrating in this direction for decades, drawn to a place that maintains some cultural ties to the rest of California (US 101 cuts right through the middle of Eureka, on its winding path toward Pasadena), but whose heavily wooded countryside, long stretches of overcast skies and rainfall, and abundance of Victorian mansions are evidence of the region's otherness. Then again, the concrete-shattering earthquakes that rip through Eureka and adjacent Arcata every decade or so give locals a shared experience with their friends in the sunny southland.

Making a living in this part of the state can be challenging. Lacking the agricultural base of an Art Town like Chico, or the tourism cash flow of Mendocino, or the proximity to technology industry jobs of Laguna Beach, Eureka is highly dependent on natural resources and the steadily expanding influence of Humboldt State University (HSU). But while HSU's financial health is underwritten by the state, there are few safety nets available for the thousands of Humboldt County jobs dependent upon the forestry, mining, and fishing industries. Economic forces that ebb and flow through multinational corporate entities may have no idea that Humboldt County even exists, but when Canadian logging companies flood lumber onto American construction sites, or when

363

Chilean salmon farmers get huge tax breaks to airfreight fish to Dallas supermarkets, it's working people in places like Humboldt County who take the financial hit.

Because there's precious little cushion in Humboldt County's economy, living here is far less expensive than in other parts of the state. There's a widespread use of barter systems in which people exchange goods and/or services for the things they need. Someone raising goats and making gourmet cheeses knows that if they need dental work done there's a possibility of working out a trade of, say, several months worth of fresh cheese deliveries in exchange for a root canal. Another aspect of the region's underground economy that influences many facets of life here is marijuana farming. It may be against the law, but the lucrative nature of this underground trade makes the threat of arrest a risk many Humboldt County growers are willing to assume.

Arts Scene

Since the sunset of the Summer of Love, artists who needed an inexpensive, isolated, and supportive place to carry on their creative pursuits have pointed their Volkswagen vans in this direction. What they found here was a place of extraordinary natural beauty whose off-the-beaten-path location made this a perfect site for focusing on one's art. They also found a relatively underutilized infrastructure built for a regional economy that had fallen on hard times. In the face of this classic staging ground for the creation of an Art Town resurgence, Humboldt County became a hotbed for the expression of creative energies. Today, the region is teeming with visual artists, musicians, fine crafts, actors, and the various technical geeks who provide the skilled labor that makes an arts scene flourish. Many of these technical whizzes have been trained in one of HSU's arts departments, and for them the region is a stepping-stone on their way to careers in San Francisco or Los Angeles's entertainment industries.

The biggest recent development on Eureka's arts scene has been the opening of the Morris Graves Museum of Art. This spectacular restoration and renovation of an early-20th-century Carnegie Library building has resulted in a first-rate visual arts institution serving the entire North Coast region. Located in downtown Eureka, the museum is named after Morris Graves, an esteemed American painter/sculptor who lived in the area from 1964 until his death in 2001. The Humboldt Arts Council manages the museum, whose exhibition areas consist of seven art galleries and an outdoor sculpture garden. The museum's vigorous exhibitions calendar is primarily focused on presenting the work of local and regional painters, sculptors, photographers, and fiber artists, which makes the museum an important arts venue for North Coast talent.

The community's other major visual arts asset is the Ink People Center for the Arts, one of the state's most innovative and far-reaching community arts centers. Located in a former schoolhouse in a quiet residential neighborhood, the Ink People Center for the Arts serves the region through a year-round, action-packed schedule of visual arts exhibitions, art workshops, lectures, performances, films, and festivals. The facility is a treasure trove of well-equipped and publicly accessible artist studios that are open to the center's hundreds of members (the Inksters) on a 24-hour basis. One of the main reasons why Eureka and Arcata are so thick with arts organizations serving this multicultural and diverse community's creative needs is because the Ink People has incubated these groups by training their leaders, lending them office space, and giving them access to everything from T-1 Internet lines to fax machines. Today, the Ink People is no less vigorous in pursuing its community arts activism goals than it was when it was established in 1979.

Another measure of this region's arts diversity is the presence of Dell'Arte Company in Blue Lake, a small town just a 20-minute drive northeast of Eureka. This unique jewel of a performing-arts training ground is devoted to the traditional arts of mime and "commedia," the ancient Italian performance discipline that taunts society to turn around and look at itself in a mirror . . . and laugh. Founded by the charismatic Carlo Mazzone Clementi, an Italian-born performer and former member of the Teatro Nazionale d'Arte Italiano, this Blue Lake facility is dedicated to training the continent's practitioners of Physical Theatre, an arts discipline that includes mime, clowning, giant puppetry, costumed comedy, and masked performance. At its Blue Lake home, Dell'Arte not only trains young artists, it also presents a year-round series of its own plays and performances in its Carlo Theatre and in the Dell'Arte/Rooney Amphitheatre. These performances are the same ones Dell'Arte tours nationally through the year, and enjoying shows here is like having the access Montréalers have to Cirque du Soleil's rehearsals. Each summer, The Mad River Festival is Dell'Arte's month-long presentation of not only its own shows but also a showcase for similar devotees of the mime and commedia disciplines from Brazil, China, Italy, Canada, Bali, and elsewhere.

The region's premier performing-arts venue is the 862-seat Van Duzer Theatre on the HSU campus. Home to CenterArts, an

Art Talk

Jim McVicker, painter.

The quality of Humboldt County's landscape still inspires me. I moved here in 1977, and at that time Eureka had this working-class ruggedness that many artists found attractive. My work was focused on the local architecture at first, and then later it turned to the coastline and farmlands. The arts scene here has continued to grow in its size and sense of integrity. Artists living here tend to be very accessible and there's a sense of cohesion you don't find in many places. Humboldt State University plays an important role in developing and sustaining the region's arts integrity. They're a stable presence in a place where art galleries tend to come and go. Our alternative venues are hugely important to artists who are coming out of HSU and are trying to make an impact on the local arts scene.

extraordinarily ambitious, and nearly year-round, presenter of top names in everything from blues music to contemporary folk, alternative rock, world music, modern dance, and touring theatre, the Van Duzer is Humboldt County's vital connection to the entertainment world's mainstream. Eureka is home to at least three, and often as many as four, or even five, theatre companies. The more stable of these are World Premier Theatre, North Coast Repertory Theatre (in Solana Beach), and the Pacific Art Center Theatre. North Coast Rep's season of six main stage plays and several black box productions is held in a former Salvation Army Hall. The Eureka Chamber Music Series, which features performances by musicians that include members of HSU's music faculty, stages its concerts in the Calvary Lutheran Church.

Eureka's historic Old Town, which is decorated with more than a dozen murals by local artists is home to a number of art galleries representing local and regional artists. One of the long-term gallery presences is the First Street Gallery, a venue exhibiting work by HSU faculty and graduate students as well as artists from the region. Old Town Art Gallery is a cooperative space that's survived more than 20 years of Humboldt's economic cycles. Outside of the galleries, an innovative program called the Alternative Gallery Project, administered by the Ink People Center for the Arts, oversees the installation of locally created art in the professional environments of Humboldt County's doctors, lawyers, retailers, businesses, and government offices.

Essentials

Visual Arts Venues

Morris Graves Museum of Art (636 F Street, 707/442-0278; www.thepalette.com) An art museum in a renovated Carnegie

Library, the Graves has strengthened the regional arts scene.

Ink People Center for the Arts (411 12th Street; 707/442-8413; www.inkpeople.org) Multidisciplinary community arts center with a vibrant exhibition program and arts education facilities.

First Street Gallery (422 First Street, 707/443-6363; www.humboldt.edu) Art space operated by HSU's visual arts department, and a great place to find up-and-coming painters, sculptors, and fine craftspeople.

Performing Arts & Events

CenterArts (1 Harpst Street, Arcata; 707/826-4411; www.humboldt.edu) Presenting top names in music and dance, this performing-arts extravaganza is an essential element of the Humboldt arts experience.

The Dell'Arte Company (131 H Street, Blue Lake; 707/668-5663; www.dellarte.com) Specializing in the traditional Italian art form of Physical Theatre, and the home of an eight-month series of performances.

Art Talk

Barbara Garza, executive director of the Humboldt Arts Council.
We opened our new art museum in January 2000 after the community came up with $1.5 million to renovate a historic library in downtown Eureka. We have seven different galleries and mount more than 30 exhibits a year, including the Redwood Art Association's fall show and our own members' show in December. During the Arts Alive events, which take place on the first Saturday of each month, we host some type of performance such as music or spoken word. A third of our exhibitions show work from the local arts community, and we feel it's important for a regional art museum to be closely connected with its local arts scene. Eureka has a surprising amount of depth to its arts scene, and a number of our artists have successfully developed national careers from here.

Ferndale Repertory Theatre (447 Main Street, Ferndale; 707/786-5483; www.ferndale-rep.org) Top-notch community theatre company presenting classics and new work in a renovated movie house.

Wine & Dine

Lost Coast Brewery & Café (617 4th Street; 707/445-4480; www.lostcoast.com) Favorite hangout for Eureka's arts crowd and a superb tap house.

Kebab Café (5000 Valley West Boulevard, Arcata; 707/826-2121) Humboldt County's premier Middle Eastern restaurant.

Curley's Grill (400 Ocean Avenue, Ferndale; 707/786-9696) Small restaurant with a great wine list and an emphasis on locally grown produce.

Accommodations

The Gingerbread Mansion Inn (400 Berding Street, Ferndale; 707/786-4000; www.gingerbreadmansion.com) An elegant Victorian mansion with lovely gardens and Humboldt County's tallest palm tree.

The Eureka Inn (518 7th Street; 707/444-8062; www.eurekainn .com) Large, comfortable hotel with a fabulous restaurant and excellent wine list.

Arcata Inn (4827 Valley West Boulevard, Arcata; 707/826-0313; www.bestwestern.com) Large, modern motel, with a pool and RV parking.

Information

Greater Eureka Chamber of Commerce: 2112 Broadway; 707/442-3738; www.eurekachamber.com

Population: 26,100

Idyllwild, California

This Art Town has a fabulous location, an inspired climate, breathtaking natural beauty, and an intimate relationship with Southern California's wilderness. It is, in other words, the perfect place for artists and art lovers. Idyllwild also has a moderate cost of living. Located on the alpine, south-facing slopes of the San Jacinto Mountains, Idyllwild's landscape is similar to that of other high-altitude communities in the desert Southwest, Art Towns such as Prescott, Arizona, and Silver City, New Mexico. On the other side of the San Jacintos is the Art Town of Palm Springs, just over an hour's drive through an amazingly diverse series of alpine and desert landscapes. Los Angeles's sprawl stops west of here, leaving the city's airports and art museums a two-hour drive from Idyllwild and its mountain-loving residents.

Artists move here for many reasons, but the stronger of the two are the desire to be within relatively easy driving distance of L.A.'s art galleries, as well as the quest to live in an affordable, safe community surrounded by incredible natural beauty. This is the kind of place where artists can live in comfortable log homes, have a studio in an adjacent barn, spend their days doing studio work in the morning, and then head out in the afternoon for hikes in the wilderness, rock climbing, fishing for rainbow trout, or even skiing at nearby Bear Mountain.

Art Talk

Jean Lubin, painter.

When I first got to Idyllwild in 1992, there were a few galleries trying to do business and a small music festival. Now it seems like there's art and music everywhere in town, and there's something going on every weekend. A lot of our visitors come in from Palm Springs, San Diego, and San Bernardino, and we're in the position of having a regional reputation as an artists' community. The Arts Academy is now an active participant in the community's arts scene, which makes everything we do in town have a much higher profile. I see artists coming up here all the time, inquiring around about places to live and show their work. This is an interesting, relaxing place to live, and it has the kind of easy access to the outdoors that artists love. I get a lot of enjoyment by being out in the landscape of this area, and it's inspired me.

Arts Scene

The local arts scene's strength is founded on two pillars: more than a dozen art galleries with monthly exhibitions and the year-round presence of Idyllwild Arts, a multifaceted academic institution running an arts-oriented school and a summer arts program. There's a summer concert series held in the Ice House parking area during July and August featuring blues, Dixieland, and jazz bands. Another major music event on the local arts calendar is the late-August Jazz in the Pines, a weekend-long festival, which for 10 years has showcased some of the best of Southern California's jazz talents in three venues on the campus of Idyllwild Arts. For more performing-arts action, locals only have to drive out of the mountains into Palm Springs or even L.A.

Idyllwild Arts is comprised of two components: the academic programs of Idyllwild Arts Academy and its Summer Programs. During the academic year the academy presents dance concerts, music events, and visual arts exhibitions on its mountainside campus. During the July and August Summer Program, things pick up dramatically when adults and youths descend on the campus for residencies in the many arts disciplines. Running parallel to the residency programs is an energetic performance and exhibitions calendar covering poetry readings, jazz concerts, chamber music recitals, and art exhibitions.

In recent years Idyllwild's gallery scene has experienced significant growth as the community's reputation has been established as an arts-focused, day-tripping destination for visitors from L.A., Palm Springs, and San Diego. This has, in turn, made it possible for a wave of landscape painters, fine craftspeople, jewelers, sculptors, and glass artists to make at least part of their living from local art gallery sales. An energetic and nearly year-round series of art walks, gallery wine-tastings, Sunday-morning instructional workshops, and an October juried exhibition have helped build the presence and impact of the community's artists and galleries. To completely make a living from one's art, it's important to have gallery representation in other high-tourist traffic places, like Palm Springs and La Jolla, and perhaps exhibit at street fairs in the L.A. area.

Essentials

Visual Arts Venues

Idyllwild Gallery of Fine Art (54225 N. Circle Drive; 909/659-1948; www.idyllwildgallery.com) Large art space featuring local and regional artists.

Two Babes in the Woods (55750 N. Circle Drive; 909/659-8100) Rustic, mountain cabin, featuring wildlife art.

Skye Gallery (54425 N. Circle Drive, 909/659-9821) Plein air painters from throughout California.

Performing Arts & Events

The Incredible Edible Art Tour (Various downtown locations; 866/439-5278; www.artinidyllwild.com) June event pairing gallery opening receptions with foods from the region's top restaurants.

Idyllwild Arts Summer Program (52500 Temecula Drive; 909/659-2171, www.idyllwildarts.com) Energetic, multidisciplinary festival of performances and exhibitions held throughout July and August.

Jazz in the Pines (see Idyllwild Chamber of Commerce below) Late-August festival of regional and national musicians.

Art Talk

Chris Maxson, gallery owner.

When I first came here in 1999 I understood the potential Idyllwild had as an arts community, so I just decided to move here. There was a need to connect the ambitions of the town's artists, galleries, musicians, and the Arts Academy, so there were hurdles to overcome, but when we did our first big event and sold out all of the tickets, I knew we were on the right path. Idyllwild, like many places, is home to a number of artists who don't necessarily see themselves in terms of being part of a group, so we had to convince people that doing things that would attract culturally aware visitors was in the town's best interests. Now, after five years, I think we've just about filled in all the holes in the town's events calendar, and there are arts events happening throughout the year. Whenever we do our gallery walks, as many as 1,200 people turn out, which is pretty incredible in a town of under 3,000.

Wine & Dine

Café Aroma (54750 N. Circle Drive; 909/659-5212) Locals' favorite buzz shop.

Restaurant Gastrognome (54381 Ridgeview Drive; 909/659-5055, www.gastrognome.com) Dark steakhouse with a hoppin' bar and a good wine list.

Good Times Pub & Grill (25985 Highway 243; 909/659-7746) Favorite artist hangout for burgers and brew.

Accommodations

Fern Valley Inn (25240 Fern Valley Road; 909/659-2205; www.fern valleyinn.com) Rustic cottages and cabins in a wooded paradise.

Creekstone Inn (54950 Pine Crest Avenue; 909/659-3342; www.creekstoneinn.com) Beautiful, lodge-style inn with enormous fireplaces.

Idyllwild Inn (54300 Village Center Drive; 909/659-2552; www.idyllwildinn.com) Cabins with fireplaces.

Information

Idyllwild Chamber of Commerce: P.O. Box 304; 909/659-3259; www.idyllwildchamber.com

Population: 2,500

Laguna Beach, California

A classic Southern California beach town within easy reach of Los Angeles, this sun-and-sea paradise has long attracted artists, gallery owners, and Hollywood entertainers. Located in Orange County, Laguna Beach is a favored weekend destination for day-tripping Angelenos, which explains why its streets are more often than not packed with traffic, making parking a seven-day headache.

While the highways leading in and out of Laguna Beach have made the community easily accessible for weekending urbanites, they've also made it possible for many to live here full time while holding down a job in the L.A.-metro area. Move here and your neighbors could be anything from accomplished screenwriters to UCLA art professors, to a landscape painter represented in one of the dozens of galleries lining the Coast Highway. Make no mistake: Laguna Beach is an expensive place to live, as is most of Southern California. But if you enjoy your art along with a healthy dose of surf, sun, and warm weather, this could be the right place for you.

An artists' colony was established here in 1903, and by 1918, when Edgar Payne opened the town's first gallery (now morphed into the Laguna Art Museum), this jewel in Southern California's sun had firmly established itself as the home of a distinctly West Coast style of Impressionist painting. To this day, California Impressionism remains a popular painting style in local galleries, and several specialize in historical works from the early and mid-20th century.

Arts Scene

Loaded with art openings, festivals, theatre performances, and museum exhibitions, Laguna Beach has a level of arts activity far exceeding what's normal for a community this size. Atop (literally) the visual arts scene is the Laguna Art Museum, which sits on a cliff overlooking Main Beach, a stretch of sand loaded with volleyball nets, bikini-clad nymphs, and musclemen. The museum, which in recent years has staked an increasingly larger claim to its slice of the Southern California contemporary arts scene, shares a 3,800-piece collection with the Orange County Museum of Art and has its own permanent collection.

Commercial art galleries are abundant in Laguna Beach, especially around the art museum and along the stretch of Coast Highway leading into and out of town. While some of these art spaces cater to the expectations of tourists, many are exceptional operations that exhibit cutting-edge work from regional and national talents. Other galleries are focused on Laguna's tradition as the center of California Impressionist landscape painting, exhibiting works by historical as well as living artists inspired by the region's amazing natural beauty. Throughout the year, Laguna's galleries time their exhibition openings to coincide with the First Thursdays Art Walk, an event that showcases art in more than three dozen spaces, all connected by shuttle buses.

Laguna's gallery scene is one of the stronger found in Art Towns on the West Coast, and its visual arts festivals are not only well organized but also wildly popular. The Festival of the Arts, which takes place across July and August, features more than 150 artists selling from booths, tents, and kiosks on a 6-acre site in Laguna Canyon. A tightly juried show, the festival coincides with the staging of the unique "Pageant of the Masters," a themed event in which members of the local arts community collaborate to re-create full-scale versions of historic works of art, but with the crazy twist of using real people, real props, and painted backdrops as a way of recapturing in three dimensions the original painted composition of the masterworks' two-dimensional forms. The pageant is staged in an amphitheatre on the festival grounds, and features its own orchestra providing background music.

The Sawdust Art Festival, which takes place during the summer months on its own site in Laguna Canyon, is a more inclusive show than the Festival of Arts, yet it's still a heck of a lot of fun and features nearly 200 artists as well as musical performances by the Laguna Community concert band. Yet another standard of the Laguna Beach summer arts calendar is the Art-A-Fair, also held on its own site in Laguna Canyon and featuring a mixed bag of arts, crafts, functional art, and home accessories. In mid-July, the Laguna Plein Air Painters Association holds its invitational exhibition, which features 50 artists working around the town to create landscape paintings that are auctioned off to the benefit of the art museum.

The two main stage organizations in Laguna Beach are the Laguna Playhouse and No Square Theatre. The Laguna Playhouse was established in the 1920s by Hollywood actors seeking a safe place to work on their new material, and has evolved into one of the nation's theatre gems. Its year-round productions include an energetic children's theatre season, as well as the North American and West Coast premiers of important new plays by emerging talents in international theatre circles. No Square Theatre stages its productions in the Laguna Beach High School's Artists' Theatre and features a wildly irreverent approach to live works on its stage, with loads of camp in its comedies and musicals.

Art Talk

Bolton Colburn, director of the Laguna Art Museum.

We have the point of view that this museum strives to find a balance between Laguna Beach's historical art and its contemporary art. We serve these two main constituencies, and we divide our exhibitions calendar right down the middle. The contemporary setting of the Los Angeles area has helped us focus our mission as an American art museum very interested in looking out to the world from a California perspective. In the past five years we've originated between a third and fully half of our exhibitions, a balance that seems to satisfy the sensibilities of our visitors. Exhibition-wise, this museum is a great space. It started as a building for the Laguna Art Association and was expanded several times. What needs to be rethought is the programmatic space in here, especially what we need available for lectures and films.

Essentials

Visual Arts Venues

Laguna Art Museum (307 Cliff Drive; 949/494-8971; www.laguna artmuseum.org) One of the museums to watch on the national contemporary arts scene, LAM also showcases historical works from Laguna's artistic past.

Peter Blake Gallery (326 North Coast Highway; 949/376-9994) One of the West Coast's most influential contemporary arts galleries.

Art Talk

Dale Terbush, painter.

I grew up in this area and have lived off and on in Laguna Beach since 1979, when it was a sleepy, quiet artists' colony. It's an influential and inspirational place for hundreds of artists, and seems to help many of us keep our perspectives on life. It's the ocean that gives me a sense of awe and makes me head back into my studio with a sense of what I want to express in my art. Laguna's art history gives me a feeling of being grounded in a place where art is, and has always been, important. Despite all of its changes this still is a place where that legacy of the great plein air painters is felt by local artists. That's why this town is filled with artists, writers, actors, you name it. No matter what happens here you just can't shut off that spirit of Laguna's past.

Redfern Gallery (1540 South Coast Highway; 949/497-3356; www.redferngallery.com) Leading gallery for California Impressionist masters.

Performing Arts & Events

Festival of Arts & Pageant of the Masters (650 Laguna Canyon Road; 949/494-1145; www.foapom.com) Large and well-selected group of visual artists and evening performances of living works of historical art.

Laguna Playhouse (606 Laguna Canyon Road; 949/497-2787; www.lagunaplayhouse.com) One of the best small theatres in the nation, featuring new works, some standards, and children's theatre.

First Thursdays Art Walk (see Laguna Beach Visitors Bureau below) Monthly event featuring more than 30 galleries and free trolleys.

Wine & Dine

230 Forest Avenue (230 Forest Avenue; 949/494-2545; www.230forestavenue.com) Innovative foods, and a great wine list.

Aegean Café Restaurant (540 South Coast Highway; 949/494-5001; www.aegeancafe.com) Spanakopita and stuffed dolmas, overlooking the Pacific.

Sorrento Grille (370 Gleneyre; 949/494-8686; www.culinary adventures.com) New American cuisine and a martini bar by chef David Wilhelm.

Accommodations

Hotel Laguna (425 South Coast Highway; 949/494-1151; www.hotellaguna.com) Refurbished hotel from the 1930s, right on the beach.

Casa Laguna Inn (2510 South Coast Highway; 949/494-2996; www.casalaguna.com) Hillside inn, with 15 rooms, local art, and great views.

Carriage House Inn (1322 Catalina Street; 949/494-8945; www.carriagehouse.com) Two blocks from the beach.

Information

Laguna Beach Visitors Bureau: 252 Broadway; 800/877-1115; www.lagunabeachinfo.com

Population: 23,900

La Jolla, California

erched along spectacular cliffsides that can be reached by just a 20-minute drive from downtown San Diego, this manicured Mecca for lifestyle refugees has the soul of an Art Town. Populated by a mix of retirees, new agers, ex-military, college professors, surfers, art students, and wealthy Europeans, this town of 29,000 full-time residents is a favored weekend destination for the San Diego region, which explains how it supports dozens of boutiques, cafés, art galleries, and antiques stores.

Living here means being surrounded by some of the most breathtaking oceanfront in North America, yet being close enough to San Diego's downtown to have easy access to amenities such as the San Diego Museum of Art in Balboa Park, the vibrant nightlife of the Gaslamp District, and the crowded streets and cafés of Tijuana. La Jolla is the kind of place where you're as likely to get run over by a rollerblading family vacationing from Spokane as you are to getting cut off in traffic by a red Ferrari. It seems that everyone's attracted by the lure of its beaches, the crashing of azure waves on the cliffs of La Jolla Cove, and the eucalyptus groves at Torrey Pines State Reserve. The flow of tourists hardly ever lets up, as winter delivers survivors from the frozen north, and summer fills the streets with heat-blasted refugees from desert communities such as Palm Springs and Phoenix.

Arts Scene

The twin peaks of La Jolla's arts scene are the San Diego Museum of Contemporary Art and the La Jolla Playhouse. Supplementing these two top-notch organizations are an energetic mix of art galleries, street fairs, music festivals, and theatre companies. The museum is an innovative facility whose focus includes the borderland Southwest, the nation, and the contemporary arts world. It presents a year-round slate of exhibitions, lectures, and films in its spectacular, Robert Venturi–designed building set high above La Jolla's cliff sides. La Jolla's commercial gallery scene is a mixed bag that includes several contemporary spaces mounting shows worthy of national attention, as well as venues exhibiting tried-and-true-seascape images. A cluster of galleries about a mile from the museum, at 7661 Girard, are notable for their focus on Southern California's leading contemporary arts talents. This sun-drenched Art Town is also home to La Jolla Fiber Arts, one of the nation's top galleries specializing in contemporary textiles.

Art Talk

Des McAnuff, artistic director of the La Jolla Playhouse.

We've had to work hard to build our presence in this community. Our location on a college campus on a hilltop overlooking La Jolla is certainly beautiful, but it also places us in a key position of serving as a contact point between the academic community and the residents of the San Diego area who come here to attend our performances. Our educational programs extend from La Jolla preschoolers to faculty members of the university. We have programs for elementary school, middle school, and high school students, and we focus on sending teaching professionals out into the community. I came back to this area in 1983 to restart this theatre company, and now we're on the verge of constructing our third theatre, a 500-seat, flexible, black box space that will allow us a state-of-the-art facility for staging the best in American and international theatre.

Located on the hilltop campus of the University of California at San Diego, the La Jolla Playhouse is one of the best regional theatre companies in North America. Many of the most popular stage hits of the past half century received their initial runs at La Jolla Playhouse, which was founded in 1947 by actors Gregory Peck, Dorothy McGuire, and Mel Ferrer as a place for Hollywood actors to hone their skills away from the prying eyes of gossip hounds and scandal sheets. Offering its audiences a powerful mix of theatre standards and new works, the Playhouse presents local residents with the opportunity to enjoy the greatest and very latest in stagecraft. A short drive from La Jolla, in the community of Escondido, is the state-of-the-art performance

Art Talk

Hugh Davies, director of the San Diego Museum of Contemporary Art. We're one of the main organizations working to ramp up the impact of La Jolla as a cultural destination, something we're pursuing through strategies such as starting Art Wave La Jolla, a first-year event in October that will coordinate major events on the community's visual arts, music, and performance fronts. For some reason La Jolla's not as well known as a culturally rich destination as it should be, so through events like Art Wave we're attempting to correct this. We've evolved from an institution that was started in 1941 as a community arts center into a collecting museum with a coherent focus on contemporary arts. We're engaged in opening exhibition facilities in downtown San Diego that will eventually give us a total of 20,000 square feet of space for regional, national, and international exhibitions in the middle of the nation's seventh-largest city.

facility of the California Center for the Arts, which has emerged as a major venue for touring theatre, concerts, and classical music. The La Jolla Chamber Music Society, which stages its performances on the UCSD campus and at MCA's Sherwood Auditorium, is another highly regarded La Jolla organization known for its innovative programming as well as its energetic community outreach programs focused on children's classical music education.

Essentials

Visual Arts Venues

San Diego Museum of Contemporary Art
(700 Prospect Street; 858/454-3541; www.mcasd.org) This jewel-like museum offers great shows by leading regional, national, and international artists and has a companion exhibitions facility in downtown San Diego.

La Jolla Fiber Arts (7644 Girard Avenue; 858/454-6732; www.lajolla fiberarts.com) Gallery representing top regional and national names in textile arts.

Tasende Gallery (820 Prospect Street; 858/454-3691) Sophisticated gallery representing international and national artists.

Performing Arts & Events

La Jolla Playhouse (2910 La Jolla Village Drive; 858/550-1070; www.lajollaplayhouse.com) An American theatre treasure, performing year-round on the UCSD campus and premiering important new works.

La Jolla Music Society (7946 Ivanhoe Avenue, #309; 858/459-3728; www.ljms.org) Energetic classical music presenter known for its SummerFest La Jolla, which takes place in August.

La Jolla Festival of the Arts (4130 La Jolla Village Drive; 858/456-1268; www.lajollaartfestival.org) Nearly 200 artists and dozens of great restaurants combine their talents for this June event on the campus of La Jolla Country Day School.

Wine & Dine

Bernini's Bistro (7550 Fay Avenue; 858/454-5013; www.berninis bistro.com) Great patio, salads, lemonade, and conversation.

Goldfish Point Café (1255 Coast Boulevard; 858/459-7407) Coffee and pastries with an ocean view.

Nine-Ten (910 Prospect Street; 858/964-5400; www.nine-ten.com) Sophisticated regional cuisine in the spectacular setting of the Grande Colonial Hotel.

Accommodations

The Grande Colonial Hotel (910 Prospect Street; 858/454-2181; www.thegrandecolonial.com) Historic hotel overlooking the center of La Jolla and its beaches.

La Jolla Travelodge (6750 La Jolla Boulevard; 858/454-0716; www.lajollatravelodge.com) Economical rooms a mile from the beach.

The Bed & Breakfast Inn at La Jolla (7753 Draper Avenue; 858/456-2066; www.innlajolla.com) Historic home, ocean views, and more than a dozen guest rooms.

Information

Promote La Jolla: 1150 Silverado Street; 858/454-5718; www.lajollabythesea.com

Population: 29,000

Mendocino, California

With its majestic location along the Pacific Coast just 150 miles north of San Francisco, this Art Town has long been a favored destination for weekend visitors from the Bay Area. For the better part of a century, since the days when Portuguese fishermen and loggers formed the heart of the region's economy, Mendocino has attracted a steady stream of artists, writers, poets, musicians, and actors. Today, the quaint and historic infrastructure that once served the needs of a quiet, coastal community has been preserved and turned into a place as seductive to the visions of landscape painters as it is inspiring to the fantasies of young lovers.

Life in Mendocino can be about as beautifully lived as anywhere in North America. Like most of the Art Towns close to major metropolitan areas, the sheer volume of tourists visiting Mendocino can be somewhat bewildering, though numbers-wise the situation isn't as overwhelming as it is in La Jolla and Carmel. Redwood trees frame the community's eastern edges, while the wind-swept Mendocino Headlands bluffs, an area patrolled by seagulls and eagles, mark the coastline. Mendocino's location places it in a transitional environmental zone, which means it gets less rain and overcast weather than does Eureka to its north, but not as much sun and warmth as does Santa Cruz to its south.

In this corner of California the entire coastline is a treasure trove of state parks and campgrounds. Living here means having easy access to rocky beachfronts perfect for ocean kayaking. And if you have a diving permit it also means being able to enjoy the popular abalone season, when these succulent shellfish are ready to be brought to your dinner table. One of the continent's greatest wine regions, the Anderson Valley, is just south of Mendocino, running southeast toward Sonoma for nearly 30 miles. That's why one of the most popular threads of conversation at Mendocino parties involves the splendors of whatever local merlot or cabernet sauvignon is newly released by an Anderson Valley winery.

Arts Scene

There's something for everyone in Mendocino's vibrant and diverse arts scene. The community's art center is a whirlwind of visual and performing-arts presentations and workshops, as well as the home of a local artists' gallery. Mendocino's gallery scene is home to nearly 20 art spaces as well as two artist-run collectives. But it doesn't stop there, with a classical music festival, two theatre companies, a surprisingly strong literary community, and even some opera tossed into the local arts mix.

The Mendocino Art Center has long served as one of the West Coast's most treasured retreats for mid-career artists looking to enhance their creative visions. The center offers short-term residencies as well as year-round teaching opportunities, a symbiosis that's never failed to attract legions of artists seeking instruction from these masters. Set among towering pines and redwoods, the center is a rambling complex of workshops, kilns, apartments, studios, and exhibition spaces. It's also the home of the renovated Helen Schoeni Theater, the community's most active performance venue. Mendocino's commercial galleries are quite good, exhibiting a strong range of landscape and non-subjective work as well as superbly designed fine crafts, primarily created by local artists who ended up living here after establishing successful careers in the Bay Area. Of special interest are the town's two artist-run galleries, Artists Co-op of Mendocino, which represents mainly painters, and Partners Gallery, a top-notch operation inside a local resort and home to many of the region's top contemporary artists.

Mendocino Theatre Company, which performs at the Helen Schoeni Theater, is a 25-year-old organization whose season schedule features an intriguing balance of new works, classic chestnuts, and children's theatre. Hit & Run Theatre, an interesting adjunct to the local thespian

Art Talk

Peggy Templer, executive director of the Mendocino Art Center.

Our status as an arts community started when a couple of artists from the Bay Area, Bill and Jenny Zacha, started coming here on weekend trips in the early 1950s. They're the ones who had the vision that Mendocino would be an ideal place for serious artists to concentrate on their work, so they decided to build the first stage of what eventually became the Mendocino Art Center. They invited their artist friends to come on up and stay for extended visits, and after a while, a number of that first group of artists decided to buy a little home and stay. Today we have a complex with 12 apartments where a group of resident artists can stay from September through May, and we offer an extensive workshop program that gets large numbers of out-of-town visitors in the summer, and mostly local residents through other times of the year. We also have several art galleries here at the center, showing work from the local arts community and our visiting artists as well as regional and national themed shows.

community, is geared toward presenting comedic performances in a variety of venues during summer months and works through local schools during the rest of the year. Opera Fresca, a beloved local institution whose supporters include many individuals associated with the San Francisco Opera, presents light opera at a variety of Mendocino venues through the year, including a holiday Sing-Along and a Christmas season Messiah. Nearby Ft. Bragg, a community with a transitioning economy about a 20-minute drive north of Mendocino, is home to the Symphony of the Redwoods, Gloriana Opera Company, and several very worthwhile art galleries.

Essentials

Visual Arts Venues

Artists Co-op of Mendocino (45270 Main Street; 707/937-2217) Located on the second story of the Sussex Building, this refuge for local landscape and seascape painters overlooks one of the continent's most spectacular sights, Mendocino Headlands.

Mendocino Art Center (45200 Little Lake Street; 707/937-5818; www.mendocinoartcenter.org) This is the place to find the up-and-coming talents on Mendocino's visual arts scene.

William Zimmer Gallery (Kasten & Ukiah Streets; 707/937-5121; www.williamzimmergallery.com) A beautiful space representing the cream of the local and regional visual arts crop.

Performing Arts & Events

Mendocino Music Festival
(P.O. Box 1808; 707/937-2044; www.mendocinomusic.com) A two-week celebration in late July featuring many of the nation's top classical music talents performing in huge tents set up on the Mendocino Headlands.

Second Saturdays in Mendocino
(see Mendocino County Tourism Alliance below) On the second weekend of each month, when Mendocino's galleries have their opening receptions, downtown's funky collection of shops stays open late, and the restaurants are filled with a mix of visitors and artists.

Mendocino Theatre Company
(45200 Little Lake Street; 707/937-4477; www.1mtc.org) Long-standing community theatre company dedicated to presenting new and classic works.

Wine & Dine

Art Talk

Joseph DuVivier, oil painter.
I've been coming to Mendocino from the Bay Area for 14 years, and my wife and I made this our permanent home five years ago. I do miss the many fun things that the city offers, like art museums, but I've adjusted to life here. Mendocino has a lot of the things artists look for in terms of natural inspiration and a better kind of life. It's a small town, the kind of place where you can meet lots of people and enjoy the sense of being in a supportive community. Many of the artists here meet for painting groups or for classes at the art center. Mendocino has a natural setting that makes you very aware of the elements of nature, and there's creative inspiration everywhere you turn. I enjoy living in a place where I can go diving to recharge my creative energy, or where walking along an undeveloped beach is something you can take for granted.

Headlands Coffeehouse (120 Laurel Street, Ft. Bragg; 707/964-1987; www.headlandscoffeehouse.com) It's a short drive to Ft. Bragg, but many of Mendocino's artists find their way to this venue for its evenings of live music, visual arts shows, and great food.

Grey Whale Bar (45020 Albion Street at MacCallum House Inn; 707/937-5763; www.maccallumhouse.com) Favorite watering hole for generations of locals, this warm and friendly pub is attached to one of the region's best restaurants.

955 Ukiah Street Restaurant (955 Ukiah Street; 707/937-1955; www.955restaurant.com) Affordable Mendocino favorite for seafood and salads.

Accommodations

The John Dougherty House (571 Ukiah Street; 707/937-5266; www.jdhouse.com) A lovely and romantic B&B in the heart of a quiet Mendocino neighborhood, with a range of rooms and fabulous gardens.

The Allen House (Comptche Ukiah Road; 510/531-7880; www.theallenhousemendocino.com) Located 6 miles outside of Mendocino in the middle of a forest, this collection of cabin, studio, and main building is a retreat offering exceptional solitude and beauty.

MacCallum House Inn (45020 Albion Street; 707/937-0289; www.maccallumhouse.com) Right in the heart of Mendocino, a Victorian inn with fireplaces and ocean views.

Information

Mendocino County Tourism Alliance: 525 S. Main Street, Ukiah; 866-466-3636; www.gomendo.com

Population: 824

Palm Springs, California

glittering, neon-encrusted oasis in the middle of a wickedly hot desert, Palm Springs exists as an anomaly to the rhyme and reason of everyday life. How hot is it here? Let's just say that if you've ever lived in Phoenix, the climate in this Art Town of 43,000, about a two-hour drive east of downtown Los Angeles, will remind you of home. It's populated by an amazingly eclectic mix of retired Hollywood stars, entrepreneurial gays and lesbians, golf-mad retirees from the Pacific Northwest, Native Americans from the Coachella Valley's tribes, Mexican migrant laborers, and a year-round flow of tourists coming here to gawk and marvel at all that overheated, only-in-Palm Springs glitz.

The good life here means living in a 1950s modernist home that looks as if it once doubled as a love shack for the Jetsons. Swimming pools, palm trees, art moderne furniture, spectacular views of the northeast-facing slopes of the Santa Rosa and San Jacinto Mountains, and a diet that includes copious amounts of locally grown dates and figs . . . that's what life here is about. But piecing together this unique sort of Palm Springs life takes a bit of doing, especially now that the Coachella Valley's spawned a building boom in nearby communities such as Palm Desert, LaQuinta, and Rancho Mirage. On the bright side of things, living here does mean having access to a top-shelf version of nightlife, thanks to the gay community's party-hard ethic. There's all the golf and tennis one can imagine, and the restaurants are as interesting as those found in most cities. The spectacular desert scenery is

Art Talk

Jayne Behman, artist.

Palm Springs was a much more affordable place when I moved here 10 years ago. There's a lot of redevelopment taking place now, a lot of people from Los Angeles and San Diego looking to buy weekend homes here, and a huge increase in the year-round community. Artists came here 20 years ago to buy modernist homes and fix them up, and sold their art to the tourists coming through. On the local level our arts scene hasn't kept pace with the real-estate scene, and for artists just starting out this can be a hard place to find representation. I show my art in my own gallery, which is in an out-of-the-way location where other artists rent out studio space, and we can teach art classes. I like being off the beaten path and like spending uninterrupted time in my studio.

breathtaking, and once you acclimate to the fact that even at midnight the sidewalks are hot enough to fry ostrich eggs, you realize that living in the desert and being just two hours from Venice Beach ain't such a bad thing after all.

Arts Scene

Between the hip, sophisticated streets of Palm Springs and the subdivided gleam of nearby Palm Desert, an exceedingly strong visual arts scene exists in this sun-bleached corner of Southern California. The region's leading cultural institution is the Palm Springs Desert Museum, a first-rate exhibition facility. Located just a short walk from the main drag of North Palm Canyon Drive, the museum offers touring national shows as well as rotating exhibitions of its permanent collection, and ongoing educational programs for adults and children. There are about a dozen galleries along North Palm Canyon Drive exhibiting a mix of regional landscape work as well as contemporary arts and photography. Two nonprofit, artist-run spaces are also part of the local arts scene, the Desert Art Center and the Jane Behman Gallery/Desert Fine Arts Academy. Alternative exhibition venues—in the form of coffee bars, restaurants, and hotel lobbies—are plentiful.

Three large spaces in Palm Desert dominate the regional gallery landscape, exhibiting works by internationally known contemporary artists. Another tier of galleries exhibits work by regional and local artists, making it possible for seasoned visual arts pros to make a living selling locally. For crafts artists the situation is even better, with events such as the Palm Springs Village Fest every Thursday evening and easily reached weekend arts fairs throughout the Los Angeles area being prime marketing targets.

Because of Palm Springs's proximity to L.A., performing arts here tend to have less of a local focus than they do in other Art Towns. The McCallum Theatre for the Performing Arts presents a year-round schedule that's action packed, diverse, and accessible. Everything from touring Broadway plays to Chinese acrobats to children's theatre makes its way to the McCallum's stage. The Fabulous Palm Springs Follies, which take place each winter at the Historic Plaza Theatre, is an over-the-top, camp hit that's been staged for more than ten years. Film festivals are always popular here, testifying to Palm Springs's lifeline connection to Hollywood. The biggest of these, the Palm Springs International Film Festival, takes place in late January.

Essentials

Visual Arts Venues

Palm Springs Desert Museum (101 Museum Drive; 760/325-0189; www.psmuseum.org) Outstanding exhibitions of international and regional art, as well as a lecture and performance series.

Jane Behman Gallery/Desert Fine Arts Academy (1000 N. Palm Canyon Drive; 760/320-6806) Local artists' gallery and studio complex.

Imago Galleries (45-450 Highway 74, Palm Desert; 760/776-9890; www.imagogalleries.com) Top international art exhibited in this gallery overlooking Palm Desert.

Performing Arts & Events

McCallum Theatre for the Performing Arts (73000 Fred Waring Drive; 760/340-2787; www.mccallumtheatre.com) Year-round slate of top entertainers in music, theatre, cabaret, and dance.

Art Talk

Janice Lyle, executive director of the Palm Springs Desert Museum.

I've been on the arts scene in Palm Springs for 20 years, and in the past several years the demographics here have shifted due to the growing interest in what Palm Springs has in its architectural inventory. A lot of our newer residents are highly aware of what's happening nationally and internationally in the arts world, and so it's been a challenge for the museum to keep up with the changing needs of our community. We're an institution that exists to bring the highest quality art into this community. We provide space for two local exhibits a year through our support councils and offer art workshops with local artists. Our exhibitions program tries to stay a little bit ahead of the community, and it's our goal to engage the community in a dialogue about contemporary arts.

Palm Springs International Film Festival (1700 E. Tahquitz Canyon Way; 760/322-2930; www.psfilmfest.org) January showcase for new works, with major celeb-spotting action.

Palm Springs International Art Fair (760/778-8415; www.psiaf.com) Major gathering of top North American art dealers in March.

Wine & Dine

Koffi (515 North Palm Canyon Drive; 760/416-2244) Sleek, modernist coffee bar with a misted patio and artsy crowd.

The Deck (262 S. Palm Canyon Drive; 760/325-5200) Watering hole and dinner spot overlooking the Palm Canyon Drive action.

Ichiban Japanese Steakhouse & Sushi (1201 E. Palm Canyon Drive; 760/318-1622) Great desert fun at the sushi bar.

Accommodations

Ocotillo Lodge (1111 E. Palm Canyon Drive; 760/416-0678) Classic Palm Springs,modern style.

Palm Mountain Resort (155 S. Belardo Road; 760/325-1301; www.palmmountainresort.com) Large resort hotel, with plenty of room for families.

Orbit In (562 W. Arenas Road; 760/323-3585; www.orbitin.com) Modernist retreat with beautiful rooms and a pool.

Information

Palm Springs Bureau of Tourism:777 N. Palm Canyon Drive; 760/778-8415; www.palm-springs.org

Population: 43,500

Ashland, Oregon

$\int$ hakespeare said it best in *The Merry Wives of Windsor*: "Defend your reputation, or bid farewell to your good life forever." Ashland, one of North America's two most Shakespearean communities (Stratford, Ontario, is the other), has carved out an international reputation for its artistic integrity and innovation. It has also aggressively defended that reputation from efforts made by several festival towns pretending to its crown. In the case of this Art Town an artistic renaissance led by forces allied with the Bard of Avon has elevated Ashland into the top tier of the continent's creative communities.

Ashland's quality of life is the stuff Art Town legends are made from. Its 2,000-foot elevation at the base of 7,500-foot Mt. Ashland means that this community has ready access to an alpine environment with its great hiking, skiing, and fishing, yet is temperate enough to have a long, sunny, and hot summer. And its location in the southwest corner of the Pacific Northwest means Ashland receives far more days of sunshine than other Northwest towns. There's an airport in nearby Medford with nonstop flights to San Francisco and Seattle, world-class white-water rafting on the Rogue River, and even Pacific coast beaches are just a two-and-a-half-hour drive west through the Siskiyou National Forest.

What's attracted a broadly based arts community to Ashland has been the presence of the Oregon Shakespeare Festival (OSF), an institution with more than 60 years of history as one of the nation's premier presenters of William Shakespeare's plays. As the festival's popularity grew, so did its number of employees, many of whom decided that Ashland was as good a place as any to buy a home and settle down during their off months. Over the years, as the festival continued to evolve, more and more talented individuals were drawn to Ashland to work at OSF and provide the technical and support services for the festival's productions. Ashland's tidy neighborhoods are now filled with individuals who work as set designers, carpenters, costumers, and lighting technicians. An increasingly important visual arts community developed along the way, as did a number of art galleries, restaurants, bakeries, bookstores, and Elizabethan-themed shops.

Living here means dealing with fast-escalating home values, which explains why some newcomer artists choose to live in the more affordable environs of Medford. In recent years, an exodus of Bay Area retirees and creative career professionals has pushed Ashland's real-estate market upward. As is the case when urbanites seek solace in Art Towns, some of these new arrivals view having an Ashland address as a necessity. The result is that many of Medford's affordable neighborhoods remain so, while Ashland at times is crawling with well-heeled folks dressed in designer sweats looking for cool places to shop.

Arts Scene

Theatre is the driving force behind Ashland's rise to national prominence as an Art Town. In large part, what exists here outside of theatre is able to survive because of the OSF's year-round economic impact. One of the hesitations that develops in people's minds when they're considering a permanent move to an Art Town is the question of "What will we do when we get there?" In Ashland, that's evolved into more of a concern about "How can we possibly manage to keep up with all the stuff going on here?" Not only is the OSF producing its February to October season of Shakespeare, classics and new works, but more than a half-dozen other theatre companies are hard at it as well, with most of those companies run by theatre pros whose résumés include substantial ties to OSF.

The festival itself is set on a surreally beautiful campus sunk right into the middle of Ashland. Its plays are produced on three stages, the largest of which is a 1,200-seat masterpiece that presents its works outdoors. There's also a 600-seat indoor theatre and a 140-seat black box, and during the summer months it's not unusual for anything and everything presented on all three stages to be sold-out, standing-room events.

During its typical season, OSF produces more than a dozen plays. Main stage fare usually includes popular Shakespearean standards such as *Macbeth*, *As You Like It*, and *Julius Caesar*, while modern plays such as *Who's Afraid of Virginia Woolf?* and *Playboy of the West Indies* highlight the schedule on the other stages. Throughout the year, OSF presents a vigorous slate of guest lectures, stage talks, readings, and other events that help connect local and visitor audiences with the work of this innovative stage company.

Ashland's year-round Oregon Cabaret Theatre (OCT) presents its performances in a renovated, 1911 Baptist church. More than 35,000 tickets are sold for OCT's entertaining slate of dinner-theatre plays, which run the gamut from pop celebrations like *Route 66* to the British slapstick comedy of traditional Panto. Ashland is also the home of Southern Oregon University, whose Department of Theatre Arts presents six plays in a November to May season for its main stage and black box theatres. The Siskiyou Singers are Ashland's chorale music organization, while the Rogue Valley Symphony, which performs from October through May in both Ashland and Medford, is the area's premier classical music organization as well as the winter home of many OSF musicians. One of the most popular music festivals in Oregon is presented by One World, which brings world music to Ashland and Medford from October to May. Many Medford concerts are presented at the Craterian Ginger Rogers Theater, a state-of-the-art facility. The Craterian is also a presenting organization whose year-round calendar brings dancers, classical musicians, and folk musicians into the region.

Nearby Jacksonville, a historic community just 15 miles from Ashland, is home to the Peter Britt Festival, an incredibly popular and successful, 40-year-old organization that's evolved into a four-month presenter of top names in rock, classical, folk, and country music, all presented in a natural amphitheatre set among ponderosa pines.

Downtown Ashland is home to more than a dozen art galleries, twice as many bakeries and restaurants, Bloomsbury Books, and a few curio joints selling sweatshirts emblazoned with Shakespeare's gaunt visage, crooked nose, and stringy hair. Taste of Ashland, an enormously successful event pairing downtown's galleries with the town's restaurants and southern Oregon's finest vineyards, takes place in mid-April and is the unofficial start of the region's visual arts season. The area's premier visual arts venue is the Schneider Museum of Art on the campus of Southern Oregon University. The Schneider showcases regional and national artists in its galleries, and serves as a lecture site and art installations site during Ashland's popular First Fridays art walks. The area's other, major nonprofit visual arts site is the Rogue

Art Talk

Charlotte Peterson, watercolor artist. I came here 31 years ago, and at that time I wasn't an artist. But living here you get a tremendous exposure to art, and there's something about Asheville that's conducive to the creative spirit. So I started out learning about painting in a regular Tuesday art class, which I stuck with for 10 years, and eventually that led me to watercolors and membership in the Oregon Watercolor Society. So now I have a lot of interest in being admitted to juried shows, and my art sales are an outgrowth of that. I'm a member of the Art & Soul Gallery, which is a cooperative space in downtown Ashland. I think our gallery gets the most traffic of any of Ashland's galleries, probably because the art is of pretty high quality and we seem able to stick around from one year to the next. Ashland has a fun, engaging environment that's somewhat protected from the ups and downs that impact economies in other places.

Gallery & Art Center in downtown Medford. Ashland's gallery scene is in a constant state of flux, with places coming and going year to year. Art & Soul, a cooperative venture formed by a few dozen local artists, is one of the places that's thrived through the past few years, as has Davis & Cline, which represents a strong group of contemporary artists from the region and also brings in work from outside the Pacific Northwest. Hanson Howard Gallery, which represents contemporary work in a variety of media, is one of Ashland's oldest galleries, while the Living Gallery incorporates visual arts into a setting that mixes furnishings and home accessories.

Essentials

Visual Arts Venues

Schneider Museum of Art (1250 Siskiyou Boulevard; 541/552-6245; www.sou.edu) Touring national, regional, and local shows as well as year-round lectures and programs.

Art & Soul Gallery (247 E. Main Street; 541/488-9006, www.artandsoulgallery.com) The region's best gallery for locally made art.

Davis & Cline Gallery (525 "A" Street; 541/482-2069; www.davisandcline.com) Contemporary Northwest and national art.

Performing Arts & Events

Oregon Shakespeare Festival (15 S. Pioneer Street; 541/482-2111; www.osfashland.org) The nation's premier presenter of Shakespearean work also stages contemporary plays during its long season.

Oregon Cabaret Theatre (1st & Hargadine; 541/488-2902; www.oregoncabaret.com) Year-round season of dinner theatre, comedies, drama, and new works.

A Taste of Ashland (Ashland Gallery Association; 541/488-8430; www.atasteofashland.com) Mid-April kickoff of the visual arts season, tying together galleries with local art, Oregon wines, and gourmet food.

Wine & Dine

Tabu (76 N. Pioneer Street; 541/482-3900) Nuevo Latino food, great music, and mojitos in the happening bar.

Chateaulin Restaurant & Wine Shop (50 E. Main Sreet; 541/482-2264; www.chateaulin.com) Fantastic onion soup, superb wine list, seafood, and Northwest cuisine.

Standing Stone Brewing Company (101 Oak Street; 541/482-2448; www.standingstonebrewing.com) Food, micro-brews, and one of Ashland's best live-music venues.

Accommodations

Art Talk

Mary Gardiner, director of the Schneider Museum of Art.

A few years ago we completed a consolidation and expansion of our campus art facilities, and we are actively searching for better storage space for the objects in our permanent collection. We're the only art museum in this part of the state that's capable of exhibiting local, national, and international exhibitions, and we do it all in a 10,000-square-foot facility. At least half of our exhibitions are concerned with what's taking place in the off-campus arts world. Our busy, summer season is when we present a general exhibition with national appeal. The arts community in Ashland is growing, and it's responding well to the challenge of staying abreast of trends in the art world. The visual arts especially have become a larger part of the region's arts economy. Restaurants, banks, and coffee bars all are exhibiting rotating shows of local art, and that's helped raise awareness of the size and integrity of the local arts community.

Bayberry Inn (438 N. Main Street; 541/488-1252; www.bayberry inn.com) Craftsman-style home, with large rooms and a three-minute walk to OSF's theatres.

The Peerless Hotel (243 Fourth Street; 541/488-1082; www.peerlesshotel.com) Historic hotel by the railroad tracks.

Ashland Springs Hotel (212 E. Main Street; 541/488-1700; www.ashlandspringshotel.com) Restored, classic hotel in downtown Ashland.

Information

Ashland Chamber of Commerce: 110 E. Main Street; 541/482-3486, www.ashlandchamber.com

Population: 20,000

Bend, Oregon

The high-desert landscape of central Oregon has attracted a steady stream of lifestyle refugees in recent years, changing Bend from a sleepy ranching community into a thriving, year-round resort Mecca with more than 52,000 full-time residents. What they're finding here is a climate that has more in common with the four seasons of northern New Mexico than it does with the gloom and rainfall of Portland, a 160-mile drive northwest of here.

Bend is an incredibly active place where nature's treasures are just a short journey from one's front door. White-water rafting on the Deschutes and McKenzie Rivers is a summertime rite of passage for locals, as is winter skiing on the pristine slopes of Mt. Bachelor's champagne powder. There are world-class mountain bike trails crisscrossing the enormity of Deschutes National Forest, and the entire region is widely considered a fishermen's paradise where seven world-class rivers are home to trophy-size rainbow and brown trout, as well as steelheads.

The fast rate of growth has meant that Bend has also become a promised land for real-estate developers. While many locals appreciate the community's improved roads, parks, and retail options, there's also a lot of concern about steadily rising costs of living, crowded roads, and subdivisions creeping across what once were verdant farmlands and forests. Getting out of Bend and into a more urban setting entails a two-hour drive across the Cascade Mountains to the university town of Eugene.

Art Talk

Forrest Rodgers, president of the High Desert Museum.

Our exhibits interpret the Intermountain West's human experience. We deal with the region's exploration and settlement, its Native American cultures, and its modern development, using exhibits about culture, commerce, industry, and artistic expression to make our points. Our two changing exhibitions galleries are generally exhibiting combinations of artifacts and art. We maintain a collection of art from the 19th and 20th centuries that illustrates this telling of the region's human history, and how the arrival of settlers impacted the traditional lives of the region's Native Americans. Our facility is a model of architectural elegance, made from natural materials found in this area and sited to look as if it naturally emerges from the landscape. In recent years Bend has become increasingly interested in the expression of its arts and culture. The downtown's art galleries have a very high visibility, and the summer art festivals are hugely popular.

Arts Scene

Downtown's streets are home to a dozen or so galleries representing local and regional work, with a smattering of cowboy art, Native American art, fine art glass, and bronze sculpture. There's another cluster of galleries in the nearby community of Sisters, 22 miles northwest of Bend in the Cascade Mountains foothills. There's a downtown Bend Gallery Walk on the first Friday of every month, an event that draws huge crowds during the busy summer months and becomes a more local affair at other times of the year. One of the art spaces in town, Mirror Pond Gallery, is run by the Central Oregon Arts Association and is located in a historic home bordering the Deschutes River.

Six miles south of Bend is the High Desert Museum, a modern and beautifully designed group of buildings dedicated to explaining the cultural heritage of the Intermountain West, an eight-state region stretching from the Canadian border to Mexico. The museum offers an amazing variety of exhibits and projects, ranging from the ecological to the historical, cultural, and artistic. This is where locals come for a year-round lecture series featuring academicians as well as changing exhibitions by regional and national artists. Less than an hour's drive north of Bend, on the Warm Springs Reservation, is one of the nation's gems of Native American art and culture, the Museum at Warm Springs.

Bend's music and performing-arts scene received a shot in the arm when the Les Schwab Amphitheatre opened in 2002 in the Old Mill District redevelopment, a complex of shops, studios, and offices on a former lumber mill site along the Deschutes River. In addition to name acts such as Lyle "That's Right, You're Not from Texas" Lovett and his Large Band, the amphitheatre hosts a summer series of free outdoor concerts featuring blues, folk, ethnic, and country musicians from across the Northwest.

Bend supports two community theatre companies, Magic Circle Theatre, which stages its plays at Pickney Center for the Arts on the campus of Central Oregon Community College, and the 2nd Street Theater, which stages its productions in a downtown black box facility behind an Italian restaurant. During late August, the Cascade Festival of Music brings a week of top-notch classical musical talent into Bend for chamber music and orchestral concerts.

Essentials

Visual Arts Venues

High Desert Museum (59800 S. Highway 97; 541/382-4754; www.highdesertmuseum.org) A modern museum covering culture, art; and history, focused on the Intermountain West

Mirror Pond Gallery (875 NW Brooks Street; 541/317-9324; www.bendgalleries.com) Popular space in a historic building, representing many of the region's top art talents.

Mockingbird Gallery (869 NW Wall Street; 541/388-2107; www.mockingbird-gallery.com) Exhibits the Pacific Northwest's top names in contemporary art, sculpture, and realism.

Art Talk

Cate O'Hagan, installations artist and director of the Mirror Pond Gallery. We're the local arts agency for a three-county region and operate programs in two locations. One is a 1907 Craftsman-style home on the river and the other is a 1911 train depot that's been relocated to the Old Mill District. The Art Station is used for our education and residency programs, and the Mirror Pond Gallery is used for exhibitions of mostly local arts. The growth of Bend's arts scene over the past decade has been impressive. Some of the reasons people come here as artists have to do with the second-home growth in this area, but there are a lot of other artists who have a full-time presence in the community. Most artists work from their homes and don't necessarily show their work in Bend but have outlets in other parts of the country. There are still some difficulties in this community when it comes to getting the message across to businesses that the arts play an important role in this town's growth. But the arts community continues to grow in spite of this problem, and they won't be able to ignore us for much longer.

Performing Arts & Events

Cascade Festival of Music (832
NW Wall Street; 541/383-2202; www.cascademusic.org) August
classical music festival at Drake Park in downtown Bend

Sunriver Music Festival (15 Sunriver Village Mall, Sunriver;
541/593-1084; www.sunrivermusic.org) Early-August classical
music festival on the grounds of a spectacular resort.

2nd Street Theatre (220 NE Lafayette Avenue; 541/312-9626)
Innovative, year-round presentations in a renovated, downtown
space.

Wine & Dine

Royal Blend (744 NW Bond Street; 541/312-4036; www.royal
blend.com) Favorite Bend spot for high-octane java fixes.

Sidelines Sports Bar (1020 NW Wall Street; 541/385-8898) Bend's
top spot for regional and national sports action, serving burgers,
sandwiches, and pizza.

Robby J's Bistro (705 SW Bonnett Way; 541/383-8220; www.robby
js.com) Innovative fusion specialties and a great wine list.

Accommodations

Lara House B&B (640 NW Congress Street; 541/388-4064) Turn-of-
the-century Craftsman-style home overlooking Drake Park; Bend's
oldest B&B.

Pine Ridge Inn (1200 SW Century Drive; 541/389-6137;
www.pineridgeinn.com) Elegant surroundings, lots of quiet rooms.

Hillside Inn (1744 NW 12th Street; 800/550-1821; www.bendhill-
sideinn.com) Close to Drake Park, with large rooms and mountain
views.

Information

Bend Chamber of Commerce: 777 NW Wall Street; 541/382-3221;
www.bendchamber.org

Population: 52,700

Cannon Beach, Oregon

I n the Pacific Northwest, where many Art Towns tout their natural assets, Cannon Beach has the full force of the raging Pacific Ocean breaking right at its doorstep. Just less than a two-hour drive from the cultural gem of Portland—which offers everything from pro sports to nonstop flights to New York City—Cannon Beach is what many artists envision when they dream about a perfect paradise. It's small, friendly, prosperous, safe, and charming. And with the big city just a short drive away, this is also the kind of town where enterprising locals, be they art-gallery owners, coffee bar operators, or country innkeepers, have plenty of opportunities to make a living.

For some, there's the issue of weather, which is one reason why Cannon Beach has kept a lid on its growth. Clear, warm days are a rarity, though when they do show up the town turns into a northern version of Santa Cruz, without the roller coaster and surfers. Real-estate values have not stopped climbing since the economic dips of the early 1990s, a situation exacerbated by newcomers trying to outdo one another with large homes designed for suburban living. Some artists moving into this area have found great real-estate deals in nearby communities such as Seaside and Astoria, a seaport with an emerging creative sector.

In a place like Cannon Beach, life tends to get boiled down to fairly simple pleasures. Morning walks on the beach, digging clams for fresh chowder, running into friends at the post office, cruising through the middle chapters of a murder mystery while sitting in a cozy coffee bar, and waiting for the darn rain to stop so you can go outside and tend to your garden. If this sounds like the place you're longing for, grab your umbrella and get moving.

Arts Scene

Once famed for having a number of artists painting seascapes on canvases framed in driftwood, the art galleries of Cannon Beach have largely made sure that those days are behind them. Oregon's art buyers have become quite savvy, and as a result the work exhibited in galleries is much more contemporary than what Cannon Beach was known for in the past. Some locals refer to Cannon Beach as the Left Edge of Oregon, a place that's attracted an extraordinary number of artists, many of whom are represented in leading galleries in Portland and Seattle. While there's some yearly turnover in Cannon Beach's galleries, nearly two dozen art sites manage to keep the local scene percolating at a lively rate.

In addition to the changing nature of the art exhibited in Cannon Beach galleries, one of the region's more notable developments in the past few years has been the arts scene in Astoria, a short drive north. Fueled by urban pioneers, Astoria's new breed of artists, musicians, and coffee bar owners has its roots in Portland's arts scene. To Cannon Beach's south, in places such as Bay City, Manzanita, Oceanside, and Tillamook, several very worthwhile galleries represent even more of the region's fine crafts artists, painters, and glass-blowers.

For locals who don't need the aggravation of a drive on wet roads to catch a play in Portland, Cannon Beach offers highly regarded community theatre in one of the most unusual settings found in any of the Art Towns. Coaster Theatre Playhouse inhabits a structure originally built in the 1920s as a skating rink. Located in the middle of Cannon Beach, this historic building has served for 30 years as the site of a year-round series of plays and acting workshops, as well as a Christmas production and even an annual arts exhibition. Astoria's Clatsop Community College presents Arts on Stage, a theatre, classical music, and dance series during the academic year. There's also the occasional country band booked into the larger hotels in Seaside.

During July and August, Portland State University uses Cannon Beach as the site of its increasingly influential Haystack Summer Program in the Arts, which focuses on visual arts instruction, writing workshops, a children's book-writing conference ,and a classical music series. Most of the classes and conferences are held at Cannon Beach

Elementary School and attract a nationally respected faculty that includes many of the top names in Pacific Northwest literary and visual arts circles.

Each summer the Cannon Beach Arts Association presents its Concerts in the Park series of (weather permitting) outdoor concerts on Sunday afternoons in City Park. The association also operates a highly regarded visual arts space just to the south of the town's cluster of commercial art galleries. In early November, the arts community gathers to collectively thumb its nose at Mother Nature's fury during the weekend-long Stormy Weather Arts Festival, which features music, drama, and jazz and world music performances at the Coaster Theatre, Chamber of Commerce Community Hall, and Sandpiper Square. The visual arts end of the festival includes a town-wide gallery walk as well as special exhibitions in each gallery and a group show at a local hotel. The year's largest tourist crowds come to Cannon Beach each June for its Sandcastle Contest, which features beach-bound artists from across the globe.

Art Talk

Craig Shepherd, actor, set designer, and artistic director of Coaster Theatre. We're located in a historic skating rink that has its original, hardwood floor, which gives us great acoustics. We have 200 seats with great sight lines and a raked seating section. As artistic director my goal is to not limit our material to comedies or standards. We present the occasional classic work, as well as new works that are a bit offbeat, and have found that challenging material gets the best reaction from our audience. During the summer season we perform three plays in repertory, which has turned out to be a very popular series with our ticket buyers, though the most popular summer shows tend to be the ones presenting straightforward entertainment. Cannon Beach has lots of full-time residents who have moved here from other parts of the country after gaining professional theatre experience, so our talent tends to rise to any occasion.

Essentials

Visual Arts Venues

Cannon Beach Gallery (1064 S. Hemlock; 503/436-0744; www.cbgallerygroup.com) Contemporary art by local painters and sculptors.

Ballantyne & Douglass (123 S. Hemlock; 503/436-0507; www.bdgallery.com) Oregon landscapes by top regionalists.

Bronze Coast Gallery (224 N. Hemlock; 503/436-1055; www.bronzecoastgallery.com) Sculpture, paintings, and fine crafts by local and regional artists.

Art Talk

Leslie Wood Garvin, gallery director of the Cannon Beach Gallery.
We're a multidisciplinary, nonprofit gallery run by the Cannon Beach Art Association, and we've been around since the mid-1980s. Our location, a number of blocks south of the main gallery district in Cannon Beach, still allows us to get our share of visitors, though they tend to be the type who is more interested in finding great art than they are in finding nice seashells. We exhibit a variety of mainly regional artists, with a changing monthly schedule of painting and three-dimensional work. The tendency is more toward contemporary arts than you'd find in most Cannon Beach galleries. This town has always attracted its share of artists, though the younger ones who move here tend to only stay for a year or two before moving on.

Performing Arts & Events

Coaster Theatre Playhouse (108 N. Hemlock; 503/436-1242; www.coaster theatre.com) Community theatre and special events in a converted skating rink.

Stormy Weather Arts Festival (see Chamber of Commerce below) Performance, music, and visual arts in the middle of the rainy season.

Haystack Summer Program in the Arts (503/725-4186; www.haystack.pdx.edu) July and August program focused on music, literature, and visual arts.

Wine & Dine

Bella Espresso (117 N. Hemlock; 503/436-2595) Java-and-jive favorite.

Pizza a' Fetta (231 N. Hemlock; 503/436-0333) Moderately priced Italian fare.

Clark's Restaurant & Bar (264 E. Third Street; 503/436-8944) Seafood dinners and a favorite live-music venue.

Accommodations

Tolovana Inn (3400 S. Hemlock; 503/436-2211; www.tolovana inn.com) Oceanfront resort, with great beach access.

Inn at Village Centre (233 N. Hemlock; 877/912-2151) Affordable and close to the beach.

Haystack Resort (3339 S. Hemlock; 503/436-1577; www.haystack-resort.com) Large, oceanfront resort, with RV parking and a pool.

Information

Cannon Beach Chamber of Commerce: 207 Spruce Street; 503/436-2623; www.cannonbeach.org

Population: 1,400

Hood River, Oregon

One of the jewels of America's outdoor recreation scene, this creative community sits in a spectacular location alongside the Columbia River just a 90-minute drive east of Portland. Once driven by the growing, processing, and shipping of fruits, Hood River's economy has diversified quite smartly in recent years. While there's still plenty of fruit grown and shipped out of Hood River's rail yards and port, this community's reputation as one of the world's greatest locations for wind surfing has led to its becoming a year-round hotbed for hundreds of athletes, many of whom are world-traveling professionals making big bucks on the wind-surfing circuit. During the winter months, some of North America's best alpine skiing is just an hour away on the slopes of 11,239-foot Mt. Hood.

Along with the outdoor recreation crowd, a new generation of artists has arrived, joining the small but thriving group of artists who were attracted here years ago by the region's opportunities for low-cost, rural living. This is the kind of place where it's possible to find a few acres of land that's home to a small fruit orchard and which can be easily converted into an ideal setup for an artist needing separate buildings for a home, studio, and storage, all within a few steps of each other. It's simply an added bonus of Hood River's lifestyle that the trees surrounding one's home and studio happen to produce cherries the size of plums and peaches the size of softballs.

Because it's close to Portland, Hood River's become one of those places that urbanites have locked onto as an ideal place to build their weekend retreats. While that's been good news for those in the construction trades, it's also led to more than a few skirmishes between locals and real estate developers wanting to slap ranchette subdivisions onto Hood River's landscape. As prices for single family homes have risen, some Hood River artists have fanned out to nearby communities such as the Dalles (where there's considerably more sunshine and cloud-free days) and even across the Columbia River to the Washington town of White Salmon.

Arts Scene

Though the eminently walkable streets of downtown Hood River are filled with more places selling wet suits than places selling watercolor landscapes, the arts community plays a highly visible role in this town's daily life. There's a lot of overlap between the artists and outdoor recreation community, with many individuals pursuing both forms of self-expression. This is the kind of place where coffee bars, restaurants, and bookstores all make room on their walls for local art. Many artists living here are making the bulk of their income through Portland art galleries as well as selling at street fairs throughout the Pacific Northwest. Others are more nationally based, with gallery representation outside the region and sophisticated Internet sales presences.

Columbia Art Gallery in downtown Hood River is the heart and soul of this town's visual arts scene. Two of the top alternative visual arts venues are Twiggs, an interior design store, and Waucoma Bookstore, where many of the best ceramists show their work. Set into the middle of fruit orchards on the outskirts of town is Mystic Mud Studio, a ceramics studio with an on-site gallery.

On summer weekends many of Hood River's artists can be found displaying their work at the Saturday Farmers' Market on Cascade Avenue. East of Hood River, in the sunny and warm climate of the Dalles, is a historic Carnegie Library building that's been converted into a nonprofit gallery. The region's biggest visual arts surprise is 40 miles east of Hood River at the Maryhill Museum of Art. This massive, Greek Revival structure overlooking the Columbia Gorge is adjacent to a full-scale recreation of the monolithic Stonehenge site. The museum hosts changing exhibitions, a film series, lectures, and seminars by art world experts and is a fascinating presence in this corner of the Pacific Northwest. Downtown Hood River is also home to the International Museum of Carousel Art, a collection of carved horses, lions, elephants, tigers, and bears, all displayed in an old bank building. The local stage troupe, C.A.S.T., performs a range of dramas, comedies, and children's theatre productions year-round in a modest facility in the basement of a downtown office building.

Essentials

Visual Arts Venues

Maryhill Museum of Art (35 Maryhill Museum Drive; Goldendale; 509/773-3733; www.maryhillmuseum.org) Historic and contemporary art, plus a full-scale Stonehenge.

Columbia Art Gallery (207 Second Street; 541/386-4512) Representing regional artists in varied media, with monthly changing exhibitions.

Mystic Mud Studio (3400 Wy'East Road; 541/354-1238) Fantastic ceramics sold nationally at galleries and design shops.

Performing Arts & Events

C.A.S.T. (105 4th Street; 541/387-8855) Community theatre presenting adults and children's plays.

Trout Lake Arts Festival (The Farm B&B, Goldendale, Wash.; 509/395-2488; www.troutlake.org/arts) This July event attracts huge crowds and top artists.

Columbia Gorge Bluegrass Festival (see Hood River County Chamber of Commerce below) Top national talents roll into town for this summer event.

Wine & Dine

Full Sail Pub (506 Columbia; 541/386-2247; www.fullsailbrewing.com) Great pub food, nice patio, and all of it inside one of America's top microbreweries.

Art Talk

Marian Dyche, manager of the Columbia Art Gallery.

We're a nonprofit, community-sponsored art gallery representing nearly 100 artists from the Columbia Gorge area. We're a 34-year-old organization and have maintained an open-door program that welcomes everyone. We recently had to relocate from a perfect space in a basement to another, but much smaller, space in downtown Hood River. We're hopeful that the community will get behind a movement to build the kind of multidisciplinary arts space that this town deserves. Artists move here because of Hood River's incredible scenery, its laid-back attitude, and its supportive community of artists. Events like the Saturday Farmers' Market let artists keep in close contact with each other. This is a congenial place but also one that attracts people with independent spirits. The cost of living in Hood River itself can be somewhat high, but there are lots of small towns that are much more affordable and not very far away.

Art Talk

Trudi Klinger, ceramist.

When I moved here I was an art student who had taken a few ceramics classes, and I happened to find a small farm for sale. It had also been a ceramics studio, so I decided to get back into ceramics work and it just grew from there. Now I've grown Mystic Mud to the point where it's a full-time career, and I do a number of wholesale shows around the country and sell to galleries all over the place. We also do an annual wholesale show right out of our own studio, which always attracts a huge number of buyers. Hood River is all an artist could ever want from a perfect community to call home. It's safe, beautiful, and while it's not as affordable as it once was, you can still find ways to buy a home if you look hard enough. This isn't a materialistic community, which goes back to Hood River's agricultural roots. If it's the environment that you value and you enjoy being disconnected from the strange things happening in other parts of the country, this is the place to live.

Pasquale's Ristorante (102 Oak Street; 541/386-1900) Regional Italian specialties.

Holstein's Coffee Co. (12 Oak Street; 541/386-4115; www.holsteins coffee.com) Java haven in downtown.

Accommodations

Meredith Gorge Motel (4300 Westcliff Drive; 541/386-1515) Affordable rooms in a restored, 1950s-style motel overlooking Columbia Gorge.

Hood River Hotel (102 Oak Street; 800/386-1859;www.hoodriver hotel.com) Historic, downtown hotel with a popular Italian restaurant.

Columbia Gorge Hotel (4000 Westcliff Drive; 541/386-5566; www. columbiagorgehotel.com) A classic beauty from the early 20th century, overlooking Columbia Gorge.

Information

Hood River County Chamber of Commerce: 405 Portway Avenue; 541/386-2000; www.hoodriver.org

Population: 5,900

Bellingham, Washington

This scenic community at the northwest tip of the United States has a lot more going for it than just its miles of Puget Sound coastline and a shabby chic, 1940s-style downtown loaded with neighborhood taverns, biker bars, and those ever-present reminders of Washington's out-of-control caffeine-addiction problem: espresso machines.

Bellingham's shifting economic foundation has been a roller-coaster ride for families dependent on the forestry and fishing industries, as well as industries such as shipping, canning, and milling. But those ups and downs have kept in check the costs of living. Tidy neighborhoods filled with hillside abodes on quiet, wooded lots abound. The main drawback to living here is the oft-gloomy weather. Bellingham's gray-cloaked skies make the annual sunshine levels in Seattle, about a two-hour drive south, seem positively tropical. Then again, there's lots of compensation in the form of access to fantastic skiing on the alpine slopes of Mt. Baker, a 10,778-foot giant in the Cascade Range, which is where many locals head to on winter weekends for a high-altitude respite from the low-lying overcast Bellingham.

Another of the aces up Bellingham's sleeve, and a main reason why this is one of the best Art Towns, is the influence of Western Washington University on Bellingham's quality of life. Home to 12,000 students, the university has carved out an outstanding reputation as one of the nation's best education values, attracting scholars, artists, and free thinkers to its spectacular, hillside campus overlooking

Bellingham Bay. With an institution of this size, Bellingham is able to not only offer well-paid jobs to many hundreds of teachers and administrators, but it is also the beneficiary of an amazingly active and culturally diverse program of year-round activities in the arts, theatre, music, film, and dance. Living here means not having to travel far to keep up with mainstream North American cultural trends.

The presence of Western's large student body also means that Bellingham is loaded with the stores and services that provide students with everything from futon furniture to used CDs to frontline fashions. Downtown's streets are a great place to window shop for the accoutrements of urban, hipster life. There's also an extraordinary number of bars and live-music clubs presenting everything from Nashville cool to urban hip-hop to Bellingham's racially diverse and politically tolerant audiences.

Yet another asset in Bellingham's favor is its proximity to one of the continent's most exciting urban metropolises, Vancouver, British Columbia. Located just 54 miles north of downtown Bellingham, Vancouver offers everything from nonstop flights to Paris to one of the largest Chinatowns outside of Hong Kong. Living in Bellingham means having the option of cruising into Vancouver for dim sum, opera, professional sports, shopping fixes, and shows at fantastic art galleries, and being home in time for dinner. In other words, Bellingham in some ways functions as an extended Vancouver suburb, in much the same way that Sarasota, Florida, relates to Tampa, or Santa Fe, New Mexico, communes with Albuquerque.

Arts Scene

With its abundance of young talent and large student population, it's not surprising that Bellingham's developed a strong and thriving independent music scene anchored by numerous live-music venues and recording studios. There are more than a dozen bars and nightclubs booking live music, and several of these venues are actively presenting a balance of both local and national acts. With urban centers to its north and south, its easy for local clubs to grab a spare evening on a touring act's Northwest itinerary, put them onstage in front of an appreciative audience, and actually make a few bucks from the show's receipts. For locally grown talent, opportunities to make career headway are easily accessible, much the same way that local live-music venues have supported thriving music scenes in Art Towns like Oxford, Mississippi, and Lawrence, Kansas. And if the word of mouth about a new band is especially favorable, venues in Vancouver and Seattle are the convenient and logical next steps up the music ladder.

Downtown Bellingham's premier music venue is the Mt. Baker Theatre, a beautifully restored, 1927 vaudeville house that now hosts nearly 200 evenings of music, dance, and theatre each year. With its 1,509 seats and Wurlitzer pipe organ, its little surprise that major classical music events such as the July and August Bellingham Festival of Music and the October to May season of the Whatcom Symphony Orchestra take place in the Mt. Baker Theatre. The theatre also acts as a music presenter, bringing national level entertainers, musicians, Broadway plays, and rock acts. A recently opened outdoor venue, Bellwether on the Bay, attracts touring national bands for summer performances on its lush, amphitheatre lawns.

Another major local presenter of music and theatre is the Western Washington University Music and Performing Arts Series. Not only can you find summer Shakespeare but also some of the most recognizable names in national entertainment circles perform here throughout the year. Western's a presenter in two on-campus venues, including a 1,100-seat main stage theatre. Downtown's Pickford Cinema, a small venue adjoining an art gallery, is a project of the Whatcom Film Association. The Pickford specializes in screening independent and foreign films and also stages a summer outdoor film series in the nearby historic community of Fairhaven.

Bellingham's visual arts scene is interwoven with the community's daily life. While some of the art action takes place in galleries, much of it happens in alternative venues such as coffee shops, restaurants, and music venues, and a good deal of it doesn't even take place inside Bellingham itself. The historic community of Fairhaven, a 20-minute drive south of Bellingham, is home to an intact, partially restored, turn-of-the-20th-century downtown that's become a favored location for artists needing affordable, loft-style studio space. Two not-to-be-missed galleries, Artwood and Lucia Douglas Gallery, are exhibiting contemporary arts in Fairhaven. Artwood, located in the ground floor of one of the community's most popular studio buildings, represents fine woodworkers, while Lucia Douglas is a first-rate art space attracting the best and brightest regional talents. Also in Fairhaven is Village Books, a multilevel independent bookseller with a gallery, café, friendly environment, and a national reputation.

There are three primary art spaces in downtown Bellingham. Allied Arts, the community's local arts agency, operates a compact space in a downtown storefront adjacent to the Pickford Theater. It has a very energetic, year-round exhibition calendar covering all media and styles.

Art Talk

Rachel Myers, executive director of Allied Arts.

Allied Arts has worked hard to become the coordinating point for the local arts community and the downtown business community. Our exhibit space is small, but we oversee the use of several alternative spaces as art exhibition venues. Our exhibition programs are focused on encouraging the growth of the new, emerging artists of Bellingham, and we like to think of ourselves as the kind of place that allows artists to do different things or to just get a public reaction to what's happening in their work. Bellingham has a great, young arts scene, and our location within easy reach of both Seattle and Vancouver means the creative community living here is in constant contact with what's taking place in the cultural mainstream.

Blue Horse Gallery, a commercial venture representing a wide range of regional historic and contemporary work, operates from the courtyardlike atmosphere of the Bay Street Village. The star in downtown's visual arts scene is the contemporary arts exhibition space operated by the Whatcom Museum of History & Art. Known as the ARCo wing, this space varies its exhibition calendar to include specially commissioned installations by local artists, retrospectives by some of the top names in Northwest arts circles, and juried exhibitions spotlighting the best emerging talents from the region's Tlingit, Hiada, and other Native American cultures. Another important local venue is the Calumet, a restaurant serving the best in contemporary Northwest cuisine, as well as presenting local art and live music.

The university's exemplary Western Gallery serves as a constant reminder to Bellingham that there's a fast-moving arts scene under way in the world around the Pacific Northwest. This is where independently curated exhibitions featuring cutting-edge work by some of the most visible names in international arts circles are welcomed through a year-round exhibition series. The university's forested campus is also home to an outstanding collection of public sculpture by nearly two-dozen top names in the arts world including Donald Judd, Bruce Nauman, Richard Serra, Beverly Pepper, Mark di Suvero, and Isamu Noguchi. Of course, if one hungers for more tastes from art's cutting-edge, the galleries and museums of Vancouver are less than an hour away.

Essentials

Visual Arts Venues

Allied Arts of Whatcom County (1418 Cornwall Avenue; 360/676-8548; www.alliedarts.org) Top-notch gallery run by local arts agency, featuring regional contemporary works.

Whatcom Museum of History & Art (121 Prospect Street; 360/676-6981; www.whatcommuseum.org) Strong, year-round exhibitions program spotlighting regional and national works.

Western Gallery (56 High Street, Western Washington University; 360/650-3900; www.wwu.edu) Specializes in cutting-edge work from the national and international arts world.

Performing Arts & Events

Fairhaven Summer Solstice Walk-a-Bout (see Whatcom County Convention & Visitors Bureau below) Annual gallery open house in June.

Bellingham Festival of Music (1300 North State St, #202; 360/676-5997; www.bellinghamfestival.org) July and August celebration of orchestral, chamber, and world music.

Chalk Art Festival (Allied Arts of Whatcom County, 1418 Cornwall Avenue; 360/676-8548; www.alliedarts.org) Downtown's sidewalks are turned into artists' canvasses during this weekend-long August event.

Wine & Dine

The Calumet (113 E. Magnolia Street; 360/733-3331) Great Northwest dining in an art-filled, live-music venue.

Boundary Bay Brewery & Bistro (1107 Railroad Avenue; 360/647-5593; www.bbaybrewery.com) Great pub food, brews, and pizza.

Pacific Café (100 N. Commercial Street; 360/647-0800) International, contemporary fusion cuisine.

Art Talk

Tom Livesay, executive director of the Whatcom Museum of History & Art. We feel a real obligation to serve the artists of this region, and our exhibitions programs make every effort to encourage and support local and regional artists from across the Pacific Northwest. This region has a strong talent base because of the educational opportunities offered at Western Washington University, which has a stunning collection of contemporary sculpture and which turns out new talents every year. We hope to quadruple the amount of space dedicated to our own contemporary arts exhibitions with a new facility that will cost in the range of $11 million. We had 24,000 schoolchildren come through the museum last year and are maxed out on our present space. This community understands that as it comes of age, the role that the arts play in Bellingham's future is becoming increasingly important.

Accommodations

Hotel Bellwether (1 Bellwether Way; 360/392-3100; www.hotelbell wether.com) Bayside luxury hotel.

North Garden Inn (1014 North Garden Street; 360/671-7828; www.northgardeninn.com) Turn-of-the-century Victorian in a historic neighborhood.

Shangri-La Motel (611 E. Holly; 360/733-7050) Downtown and affordable.

Information

Whatcom County Convention and Visitors Bureau: 904 Potter Street; 360-671-3990; www.bellingham.org

Population: 59,000

forks, Washington

With its rugged, ocean beaches and towering mountains, what's come to be known as the West End of Washington's Olympic Peninsula is as remote a place as exists in the fast-developing Pacific Northwest. This is also the home of a genuine rain forest, one of the few existing anywhere in North America, which means that liquid sunshine is so typical of the region's weather pattern that locals here are pleasantly surprised, if not somewhat astonished, whenever the sun breaks through the clouds.

The Art Town of Forks, home of the Forks Timber Museum, is located along the western edge of Olympic National Forest, which adjoins Olympic National Park. Once exclusively a logging community, in recent years Forks has diversified its economy, placing a new emphasis on outdoor recreation tourism, cultural tourism, and development alliances with the nearby Makah and Quileute Indian Nations.

The types of artists who have found their ways here tend to be attracted by the town's low housing costs, its near-complete isolation through the rainy season, and their instant access to a mind-boggling array of outdoor recreation options. This is the kind of place where hikers may or may not run into someone else on one of the National Forest's dozens of trails. Wildlife is plentiful, with large populations of bear and elk as well as endangered species like the Northwest spotted owl.

Living here involves coming to terms with and celebrating nature's bounty. Digging for razor clams, fishing for rainbow trout and salmon, rambling hikes through old-growth forests, rides along single-track mountain bike trails, and some of the best rock climbing in the world are practically at one's doorstep. If your idea of a great place to live involves working in your studio until noon, then heading out to commune with nature until dusk, then Forks might be the paradise you're searching for. Just don't forget your umbrella.

Arts Scene

While Port Townsend may attract the bulk of the Olympic Peninsula's cultural tourists, artists living in and around Forks have learned a thing or two about how to attract visitors. They've organized themselves into a self-guided gallery and studio tour, the Olympic West Arttrek, centered around more than a dozen sites in Fork's environs. While some of the art highlighted on the tour veers toward the kitschy and crafty, most of it is created by seasoned art professionals who have made a living from their work for a number of years.

There are also two important Native American arts components of the Arttrek, the Makah Cultural & Research Center in Neah Bay, and the Indian Craft Shop in LaPush. The shop in LaPush is filled with traditional work by members of the Quileute Nation, whose artists are famed for their beadwork, carved wooden paddles, and ceremonial masks. The Makah Center's gallery is a tribally run operation representing some of the most revered names in the basketry art world, along with sterling silver jewelry bearing the distinctive designs of the Northwest coast's Native Peoples.

Celebrating their utter disregard for the darker side of nature's demeanor, Forks' arts community springs into action each April with its annual RainFest, a three-day exercise in using the arts as a platform for shouting out to the rain gods: "We're mad as hell, and we're not gonna take it any more." The festival runs its activities both day and night, with the days taken up by art exhibits, a kids umbrella-painting workshop, and an umbrella parade down the middle of Spartan Avenue. At night there's music performances in the high school's commons, live theatre by the Rainforest Players, and performances by bands and folk musicians in local restaurants and coffee bars.

The Rainforest Players, an innovative partnership with the West Olympic Council for the Arts, has stepped up to the plate in recent years as a year-round presenter of serious music and theatre. Its two annual plays, one performed during RainFest, are carefully selected for their thought-provoking potential, which is why they've put on material such as *Blithe Spirit* and *Visit to a Small Planet*. Operating out of a building in downtown Forks, the Rainforest Players have also become a presenter of chamber music and poetry, as well as a venue for readings of original plays and acting workshops.

For visual artists the name of the game involves securing a spot in one of the venues exhibiting local work, and then joining one of the area's two local arts associations in order to make important professional contacts as well as become part of these organizations' very popular exhibitions. The Far West Art League, which is the older of the two associations, stages juried exhibitions in the lobby of the local Bank of America (BofA) branch. These shows, which range from photography to landscape painting to fiber art, include a summer July 4 headliner event. The Messy Palettes Art League, which is based slightly north of Forks in the oceanfront town of Clallam Bay, uses the Clallam Bay branch of B of A as its main exhibition venue, and then goes a significant step further by showing work year-round at a local restaurant and even at the medical clinic.

Art Talk

Cheri Fleck, president of the West Olympic Council for the Arts.

Our arts center is the old Odd Fellows building, up two flights of stairs. The city asked us and the Rainforest Players to take over the space, so we now have a 5,000-square-foot ballroom for visual arts, theatre, music, and dance. Opening this building as an arts center has had a fabulous impact on this community. Now we've got a central place to organize and present our events, and that's raised the local interest in the arts. Our roster of local artists includes more than 100 names, and many of them are recent arrivals who came here for the remoteness and the beauty of the area. When you average 12 feet of rain a year, enjoying the time you spend in your studio creating art is what keeps you sane.

Essentials

Visual Arts Venues

Rainforest Arts Center (West Olympic Council for the Arts; 35 N. Forks Avenue; P.O. Box 2419; 360/374-0789) Former Odd Fellows Hall converted into a year-round visual arts exhibition space and performing-arts facility.

West Wind Gallery (120 Sol Duc Way; 360/374-7795) One of the best-run artists' cooperative galleries in the region, this is the place to find many of the Olympic Peninsula's top creative talents in visual arts and fine crafts.

Art Talk

Susan Gansert Shaw, watercolor and pastels artist.

The remoteness and peacefulness of this community is important to me. If I want, I can easily get into the city for an art museum visit, but it's always wonderful to get back here and work. Forks attracts independent artists who don't rely on a lot of technology to do their work. This is an amazing place to live. We're very close to these rugged beaches with the most beautiful tide pools, and if you like the rain and enjoy walking a few miles each day in your Gore-Tex coat, this is paradise for an artist. You have to be the kind of person who doesn't shut down when the weather turns. If anything, you have to be inspired by rain and dark clouds.

Makah Cultural & Research Center (1880 Bayview Avenue, Neah Bay; 360/645-2711; www.makah.com) Art and artifacts from one of the continent's oldest indigenous peoples, with a fantastic gift shop representing tribal basket-akers, jewelers, and clothing designers.

Performing Arts & Events

RainFest (West Olympic Council for the Arts; 35 N. Forks Avenue; 360/374-0789) Forks's biggest annual arts blast takes place in downtown on a (hopefully) soggy April weekend.

Rainforest Players (see Chamber of Commerce listing below) An energetic, year-round presenter of theatre, poetry, and music.

Quileute Days (Quileute Reservation, LaPush; 360/374-6163) A mid-July celebration of the tribe's arts and culture, featuring a salmon bake and dances.

Wine & Dine

South North Garden (140 Sol Duc Way; 360/374-9779) Top spot in town for Chinese food and cocktails with umbrellas.

Forks Coffee Shop (241 S. Forks Avenue, 360/374-6769; www.forkscoffeeshop.com) The best place to get a caffeine buzz and the local gossip.

Smoke House (193161 Highway 101; 360/374-6258) Favorite hangout for the steaks-and-brew crowd.

Accommodations

Bagby's Town Motel (1080 S. Forks Avenue; 360/374-6231; www.bagbystownmotel.com) Comfortable and affordable.

Eagle Point Inn B&B (Stormin' Norman Road, Beaver; 360/327-3236; www.eaglepointinn.com) Rustic lodge 10 miles north of Forks on the Sol Duc River.

Olympic Suites Inn (800 Olympic Drive; 360/374-5400; www.olympicsuitesinn.com) Modern place, with room for families.

Information

Forks Chamber of Commerce: 1411 S. Forks Avenue; 360/374-2531; www.forkswa.com

Population: 3,200

Friday Harbor, Washington

Reached via an hour-long ferry ride from the mainland at Anacortes, this largest community in the San Juan Islands chain is one of the most beautiful of all the continent's Art Towns. Nestled into sloping hills at the edge of waters deep enough to be home to pods of orcas, Friday Harbor is a compact and historic community. Many locals are self-employed through the arts, and with the island's busy summer tourist season, it's possible for artists to make a living selling locally.

Outside of the town of Friday Harbor, San Juan Island itself is a bucolic paradise whose rolling hills and miles of shoreline bear more than a passing resemblance to the equally historic island Art Town of Nantucket, Massachusetts. As if to emphasize the similarities that exist between these two isolated hotbeds of creativity, one of Friday Harbor's most popular attractions is its Whale Museum, which is focused on the protection, rather than exploitation, of this ocean mammal.

While some of Friday Harbor's artists choose to live inside the town's square mile of tidy homes, two-story commercial buildings, and scattered apartments, the name of the game for most local artists is to find a place with some land, a few farm/studio buildings, and a place to grow vegetables. The tricky part is finding all of this in an affordable price range. The average cost of a single family home in Friday Harbor is steadily rising, a condition that's caused some local artists to search for affordable housing on other nearby islands such as Orcas and Lopez. Of course, what one gains in terms of affordability on these other islands is paralleled by what one loses in terms of access to goods and services, but that's a tradeoff many artists don't seem to mind.

Arts Scene

One of the most pleasant surprises of the island's arts scene is the energetic and versatile programming presented by the San Juan Community Theatre. Operating from a spacious performing-arts center just up the hill from Friday Harbor's business district, the theatre company is busy year-round with plays for adults and kids, as well as performances by touring musicians working the Northwest's circuit. During the summer months there's also the San Juan Chamber Music Festival, a Playwrights Festival and even the Barbershop Bonanza, a festival of singing fellas dressed in striped shirts and straw hats. The Community Theatre organizes its energetic Lobby Art Gallery program, which rotates monthly visual arts shows through the building year-round. The shows feature everything from schoolkids' art to work by masters of the island's accomplished arts community.

Friday Harbor's art galleries are sprinkled through it's quaint and walkable downtown. As many as a dozen galleries can be found on the town's side streets, depending on who is making a run at this tricky but rewarding business. Rainshadow Arts Gallery exhibits some of the most interesting gourd art anywhere, while Arctic Raven Gallery is small and compact, yet is also one of the Northwest's best places to find Native American, Alaskan, and Canadian First Nations art. Island Studios is a slightly funky gallery representing practically anyone and everyone living on the island who calls themselves an artist, while Napier Sculpture Gallery is owned and operated by an island bronze artist who is represented in galleries across the West.

There are two wine makers on the island, Island Wine Company, which produces its San Juan Cellars wines, and San Juan Vineyards, an accomplished producer of white wines (chardonnay, gewürztraminer, semillon) and whose tasting room is in an old church building. A 19-acre site at the north end of San Juan Island is home to the Wescott Bay Nature Reserve and Sculpture Park, a fascinating installation of as many as 50 works of art in a stunning outdoor setting at the entrance to the upscale Roche Harbor Resort. The number of sculptures vary, but the work is of top-notch quality and a must-stop on any island visitors' itinerary.

Art Talk

Merritt Olsen, executive director of the San Juan Community Theatre.
In the mid-1980s some local people decided that having a community theatre on San Juan Island would be a good thing, and while our early years were great, in the mid-1990s we fell on some hard times. But belts got tightened and we're healthy again, with an annual budget close to $450,000 and we're meeting our expenses. Our community theatre does three big plays each year, with another three or four in our black box. Our building is used for more than 50 events a year, and we have great acoustics. Our busiest season is from July to September and most of our audience is locals. We get great support from the county's bed tax. There's a move under way to build a visual arts center on the island, and that would be a great thing.

Essentials

Visual Arts Venues

Arctic Raven Gallery (1 Front Street; 360/378-3433; www.arctic ravengallery.com) Outstanding selection of visual arts, fine crafts, and jewelry by Native artists of North America.

Island Studios (270 Spring Street; 360/378-6550; www.island studios.com) Wide-ranging selection of arts and fine crafts from across the San Juan Islands.

Napier Sculpture Gallery (232 A Street; 360/378-2221; www.napier gallery.com) Wildlife sculpture in stone and bronze.

Performing Arts & Events

Wescott Bay Reserve (8607 Cattle Point Road, Roche Harbor; 360/370-5050; www.wbay.org) May gathering of many of the Northwest's top names in three-dimensional art, with artist demonstrations at Wescott Bay Nature Reserve and Sculpture Park.

Summerfest (San Juan Community Theatre; 100 Second Street; 360/378-3210; www.sanjuanarts.org) A June through August season of plays and performing arts at San Juan Community Theatre.

San Juan Island Artists Studio Open House (see San Juan Island Chamber of Commerce below) Memorial Day weekend tour with more than two dozen self-guided stops.

Wine & Dine

Downriggers (10 Front Street; 360/378-2700) Waterfront dining overlooking the ferry dock.

Duck Soup Inn (50 Duck Soup Lane; 360/378-4878; www.ducksoup inn.com) Gourmet Northwest cuisine.

Vinny's (165 West Street; 360/378-1934) Great Italian foods, just like mama used to make, plus a nice wine list.

Accommodations

Roche Harbor Village (P.O. Box 4001, Roche Harbor; 360/378-2155; www.rocheharbor.com) Historic hotel on an isolated tip of the island.

Argyle House B&B (685 Argyle Street; 360/378-4084; www.argyle house.net) Comfortable inn and a historic home with great water views, hot tub, and lots of local charm, just a few blocks from the ferry dock.

San Juan Inn (50 Spring Street; 360/378-2070; www.sanjuan inn.com) Victorian inn just a two-minute jaunt from the ferry dock

Information

San Juan Island Chamber of Commerce: P.O. Box 98; 360/378-5240; www.sanjuanisland.org

Population: 2,100

Art Talk

Jason Napier, sculptor and owner of Napier Sculpture Gallery.

We leave for four months each winter and head to Arizona to do different art shows, because there's just not much happening in Friday Harbor in the winter. In the summer this place becomes very busy and very entertaining. I'm a wildlife sculptor, and I love living in a place that's so close to such an amazing variety of wildlife. On a small island like this you really don't have much to get you distracted from your work. The island is an expensive place to live, and just to see a movie you've got to take a ferry ride. But our buyers find us and come here from across the country. Artists are continually moving here, trying to make a go of things. If you can run your life as a business, you can make a living here.

Langley, Washington

L ong a favorite destination for weekending and second-home-owning Seattleites, the Art Town of Langley on the south end of Whidbey Island has great proximity to the urbanized mainland through a ferry service. This makes full-time living here a reality for some commuters and artists, as well as machinists working at the Boeing aircraft facility in nearby Everett. The island's north end is reached by a 90-minute drive from Seattle that traverses Deception Pass. There's even a roundabout way to approach the island from the west, which involves taking a ferry from the Art Town of Port Townsend to a landing along the island's midpoint.

Besides being home to hundreds of small farms and several waterfront towns with tidy, business districts, Whidbey is also home to a naval air station at Oak Harbor. Because of the way the island's geography works, the runways and big box retail necessary for this small military base are largely tucked out of the way and present a minimal intrusion upon the island's bucolic lifestyle. Oak Harbor offers islanders an accessible range of goods and services, as well as a thriving town with lots of employment opportunities. If you live here and need, say, a 48-roll package of toilet paper, you don't need to consult the ferry schedule to figure out the logistics of a mainland shopping trip, because its all in Oak Harbor.

Besides offering its residents peace and quiet, Whidbey Island is large enough to support several artistic communities. Langley, on the island's southeast side, is an upscale kind of place where Seattleites feel perfectly comfortable shopping in trendy stores, dining in sleek restaurants, and entertaining guests in homes built with the spoils of the dot-com boom. Clinton, also on the island's south end, is a less-organized place that lacks Langley's charm but has lots of small and medium-sized homes, some with stunning night views of Seattle's distant office towers. Coupeville, at the island's midpoint, is a quiet and pleasantly ramshackle sort of place whose blue-collar roots haven't yet been paved over or turned into coffee joints. Just north of Deception Pass is Anacortes, a maritime and industrial community whose funky north end has in recent years become home to several art galleries and a low-cost, loft-and-studio scene pioneered by artist refugees from Seattle and Bellingham. Finally, on Whidbey Island's east side and across Saratoga Passage is Camano Island, an artist-filled place of less than 1,000 residents and home to several glass artists with national reputations.

Arts Scene

Living here means having easy access to the big city's museums, theatre, concerts, and opera. And because the 30-minute ferry ride to Port Townsend is such a breeze, Whidbey Islanders also have no trouble attending performances at Centrum's sprawling campus, or dropping by for the town's monthly ArtWalks.

The Whidbey Playhouse in Oak Harbor is the island's longest-standing community theatre, with a season stretching from winter through spring and early summer. The fare's typical of community theatre companies (Arthur Miller, *Nutcracker,* etc.). Whidbey Island Center for the Arts, a modern facility adjacent to Langley's middle school, is home to a resident theatre company performing from October through June, and is also a stop for national talents touring the region's performing-arts circuit. In October, the arts center hosts one of the most innovative of any Art Town performing-arts festivals when it becomes home to Djangofest Northwest, a weeklong celebration of the life and musical genius of Django Reinhardt. A seminal figure of Paris's café scene in the 1930s and '40s, Reinhardt founded what's come to be known as the sound of Gypsy Jazz. This well-attended festival attracts Django lovers and Gypsy Jazz musicians from across North America, and is bolstered by an extensive local program of performances, workshops, and seminars.

Concerts on the Cove stages musical performances year-round in the Coupeville High School's Performing Arts Center and sponsors the summer-long Sundays in the Park series of concerts at Coupeville Town

Art Talk

Howard Hamsa, ceramist.

South Whidbey Island is flourishing. We're not far from the sea, not far from the city, and more affordable than many places. As long as you don't need to live in a home with a water view, life here is still pretty affordable. I do functional and decorative pottery work, along with Carol Bauer, my wife. We leave here to do about 20 shows a year, mostly along the West Coast, and we do retail out of the Artists Cooperative Gallery, which represents about 40 artists. All through the late spring and summer this place is pretty busy, and even winter weekends can be active. The island has a real mix of artists, with a percentage of them being older artists, and a fair share of younger artists who have moved here to start their careers.

Park. One of the nation's premier fiber arts communities is concentrated around Coupeville. The Coupeville Arts Center offers year-round classes as well as special seminar weeks in various aspects of traditional and contemporary fiber arts.

The island's two main clusters of art galleries are in Coupeville and Langley. Both areas are perfectly walkable, with the galleries interspersed among cafés and gift shops. There are quarterly Art Walks in each community, as well as an August Arts & Crafts Festival along the streets lining Coupeville's waterfront.

Essentials

Visual Arts Venues

Museo (215 First Street; 360/221-7737; www.museo.cc) A slice of urban contemporary style in the middle of historic Langley, Museo represents artists working in painting, sculpture, fine crafts, and jewelry.

Artists Cooperative Gallery (314 First Street; 360/221-7675) A large and eclectic space representing many of the island's best artists and craftspeople.

Whidbey Island Center for the Arts (565 Camano Avenue; 360/221-8268; www.wicaonline.com) Year-round community theatre, visual arts, and music.

Performing Arts and Events

Whidbey Playhouse (730 SE Midway Boulevard, Oak Harbor; 360/679-2237; www.whidbeyplayhouse.com) Strong and stable community theatre company presenting adult and kids' plays.

Djangofest Northwest (see Whidbey Island Center for the Arts above) Innovative, international music festival staged in October.

Coupeville Arts & Crafts Festival (360/678-5116; www.coupeville arts.org) August outdoor showcase of top island visual and fine crafts artists.

Wine & Dine

Whidbey's Coffee Company (224 First Street, Langley; 360/221-8676) The island's favorite choice for java and conversation.

Whidbey Island Winery (5237 South Langley Road, Langley; 360/221-2040; www.whidbeyisland winery.com) Small, family-owned vineyard, with a year-round tasting room.

Cafe Langley (113 First Street, Langley; 360/221-3090) Gourmet dining with a Mediterranean emphasis. Cozy location on the waterfront.

Accommodations

The Captain Whidbey Inn (2072 W. Captain Whidbey Inn Road, Coupeville; 360/678-4097; www.captainwhidbey.com) High-end elegance with a marina.

Inn at Penn Cove (702 North Main Street, Coupeville; 360/678-8000) Affordable, Victorian B&B with great water views.

Best Western Harbor Plaza (33175 SR 20, Oak Harbor; 360/679-4567; www.bestwestern.com) Modern motel, with accommodations for families.

Information

Central Whidbey Island Chamber of Commerce: 107 South Main Street, Coupeville; 360/678-5434; www.centralwhidbey chamber.com.

Population: 970

Art Talk

Stacie Burgua, executive director of the Whidbey Island Center for the Arts. This town has always attracted a large number of artists and creative spirits. I moved here in 1978, and it was happening then and has only grown from there. People who move to the island or who want to own a second home here are attracted by the ways the arts are so visible on the island. We're an eight-year-old organization that has built its own facility and uses it to present and produce performing-arts programs. We produce about five shows a year and offer original works by local playwrights each year. Djangofest, which we started as a lark a few years ago, has grown into this national event that's taken everyone by surprise. Now the town has caught the Django fever and is promoting the festival as another great reason to visit the island.

Port Townsend,
Washington

While there are several Art Towns whose architectural roots are grounded in Victorian-era aesthetics, few have the magical combination of spectacular location along with the abundance of authentic Victorian mansions that characterizes Port Townsend. Located on the northeast tip of Washington's Olympic Peninsula, this community is ideally sited within reach of Seattle, yet remote enough to serve as a quiet, creative refuge. The two-and-a-half-hour drive and ferry ride into the big city puts Port Townsend within range of weekending urbanites with money to spend on art, wining and dining, as well as the handsome guest rooms in Port Townsend's many B&Bs.

This historic seaport is even closer to the Vancouver Island city of Victoria, which is but a ferry ride away (though the ferry terminal is in nearby Port Angeles), across the Strait of Juan de Fuca. That's one reason why the summer arts festivals at the Centrum Foundation, which attract national talents in jazz, dance, music, and literature to a former military base on Port Townsend's outskirts, are typically loaded with Canadian visitors.

While Port Townsend is small enough to allow locals to know their neighbors' shopping habits as they prowl the aisles of the ever-popular Food Co-op, it also is large enough to offer activities such as golf, whale watching, yachting from a well-equipped marina, and a large library originally built as a Carnegie Library in 1913. Downtown's streets are located at the base of a bluff and skirt the town's beautiful, historic waterfront. There are mini-parks, superb restaurants, coffee bars, and bookshops everywhere. While some homes' values rode the bubble of Seattle's dot-com boom of the late 1990s, Port Townsend largely escaped the steep home-price increases that irrevocably changed the face of some Puget Sound communities.

Arts Scene

Port Townsend's arts scene carries on throughout the year, though May's kickoff of the Centrum Arts Festival in Fort Worden State Park signals the arrival of this Art Town's jam-packed summer arts season. Staged in two historic venues on a decommissioned, turn-of-the-century military base (one of the venues was built as a hangar for US Army blimps), the Centrum summer season runs through August and attracts top name national performers. Outside of the summer season, Centrum also provides the cultural underpinnings to this community's local arts scene through its year-round program of youth arts-education workshops, professional artist residencies, and Elderhostel programs.

Port Townsend's nightclubs are well known as the stopping-off point for many a professional career, and venues lining downtown's Water Street are home to a number of clubs such as Maxwell's Brewery & Pub, which is in a historic building and features local, regional, and national music acts year-round on its postage-stamp-sized stage. During the summer months, nearby Quilcene hosts the Olympic Music Festival, showcasing the talents of the Philadelphia String Quartet in the gorgeous, restored barnhouse of a 55-acre dairy farm. From late June to early September, classical music lovers trek here for outstanding performances, nibbling on cheesesteaks while savoring the sounds of world-class musicians.

The local theatre community's leading organization is the Key City Players, whose year-round performances are staged in downtown's Key City Playhouse. The players mix up their seasons with a range of material covering the likes of children's plays, Neil Simon classics, and original work. Port Townsend's downtown Rose Theatre is a historic, 1908 masterpiece featuring first-run Hollywood flicks in an environment where the popcorn and espresso are fresh and affordable.

While the town's visual arts galleries tend to have some turnover from year to year, there are usually a dozen or so venues participating in the monthly Gallery Walks. For the most part, the gallery scene is clustered around downtown's Water Street, though the excellent Port

Art Talk

Carol Heath Stabile, pastel artist.
People visiting Port Townsend know it's a great place to find artists, and local art is one of the big draws for tourists. It's exhibited everywhere, from the galleries to the restaurants and coffee bars, and even the ice-cream shop. I joined the Port Townsend Gallery in 1998, back when it had eleven members. We're up to 30 members now, with a small space in a fantastic location on a historic block, and have a waiting list of artists wanting to get in. This community promotes itself as a place filled with the spirit of creativity, and the arts in Port Townsend receive broad support from the business community. A new generation of younger artists has settled into Port Townsend, and while they have to scramble a bit for exhibition and performance space, their presence is being felt more each year.

Townsend Open Studio & Gallery, an artist-run cooperative featuring some of the best contemporary artists in the Pacific Northwest, is located south of downtown in a commercial strip. Because of the high volume of tourist traffic, some of Port Townsend's galleries are operated as affairs catering to less demanding tastes. This isn't the case at venues such as Ancestral Spirits Gallery, Earthenworks Gallery, and the Port Townsend Gallery, all of which have great locations and take pride in selling locally created art.

Essentials

Visual Arts Venues

Port Townsend Gallery (715 Water Street; 360/379-8110); Top-notch, local, artist-run, and affordable.

Earthenworks Gallery (702 Water Street; 360/385-0328; www.earthenworksgallery.com) Strong selection of ceramics, glass, metalwork, and fiber arts.

Ancestral Spirits Gallery (701 Water Street; 360/385-0078; www.ancestralspirits.com) Tremendous selection of Native American arts and fine crafts, as well as work by Canada's First Nations artists.

Performing Arts and Events

Centrum Arts Summer Festival (Battery Way, Fort Worden State Park; 360/385-3102; www.centrum.org) Popular summer music, arts, and dance festival covering many styles, also offers year-round programs for visual artists and writers.

Olympic Music Festival (see Port Townsend Visitors Center below) One of the West Coast's premier summer classical music festivals.

Key City Players (419 Washington Street; 360/385-7396) Year-round, innovative theatre for kids and adults.

Wine & Dine

Tyler Street Coffee House (215 Tyler Street; 360/379-4185) Favorite hangout for artists, with local art on the walls.

Bread & Roses Bakery and Café (230 Quincy Street; 360/385-1044) Breads, sandwiches, coffee, and a great place to wait out a rain shower. But where are the roses?

Silverwater Café (237 Taylor Street; 360/385-6448; www.silverwater cafe.com) Port Townsend's top place for locally caught salmon and fresh farm produce.

Accommodations

Palace Hotel (1004 Water Street; 360/385-0773; www.palace hotelpt.com) Old-time elegance in the heart of the arts district.

Harborside Inn (330 Benedict Street; 360/385-7909; www.harborside-inn.com) Full-service hotel with a marina within walking distance of downtown.

Ann Starrett Mansion (744 Clay Street; 360/385-3205; www.starrettmansion.com) Victorian elegance.

Information

Port Townsend Visitors Center: 2437 E. Sims Way, 360/385-2722, www.ptguide.com

Population: 8,450

Art Talk

Keven Elliss, director of marketing for Centrum

We're an interdisciplinary arts organization with an emphasis on presenting performing arts and on developing unique educational opportunities. We're located on a 500-acre state park and our workshop programs usually last a week or longer. During our festival days downtown Port Townsend turns into one giant club scene. We attract a range of students and artists to our programs, from talented high schoolers to retired second-stagers, all of whom come for the pleasures of a vacation and learning experience. We try to provide Port Townsend with a spark of creative energy to keep the local arts scene fresh and new, and we encourage the cross-pollination that takes place when our students and faculty work with and within the local community. To me this community feels like a college town, but without the college.

Canada

Nelson, British Columbia

The outdoor recreation paradise that's British Columbia's Kootenay region embraces some of the most spectacular lakes, mountains, and rivers on the continent. Silver mining is what made this area's fortunes and provided the wealth for building its collection of charming, turn-of-the-century towns. Nelson, a community north of Spokane and nearly six hours east of Vancouver, is an arts-crazed place in a spectacular location on Kootenay Lake. Its economy has suffered through more ups and downs than an elevator repairman, which is why the homes here are still affordable. There's no security anymore in logging, mining, or even manufacturing, and so Nelson's made the smart move by backing its two best-performing growth sectors: arts and tourism.

Downtown Nelson's Baker Street is the sort of classic main drag that Hollywood seeks to re-create on back lots, except that here in Nelson the ice-cream shop uses real cream and the shoe repairman isn't a moonlighting bartender from Spago's. This is a place filled with picture-perfect downtown lofts and studios, as well as affordable apartments that are within easy walking distance of supermarkets, drugstores, nightclubs, and the town's amazingly scenic Lakeside Park. The winters in this part of Canada are cold and long, which is why the Nelson Leafs hockey games are played before standing-room crowds loaded up on antifreeze. Artists in the region who can finagle a way out of the Kootenay winters will jump on the opportunity, which is why the bars in places like Puerto Escondido, Oaxaca, are a second home to so many B.C. refugees. While there's not much opportunity to sell art in Nelson, living here does afford artists the chance to live and work quietly and affordably in an arts-supportive setting. The key to surviving is either having gallery representation in places such as Vancouver, Calgary, Salt Spring Island, and Banff, or making one's living from the wealth of summer arts fairs that explode across Canada from early May through September.

Arts Scene

While the foundation for Nelson's arts identity has traditionally been provided by the widely acclaimed Kootenay School of the Arts (KSA) and the steadily growing presence of artists from across Canada who come here to live and work, it took the 1997 arrival of StreetFest, a weekend-long extravaganza dedicated to the genius of street buskers (jugglers, mimes, acrobats, and the like) for the arts community to fully demonstrate its economic muscle. In a town that had not known an outdoor summer arts fair, StreetFest grew in just two years into an event that attracted more than 50,000 tourists to Nelson for three days of free performances on a dozen stages set up along Baker Street and Ward Street. In its first few years, StreetFest's skyrocketing growth took the downtown business community by complete surprise. In StreetFest's first year, when 20,000 attended the event, many Nelson pubs ran out of beer. So the following year, when the pubs braced themselves for a similar turnout, the crowds nearly tripled, and the pubs again were sucked dry. By now, everybody's learned their lesson. StreetFest is the biggest party to ever hit Nelson, and a must-see on the region's summer arts calendar. And the beer never stops flowing.

KSA, whose focus is on fine crafts as well as ceramics and studio glass, employs many local artists as instructors for its year-round programs on its downtown campus. The school also operates Nelson's only year-round art gallery, though in the summer months the visual arts focus shifts to Artwalk, a long-standing event through which a dozen downtown Nelson businesses are used as rotating art galleries for exhibitions by regional artists. Monthly opening receptions for the freshly hung shows draw substantial numbers of art lovers into downtown and result in surprising numbers of sales. Since the last edition of this book, the David Thompson Cultural Society has divested itself of its performance space and is looking for a new home. The Nelson Museum, once a primarily historical institution, has expanded its reach after moving into a new venue, allowing a fuller range of exhibitions of regional and national artists in its new art galleries, as well as more shows of locally created work.

Nelson's premier performing-arts venue is the Capitol Theatre, a 1927 Vaudeville house whose art deco majesty was restored in 1988. Operated by the city, the theatre is home to events such as the Overture Series of classical music performances by top soloists from Vancouver, Calgary, and elsewhere. Touring dramatic presentations generally packaged out of Vancouver; concerts by Canadian bluegrass, folk, and maritime musicians; and occasional local productions from presenters such as Rossland Light Opera and Shameless Hussy Theatre also use the Capitol.

Essentials

Visual Arts Venues

Kootenay School of the Arts (606 Victoria Street; 250/352-2821; www.ksac.bc.ca) One of Canada's best schools for studies in fine crafts, ceramics, and fine glass, KSA has produced many of the top craft artists in British Columbia.

Kootenay Gallery of Art, History & Science (120 Heritage Way, Castlegar; 250/365-3337; www.kootenaygallery.com) A contemporary art gallery, the Kootenay Gallery is the region's premier showcase for visual arts talents as well as touring national shows.

The Nelson Museum (402 Anderson Street; 250/352-9813; www.nelsonmuseum.ca) Expanded, relocated institution with a collection of historic artifacts and exhibitions of local and regional arts.

Performing Arts & Events

Nelson International Street Performers and Arts Festival (a.k.a.: StreetFest) (P.O. Box 386; 250/352-7188; www.streetfest.bc.ca) The

Art Talk

Shawn Lamb, director of the Nelson Museum.

We're located in the old City Hall, a 1902 building that also was a post office. We've acquired more than five times the space as we had in our old, 3,750-square-foot building, plus we now have classroom space and about 5,000 square feet for storage. We're in the heart of downtown Nelson, and with this new facility we have become the hub for the community's arts scene. Our 10, small shows each year have been expanded to include traveling national exhibitions, and we now do much larger presentations of local and regional art. Nelson's art economy has been estimated to have an annual impact of $7 million, and lots of our artists make their living by selling their work in the States. We're still a safe, unpolluted, and affordable place in the middle of incredible natural beauty.

Art Talk

Barry Auliffe, director of the Kootenay School of the Arts.

We've become a private school in the past few years with a more international student body. Our appeal is three-fold: we're located in a cosmopolitan, mountain town; we have a program centered around studio work; and when students leave us they're ready to step into careers. The courses that fill up the quickest are the ones in clay, jewelry, and metal design. We now have 90 students, but our student capacity is 150. The arts in Nelson are in a continued state of growth, and our new art museum site has been a big asset to the entire community. There is a scarcity of venues for exhibiting art, but I feel that, too, will change in the next few years.

biggest event on Nelson's summer calendar is this three-day July celebration of street performers from across the globe.

The Capitol Theatre (421 Victoria Street; 250/352-6363; www.capitol theatre.bc.ca) The community's restored, art deco performance space is used for touring theatre companies, local musicians, children's summer drama camp and classical music concerts.

Kaslo Jazz Festival (Kaslo Bay Park; 250/353-7538; www.kaslojazzfest .com) This three-day August music festival on the shores of Kootenay Lake draws blues, jazz, and world musicians from across Canada.

Wine & Dine

All Seasons Café (620 Herridge Lane; 250/352-0101; www.allseasons cafe.com) The favorite of local artists, All Seasons has innovative cuisine, a great selection of B.C. wines, and lots of local art on its walls.

Café Danube (415 Hall Street; 250/354-0566) Great place for crepes, pastries, and local art.

Fiddler's Green (2710 Lower Six Mile Road; 250/825-4466; www.fiddlersgreen.ca) Elegant dining in a country home on the outskirts of Nelson. Great wine list and a lovely patio garden.

Accommodations

New Grand Hotel (616 Vernon Street; 250/352-7211; www.new grandhotel.ca) Restored, boutique-style hotel in downtown Nelson with 34 rooms and Art Deco charm.

Inn the Garden (408 Victoria Street; 250/352-3226; www.innthe garden.com) In-town B&B with cozy rooms, great breakfasts, and lots of local art on the walls.

Dancing Bear Inn (171 Baker Street; 877/ 352-7573; www.dancing bearinn.com) Full-service hostel with shared baths, local art, and affordable rates.

Information

Nelson and District Chamber of Commerce: 225 Hall Street; 250/352-3433; www.discovernelson.com

Population: 9,600

Salt Spring Island, British Columbia

D o you think of Canada as wind-whipped, snow-packed, and frozen for eight months out of the year? Then it's time you visit Salt Spring Island. Located in the Gulf Islands of British Columbia, this beautiful and artistic refuge is Canada's answer to places like Santa Cruz, California, and Key West, Florida.

On a clear night in Ganges, the harborside community at the heart of Salt Spring's artistic and commercial activity, it's easy to see the glow of the nearby metropolis of Vancouver, which is an hour's ferry ride from the island. To the south of Salt Spring is the historic and very lively city of Victoria, again reachable by ferry; yet the boat makes the trip in about half the traveling time to Vancouver.

This magnificent location, north of Washington State's San Juan Islands, guarantees that Salt Spring's climate rarely gets too hot or too cold. Summer days are reliably in the 70s, while winter stays damp and temperate, with small amounts of snow and lots of overcast days perfect for helping artists focus on their studio work. That climate is also the reason Salt Spring is such a green paradise, profuse with flower beds and vegetable gardens, all nestled among the island's deep forests of towering pines.

While the full-time islander community numbers slightly more than 10,000, during summer weekends that number can easily double, if not triple, with vacationing urbanites from nearby Vancouver, Victoria, and occasional weekending clam diggers from as far away as

Calgary and Edmonton. This being an island with limited job opportunities (fishing, construction, and forestry are the leading employers), it's little surprise that the year-round community includes many hundreds of artists and artisans engaged in everything from crafting goat cheese to writing Hollywood scripts, as well as a number of internationally famous entertainers making regular trips to Vancouver's airport for early flights to Los Angeles.

While Salt Spring has its share of self-employed creative professionals, some of whom make their living selling to the island's year-round flow of tourists, and many marketing their work through art galleries and crafts fairs across the United States and Canada, what keeps the island's economy popping along is the influx of second-home owners from across North America venturing here in pursuit of the island's laid-back quality of life. These are the folks who are building $600, 000 homes along the island's sheltered coves and on the slopes of its mountains and ridge tops, buying lots of local art, not to mention appliances, wood-burning stoves, and Range Rovers. Catering to the needs of these homeowners has allowed many of Salt Spring's artists and artisans to survive in the face of the island's typically erratic economy.

Ferry schedules being what they are, it's a lot easier for Salt Spring's residents to get their fix of big-city life (and shopping malls) in nearby Victoria. Victoria offers a downsized, yet completely satisfying, version of what's available in the larger metropolis; the ethnic restaurants, art museums, outdoor markets, and nightclubs in Vancouver are truly world-class. Salt Spring is located at the crossroads of these media markets, thus, radio stations from both these large cities come in loud and strong.

Arts Scene

To survive here as an artist is as much a matter of mastering one's career timing as it is coming to terms with the reality that success as an artist living on an island in Western Canada is achieved after years of hard work. In much the same way that high-spending professionals from Boston and New York City turn Art Towns, such as Nantucket, Massachusetts, and the Hamptons, New York, into weekend marketplaces for everything from $50 French beach towels to $5,000 bronze sculptures, so does Salt Spring's action in its arts sector hit and sustain a high note from mid-May through September.

Artists living here have to be both entrepreneurial and full of energy in their pursuit of the sales opportunities presented by the visitors.

While there's a substantial amount of weekend traffic throughout the year on Salt Spring, nothing quite matches up to what happens here during summer. There are some artist exceptions to the rule, primarily individuals who have spent the bulk of their careers elsewhere and have moved to Salt Spring only after firmly establishing their reputations in art galleries, art museums, theatre companies, movie-production studios, and recording companies across Canada and the United States. In this sense, Salt Spring operates as a magnet for established Canadian artists in much the same way that Santa Fe, New Mexico, does for artists in the United States. This is a fantastic place to live, especially if what you need to do in order to make ends meet is work like mad in your studio all week long, then call FedEx to pick up your creative output (paintings, rings, carved totems, glass bowls, and the like) and deliver those treasures to the five or six art galleries representing your work.

But even for artists and creative professionals who haven't lined up their careers by the time they get to Salt Spring, making a living here isn't a matter of blind luck. One of the most effective ways for artists to make ends meet is to participate in the year-round, self-guided studio tour that takes place from Salt Spring's northernmost tip right down to the ferry landing at Fulford Harbour. More than 30 artists participate in the tour, and while some studios are only open on weekends from May to September, the majority of studios welcome visitors year-round. Every imaginable art, craft, or home furnishings object is available on the studio tour, whose stopping points are found by clearly marked roadside signs, as well as through widely distributed tour maps available throughout the island.

The main cluster of art galleries is concentrated in the village of Ganges, which is the island's commercial center and also the location of the Saturday Market, an April through October weekly invasion of downtown Ganges's Centennial Park by dozens of flower vendors, cheese makers, bakers, organic vegetable growers, crafts artists, jewelers, and metal smiths. Ganges is also the location of ArtCraft, a gallery operated by the Gulf Islands Community Arts Council, that opens its doors from May through September in the historic, church-like Mahon Hall and represents the work of more than 200 artists from Salt Spring as well as from nearby creative havens such as Chemainus, Saturna Island, Pender Island, and Mayne Island. ArtCraft also opens for 10 days around the holiday season for the annual Guilds of Christmas Sale. There are a dozen or so commercial galleries strewn around Ganges, including the Stone Fish Sculpture Studio, the always-interesting Pegasus Gallery of Canadian Art, and the Thunderbird Gallery, which represents sculpture, jewelry, and painting by First Nations Peoples of Canada.

The artistic heart of this multicultural island is ArtSpring Island Arts Centre. Long in planning, this contemporary, hillside structure in Ganges serves as a multidisciplinary performing- and visual-arts facility for the island's resident arts community as well as a venue for performing artists and entertainers from across Canada. ArtSpring's 270-seat theatre is an ideal setting for dance, drama, and music, while its adjacent art gallery spaces provide the island with its best venue for large-scale paintings and sculpture. Every April, ArtSpring hosts the island's most prestigious visual arts show, the Salt Spring Painters Guild Exhibition, and every August the annual exhibition of the Alliance of Salt Spring Artists rolls into ArtSpring. The island's resident drama company, Graffiti Theatre Company, stages its four annual productions at ArtSpring, as does a newer drama troupe, Chicken and Egg Productions.

While Salt Spring's calendar is sprinkled with family events such as the Fall Fair in mid-September, Sea Capers in June, Canada Day in early July, the annual Garlic Festival in August, and the Island Treasure Fair in July, two performing-arts festivals are staged each summer that draw in crowds from across British Columbia. The Salt Spring Festival of the Arts at Meaden Hall, and at ArtSpring during the entire month of July, covers everything from local music and comedy to performances by Acadian dancers from Canada's Eastern provinces. Festival ArtSpring, which stages its events across the first half of August, strives for a different terrain with a program that includes chamber music, Broadway sing-alongs, and Shakespeare.

Art Talk

Lorna Cammaert, president of the Gulf Islands Community Arts Council. We have a growing arts scene and ArtCraft's success is one indication of that. Our studio tour gets larger every year and our Saturday Market has reached the point where it can no longer accommodate all those who want to sell there. Artists come here because they share similar values and enjoy being around other artists, who tend to have a cooperative sense of support for each other. ArtCraft has 35 years of experience launching local art careers. Some artists exhibit here for a few years, get their careers moving, and leave us. Others stay on for long stretches, and we now have work from 180 artists in the gallery. The quality of work that's presented to our jurors each year is simply amazing.

Essentials

Visual Arts Venues

ArtCraft (114 Rainbow Road; 250/537-0899; www.artcraftgallery.ca) A summer seasonal gallery, featuring artists from across the Gulf

Art Talk

Paul Gravett, executive director of ArtSpring.

Salt Spring is a unique place that's recently started attracting a number of Americans building second homes. We want our new residents to take part in the community and not react to the island as just a part-time place. ArtSpring is only five years old but it has had a great impact on the community. We're essentially a community arts center and are supportive of all the art events taking place on the island. We offer a great sound system, and our gallery has a very professional look. Our classical music and jazz series do very well, and we feel we do best when we present talent that doesn't normally get a lot of exposure on the island.

Islands. It also has a holiday-season market.

Pegasus Gallery of Canadian Art (1–104 Fulford-Ganges Road; 250/537-2421; www.pegasus galleryca.com) Representing many of Canada's premier artists, with work ranging from glass and sculpture to jewelry.

Studio Tour Group (see Salt Spring Island Chamber of Commerce below) Self-guided, year-round studio tour to several dozen sites.

Performing Arts & Events

ArtSpring (100 Jackson Avenue; 250/537-2125; www.artspring.ca) ArtSpring's 270-seat performing-arts theatre serves as the island's premier venue for music, drama, and dance. Home of Festival ArtSpring each August.

Salt Spring Festival of the Arts (100 Jackson Avenue; 250/537-2125; www.artspring.ca) This annual July event is a multidisciplinary performing-arts showcase featuring top Canadian acts.

Graffiti Theatre (see Salt Spring Island Chamber of Commerce below) Year-round, local drama company founded by Vancouver theatre pros.

Wine & Dine

Salt Spring Roasting Company (109 McPhillips Avenue; 250/537-0825) The island's favorite hangout for the caffeine-deprived. Dog owners congregate by the outdoor tables when the weather's cooperating.

Moby's Marine Pub (124 Upper Ganges Road; 250/537-5559; www.mobyspub.com) A great place for late-night seafood and music, down by the waterfront.

Artists Bistro (115-3106 Fulford Ganges Road; 250/537-1701; www.artistsbistro.com) Local sensibilities, seafood, and British ingredients.

Accommodations

Harbour House Hotel (121 Upper Ganges Road; 250/537-5571; www.saltspringharbourhouse.com) An affordable, nicely maintained motel by the waterfront. Features a busy liquor store in its rear parking lot.

Cusheon Lake Resort (171 Natalie Lane; 250/537-9629; www.cusheonlake.com) Secluded hideaway, with hot tubs and fireplaces.

Anchor Point B&B (150 Beddis Road; 250/538-0110; www.anchor pointbb.com) Harbor views, huge breakfasts, and luscious gardens.

Information

Salt Spring Island Chamber of Commerce: 121 Lower Ganges Road; 250/537-4223, www.saltspringtoday.com

Population: 10,850

Antigonish, Nova Scotia

This community on Nova Scotia's Sunrise Trail is home to one of Canada's premier Catholic colleges and its vibrant student body of 2,300, free-spending sybarites. There's year-round cultural activity in Antigonish, and even the makings of a night life despite the region's deep-freeze winter temperatures. A town whose residents are grateful to St. Francis Xavier University for its hundreds of jobs and wealth of lavishly funded research and entertainment facilities, Antigonish has been smartly wrapping its tourism appeal around the talent attracted by the school, which is referred to as StFX. Summer performing-arts events highlight the community's entertainment calendar, while winter's performing-arts series and theatre presentations as well as the hockey games of the college's X-Men and Antigonish's Junior A Bulldogs are huge draws.

Living here means having an affordable home in a place where it's easy to find houses that have lots of room for gardens and studios. The community's Saturday-morning Farmers' Market is a treasured gathering point for the region's creative community, as well as a great place to find local fine crafts and jars of clover honey. Antigonish was settled by kilt-wearing Scotsmen in the late 1700s, and to this day the region proudly expresses its cultural identity through events like the Highland Games in July (caber toss, anyone?), exhibits at the Heritage Museum (a 1908 railroad depot), and the lecture series offerings of StFX's Celtic Studies Department. There's a French Acadian community in nearby Pomquet, a community of 500 whose Pomquet Beach

Park is the region's favorite skin-spotting spot from mid-June through August.

Because the Sunrise Trail region is thinly populated, people here tend to think and act regionally. Culture jaunts into Halifax, a 90-minute drive if the roads are clear, are a must for anyone interested in Thai restaurants, art museums and shopping, while outdoor recreation along the hiking trails in Arisaig Provincial Park on Cape George affords ideal settings for mountain bikers, snowmobilers, and cross-country skiers.

Arts Scene

Antigonish is loaded with visual and performing artists who choose to live here because of the region's tremendous natural beauty and the many amenities of living in a college town. The community's location on St. Georges Bay means that lobster and salmon are readily available, while StFX provides teaching jobs for many of the best local artists. The regional arts council uses the nearby communities of Guysborough and Pictou as venues for its popular Gathering of the Arts, a summer show that starts at Antigonish's Courthouse during the Highland Games and travels the region into early August. There are free musical performances during the summer months at the Chisholm Park gazebo, and outdoor sculpture decorates the town's urban walking trail. Several art galleries make a living by selling to the Sunrise Trail's busy summer tourist market, and an artists' studio tour is one of the year's most popular visual arts events. The leading visual arts venue is the StFX Art Gallery, which exhibits works from students, faculty, and the local arts community as well as touring exhibitions of important Canadian and international artists.

While the region's vibrant Celtic music scene is reinforced by its presence on CJFX, the university's radio station, live bands are a regular feature of the weekend fun at the campus's Golden X Inn. There's a fall through spring performing-arts series that uses Immaculata Auditorium as a venue for touring classical, jazz, and world musicians (including the prestigious Debut Atlantique classical recital series), while Theatre Antigonish uses the 200-seat Bauer Theatre for its winter season of five plays using student as well as local performers. The community's premier summer arts event is Festival Antigonish, a 15-year-old celebration of Canadian theatre talent that runs practically nonstop for two months on three stages. While the festival's Theatre Camp attracts dozens of youths and adults interested in honing their

Art Talk

Jeffrey Parker, coowner of
Lyghtesome Gallery.
The environment here, both in the physical and the psychological sense, suits the
arts very well. We're rural yet close to
urban amenities and this gives us the
peace required to create art. This community has a great respect for creativity, and it
even accommodates eccentricity, which
has allowed the artists of this area to band
together and deal with the challenges of
making a living in a community far
removed from the major art markets.
From July through October we're very
busy with visitors from Canada and the
United States, and the local arts scene has
had steady growth over the past decade.
There are lots of rural homes and studios
available at a very reasonable cost, and
artists are moving in all the time.

stage skills, Festival Antigonish serves
as a summer getaway for many of the
top actors and technical experts connected with Halifax's vibrant stage
scene. A series of children's theatre performances is part of the mix, as is a
main stage series featuring works by
the likes of A. R. Gurney and Agatha
Christie. The star of the festival is its
Late Night Series, a group of four or five
new works that are performed starting
at 10:30 PM at the Bauer. These plays,
which are for adult audiences, represent the cutting edge of Canada's
drama scene.

Essentials

Visual Arts Venues

StFX Art Gallery (StFX campus,
11 West Street; 902/867-2303;
www.stfx.ca) The region's most
prominent visual arts venue, featuring works from the campus community, region, and nation.

Lyghtesome Gallery (166 Main Street; 902/863-5804; www.lyghte
some.ns.ca) The region's top commercial art space, representing
the best in landscape painters and fine crafts.

Silver Glen Centre for the Arts (Mount Cameron Estates, 31
George Street; 902/867-1123; www.silverglenart.com) July through
September series of workshops on a beautiful estate. Everything
from seascape painting to pasta making.

Performing Arts & Events

Festival Antigonish (StFX campus, Bauer Theatre, 11 West Street;
902/867-3333; www.stfx.ca) July and August series of children's
plays, main stage classics, and an edgy, bold, New Plays series.

Antigonish Highland Games

(274 Main Street; 902/863-4275; www.antigonishhighland games.com) Canada's oldest Celtic celebration, this July event on Main Street's Columbus Field traces its roots back to 1861 and features music, art, dancing, and strength contests.

Antigonish Performing Arts Series

(StFX campus, Bauer Theatre, 11 West Street; 902/867-3333; www.stfx.ca) A fall through spring series of classical, world, and Canadian Maritime musical performances.

Wine & Dine

Sunshine on Main Café

(332 Main Street; 902/863-5851; www.sunshine onmain.com) Art-filled and innovative, this is the creative community's favorite gathering spot.

Golden X Inn

(StFX campus, Bloomfield Centre, 11 West Street; 902/867-2444; www.stfx.ca) Favorite nightspot of the young and restless, with DJ's and live music.

Art Talk

Bruce Campbell, director of the St. Francis Xavier University Art Gallery. Our main constituency is the university, but given our location in a small town we also reflect the amazing talent and diversity of cultures that are in this area. Even though Antigonish is isolated it maintains a high level of critical discourse in the arts. As a gallery it seems we can never move fast enough to keep up with the creative energy of where our students are going. We have demands placed on us all the time to do exhibitions relevant to what's taking place in society. There's not as much of an emphasis on contemporary art in the community as there is on the college campus. The area seems to have a taste for representational work, but there is also a thirst for knowledge here, and a sense of tolerance for different viewpoints.

Gabrieau's Bistro & Coffee Connection

(350 Main Street; 902/863-1925; www.gabrieaus.com) The best place in northern Nova Scotia for onion soup and a glass of chablis.

Accommodations

Victorian Inn (149 Main Street; 800/706-5558) In-town B&B with turn-of-the-20th-century charm.

Maritime Inn (158 Main Street; 888-662-7484; www.maritime inns.com) Large motel with RV parking and a restaurant.

Whidden's Cottages & Campground (11 Hawthorne Street; 902/863-3736; www.whiddens.com) Quiet refuge popular with visiting artists.

Information

Antigonish Regional Development Authority: 20 St. Andrews Street; 902/863-3330; www.antigonishrda.ns.ca

Population: 4,750

Baie St. Paul, Québec

The beauty of Eastern Canada's Charlevoix region has long had a magnetic lure for French Canadian painters, sculptors, and fine crafts artists. Rolling northeastward from the historic and culturally vibrant city of Québec, the Charlevoix follows the broad contours of the St. Lawrence River through miles of cliff sides and farmlands, framed on its north by the Laurentian Mountains. Halfway to the Charlevoix's boundary at the mouth of the Saguenay River is the Art Town of Baie St. Paul, a community located just over a one-hour's drive from Québec City. A spectacular place whose hillside vistas have transfixed generations of artists, Baie St. Paul is, block for square block, loaded with more French-speaking painters and sculptors than any town outside the paradise of Provence.

Artists have settled not only among the garrets of Baie St. Paul's eminently walkable historic district, a place filled with galleries, ateliers, cheese shops, and delis selling Montréal-style bagels, but have also fanned out to nearby communities such as Isle aux Coudres, St. Joseph de la Rive, and Petite Riviere St. Francois. Each is a historic, culturally rich place whose residents, like the residents of northern New Mexico, trace their European ancestry back well prior to America's Revolutionary War. To live here is to be aware of the past and of the unique, separate historic pathway French Canada has traveled.

Within Canadian arts circles, Baie St. Paul has developed into a destination of legendary stature. In large part, this has been the result of the integrity with which local artists of all styles, be they contemporary sculptors or traditional landscape painters, conduct their professional activities. But it also has to do with the amazing and unexpected way the local arts scene continually reinvents itself and expands upon its successes. Certainly, galleries (as well as restaurants) come and go. But what's also taking place here involves major investment in the development of summer fine arts festivals and in arts infrastructure. It's been a slow, methodical process, but through the steady application of effort, Baie St. Paul has developed a first-rate selection of fine arts venues and an irresistible array of must-see events that are liberally sprinkled across the height of its May to October tourist season.

Arts Scene

The decidedly visual arts slant to Baie St. Paul's stature as an Art Town is rooted in its long-standing tradition of being a refuge for painters of the Charlevoix landscape. They would travel here during the summer months from places such as Montréal, Québec, and even Paris in search of peace, quiet, cool breezes, and affordable studio space. Fortunately, all of those factors still exist in Baie St. Paul, though its streets get a bit crowded in mid-summer, when hordes of tourists descend upon the Charlevoix in pursuit of the region's treasures. Everything from local cheeses (several producers are in the area) to giant salmon hooked in the St. Lawrence River attract these visitors, who flood into the town's art galleries after their bellies are filled.

Clarence Gagnon and René Richard are the seminal artists who committed large parts of their lives to developing Baie St. Paul's reputation. Now that they're deceased, the torch has passed on to a new group of artists similarly committed to this community. Their studios and the galleries selling their work are scattered throughout Baie St. Paul and its surrounding towns, and during clear stretches of weather it's not uncommon to spot a few painters with their easels set up on roadsides, capturing the Charlevoix landscape in the tradition of plein air painting.

The most impressive visual arts amenities in Baie St. Paul are Le Centre d'Art and the Centre d'Exposition. Both are actually part of the same cultural complex, though each serves a different role. The Centre d'Exposition is a three-level, contemporary arts museum with its own permanent collection and a year-round exhibition program focused on local, national, and international shows. Many of Canada's best contemporary artists have shown their work here, and the facility also stages major shows of historical art. The Centre d'Art has a more localized focus, with a year-round series of lectures and workshops as well as a for-sale art gallery and several exhibition galleries dedicated to local painters and sculptors inspired by the Charlevoix art traditions.

At Domaine Forget in nearby St. Irenee, a spring through autumn performing-arts festival attracts top dancers, musicians, and composers into the area for individual performances as well as a summer-long residency program. The shows take place in a 600-seat, state-of-the-art concert hall, while on Sunday afternoons casual brunches featuring live musical entertainment are offered on a terrace overlooking the St. Lawrence River. More than 30 concerts highlight the summer season, while in September and October the focus shifts to more popular music. La Roche Pleureuse and Theatre de Charlevoix de l'Auberge la Coudriere are two summer theatre institutes on Isle aux Coudres presenting everything

Art Talk

Chantal Boulanger, director of Le Centre d'art de Baie St. Paul.

Baie St. Paul is mostly devoted to commercial art, so our mission of being an art museum in a community this size is somewhat difficult. We organize a lot of conferences and lectures, and our annual symposium attracts artists from across Canada and Europe. Through our month-long artist residencies we bring in artists from across the world to meet and work with artists from this area. More contemporary artists are starting to move into the area, and I think it's because of our wonderful environment. What works in the local galleries is crafts and traditional arts, so if you do live here and work in contemporary styles then you have to have galleries selling your work in Montréal or Québec.

from historical pageants of Charlevoix history to cutting-edge new works by Montréal playwrights. The main event on Baie St. Paul's autumn arts calendar is Reves d'Automne, a two-week arts festival that features performances, street painting, and instructional art workshops, while the summer's highlight is the August-long contemporary arts symposium, competition, and exhibition held at Le Centre d'Art and the Arena.

Essentials

Visual Arts Venues

Le Centre d'art de Baie St. Paul (4 rue Ambroise-Fafard; 418-435-3681; www.centredart-bsp.qc.ca) Located in the heart of Baie St. Paul, this modern art center stays active year-round with

Art Talk

Stephane Bouchard, coowner of Galerie d'art Iris.

In the past fifteen years this town has changed quite a lot for the better. The center of the community has been revived and we've become one of the most popular places for tourists in eastern Canada. The popularity of our artists has attracted lots of new investments by restaurants and hotels, and even the ski area has expanded. Artists love living here because of our historic connection to Québec's art traditions. The scenery is breathtaking, there is a new generation of younger artists moving into town, and many of Canada's best artists keep at least a part-time residence here. For galleries this is a very competitive place and what we're now seeing is more of the galleries staying open year-round in response to our growing numbers of tourists.

workshops, lectures, and a regionally oriented exhibition program.

Le Centre d'exposition de Baie St. Paul (23 rue Ambroise-Fafard; 418/435-3681; www.centredart-bsp.qc.ca/cexpo) A three-level contemporary arts center and museum with a permanent collection and rotating national and international shows.

Galerie d'art Iris (30 rue St. Jean-Baptiste; 418-435-5768; www.galerie iris.com) A large, multidisciplinary gallery representing living painters who work in traditional Charlevoix styles.

Performing Arts & Events

Domaine Forget (5 rang St. Antoine, St. Irenee; 418/452-8111; www.domaineforget.com) This hillside former estate is home to a seven-month program of music and dance, as well as 30 summer concerts staged indoors and outdoors.

Rêves d'Automne (4 place de L'Eglise; 418/435-5875; www.revesautomne.qc.ca) A weeklong arts and cultural festival in late September and early October that includes dozens of arts events, held during the height of fall colors.

Le Symposium International d'Art Contemporain (23 rue Ambroise Fafard; 418/435-3681; www.centredart-bsp.qc.ca) Annual August series of events featuring artists from Québec, Canada, France, and elsewhere.

Wine & Dine

Au Pierre-Narcisse (41 rue Ambroise-Farfad; 418/435-2056; www.aupierrenarcisse.com) Classic French Canadian fare in the heart of town, famed for its *moules et frites*.

La Pignoronde (750 boulevard Monseigneur de Laval; 418/435-5505; www.aubergelapignoronde.com) Art-filled gourmet restaurant with an extensive list of French wines on the outskirts of Baie St. Paul.

La Grande Maison (160 rue St. Jean-Baptiste; 418/435-5575) Victorian-style inn serving classic, haute-French cuisine.

Accommodations

Le Balcon Vert Auberge (22 côte du Balcon Vert; 418/435-5587; www.balconvert.charlevoix.net) Inexpensive hotel and hostel, with a jazz club and international clientele.

Hotel Baie St. Paul (911 boulevard Monseigneur de Laval; 418/435-3683; www.hotelbaiestpaul.com) Large hotel with RV parking and places to park snowmobiles.

Gite au Perchoir (443 Chemin Cap aux Rets; 418/435-6955; www.auperchoir.com) Relaxed B&B with spectacular river views owned by an artist couple.

Information

Association Touristique Regionale de Charlevoix: 444 Boulevard Monseigneur de Laval; 418/435-4160; www.tourismecharlevoix.com

Population: 7,300

Owen Sound, Ontario

This remote community on Lake Huron's Georgian Bay is 140 miles northwest of Toronto and has long been a favored summering destination for Toronto artists seeking relief from the crowded city's hot and humid streets. Though many return to their urban studios in late August, enough have decided to stay put and sink their roots here that Owen Sound in the past decade has developed a strong, year-round arts scene of its own. In American history books, Owen Sound is famed for being the northernmost terminus of the Underground Railroad, a confederation of pre–Civil War abolitionists dedicated to liberating escaped slaves.

What keeps the arts community going in Owen Sound is the region's tremendous flow of summer tourists. Selling to them at one of the many festivals dotting this town's summer arts calendar is vital to making a living from one's art. Artists of all types are drawn here by the area's fantastic natural beauty, its proximity to the Bruce Peninsula National Park and the Chi-Cheemaun ferry's two-hour ride to Manitoulin Island, by the hiking trails and 50-foot waterfalls that follow the Niagara Escarpment through thousands of acres of conservation lands, and by the lake's incredible fishing opportunities for 40-pound chinook salmon and rainbow trout.

The region's economy is based on the maritime, forestry, agriculture, and tourism industries. It's also home to one of the oldest farmers' markets in Ontario, a place where beekeepers sell local honey alongside basket makers and maple syrup producers. Winters are long and difficult, with terrific storms blowing into town every few days.

There are hundreds of miles of snowmobiling trails crisscrossing the countryside, and more than a few cases of Labatt's are sucked dry in the legions of ice-fishing shacks that pop up along the shorelines each November.

Arts Scene

Owen Sound's visual arts community is so strong that it's able to support two artist-run facilities (a gallery and a studio collective) as well as a gallery/museum dedicated to the legacy of Tom Thomson, a member of the Group of Seven who was originally from this area. The Art Town Collective (love that name!) is a group of nearly two dozen of the region's most experienced artists sharing studio quarters in a three-story brick building in downtown Owen Sound. Many of them are painters and fine craftspeople represented in galleries in Toronto and Ottawa, and many also work Canada's summer arts fair circuit. The Owen Sound Artists Co-op is the other artist-run operation, and its efforts are represented in a well-run art gallery right in downtown on 10th Street East. Many of the region's top ceramicists, jewelers, and silversmiths are represented here.

The Tom Thomson Memorial Art Gallery has a superb permanent collection of Canadian masterworks as well as an energetic and ambitious program of contemporary art exhibitions showcasing the work of Owen Sound artists. Home to a year-round series of art classes for children and adults, the Thomson gallery also sponsors the community's very popular Gallery Night at the Movies, in which foreign flicks are brought into town for one-night screenings at the Galaxy Cinema. With its year-round program of exhibitions, events, classes, fundraising galas, and films, there's no underestimating the impact that native son Tom Thomson has had on developing the continued strength and integrity of Owen Sound's arts scene.

The biggest performing-arts event on Owen Sound's annual calendar is Summerfolk, a three-day music festival in August that's staged on the shores of Georgian Bay. It pulls in more than 10,000 visitors each year despite a history that's checkered by regular rainstorms. But the talent is top notch, the vibes are great, and if you can't tolerate a few raindrops you probably should move to Tucson. During the cold months, the same organization that pulls together Summerfolk also presents Winterfolk, a program of performances by national recording acts, staged in venues such as the Grey Granite Club. The Roxy Theatre, a restored, art deco movie house, serves as the home venue for both the

Art Talk

Jim Louie, ceramist and sculptor.
The diversity of the people living here and the sophistication of the people moving here have given Owen Sound a base of individuals who appreciate art and value creativity. We have beaches, wildlife, and water, and these entities tend to influence our creative ideas. It's affordable here, which allows a lot of artists to survive on their summer sales. Lots of us moved here from Toronto, and we're still closely in touch with what goes on there. Lots of people from the city drive out here on weekends or for the amazing shows at the Thomson gallery, which backs up our local arts scene and gives all the artists here a sense of legitimacy. The influx of out-of-towners has made Owen Sound a tolerant place, and you can be anyone you want to be here and nobody will bother you.

Owen Sound Little Theatre's calendar of standards as well as the performances of touring music acts and theatre companies from Toronto. There's also a Celtic Festival of music every September, and on summer evenings the outdoor music program of Harbour Nights brings family music performances to Owen Sound's lakefront.

Essentials

Visual Arts Venues

Tom Thomson Memorial Art Gallery (840 First Avenue West; 519/376-1932; www.tom thomson.org) A superb visual arts facility dedicated to the legacy of one of the Group of Seven, this gallery exhibits masterworks as well as touring national and regional contemporary shows.

Owen Sound Artists' Co-op (279 10th Street East, 519/371-0479; www.osartistsco-op.com) Well-run art gallery in downtown Owen Sound with representation from fine crafts artists, jewelers, and painters.

Art Town Collective (781 2nd Avenue West; 519/371-0164; www.makersgallery.com/arttown) Group of experienced artists sharing a large building in a downtown neighborhood.

Performing Arts & Events

Summerfolk (P.O. Box 521; 519/371-2995; www.summerfolk.org) The largest event on Owen Sound's yearly arts calendar, this three-day August celebration of folk, blues, and world music is staged outdoors come rain or shine.

Roxy Theatre (251 9th Avenue East; 519/371-5467) This 400-seat venue is geared for live theatre and music.

Owen Sound Celtic Festival (see Owen Sound Tourism below) This three-day festival in mid-September draws Celtic artisans and musicians from across Canada.

Wine & Dine

Jazzmyn's Tapas & Taps (261 9th Street East; 519/371-7736) Favorite live-music and cocktail lounge featuring Mediterranean cuisine.

Stark's Dining (2010 16th Street East; 519/376-0059; www.starks dining.com) Fine-dining house with innovative cuisine and a great wine list.

Martini's Bar & Café (209 8th Street East; 519/371-1887) Great place for stiff drinks with lots of local attitude.

Accommodations

Victorian Gardens Bed & Breakfast (518 10th Street 'A' West; 519/376-5207; www.victorian/gardens.com) Elegant B&B in a historic home, and within walking distance of downtown's arts amenities.

Comfort Inn (955 9th Avenue East; 519/371-5500; www.choice hotels.com) Affordable rooms in downtown.

Best Western Inn on the Bay (1800 2nd Avenue East; 519/371-9200; www.bwinnonthebay.com) Large, full-service motel, with RV parking and a swimming pool.

Information

Owen Sound Tourism: 519/371-9833; www.owensound.ca

Population: 22,000

Art Talk

David McLeish, president of Summerfolk.

We feature an eclectic lineup of musicians, from country and folk to new singer/songwriters and world music. Our crafts festival pulls in about 40 artists to complement our 40 performing acts, and we also have a youth arts festival. We started a March showcase called Last Chance Saloon with 12 acts as a way to honor the many local volunteers who support us year in and year out. One of our biggest challenges involves getting airplay for our acts. Even our local radio stations ignore us, and they overlook the fact that we attract 5,000 people each day for our events. Our Winterfolk concerts happen three or four times a year at places like the Roxy and draw a large part of their audiences from the greater Toronto area.

Stratford, Ontario

This theatre-mad community is dedicated to the highest standards of dramatic presentation and is guided by the inspirational power of the works of William Shakespeare. Located 100 miles from the multicultural neighborhoods of Toronto, Stratford has hooked a large part of its economic destiny to the ever-expanding vision of the Stratford Festival of Canada, a 50-plus-year-old organization that produces an April to November series of classic and cutting-edge stage works that plays to international audiences who travel far and wide in journeying to this Canadian Art Town.

The place is pure Canadian confection. Set amid one of the continent's most prolific agricultural regions, Stratford is surrounded by family farms raising everything from alpacas to Angus steers. Roadside produce stands line the narrow blacktop roads leading into Stratford, and the community's Saturday-morning farmers' market at the fairgrounds is one of the best in the province, loaded with treats from handmade crafts to clover honey, sweet cherries to fresh-baked pies. Victorian in architectural character, Stratford has maintained most of its historic infrastructure in large part because of the festival's strong influence. Since 1953, the festival's directors have encouraged and financially supported many historic renovation and restoration projects in and around downtown Stratford, helping the town to dodge the development of generic-looking business districts and maintain an authentic sense of place and regional culture. The appropriately named Avon River meanders through the middle of Stratford, providing a focal point for a riverside park that features 100 flower beds. One of Canada's largest floral exhibitions takes place at the Coliseum in March, drawing thousands of visitors. More than 1,000 acres of city-maintained parks are scattered throughout Stratford, and during the summer months musicians perform on floating barges on the Avon, while fine crafts artists set up each Wednesday, Saturday, and Sunday in Lower Queens Park for the June through September Art in the Park series.

Arts Scene

For any Art Town to have the capacity to attract a half-million or so annual visitors, something extraordinary must be taking place. Stratford's flow of free-spending cultural tourists rivals the likes of Art Towns such as Provincetown, Massachusetts, and Carmel, California. For generations, art lovers excited about top-shelf theatre have made pilgrimages to this corner of Ontario a summer ritual, and Stratford has measured up to the challenge by spawning an exciting visual arts scene as well as a wealth of fabulous restaurants and charming country inns.

It all starts with the Stratford Festival, a performing-arts organization that actors, technical pros, costumers, publicists, and even ushers compete against other talents to secure places anywhere in the organization's 30-week season of productions on several stages. Shakespeare remains at the core of Stratford's seasonal offerings, with plays showcased at the 1,820-seat Festival Theatre, 1,107-seat Avon Theatre, and the 410-seat Tom Patterson Theatre. The festival has made a substantial investment in not only its own future but that of many generations of Canadian actors and playwrights by developing the new Studio Theatre in downtown Stratford. This 278-seat venue is dedicated to the performance of new works as well as rarely performed theatre classics and creates a dynamic synergy with other Stratford events such as the fall season classical theatre classes for university students, the fall and winter Music Conservatory, and the October Canadian Playwright's conference. During its extensive spring, summer, and fall season offerings, the festival presents nearly two-dozen plays, as well as a Monday-evening classical music series. Jack Scoffield, a local wag who knows more about the festival's backstage workings than anyone else in town, is a Stratford celebrity famed for his hour-long lectures about the festival and its plays.

Classical music is also the focus of Stratford Summer Music, an innovative organization whose July and August performance series is staged in eclectic venues such as churches, restaurants, parks, and even

Art Talk

Jennifer Rudder, executive director of Gallery Stratford.

Artists like living here and arts organizations flourish here because of the presence of the Stratford Festival, which has reinforced the local and summer audiences' sense of appreciation for all the arts. There's lots of work available in Stratford for artists, and the entire community understands how its economic development is tied into the festival and its impact. We're a municipally and provincially supported organization that serves locals and visitors. We schedule our biggest shows for the summer and use the rest of the year to focus on our local and regional artists and programs. Our emphasis is on cutting-edge, experimental work, and we try to keep some sort of connection to the theatre through our exhibitions program.

city hall. Jazz on the River, which takes place from June to September, features the '39 Casino Band performing on an Avon River barge on Wednesday and Friday evenings.

While Stratford's most popular annual arts events are the twice-yearly Rotary Arts & Crafts Shows at the Coliseum in May and November, the jewel of the region's visual arts scene is Gallery Stratford. This Tudor-style facility, within walking distance of the Festival Theatre, is a hotbed of contemporary and classical visual arts exhibitions, kids' art workshops, artist and guest curator lectures, a superb fine crafts gallery, and even a Monday-night film series. Gallery Stratford is a gathering point for the region's visual artists, and it serves as an influential venue for exhibitions by local and national painters and sculptors. Several commercial art spaces are sprinkled around downtown Stratford, and some great local art shows up on the walls of local restaurants and coffee bars.

Essentials

Visual Arts Venues

Gallery Stratford (54 Romeo Street South; 519/271-5271; www.gallerystratford.on.ca) A visual arts exhibition facility and fine arts center exhibiting regional and national work, as well as offering educational and entertainment programs throughout the year.

Gallery Indigena (69 Ontario Street; 519/271-7881; www.gallery indigena.com) One of Canada's foremost contemporary art galleries specializing in the work of First Nations artists from Nova Scotia and British Columbia.

Gallery 96 at Discovery Centre

(270 Water Street; 519/271-4660)
A contemporary arts gallery run by
local artists, this popular cooperative
art space is located next to the
Festival Theatre.

Performing Arts & Events

The Stratford Festival of Canada

(55 Queen Street; 800/567-1600;
www.stratfordfestival.ca) Premier
theatre organization dedicated to the
works of Shakespeare, this festival's
vision also includes producing new
Canadian plays.

Stratford Summer Music (see
Tourism Stratford below) A superb,
action-packed, two-week program of
top Canadian and international classical music performers playing at several Stratford venues in late July and
early August.

**Monday Night Festival Fringe
Concert Series** (see Stratford Festival
above) This innovative, summer-long
series of popular music concerts at the Festival Theatre brings the
very best international entertainers into town for one-night stands
throughout the summer-theatre season.

Wine & Dine

Balzac's Coffee Roastery (149 Ontario Street; 519/273-7909;
www.balzacscoffee.com) This independent buzz shop is the best
place in town to catch up with everyone from main stage stars
from the Stratford Festival to local visual artists.

Bistro 104 (104 Downie Street; 519/275-2929; www.bistro104
.com) The artistic, casual, and comfortable Bistro 104 captures the
best of Canadian modern culinary trends, and offers an exceptional wine list.

Art Talk

Cindy Hubert, director of
Gallery 96.

We're a 30-year-old organization that was
founded by a group of artists who were
working in the theatre, and our mission
involves exhibiting the work of existing
members as well as bringing new art into
the community. We close for three months
each winter, but when we're open we're
very busy with shows by artists from here
as well as places like Toronto, New York
City, and Ottawa. About half of our member artists also have jobs in the theatre
community, and some even teach art
classes here at the gallery. There's a rising
level of recognition for the integrity of
Stratford's visual arts scene, and it's to the
point where some visitors are attracted
here more for the galleries than they are
for the theatre.

The Church Restaurant & Belfry Grill (70 Brunswick Street; 519/273-3424; www.churchrestaurant.com) Stratford's most elegant dining spot is a must-do, offering everything from caviar to local lamb. The Belfry is a great place to meet actors and actresses out for a night on the town.

Accommodations

Ambercroft B&B (129 Brunswick Street; 800/794-2515; www.ambercroftbandb.com) A comfortable and affordable Victorian inn right in the heart of town.

Festival Inn (1144 Ontario Street; 519/273-1150; www.festival innstratford.com) Large hotel, with a pool.

As You Like It Motel (379 Romeo Street North; 519/271-2951; www.asyoulikeit.on.ca) A family-owned motel at the north end of town with lots of parking for RVs and a swimming pool.

Information

Tourism Stratford: 47 Downie Street; 519/271-5140; www.city.stratford.on.ca

Population: 29,500

Index